The Complete Book of HyperTalk® 2

The Complete Book of HyperTalk® 2

Dan Shafer

Addison-Wesley Publishing Company, Inc.
Reading, Massachusetts   Menlo Park, California   New York
Don Mills, Ontario   Wokingham, England   Amsterdam   Bonn
Sidney   Singapore   Tokyo   Madrid   San Juan   Paris
Seoul   Milan   Mexico City   Taipei

Many of the designations used by manufacturers and sellers to distinguish their products are claimed as trademarks. Where those designations appear in this book and Addison-Wesley was aware of a trademark claim, the designations have been printed in initial capital letters (e.g., Macintosh is a registered trademark of Apple Computer, Inc.).

Library of Congress Cataloging-in-Publication Data

Shafer, Dan
    The complete book of HyperTalk 2/Dan Shafer
        p.   cm.
    Updated ed. of: HyperTalk programming. Rev. ed. 1988.
    Includes index.
    ISBN 0-201-57082-3
    1. HyperTalk (Computer program language) I. Shafer, Dan.
HyperTalk programming. II. Title. III. Title: Complete book of
Hypertalk two.
QA76.73.H96S52 1990   90-19617
005.265--dc20   CIP

Copyright © 1991 by Dan Shafer

Sponsoring Editor: Carole McClendon
Technical Reviewer: Steve Michel
Cover Design: Ronn Campisi
Text Design: Copenhaver Cumpston
Set in 10 point Palatino by Don Huntington

ISBN 0-201-57082-3

2 3 4 5 6 7 8 9 10 - MW - 94939291
Second printing, June 1991

For patience beyond endurance,

support beyond expectation,

love beyond measure,

joy unsurpassed . . .

For Carolyn

. . . with renewed conviction

Contents

6 System Messages 73

7 Mouse, Keyboard, and File I/O 95

8 Control Structures and Logical Operators 111

Preface

Writing this revised edition of my best-selling book on my favorite computer program and language has been great fun. It has enabled me to renew my acquaintance with HyperCard and to wonder anew at the approachability of HyperTalk. It has reaffirmed my initial affection for the Macintosh. And it has given me a chance to experiment with the ever-changing world of programming.

If you bought the original or revised versions of this book, you will by now have recognized that the cover and the version of HyperTalk we discuss are not the only changes. This edition has a new publisher, Addison-Wesley. I must say I am quite excited at the prospect of Addison-Wesley publishing this book. Their reputation in the Macintosh book marketplace — built on their close working relationship with Apple Computer on the official Macintosh Technical Library — is legend. I look forward to a long and interesting association with them.

The changes to HyperCard in Version 2.0 are detailed throughout the book, but it may be interesting to take a step back and provide a kind of bird's-eye view of the product in its latest incarnation. On some level, at least, I was surprised by what I saw in HyperCard Version 2.0 as it began to emerge through several beta releases. It seems clear that Apple Computer chose to emphasize the programming and development aspects of the product, singling them out for the most significant improvements. That's good for those of us who spend our days scripting and hacking away at stacks. It's not clear yet how much benefit users will realize from these modifications, but I hope the developer community will see the enhancements in this release of Hyper-Card as a signal from Apple that it considers HyperTalk a valid and viable programming language worthy of support. It now includes moderately good debugging (discussed in detail in Chapter 19), significantly enhanced reporting capabilities (covered in Chapter 18), and numerous extensions to HyperTalk that have been requested by thousands of developers and users during the first three years of HyperCard's life.

Wherever I have described any of this new functionality, I have tried to be careful to point out that it is new with Version 2.0 so that if by chance you are working with an earlier version, you won't find yourself stumbling around too much. In addition, Appendix A marks every new function, command, operator, system message, and other addition to the HyperTalk vocabulary, as well as those that existed in earlier versions but have changed with this release.

There was so much new material in this edition of the book that we had to eliminate some material from the earlier versions. That turned out to be a good decision for more than one reason. The things we eliminated were arguably important when HyperCard and HyperTalk were new entities with little support software around. Now, though, the product is much more mature; so much of that helpful material is no longer current or as valuable as it once was. I trust you'll agree that we've retained the important parts of the first versions and added substantially to this edition.

Happy scripting!

Dan Shafer

Redwood City, California
August 1990

Acknowledgments

You might think, as I once did, that revising an existing book would be much easier than writing one from scratch. Like me, you'd be wrong. This book put a lot of people through contortions before we could get it out the door. I'd like to acknowledge their help publicly.

The people on the Addison-Wesley team have been helpful, enthusiastic, understanding, supportive, and professional throughout the development of this book. Carole McClendon, Joanne Clapp Fullagar, Rachel Guichard, and Diane Freed deserve a big vote of thanks. So, too, does Tema Goodwin, whose copy edit of the manuscript included the onerous task of cross-checking dozens of chapter references as well as finding little things that were still wrong with the original book from which we worked.

Production of the manuscript itself fell into the capable hands of my good friends Don and Rae Huntington. With their usual aplomb and refusal to be ruffled, they completed the complex assignment of weaving together three sets of changes into a coherent manuscript. That they did this while on a houseboating "vacation" on the Sacramento River Delta makes the whole thing border on astounding.

Scott Knaster, Series Editor of the *Macintosh Inside Out* series, and Steve Michel, technical reviewer for this manuscript, performed service above and beyond the call. Both found lots of small errors in first drafts, pointed out better ways of doing things, and questioned approaches and omissions in such a way that they significantly improved the quality of the product.

Any book project requires time. My life partner and wife, Carolyn, and my new business partner Paul Rice, conspired to ensure that I was insulated from as much of the day-to-day administrivia of running a consulting and writing business as possible so that I'd have time to get this book out. The fact that the home and business are still intact after this experience is a greater testimony to them than to me.

In the three years that have transpired between the publication of the first edition of this book and this latest incarnation, I've learned a lot of HyperCard and HyperTalk techniques from lots of other scripters, clients, developers, colleagues, friends, associates, and hangers-on. There is not room here to thank all of them. Hopefully, I've done so privately as we've gone along.

Of course, any errors or omissions you find in this book are strictly my doing and none of these good people who have been kind enough to help nurture this manuscript to publication should be held accountable for them.

Introduction

The focus of this book is on the HyperTalk language, not on how to design and build stacks. The book helps you take advantage of the awesome power of HyperTalk to control your Macintosh world the way you want it controlled. If you are an experienced programmer, you will be exposed to the inner workings and object-like concepts in HyperTalk so that the underlying elegance of the language is revealed. If HyperTalk is your first language — or if you are one of the hundreds of thousands of people who learned BASIC but gave up programming since the advent of more difficult-looking Pascal and C — you will gain a ground-level introduction to HyperTalk as a language and be taken all the way through complex script development.

▶ What's in Here?

This book has 21 chapters and an appendix. Chapters 1 and 2 cover background material about HyperTalk and the HyperCard environment. Chapter 3 is a refresher course in the basics of HyperCard design. Chapters 4 and 5 introduce essential, practical information about HyperTalk programming, such as how to use the script editor and HyperTalk naming conventions.

Then in Chapter 6 we begin our exploration of the operation of the HyperTalk programming language itself. We cover intensively the following topics:

- system messages (Chapter 6)

- mouse, keyboard, and file I/O operations (Chapter 7)

- control structures and logical operators (Chapter 8)

- controlling stack flow, card flow, and interaction (Chapter 9)
- text and data management routines (Chapter 10)
- dialog boxes and their use in HyperTalk (Chapter 11)
- menu management (Chapter 12)
- the use of visual and graphics effects (Chapter 13)
- sound and music (Chapter 14)
- math (Chapter 15)
- action-taking commands (Chapter 16)
- property-related commands (Chapter 17)
- report-printing commands and techniques (Chapter 18)
- script-related commands and debugging tools (Chapter 19)

Chapters 20 and 21 cover more advanced topics. In Chapter 20, we look at the issue of how to design your HyperCard stacks for maximum flexibility and ease of use. Chapter 21 focuses on how to extend the HyperTalk environment using resources such as external commands, sounds, and cursors. Appendix A is a complete alphabetical vocabulary listing of HyperTalk's commands, operators, functions, messages, and properties.

In keeping with one of the key principles of hypertext called "chunking," several of the chapters are short. I've done this so that material about one topic is all together, without extraneous material to distract you.

Hands-On Exercises

In hands-on exercises throughout Chapters 6-18, you build small demonstration scripts that show how commands work and interact.

When you see one of these sections, plan on being at your Mac and ready to type in a script or message to see how something works. I have emphasized hands-on experiments because HyperTalk is not the kind of language you can learn by sitting passively and reading this, or any other, book. HyperTalk, like the Hyper-Card environment of which it is an integral part, requires interaction on your part. Don't just *read* these exercises, *experience* them.

▶ Programs Mentioned

Throughout the book I mention free and shareware programs. You can usually obtain these programs from several sources.

Shareware programs are developed by people who enjoy "hacking" at the Macintosh and would like to see some reward for their efforts but don't want to put their programs into the usual marketing channels. Some incredibly good software is shareware. But shareware only lasts if people who use shareware products pay the usually nominal fee to the developer. So if you use and enjoy someone's shareware product, take the time to send him or her a check. You'll contribute to the likelihood that more good shareware will appear over time.

I should add that, for the most part, mentioning these programs does not mean that I recommend them, or that they are the best of their kind available. It means only that I've used them, they work for me, and I think you might find them helpful. If you find more useful stacks and programs, let me know.

▶ Contacting Me

I try to be accessible to my readers. After all, you are the most important ingredient in the recipe of whatever success I may ultimately enjoy.

If you find a bug, have a question, want to argue, or have things to share for future editions of this book or related books, please contact me. I can be reached electronically on CompuServe (71246,402, Connect or AppleLink (DSHAFER). Or you can write me at 277 Hillview Avenue, Redwood City, California 94062. But please don't call me at home; I'm buried under stacks anyway.

▶ Enough of the Commercial Already

I know you're itching to get into scripting, so I won't take any more of your time. Thanks for buying this book and realizing the immense potential of HyperTalk. I think you'll be pleasantly surprised at the elegance of the language and how easy it is to learn and use.

Enjoy!

1 ▶ Building Your Own Stacks

In this chapter, you will

- examine the step-by-step process of stack creation using HyperCard
- see the role played by scripting in HyperCard's built-in HyperTalk language

▶ Why Build Stacks?

You have some interest in building and programming HyperCard stacks or you wouldn't have bought this book. But you may have some lingering doubts about the wisdom or value of constructing your own stacks as opposed to buying them. Or you may be planning to build stacks for other people and you want some idea of which stacks are likely to be most useful.

▶ Build versus buy

The question of whether you should buy a ready-made stack or plunge into this book and the joys of HyperTalk programming is subjective enough that you shouldn't expect a hard-and-fast answer. But we believe that designing and even scripting your own stacks is neither so hard as to be intimidating nor so time-consuming as to be prohibitive if programming isn't your primary occupation.

Still, there are trade-offs. Constructing and scripting a stack for your own use takes time, though it takes substantially less time than programming a Mac application any other way. Particularly when stacks are being sold inexpensively and even given away so freely in the Bill Atkinson-generated spirit of HyperCard, it may be tough to justify to yourself, your spouse, or your boss spending any time developing your own stack. It's the old "build versus buy" decision brought down to real micro-economics. So here are some good reasons for doing your own stackware.

1. If you want something done right, you have to do it yourself. That old saw is another way of saying that some of your needs for a particular stack are probably unique. HyperCard gives you such enormous flexibility about the way the stack looks and how you use it that it seems a shame to let someone else make those decisions for you.

2. You understand better how to use something that you've designed. We all know people who have been using very powerful programs on the Mac but using them in limited ways, not taking advantage of all their capability. Part of the reason is a lack of understanding of what the programs can accomplish. If you design the stack, you will certainly be able to take advantage of all of its functionality.

3. The creative process itself is rewarding and enjoyable.

4. In designing a stack to solve a problem, you will gain some insight into the nature of the problem itself. You may find out that the problem you are trying to solve with the stack is a completely different one from what you first thought. This added insight makes you a better problem-solver.

▶ Building stacks for others

If you are a programmer or a designer and are asked to develop stacks for other people, you don't need to be convinced of the value of stack design. You've been doing custom programming long enough to understand its strengths and weaknesses. Your concern probably lies more with the issue of whether HyperCard is an appropriate vehicle for solving a specific problem.

The brief answer is that you can do anything with HyperCard, particularly with its extensibility (discussed in Chapter 21), that you can do with any other programming language. Even without extension, HyperTalk is, as you will see in this book, a very powerful programming environment that is rich in functionality. The language also brings an ease to programming Macintosh applications that no other language has approached.

But you have to deal with some realities if you decide to use HyperCard and scripts to solve problems for clients and customers. Before HyperCard 2.0, builders of HyperCard stacks were limited to a single window showing a single card from a single stack on the screen at one time. HyperCard 2.0 relaxes this limitation somewhat. You can now have several stacks open at once, each in its own window. However, you can only have one window open per stack, which means that the user can only see one card per stack at a time. Also before HyperCard 2.0, the size of a card was fixed at the size of the smallest Macintosh screen. The card could not be resized, though it could be relocated if the monitor was larger than the small nine-inch displays on the Macintosh Plus and SE series. In HyperCard 2.0 you can create cards and windows of any size, although all of the cards in a given stack must be the same size. You can resize the window either from within a script or by using the "Scroll" option from the Edit menu to cause the resize box, which is normally hidden, to appear. If you make the window smaller than the card size set for the stack, the window shows only part of the card. The user can then scroll around in the window to examine various parts of the card.

Another sometimes significant limitation of HyperCard from a programming standpoint is the way it shields you from Macintosh ROM Toolbox routines. This can be a real advantage: The ROM is mysterious and difficult to understand and manage in many ways. And it is true that you can extend HyperTalk with external commands and functions that do access the Toolbox. But if you confine yourself to HyperTalk as it is designed and delivered by Apple Computer, you're apt to feel a loss of control over the application.

These limitations are minor when you compare them to the staggering power and ease of programming in HyperTalk. But you are probably not going to design the next spreadsheet program in HyperCard. And it's not well suited to designing a full-powered word processing program. But tasks that involve the things at which HyperCard excels can be a pure joy to design and program in HyperTalk. Here's a list of some of the particular strong points of HyperCard:

1. You will probably never need to worry about local coordinates, global coordinates, and the location of buttons and fields on the screen. Hyper-Card uses its own set of coordinates anchored to the upper-left corner of the card for almost everything you do. But more important, a button's location has no effect on your scripts. If the user moves the button, your script need not be aware of his or her action. The script goes with the button, wherever the button goes.

2. Designing the most useful interface objects is as easy as using a painting or drawing program. Even scrolling fields, a difficult and demanding task even for a proficient Mac programmer, snap into place with a few clicks of the mouse.

3. HyperTalk, as we will see, includes powerful control structures, high-quality visual effects, and full program access to and control of menu interaction. It is a complete programming language in its own right.

4. When you write scripts, you can be as verbose (and readable) or terse (and efficient during coding) as you like, within broad limits. Many commands have several forms of syntax, depending on how readable you want your scripts to be.

5. The modularity of having each script connected to an object means the notorious "ripple effect" of conventional programming practices all but disappears. (The "ripple effect" refers to the fact that a change in one part of a program often causes new problems to ripple through other parts of the program.) If a handler for a particular event connected to a button works in script A, it will work identically in scripts B, C, and D, with little or no modification.

6. HyperTalk is designed so that it tries — very hard, in fact — to make sense out of your code. Only when it has exhausted a fairly thorough search of its understanding of the HyperCard environment will you get an error message. And when you do get an error message, you can move with a single mouse click to the script to find the cursor blinking at precisely the point where the error occurred. Debugging is streamlined.

You will discover dozens of other advantages to HyperTalk scripting as you work through this book and begin to build your own stacks. We believe that HyperCard as a paradigm and HyperTalk as its programming environment are a leap in Mac program design. Before you are done with this book, we're confident you will agree.

▶ Step-by-Step Design

Now that you are convinced that designing and scripting your own stacks will be rewarding and pleasant, how do you begin? How do you move from an idea for a new product or a problem to the solution itself?

The steps in building a HyperCard stack are not so different from programming in more conventional languages. They are summarized in Figure 1-1. Those unique to HyperCard or that require further amplification are discussed in the following sections.

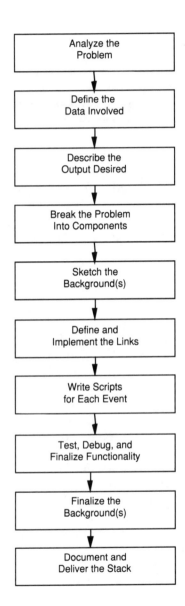

Figure 1-1. Steps in HyperCard stack design and construction

▶ Design process

The first four steps in the process of designing a stack as shown in Figure 1-1 are identical to those in any other application development environment. They are beyond the scope of this discussion. Any book about basic programming techniques contains information on these steps.

▶ Sketching the backgrounds

Every stack has at least one card. Every card has one background. Sometimes the backgrounds in your stacks are graphically elaborate. Other times, they are simple and relatively sparse. Because the background can be detailed in later, it is a good idea simply to rough out the ideas and put in the necessary buttons and fields at this stage.

▶ A word about "borrowing"

One of the principles of Macintosh software design that became established very early in the computer's history was the principle that "nobody does it from scratch." If you've done any serious Mac programming, you know that programmers frequently reuse the main event loops and common procedures of other programmers. There is, by and large, only one way to do many things on the Mac.

HyperCard extends the idea of borrowing to a new level. Unlike almost any phenomenon since the first days of BASIC on microcomputers, HyperCard has fostered a spirit of giving and sharing among its users and developers. We've seen programmers who wouldn't share three lines of their preciously thought-out and painstakingly crafted Pascal code go to great lengths to make sure that anyone who wanted a copy of their latest whiz-bang script got it. As a result of this spirit, you can go to hundreds of places to get ideas for backgrounds and card designs. You may stumble onto one that is exactly what you need for your stack. Or you may find one or more from which you can borrow elements to build what you need. This sort of borrowing — dubbed by one writer as "standing on other people's shoulders, not their toes" — is encouraged and generally positive.

But be careful about what you borrow and for what purpose. A great deal of stackware is freeware or shareware that you can use at little or no cost. But check your source. "Borrowing" cards, buttons, scripts, backgrounds, and designs from copyrighted stacks may be illegal and is certainly dishonest. If you really need something that a copyrighted stack contains and you are not planning to market the product that incorporates it, drop the copyright holder a note. Quite often, he or she will be happy to give you a release for the limited purpose of your stack; after all, imitation remains the sincerest form of flattery.

▶ Defining and implementing links

If you have worked with HyperCard in its authoring mode, you know that much of the readily apparent power and flexibility of the program stems from its elegant implementation of dynamic links. Connecting one card or idea to another is child's play.

When you design a stack, it's a good idea to think very early about these links. At least two major benefits derive from this approach.

First, deciding on the links often helps you structure the stack in the way that the casual browsing or typing user will find comfortable and natural. Before all the functionality and relative complexity of scripts and dozens or hundreds of cards are in the way, you can think about this issue concisely and somewhat abstractly. Also, this often enables you to gain insight into the design of the stack itself, sometimes leading you to change or enhance the design.

Second, implementing the links is easier when the stack is new and there aren't a lot of visual or conceptual impediments to seeing the path clearly. Efficiency will result.

▶ Writing scripts

This book is entirely about writing HyperTalk scripts. These collections of HyperTalk "code" are not nearly so much like programs in the conventional sense as they are like Pascal subroutines or Smalltalk methods. (We'll have more to say on this subject in the next chapter.)

A script is exactly what its name implies. It consists of a series of handlers, each of which is responsible for dealing with or responding to certain messages from HyperCard objects such as buttons and fields. And a script tells the object to which it is connected how to behave, which is exactly what a TV or theater script does.

You may develop your scripts modularly, dealing with one event at a time. "What do I want to have happen when this button is pressed?" is one question that is answered by a script.

▶ Testing and debugging

Like the first four steps of this process, testing and debugging a script is very similar to programming in other languages and won't be covered in this book. Suffice it to say that you should make sure the script is working under all circumstances you anticipate the end user may expect.

In HyperCard 2.0 Apple added a great deal of support for the formerly insidious task of debugging your HyperTalk scripts. With a built-in debugger, the ability to create checkpoints, and variable-watching, you can now do a decent job of debugging your complex HyperTalk handlers. We will have much more to say on this subject in Chapter 19.

▶ Finalizing the backgrounds

After you're sure the stack and all its scripts are working, you can confidently fill in the graphic, visual, and other details of the backgrounds. We are not talking about the functional or operational aspects of the background such as buttons and fields but rather of cleaning up fixed-text labels, adding graphic interest, detailing existing rough sketches, and the like.

▶ Documenting HyperTalk

As mentioned, HyperTalk permits you to write scripts that are easily read by other people, even those who are not proficient scripters. Throughout this book, we encourage this verbose, readable style for many reasons. If you are interested in some of the most cogent arguments for ensuring the readability of code, get a copy of Dr. Adele Goldberg's article, "Programmer as Reader," which appeared in the September 1987 issue of *IEEE Software* magazine. Among other things, she says, "Readability is an issue because we read to learn to write, and we read to find information, and we read in order to rewrite." We firmly agree.

One important and relatively easy way to make your HyperTalk scripts more readable is by choosing to use the verbose forms of many HyperTalk commands, operators, identifiers, and other key words that also have shorthand abbreviations. For example, both of the following lines mean the same thing, but you can easily see that one is far more readable than the other:

```
put "Help" into cd fld 3 of cd 14 of bg id 3097
put "Help" into card field 3 of card 14 of background id 3097
```

Another essential step in creating more readable HyperTalk scripts lies in commenting your scripts and handlers liberally. In HyperTalk you can include a comment on a line by itself or at the end of an executable line. HyperTalk ignores everything that follows the comment markers on a given line. Comments are indicated by the use of two hyphens next to each other (--). No space should appear between the two hyphens.

One other way to create readable scripts is to use descriptive variable names. Sacrifice brevity for readability.

But beyond writing your scripts in a verbose way and commenting them liberally (even though it requires a few extra keystrokes when you're typing the script), you should also be sure to include a Help function in your stack. Users are accustomed to seeing a question mark (see Figure 1-2) on which they can click to get help. The help screen that appears when you click on such a button is just another card or a pop-up field on the current card.

Figure 1-2. Typical HyperCard help-button icons

A final level of documentation involves the judicious use of buttons that are intuitive and visual effects that convey information to the user. These topics require an understanding of how HyperTalk works and deals with the user.

▶ Summary

In this chapter, you examined some of the reasons for doing your own HyperCard stacks and scripts. We discussed the process of designing stacks and examined the steps that are unique to HyperTalk.

Before you begin learning the HyperTalk language, however, you will be well served by taking a more conceptual look at HyperTalk and its HyperCard environment. This process begins in the next chapter, where we relate HyperTalk to the concepts of object-oriented programming.

2 ▶ Object-Oriented Programming

In this chapter, you will learn

- the important new role being played in software development by concepts grouped under the rubric "Object-Oriented Programming" (OOP)
- how HyperCard parallels some of those concepts and goes its own way in others
- how an understanding of OOP can help you be a better HyperTalk programmer

▶ HyperCard: Object-Like Programming

Let us be clear at the outset of this discussion. HyperTalk is not object-oriented programming in the "traditional" sense. We know it lacks some essential features of true OOP. But our interest in this chapter is how closely some key ideas in HyperCard resemble those in OOP. The objective is to see what the world of OOP has to offer would-be HyperTalk gurus.

To describe HyperTalk and its somewhat loose ties to OOP, we have coined the phrase *Object-Like Programming* (while not suggesting that we refer to it as OLP). HyperTalk is object-like in that it uses some of the same terminology, adopts some of the same methods and adapts others, and in many ways looks and "feels" like OOP.

Before you can appreciate the validity and utility of all this, though, you need a basic understanding of OOP. The next section presents some of the fundamental ideas in OOP, but it is not an exhaustive treatment of the subject. (For a more thorough treatment, see *Programming with MacApp* by Dave Wilson, Larry Rosenstein, and Dan Shafer, published in 1990 by Addison-Wesley as part of the Macintosh Inside Out series.) If you are already familiar with OOP, you might want to skim or skip the next section.

▶ OOP Fundamentals

Object-oriented programming is a way of looking at programming tasks that differ from the traditional approach. In procedural programming with Pascal, C, and other similar languages, you describe functions and procedures that operate on certain types of data. The data is separate from the functions that operate on it. In OOP, data and procedures that operate on the data are together, packaged in something called an *object*.

There are five central ideas in OOP: objects, messages, methods, classes, and inheritance. Although we explain each of these ideas briefly, they are so intertwined that an understanding of each depends on an understanding of the others.

▶ What are objects?

Viewed abstractly, an *object* is a single programming entity that combines data and procedures or functions that operate on that data. Viewed from a programming standpoint, objects are the elements of an OOP system that send and receive messages. We discuss messages in greater detail in the next section.

If you write a procedure to invert something in Pascal, you have to know in advance what kind of data the procedure will operate on. For example, inverting text might mean changing it from black letters on a white background to white letters on a black background. Inverting a matrix, however, is a complex mathematical operation unrelated to text color display. Similarly, inverting a graphic object like a pyramid is different from inverting text or numeric matrices. If you want a program to be able to invert any of these types of data, you would write a separately named procedure for each type of data, check in your program for the type of data to be manipulated, and then call the appropriate procedure. This process is depicted in Figure 2-1.

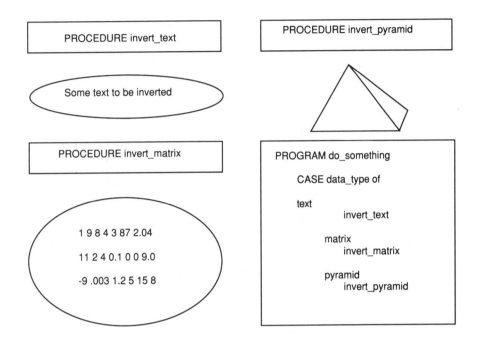

Figure 2-1. Data, procedures, and programs are separate in traditional programming

Object-oriented programming, however, permits the designer to say, in essence, "I want to invert whatever object I've been working with, so I'll just use an invert command and let the system take care of the problem." In OOP parlance, this command is referred to as a message. An object called, for example, matrix receives a message called invert and carries out its own processing in response to the message. There are still three separate invert routines, but the part of the program that inverts an object doesn't need to be aware of them. This situation is represented in Figure 2-2.

You can probably see an advantage to the OOP approach. If you want to add a new type of object to a procedural language application — for example, a list of items where invert means "reverse the order of" — you have to define a new procedure and add a new case to the main program. In other words, everything will change. Thanks to the well-known ripple effect, the consequences of this could take a long time to resolve. In an OOP world, though, you simply create a new object and add to it the ability to invert itself. Any other objects that send this new object an invert message do not need to be modified. The change is isolated and, therefore, manageable.

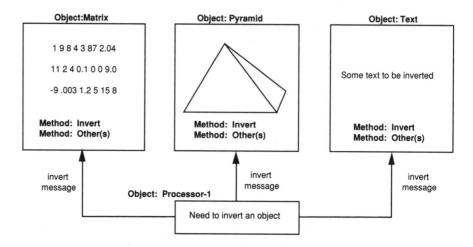

Figure 2-2. Data, messages, and methods in OOP

▶ What are messages?

We have talked glibly about messages as if it were obvious what they are and what they do. Although they may constitute a new *programming* idea, the concept of messages is not novel. When you call a friend across town and he or she answers the phone, you are sending messages. When you mail a letter to someone and the person on the other end opens it and reads it, you're sending messages. In fact, you probably do most of your work by sending messages of one kind or another to other people and to machinery or electronic equipment.

A *message* in an OOP world corresponds to a procedure or function call in a procedural language. Everything in OOP is accomplished only one way: One object sends a message to another object and the receiving object reacts. There are no alternate ways to get things done. The simple elegance of this model makes programs written for an OOP environment easy to understand.

▶ What are methods?

The idea of a *method* is the easiest of the five basic OOP concepts to explain. A method corresponds almost exactly to a function or a procedure. A method is the code in an object that tells the object how to react when it receives a message with the same name as the method.

In the previous example, each type of object had an *invert* method. When an object receives an *invert* message from another object, it simply carries out the instructions in that method. Sometimes, it sends a message back to the sending object indicating it has completed the instruction. Other times, it might trigger another method in another object, perhaps even a different *invert* method in another object, to accomplish its goals. To do so, it sends a message to that object.

If a message is sent to an object that does not have a method of that name defined, the system generally handles the problem with an error message such as "Object pyramid doesn't understand how to invert." Objects in OOP can have from zero to any theoretically large number of methods that they understand and that mold their behavior in reaction to messages from other objects.

▶ What are classes?

Groups of objects with sets of common characteristics are called *classes*. The most important thing objects in a class have in common is the way they react to one or more messages. If we had to write the same method for every single object, some of the advantages of OOP discussed in the next section would be lost in a mass of code. But if we define a class, each object we create as a member of that class will already know how to behave in response to the messages the class contains. The class, like everything else in an object-oriented world, is itself an object.

Individual objects are referred to as *instances* of a class. Because a class is also an object, an object can be both a class and an instance of another class. The concept that makes classes significant is the fifth OOP central idea: inheritance.

▶ What is inheritance?

In a true object-oriented world, objects *inherit* behavior from their *ancestors* in an ever-expanding and descending chain of heredity. All objects in OOP have at least one ancestor. The closer an object is to the root object class from which all other objects and classes spring, the fewer ancestors it has. This structure resembles an outline or a classification scheme.

Figure 2-3 depicts a classification structure for a class called Furniture. As you can see, this class has subclasses called Seating, Table, and Lamp. The subclass Seating, in turn, has other subclasses, and so on.

The key idea in inheritance is that if the class Furniture has a method called, for example, moveIt, every member of every subclass can use that method in the same way. If you send the message moveIt to a love seat, it need not have a method called moveIt. It simply passes the message up the hierarchy to its immediate ancestor (in this case, Sofa), which reacts if it has a method named moveIt or passes the message on if it doesn't have a corresponding method.

Class: Furniture
    Class: Seating
        Class: Chair
            Instance: armchair
            Instance: easy chair
            Instance: secretarial chair
        Class: Stool
            Instance: milking stool
            Instance: bar stool
            Instance: snack counter stool
        Class: Sofa
            Instance: sofa bed
            Instance: sofa
            Instance: love seat
    Class: Table
    Class: Lamp

Figure 2-3. Typical classification scheme

Generally, you can override a method that a class has in common so that an individual instance can react differently to that message. If you find yourself doing this too often, the method may be one that isn't really a good one around which to build a class.

▶ Object-oriented programming summary

Let's see if we can capsulize this sketchy look at object-oriented programming. Everything in an OOP environment is an object. Each object (except the one central object from which all others are descended) has at least one ancestor. An object inherits methods from all its ancestors in the chain that tell it how to respond to messages. Everything in an OOP environment is accomplished by objects sending messages to other objects.

▶ Why Object-Oriented Programming?

Why has OOP become such an important idea in the past few years? It really seems to be just a new way of looking at programs and data. So what's all the excitement about?

The characteristics inherent in OOP create numerous advantages in software design and development. Let's take a look at the three main ones often singled out by proponents of the OOP approach to computer programming. These are

- the natural "feel" of the OOP model of the problem
- the high degree of code reusability
- the ease of maintenance and modification

▶ OOP is "natural"

The world in which we live is composed of objects. And as we saw earlier, we accomplish much of what we do by sending messages to other objects in our world and reacting to their messages. Furthermore, we generally do things by telling other objects *what* we want done rather than by explaining in great detail *how* to do it. The *how* describes the procedure and is part of the procedural programming model. The *what* describes the task, the problem, and its solution in descriptive, or declarative, terms, and is part of the *declarative* programming model of which OOP is a prime example. When you give your Macintosh a print message, you don't tell it, "Now I want you to take this document that I've just finished creating and analyze its bit map structure. Got it?" You just tell it to print and expect its behavior to follow.

Similarly, if you give an assignment to a subordinate, you generally say, "I need the quarterly objectives report on my desk by 3:00, Jim." You don't say, "Jim, I want you to sit down at your desk. Take out a piece of paper and a pencil. Now, put at the top of the paper...."

But these descriptions — simplified for illustration — are good summaries of the differences between procedural programming and OOP. The world just doesn't work procedurally. Consequently, it is much easier to write programs designed to emulate or simulate reality and intelligence in OOP environments than in more procedure-oriented environments.

Note ▶ We should not leave the impression that the dichotomy is between procedural languages and OOP. The distinction is between procedural and declarative languages. OOP just happens to use a declarative style. Prolog, for example, is virtually never used in OOP environments but is a declarative language.

▶ Code reusability

If you can define one object that is usable in several different systems, you can move it from one system to another with great ease in an OOP environment. There is nothing new to declare in the second system, no data structures to worry about, no other objects or procedures to modify. Simply pick up the object from program A and plop it down in program B and run it.

Consequently, if a programmer is proficient in and comfortable with OOP design concepts, he or she spends a great deal of time building reusable tools and objects. After that, a large percentage of programming time is spent simply assembling the appropriate objects into new "worlds," or systems. Very little time gets used up by reinventing wheels.

▶ Ease of maintenance

As we saw earlier, the ripple effect that causes so many software maintenance headaches all but disappears in an OOP environment. If the object behaves in a certain way in system A, it is guaranteed to work the same way in system B. Debugging is effectively (though not totally) reduced to finding messages sent to inappropriate objects, messages sent with the wrong number of arguments, and missing or undefined objects and methods.

▶ OOP and HyperCard

So what does all of this have to do with HyperCard and HyperTalk? After all, we've already pointed out that HyperTalk is not an object-oriented programming language.

There are some strong parallels between HyperTalk and true OOP systems, though, and these parallels are neither accidental nor incidental. Although the parallels are not exact and don't hold up throughout the architecture of HyperTalk, they are interesting and important enough to merit our attention. Our hope is that by seeing the aspects of design and programming that HyperTalk and more traditional OOP languages have in common, you will see how to take advantage of OOP concepts in designing stacks.

▶ Objects in HyperTalk

There are five types of objects in HyperTalk: stacks, backgrounds, cards, buttons, and fields. Like OOP objects, each of these can send and receive messages. Each type of object can be associated with a *script* that contains *handlers,* which correspond to methods (as we'll see in a moment). So the object and the program code that enables it to respond in a specific and predictable way to a message are packaged together, exactly like objects in an OOP environment. (For some purposes, windows might be considered objects. They have properties, which are discussed in Chapter 17. But since you cannot attach a script to a window and since a window is not part of the hierarchy of inheritance, which we'll discuss shortly, we will not treat windows as objects in this book.)

▶ Messages in HyperTalk

The parallel between OOP systems and HyperTalk continues when we examine the subject of messages. HyperTalk uses the same term to describe the communications that take place between objects.

HyperTalk includes system messages that are sent as a result of events triggered by stack users. Each type of message can be addressed to one or more of the types of objects encompassed by HyperCard.

When an event takes place, a system message is generated and sent to the object of which the event is the target. That object reacts as called for in the handlers contained in its script. The parallel with OOP is quite strong.

▶ Methods in HyperTalk

As we have pointed out, each type of object in the HyperCard hierarchy can have a script associated with it. In each script there can be one or more handlers. These handlers correspond closely to OOP methods. A handler is associated with each type of message the object can receive.

There are two types of handlers in HyperTalk scripts: function handlers and event handlers. The latter derive their name from the fact that they are typically triggered by an event, as described in the preceding section.

All HyperCard objects also have properties associated with them. Properties are an important concept; they are discussed in depth in Chapter 17. Some properties bear a close resemblance to methods as well. For example, a button can have a property of being automatically highlighted when it is pressed. This is a character trait, or behavior, of the object, and so it corresponds at least roughly to a method.

▶ Classes in HyperTalk

There is no strong analog in HyperTalk to OOP's concept of *classes*. The hierarchical form of inheritance (see the next section) used in HyperTalk is not precisely parallel to that of object-oriented programming, due in part to the lack of classes for objects. For example, there is no class called a button class to which all buttons belong and which has individual instances of buttons. Although there is some commonality of behavior among buttons — they all, for example, cause something to happen when they are pressed — there is really no classification scheme resembling OOP classes.

The concept of card *backgrounds*, however, comes close to emulating an OOP class. All cards in a stack with the same background have many common characteristics. They usually look the same, and buttons that appear on backgrounds look and act identically from card to card within the background group. When you design a stack, you generally group cards with similar functions into backgrounds in the stack. Complex stacks almost always have more than one background.

But because you put specific card types into the same background group rather than have them formed by the program as a consequence of their functional similarity or as a direct result of a command, the parallel with OOP classes is not quite complete.

▶ Inheritance in HyperTalk

There is no true inheritance in HyperTalk. Messages pass through a definite hierarchy (see Figure 2-4), and this hierarchy has some of the characteristics of OOP inheritance structures, but the analogy is less complete when it comes to inheritance than on any other point.

The hierarchy in Figure 2-4 is up from the button or field, where the action takes place that triggers the event, to the card, background, and stack, then to the Home stack, and finally to HyperCard itself.

A message that originates with the press of the mouse on a button gets passed up the hierarchy until one of two things happens: A handler with the same name is encountered and executed or the top of the hierarchy is reached with no handler having intercepted and acted on the message. This behavior is quite similar to the message-processing approach of OOP systems.

But the opposite is not true. In other words, just because a particular button on a card has the ability to respond to a specific type of message does not mean that all other buttons have the same capability. The same can be said of backgrounds and cards. If you create a new card using the Edit Menu's New Card option, the new card has the same background as the currently visible card unless you specifically choose not to copy that background (in which case you end up with a blank new card). If the background has a handler for a particular system message, the copy also has that same handler. But this is not inheritance so much as it is copying, because the new card of the same background is not a descendant of the original; both are on the same level of the hierarchy.

You can also modify the inheritance path dynamically in your scripts to a limited degree. Beginning with HyperCard 2.0, you can place up to ten existing HyperCard stacks into the message hierarchy between your stack and the Home stack. This makes it possible for you to redefine at least a significant part of the hierarchy and to create libraries of scripts that can be shared among other stacks only when they are needed.

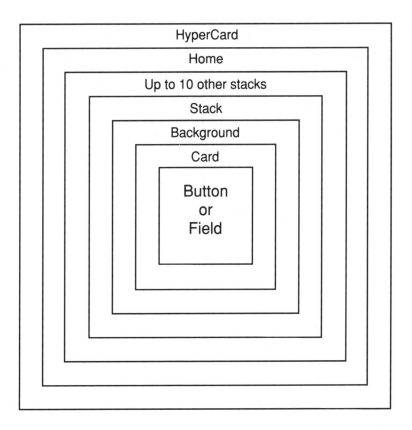

Figure 2-4. HyperTalk hierarchy of inheritance

▶ How OOP thinking helps in stack design

You can see why we said at the outset of this discussion that HyperTalk is not true OOP but shares enough with that approach to software design to merit consideration of the parallels.

We mentioned that code reusability is a major advantage of OOP systems. Because of the absence of true inheritance, that advantage does not accrue to HyperTalk. Thanks to the Macintosh's marvelous cut-and-paste editing power, you can easily copy scripts and handlers from one object to another object of the same type (or even a different type). But this manual process, no matter how facile, hardly qualifies as inheritance of behavior from object to descendant object.

On the other hand, the isolated nature of a handler and its ease of modification mean that maintaining scripts is much easier than modifying and managing traditional procedural programs. If the handler works in response to the message it handles in one card or button, it will work correctly in another place. Similarly, if a script has more than one handler, even if they interact, the functionality is isolated to a sufficient degree that software maintenance is quite straightforward.

Finally, and perhaps most significantly to HyperTalk programmers, the language does a remarkably good job of emulating the world of which it is a model: that of the Macintosh application. It makes working with the complex world of objects much simpler, more readable, and more enjoyable than any other Macintosh product since the first desktop appeared on the first 128K Mac screen several years ago.

Partly because of its strong object influence and partly because of the nature of the Macintosh world that lends itself well to such object emulation, HyperTalk removes many of the barriers between programmers and elegant, usable, Mac-like applications.

▶ Summary

In this chapter, we looked at the basic concepts of the new software idea called object-oriented programming (or OOP) and saw how they relate to the HyperTalk programming language. We also saw that the parallels between the two approaches are strong but not complete. We learned some of the advantages of OOP and saw how those advantages translate into the world of HyperTalk design and programming.

Chapter 3 is a refresher course in how HyperCard works from the viewpoint of a browser or author.

3 ▶ HyperCard Refresher

This chapter reviews some of the basic ideas in HyperCard as seen by the users of your stacks. Topics include

- user preferences
- navigation techniques
- links
- using **find**
- authoring tools
- field creation and characteristics
- button creation and characteristics
- copying, moving, and sizing objects
- using HyperCard on read-only media, such as CD-ROM

▶ The User's Viewpoint

Before we launch into a discussion of programming in HyperTalk, let's pause and take a telescoped look at HyperCard from the perspective of the users who do not generally program their own stacks. Until now you were probably in this category. So it may seem redundant to spend any time on the *use* of HyperCard. After all, you bought this book to learn to *program* HyperCard your way, not to learn to use it.

But our objective here is not to teach you to use HyperCard. It is rather to refresh your recollection about aspects of its use that may by now have become so familiar that you don't think about them much. Additionally, we look at some of the authoring techniques that you'll need to emulate in your scripts with commands. You are used to performing techniques with explicit mouse-and-tool manipulation. But running these tools by remote control, through a HyperTalk script, has a slightly different feel. By spending these few minutes, you will also understand the user's relationship to HyperCard. That will make the rest of your exploration of this book more fruitful.

▶ What kind of user?

When we talk about the user's perspective, what kind of user do we have in mind? Given that there are several levels of user below that of scripting, what level are we talking about here?

Throughout this book we will focus on designing and providing stacks for users who are browsers and typers. We are convinced that most HyperCard users fall into those two categories, at least in terms of the way they use stacks built by others. Interestingly, far more HyperCard users than anyone ever anticipated end up doing at least some scripting as part of their experience with the product.

You will probably want to design your stack so that the user who wants to do authoring can't get into your scripts and change anything fundamental. And you will probably not want your users to be able to relocate buttons and fields, particularly if you rely on their position for some of the tasks in your scripts.

So the primary emphasis is on the user who wants to get at a stack of information, put new data into a stack, and use the knowledge stored there without moving things around or changing the way they work.

But we also discuss authoring techniques and tools. By now you probably have some experience with these aspects of HyperCard. Although we don't expect the user of your stacks to understand these tools, you will often use the techniques described in this chapter to build basic cards and backgrounds. And you'll be doing object manipulation that originates in the authoring environment from within scripts.

▶ User preferences

HyperCard has five levels of user involvement. These are outlined in settings on the User Preferences card in the Home stack, as shown in Figure 3-1. Each higher level of control gives users access to additional tools.

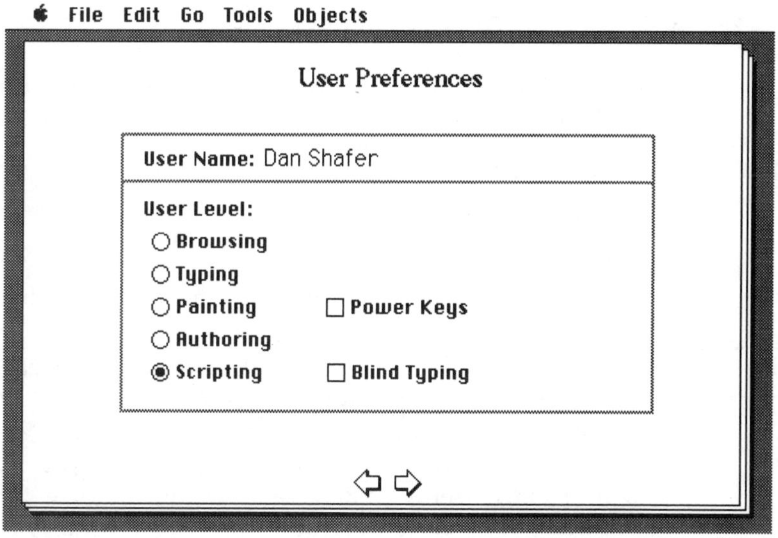

User Preferences

User Name: Dan Shafer

User Level:
○ **Browsing**
○ **Typing**
○ **Painting**   □ **Power Keys**
○ **Authoring**
◉ **Scripting**   □ **Blind Typing**

⇦ ⇨

Figure 3-1. User preferences settings

At the *browsing* level, users can only look at information in a stack. This corresponds to traditional read-only access. Moving to the *typing* level, users can enter and edit text in card fields, giving them read-write access to data but still restricting them from changing the stack's structure.

When users have *painting*-level control, they can add graphic objects to the stack or to any card with the powerful paint tools built into HyperCard. At this point, users can change the stack's appearance but not its functionality.

Users with *authoring* access can modify fields and buttons, create new backgrounds, and generally modify anything about a stack except the scripts attached to objects. This is the highest level of control over HyperCard you can use without learning to program in the HyperTalk language.

Only by setting the level to *scripting* can users gain access to scripts and HyperTalk commands for permanent modification of the stack.

Note ▶ To do the work in this book, make sure you have set your user level to scripting on the User Preferences card of the Home stack. It's probably a good idea to do that now if you haven't previously done so.

▶ Modifying the user's level

As you will see in Chapter 17, one of HyperCard's global properties that your script can monitor and modify is the user's access level. You can be in control of this the entire time your stack is running. If you want to disallow access above the browsing or typing level because such access could be dangerous to your stack, you can

- set the user level in your script
- intercept and prevent any effort by the user to modify the level

| Caution ▶ | If you do find it necessary to change the user's access level during the use of your script, be sure to change it back to its original setting when your script is finished and the user is returning to the Home stack or going on to other work. If you fail to do so, you may find yourself with some highly irritated users who find themselves unable to perform tasks they should be able to perform on other stacks after using yours. |

▶ Browsing-Level Operations

Even a browsing-level user can perform a number of functions in HyperCard. We will concentrate on two activities that constitute most of those actions and, not coincidentally, the bulk of the browsing-level commands in HyperTalk: navigation (moving between cards and stacks) and finding information in fields.

▶ Navigation functions

As you design and construct stacks, keep in mind the ways in which the casual user is accustomed to moving around in HyperCard.

Most stacks have buttons the user can click to move forward or backward in the stack, to the beginning of the stack, or to the last card in the stack. These buttons often look like those shown in Figure 3-2, though, of course, they need not look like them at all. The buttons in Figure 3-2 are included with Hyper-Card in the Ready-Made Buttons stack.

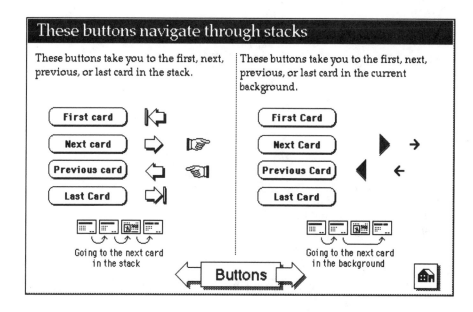

Figure 3-2. Typical navigation buttons

Because browsers are accustomed to buttons of this type for navigation, you should consider including such buttons in your stacks and retaining their usual meanings. Placing a right arrow button in your stack and expecting the user to know that the button increases the value of a number in a field, for example, is not a terrific design idea.

On the other hand, feel free to invent new icons or shapes for buttons that are, at least to some degree, self-evident. For example, if you want to let a reader who has clicked on the turned-up corner of a card move forward and backward in the stack, this is relatively easy to do and may be sufficiently evident that the user figures it out easily and becomes comfortable with it.

Clicking on buttons is not the only way users can navigate, of course. They can choose items from the Go menu (see Figure 3-3) or type their keyboard equivalents. All these navigation techniques are available to the browsing user.

It is unlikely that you will design a stack in which you don't want the user to be able to navigate. But if you do design such a stack, not only will you want to exclude the usual navigation buttons, you will also want to design handlers to trap both key combinations the user can type to navigate and menu selections.

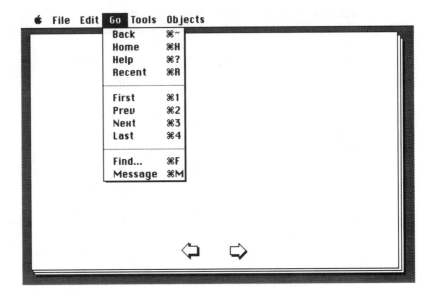

Figure 3-3. Go menu

▶ Using find

Another common task the browsing user performs is locating information stored in fields by using the **find** command. This command can be invoked by a menu selection from the Go menu or by typing Command-F from the keyboard. When the user selects a **find** operation, the Message box appears (if it was previously invisible), with the word *find* already typed and the cursor flashing between two quotation marks (see Figure 3-4). The user then types in the string to be searched for in the stack. When HyperCard finds the string, it stops on the card and draws a rectangle around the located text (see Figure 3-5).

Quite often the user types in more than one word to find. In that event, HyperCard finds a card on which all of the words appear, regardless of their order, relation to one another, or even if they are all in the same field. For example, if the user searches for New England, a card that describes the new Prime Minister of England is found, with the word new marked.

With HyperCard versions beginning with 1.2, the user can force HyperCard to find multiple-word groups only if they appear in one field and in exactly the order given. This **find whole** function is invoked when the user presses Shift-Command-F from the keyboard or uses the command inside the Message box or a script.

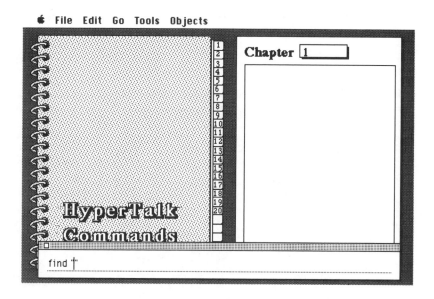

Figure 3-4. The find Message box

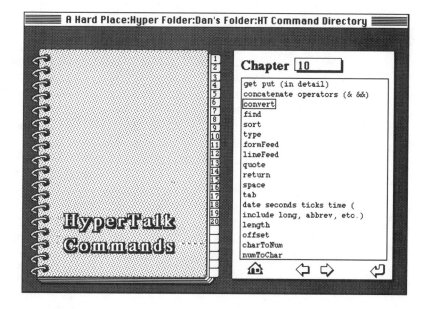

Figure 3-5. HyperCard finds text

If you are designing a stack that involves data management (see Chapter 10), you may want to include more sophisticated **find** capabilities in your scripts. You can, for example, let the user confine the search to a single field. But the basic **find** process is the same.

▶ Authoring-Level Operations

At the authoring level, the user can perform an almost endless variety of functions. The ones with which we are most concerned, however, involve manipulating HyperCard objects, particularly buttons and fields. Some of these functions in turn involve the use of tools other than the browsing tool. We discuss the following operations in the context of scripting:

- adding and deleting cards
- tool selection and use
- creating fields
- creating buttons
- copying, moving, and resizing buttons and fields

▶ Adding and deleting cards

Because the New Card, Delete Card, and Cut Card options appear on the Edit menu, you might think the browsing-level user has access to them. After all, the Edit menu is displayed when the user is a browser. But there are two different Edit menus in HyperCard, one for browsing users and one for all other levels. The menu on the left of Figure 3-6 shows what facilities the browsing-level user has available. The one on the right is the full Edit menu.

As you will see when we begin exploring HyperTalk's commands, you can design handlers to intercept the user's attempts to delete cards, cut cards, or create new ones. Sometimes you want special control over these functions if your stack allows their use. For example, you might not want to let users delete a card that has an outstanding value in a field. Or you might not want to let users delete anything unless they have a special password that the manager of the script-using team gives to only certain members of the group.

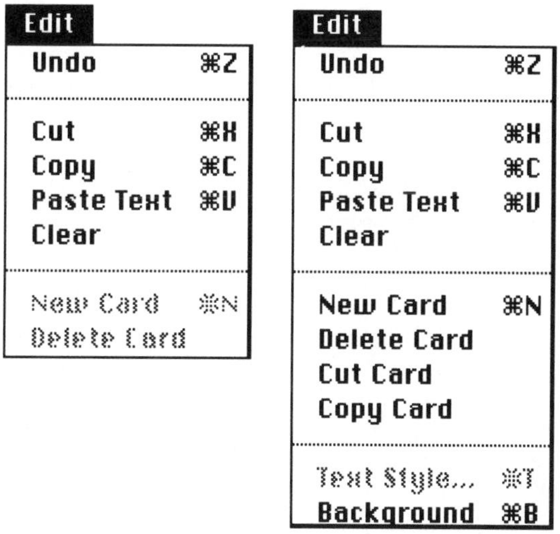

Edit menus shown:

Edit	
Undo	⌘Z
Cut	⌘H
Copy	⌘C
Paste Text	⌘U
Clear	
New Card	⌘N
Delete Card	

Edit	
Undo	⌘Z
Cut	⌘H
Copy	⌘C
Paste Text	⌘U
Clear	
New Card	⌘N
Delete Card	
Cut Card	
Copy Card	
Text Style...	⌘T
Background	⌘B

Figure 3-6. HyperCard's Edit menus

▶ Tool selection and use

Authoring-level users of HyperCard can also access the button, field, and painting tools from the Tools menu (see Figure 3-7). Using these tools, users can modify basic information about buttons and fields or alter the appearance of a card or a background.

The three tools across the top portion of the Tools menu are the browsing tool, button tool, and field tool, respectively. All tools below the dotted line in the menu are painting tools. Depending on the tool selected, the user can perform various tasks using the tools directly or accessing menu options that only appear when a specific tool is chosen.

From within a script, you can choose a tool and then use various commands to manipulate it as if by remote control. You can also intercept an attempt to access a specific tool and either prevent it or post a warning notice that lets users proceed only after acknowledging that what they're about to do could damage the stack or card content.

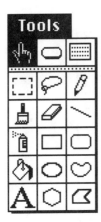

Figure 3-7. Tools menu

▶ Creating fields and buttons

Users with authoring-level access to HyperCard can create new objects besides cards. They can add buttons and fields to a card or background. (They can also modify them, as we will see in the next section.) Because these operations can alter the nature of your stack and the execution of your scripts, you may want to provide intercepting handlers.

Users can create a new field in two ways. They can choose the New Field option from the Objects menu, or they can use the field tool to select and copy an existing field, then move it to a different place on the card or background. New button creation is a similar process. Copying can be done either with a menu option or by dragging the selected object with the Option key held down. If you are faced with users who have authoring-level access to Hyper-Card, you will want to be sure to either permit such modifications and plan for them or provide handlers to intercept the user's attempt to manipulate the stack via menus or tools and provide appropriate barriers or warnings.

▶ Altering fields and buttons

Besides adding new buttons and fields, users can delete, copy, move, and resize existing objects if they have authoring-level access to your script. As is the case with creating new objects, they can modify existing objects either by using the right tool and selecting the object manually or by using menu choices.

For example, the user can delete a button after it is selected by

- pressing the Backspace key
- choosing "Cut Button" from the Edit menu
- choosing "Delete Button" from the Edit menu
- pressing Command-X at the keyboard

Deleting other objects is also easy to do and there are many ways to accomplish the deed. Your script will have to deal with each of these possible situations to avoid serious damage to your stack.

Users can also use the appropriate tool to select an object, then drag it to a new location or resize it or both. Most of the time, this will not affect your scripts, because the object's location on the screen is not vital to your script's execution. Wherever the user drags a button, it will still carry out its task when it is pressed. But if you have script commands that depend on the exact screen locations of objects, you will want to monitor the changing of those locations by the user.

▶ Protecting the User...And Your Stacks

As you can tell from the preceding discussion, there are times when you need to be able to protect the user from making fatal or serious mistakes purely out of a lack of understanding of the consequences of certain actions. At the same time, you may need to protect the integrity of your stacks against such ill-advised alterations.

There are three basic ways of handling this protection:

- by setting certain card properties in the information dialog for cards
- by setting those same card properties — as well as others, plus stack properties that are not accessible via the dialog boxes — in your scripts
- by writing handlers to trap the user's activities and change or override the attempted actions on the fly

You can designate certain cards as not deletable by the user, for example, either by clicking on the "Can't Delete" button in the Card Info dialog box or by using a script command to set the card's **cantDelete** property to true. Similarly, you can prevent the user from looking for button objects with the Command-Option key combination by setting a stack's **cantPeek** property to true, and from stopping your scripts from executing by setting the stack's **cantAbort** property to true. We will have much more to say about these and related subjects in Chapters 9 and 17.

▶ Avoiding user paranoia

It may seem as if we are suggesting that you spend a great deal of time and effort worrying about how to protect your stack and its users. One word of advice and clarification is in order: Don't.

Macintosh users are accustomed to a great deal of freedom and flexibility when they run applications. The Macintosh's design philosophy is that the user, not the programmer, is the boss. If you design a script so that users can do exactly what you want them to do and nothing else, you may find the script is not well-received, at least by experienced Macintosh users.

Ultimately, you must balance the need for your stack to stay relatively unmolested and predictable against the user's right to and expectation of a great deal of flexibility, freedom, control, and power.

▶ HyperCard and CD-ROM

From the time of its introduction, HyperCard was clearly perceived by many people to be the key for unlocking the potential of such huge mass-storage media as CD-ROM (Compact Disc Read Only Memory) and laser discs. In its first releases, however, HyperCard could not work directly on locked (that is, read-only) media, which limited its usefulness for such activities.

Beginning with Version 1.2, however, HyperCard can work with locked media.

▶ Summary

This concludes our discussion of how HyperCard works from the user's perspective and how those operations should affect your thinking as you script stacks. You have seen that users can perform many tasks, some of which may be undesirable. And you know that there are ways to intercept users' actions and either prevent them or at least warn of the consequences before allowing them to proceed.

Chapter 4 describes the basic building blocks of which all HyperCard applications are composed and begins our study of the HyperTalk programming language.

4 ▶ HyperTalk Building Blocks

In this chapter, you will learn about the items that make up HyperTalk, including

- action elements
- passive character traits
- objects

This chapter presents an overview of these HyperTalk building blocks; each is discussed in detail in one or more places later in the book.

▶ Naming Things in HyperTalk

Before we begin our examination of the components of the HyperTalk programming language, we should pause to discuss the rules regarding the names of things in HyperTalk.

Action elements and variables in the HyperTalk language are generally made up of one word. Action elements include functions, commands, and messages. If you define a new function designed to reverse the characters in a string, for example, you can call it *reverse, reverseString, reverseIt*, or something similar. But you cannot name it *reverse the string* because that name has more than one word. Similarly, variables, a type of special item called a *container* in HyperTalk, must also have one-word names.

Passive elements other than variables are not generally named; they are more correctly viewed as part of the structure of the language, as we will see in a few moments.

Objects can be named almost anything you wish, using as many words as you like. Thus, you can have a stack named *My Important Stuff* and a card named *Books and Magazine Articles*. Buttons frequently have two-word or three-word names (though you have to watch the length and make sure it can be seen through the button if you have HyperCard show the name on the button). This makes HyperCard friendlier for users. A button named *Do It!* is more communicative than one called *doIt*, which might in fact also be misread.

▶ Several words in one

One naming technique HyperTalk scripters often use is to run two or more words together into one and then capitalize the first letter of each embedded word. You'll see labels like *currentStackName*, *mouseUp*, and *passMeTheSalt* sprinkled through the HyperTalk script examples in this book and other scripts.

This approach to naming things is not unique to HyperTalk. Programmers have been using the technique for many years. But some programming languages have limits on the lengths of names that make the use of such an approach marginally useful at best. In HyperTalk you won't encounter any limit that will become problematic. A button or field, for example, can have a name up to 253 characters long.

▶ The first character is important

It is a good idea to avoid beginning the name of any HyperTalk item with a number, although it is not, strictly speaking, illegal. HyperCard stores everything as strings of characters and tries to interpret the nature of this information from its context. The matter is further complicated because HyperCard automatically assigns identification numbers to objects other than stacks when they are created. Suppose you name a card *1234Alpha* and then try to tell HyperCard to **go** to that card. HyperCard is likely to assume from the first digit that this label is a card ID. As a result, it won't find the card. Begin names with a letter, and you'll avoid a lot of confusion!

▶ Active Elements of HyperTalk

An active element, for the purpose of our discussion, is any component of HyperTalk that results in something happening in the environment. Messages are the basic active element, but there are several others, including

- commands
- handlers
- functions
- scripts

These elements and their use occupy much of our attention in this book. The following brief discussion simply puts those future discussions into perspective rather than providing an exhaustive treatment of each subject.

▶ Messages

We have spent some time in Chapter 2 describing messages and their role in HyperTalk. Now let's examine a message structurally.

All HyperTalk messages consist of only one word. That important idea is sometimes hard to remember. Because HyperTalk includes the ability to add *throw-away* words, some messages look like they're longer than one word. For example, in Chapter 13 we'll see the use of visual effects in HyperTalk. These effects can be called with the message **visual**. But they can also use the optional second word **effect** so that the command looks like **visual effect zoom open.**

But only the first word of a message is the message itself. Everything that comes after is either a parameter or additional descriptive information (to tell HyperTalk what object to affect with the message, for example).

The rule that only the first word of a message is its name becomes important when you write handlers to respond to messages. The handler must be associated with a message name. Requiring that all message names be one word makes life much easier for us scripters!

▶ Handlers

There are two types of handlers in HyperTalk: event handlers and function handlers. An event handler always begins with the key word **on** followed by the name of the message it is designed to handle. It also ends with the key word **end** followed again by the name of the message it handles. Most handlers you write will be event handlers.

A function handler begins with the key word **function** followed by the name of the function it defines. The purpose of this handler is to allow you to define new functions that can be used by other event handlers. This type of handler also ends with the key word **end** followed by the name of the function involved.

After you define a function in a function handler, it is available to all other event and function handlers in the same script or lower in the HyperTalk hierarchy. A function handler cannot be defined within another function handler or an event handler.

There are some operational differences between these two types of handlers. This subject occupies much of our attention in Chapter 5.

▶ Functions

Functions are of two types: built-in HyperTalk functions and user-defined functions. HyperTalk has approximately 60 functions that can be used in any handler. These functions involve such tasks as

- mathematical calculations

- locating and managing the mouse and its button

- dealing with date and time

In addition, you can define any function you need in function handlers. (It is also legal to define a function with the same name as a predefined one, but then you bear the responsibility for its proper use everywhere in your stack.)

▶ Scripts

A script in HyperTalk is a collection of one or more handlers — some or all of which may be empty — associated with a particular object.

You can think of a script as a program, but as you know from Chapter 2, that is a simplification. There are no programs in a HyperCard stack. Instead, you have one or more scripts, each composed of one or more handlers, which, taken together, constitute the methods describing the stack's behavior in response to messages.

▶ Passive Traits

Not everything in HyperTalk is active. Some elements of the language are for the convenience and use of active elements. These include

- variables
- properties
- control structures
- "chunks"

▶ Variables as containers of information

Throughout this book and other HyperCard and HyperTalk documentation, you will find the term *container* used quite frequently. It is easy, after a brief acquaintance with the term and its use, to conclude that a container is nothing more than a variable in a conventional programming language. That view, however, is too simplistic to be useful or accurate.

A variable is a type of container. But in the broader sense a container is anything that can be a repository of a value. Fields, the **message box**, and two special HyperTalk variables called **It** and **selection** can also hold information and so are containers.

All programming languages embody the concept of a variable. A variable is any word or symbol whose value can change as the program executes or from one execution of the program to another. This variability of value is where variables get their name.

In many programming languages, you have to define or declare variables explicitly before you can use them. This is not the case in HyperTalk. The rule is simple: When HyperTalk encounters a word in a script that cannot be interpreted as the name of an object or as a chunk of an object's contents, it assumes the word is a variable.

It really is that simple. In practical terms, this means that to use a variable in HyperTalk, you simply use it. No need to declare it, define its type, or otherwise alert HyperTalk to its existence or nature. Just use it and HyperTalk takes care of the details. Attempting to read from or evaluate a container before putting anything into it, however, generates an error in HyperTalk just as it would in any other programming language.

There are actually three types of variables in HyperTalk. *Global variables* are accessible to any handler in a script and to other scripts in the HyperCard environment. They must be explicitly declared global using the key word **global** in any script or handler where they are used. *Local variables* are known only inside the handler in which they appear and require no special handling. *Special variables* are furnished by the system and include **It**, **selection**, and **message box.** We will have more to say about these variables as they are used in subsequent chapters.

► Properties

All objects (except windows) have certain properties associated with them. For example, they all have system assigned ID numbers and optional names. They also have properties such as location, font characteristics, border, shape, and style.

These properties are all accessible to your scripts, and many can be changed from a script (as well as, more conventionally, through dialog boxes or other user-oriented means). Properties are often examined and decisions made based on the outcome of the examination. For example, you might want to check if a particular object is visible and, if not, to make it visible. Its visibility is a property that your script can both examine and change. Properties are a very important idea in HyperTalk. We devote all of Chapter 17 to their use.

► Control structures

Most programming languages embody elements called *control structures* that permit the programmer to alter the normal sequential flow of processing. HyperTalk is not an exception to that general rule. Both **repeat** loops and **if-then-else** conditional processing constructs are built into HyperTalk. These form the subject of Chapter 8.

► Chunks

The idea of chunking is unique to hypertext; HyperTalk, true to its roots, incorporates the use of chunks in its programming.

Simply stated, a chunk is any arbitrary portion of any container. A *chunk expression* uniquely identifies any given character(s), word(s), item(s), or line(s) in a container. You will come to appreciate chunks as you learn to program in HyperTalk.

Using chunking expressions, you can access individual elements of a container as easily as stringing together a kind of map to their locations. The map is built "inside-out," though, beginning with the smallest unit and moving out to the larger. Here are some examples. (Don't worry if some of the terminology isn't clear; it will be soon.)

```
second character of word 3 of fifth line of field 1 of card "Help"
char 5 to 8 of third word of testVariable
third item of It
```

You can see how powerful an idea chunking is. It permits you to gain precise control over many situations and data elements in a HyperTalk script. Soon after you begin scripting, chunking becomes second nature.

▶ Objects

We have spent a lot of time looking at objects in HyperTalk (see Chapter 2). Most of these concepts are familiar even to a browser of stacks, so they don't bear much further examination. However, we will take a brief look at each object type from a programmer's perspective and spend a fair amount of time on backgrounds, which are largely transparent to users and play potentially important roles in scripting.

▶ Stacks

Every stack has a name. When you choose "New Stack..." from the File menu, a standard file-creation dialog box appears as shown in Figure 4-1. You must give the stack a name by which it will be known to the Finder.

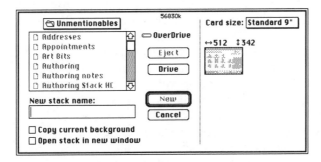

Figure 4-1. Stack-creation dialog box

All stacks have a Stack Info… dialog associated with them, which you can view by selecting the menu option with that name from the Objects menu. Figure 4-2 shows a typical stack information dialog. You'll learn more about individual characteristics of stacks in Chapter 17.

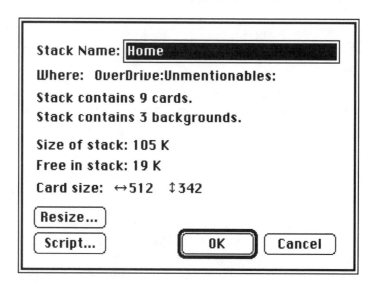

Figure 4-2. Stack Info… dialog box

▶ Backgrounds

If you've built some stacks in authoring mode, you are undoubtedly familiar with the concept of layers in HyperCard. We have also discussed backgrounds briefly in Chapter 2 as a means of subclassifying card types within a stack. Now let's take a deeper look at backgrounds from the viewpoint of the stack designer.

Every stack has at least one background and one card when it is created. If you create a new stack with the copy current background check box in the stack-creation dialog box of Figure 4-1 checked, you get a new stack with the same background as the one that is active when you create it. If you do not check that box, you get a blank white slate as your background.

The background is the most basic building block of a stack. It dictates the shape of all cards in the stack (assuming you have just one background) as well as their default graphic content and other characteristics. Following the idea of inheritance discussed in Chapter 2, anything that appears on the background appears automatically on all cards that share that background. The background is part of the card's appearance unless you specifically remove it.

But layered on top of this background are background object layers. Each button and field you define as a background button or field has its own layer. These layers are transparent overlays on top of the basic background. Like everything else that appears on the background, any background object appears on all cards sharing the background.

Any function or script that you want all cards of a specific background to have should be placed on a *background object layer* or attached to an object there. For example, if you want all cards of a particular background to have a title field at the top where large, bold type is used to display a brief title, define that field as a background field.

Fields that exist on backgrounds can work in one of two ways. They can either act merely as a repository that is common to all cards in the background, with each card managing its own contents for the field, or they can be designed to contain the same information on all cards. This latter approach is useful when you have a title you want to appear on every card in a stack. In that case, you have a choice between using a background field that shares its text content across all cards in the background or painting the title directly onto the background as part of the background picture.

Sometimes you will want all but a few cards of a given background to have a certain graphic or contain a certain field or button. In those cases, define the item as a background item and then use a technique such as designing an opaque button or using a paint tool to obscure it from view on those few cards where you don't want it to appear. This is more efficient than making the item a card-level item and placing it on all the cards you do want it on.

Most of the stacks you have designed in authoring mode probably had one background. In fact, most stacks have one background. But sometimes you will find it advantageous to use two or more backgrounds in a single stack.

You always have to make a trade-off in such situations. You can give a distinct appearance to cards that have different functions or contents by using contrasting backgrounds or by creating new stacks with single backgrounds.

Beginning with HyperCard 2.0, Apple made this trade-off decision somewhat more complex by making it possible to have multiple stacks open, with each stack limited to a single window. This means that some designs that formerly used multiple backgrounds for efficiency might now be improved by turning them into multistack designs, allowing the user to see each former background independently of the others and more than one type of background at a time.

▶ Cards

Every card can have its own fields, buttons, and graphics that don't automatically appear on any other card in the stack. These buttons and fields are accessible only from the card on which they appear, though it is perfectly permissible for them to send messages to objects on other cards, on the background, or higher in the HyperTalk hierarchy.

Like stacks, cards have an information dialog box (see Figure 4-3) that gives you some information about them. This identifying information is often used in scripts.

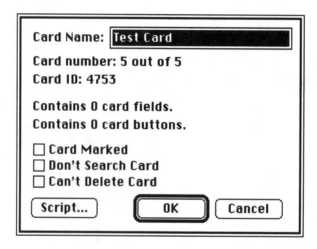

Figure 4-3. Card Info... dialog box

▶ Windows

A card window is unlike the other building blocks we've been talking about in a number of ways. You don't create it explicitly; it comes along for free whenever you open a stack. Each stack has one and only one card window, the size, location, and visible area of which you can control in your scripts.

Because you don't create them explicitly, card windows don't have a dialog box associated with them. They also have no protection property associated with them; if the stack or card they contain is protected from deletion, the window is also clearly not subject to deletion.

▶ Fields

Fields in HyperCard hold information. Everything in a field is stored as a text string. HyperTalk attempts to discern from the context of the way scripts use or refer to the data whether it is text information, numeric information, date and time information, or some other form of data.

A field's content is frequently the target of chunking expressions (discussed previously in this chapter). Fields can be any of several types. They also have identifying information associated with them, as you can see in the Field Info... dialog box in Figure 4-4.

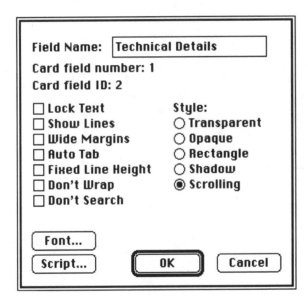

Figure 4-4. Field Info... dialog box

▶ Buttons

HyperTalk buttons are the objects most frequently used by browsers and other script users. Most of the scripts you write will be button scripts that activate when the user releases the mouse button. Buttons can be of several types and almost any arbitrary shape. They are the only object that a nonscripter can "program" in the sense of giving them some instructions to perform when they are activated.

Figure 4-5 shows a Button Info... dialog box for a new button. The values shown are the defaults for a button.

A button is the only object whose script starts out with some information in it. Figure 4-6 shows what a button script looks like before you put anything into it. HyperTalk furnishes the skeleton of a **mouseUp** handler because most buttons have at least this handler if they are going to be useful.

Figure 4-5. Button Info... dialog box

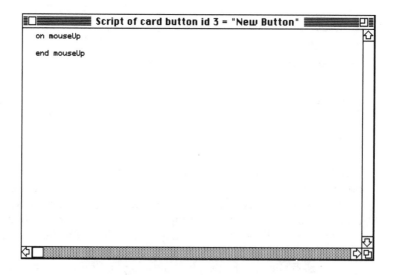

Figure 4-6. Starting button-script template

Note ▶	Actually, there is no script stored with the button unless you put some commands between the lines HyperTalk provides when you open the script editing window. If you open the script editing window and close it without creating any commands, the script will be empty. HyperTalk simply gives you a helping hand when you open a button's script and no handlers have yet been defined. This becomes important when we consider that messages are "trapped" by handlers and not passed up the hierarchy. The **mouseUp** message is not trapped by an empty button script.

▶ Pictures

Any artwork drawn using HyperCard's built-in painting tools on a card or a background becomes a card or background *picture*. Only one such picture can be associated with each card and each background.

Card and background pictures can be shown or hidden using scripting commands (see Chapter 13) or by setting a property that determines their visibility (see Chapter 17).

▶ Summary

You now have a good idea of all the pieces that make up a HyperTalk script. You know there are active elements that process information, determine the outcome of requests, and manage the environment. You also know that these active elements sometimes use passive elements. Finally, you know more about the functionality associated with each object type in HyperCard.

Chapter 5 introduces the concept of scripting and the basic techniques of HyperTalk stack design and construction.

5 ▶ HyperTalk Basics

In this chapter, you'll learn about
- the mechanics of entering, editing, printing, and managing scripts
- handlers and their crucial role in HyperTalk scripting
- messages and how they are passed inside HyperCard
- variables and how they are referred to and manipulated
- the special concept of a container and how it is used
- addressing the components of a field in an English-like way

This is a lot of ground to cover, but as you will soon see, learning HyperTalk is enjoyable and far less difficult than learning any other language you've tried. So get comfortable in front of your favorite Macintosh, and prepare to master the basics of HyperTalk.

▶ Script Mechanics

As you already know from our discussions in Chapters 3 and 4, HyperTalk scripts are attached to HyperCard objects. Any stack, card, field, or button can have a script associated with it. Any time you edit one of these objects — and assuming you have scripting access — one of the buttons that appears in its information dialog window is a Script button. Figure 5-1 shows such a button for a HyperCard field. You can gain access to the script for any HyperCard object by clicking the Script button in its Info... dialog.

Note ▶   In this discussion, we assume you are working with the built-in default script editor that comes with HyperCard. Beginning with Version 2.0, HyperCard permits you to define a third-party editor as your script-editing environment. If you are working in one of those tools, of course, the following discussion won't be accurate in most details. Refer to the user manual for the particular editor with which you are working.

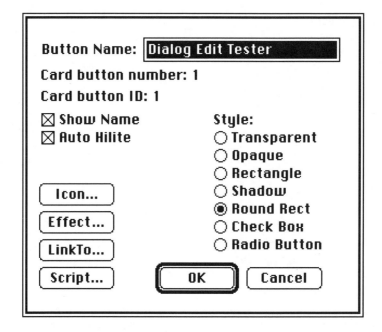

Figure 5-1. Script button gives access to object's script

You can look at the script of an object two other ways. First, you can select the appropriate tool, then double-click on the object while holding down the Shift key. Second, you can use the "peeking" method available in HyperCard Version 1.2 and later. This method uses the Option and Command keys, sometimes in combination with other keys, to open the script-editing windows of various HyperCard objects.

The Option-Command key combination with a mouse click opens any button script. Hold down the Shift key with the same combination and open a button or a field script: Option-Command-c opens the card's script; Option-Command-b, the background's script; and Option-Command-s, the stack's script.

Having opened a script-editing window by any method, you can close it one of three ways: by choosing "close script" from the script editor's File menu, using its keyboard equivalent, Command-W, or by holding down the Option and Command keys and clicking the mouse or pressing any key. If you have changed the script, HyperCard asks whether it should save the changes before it closes the editing window. You can also either choose the "Save Script" option from the script editor's File menu or use its keyboard equivalent, Command-S, to save the script any time during editing and before closing the script.

After you have opened the script-editing window for an object, you will see a screen similar to Figure 5-2. In most cases, the window will be empty. There are two exceptions to this rule. If you open a button script, HyperTalk supplies a framework for the most likely script you'll want to write by presenting a screen like that shown in Figure 5-3. The other exception to the empty-script rule: when you open the script window for an object that already has a script.

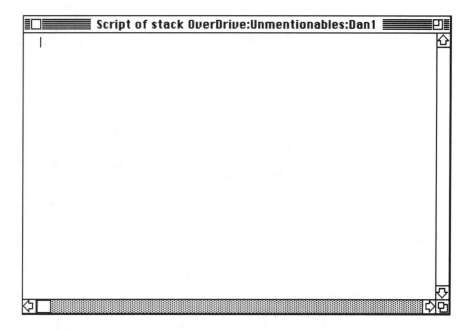

Figure 5-2. Typical empty script window

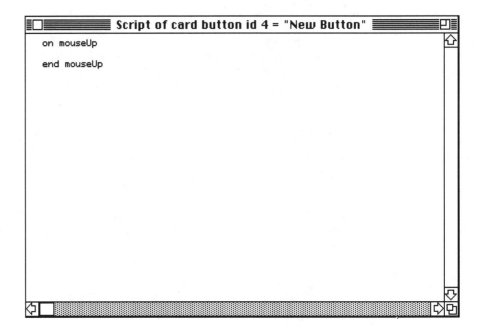

Figure 5-3. Button-script window on opening

After you are in a script window, you have the full range of editing capability you'd expect in a Macintosh editor. You can cut, copy, and paste using the usual command-key equivalents of Command-X, Command-C, and Command-V respectively or you can use the Script editor's special Edit menu beginning with Version 2.0. One particularly intelligent feature of the HyperTalk script editor is that it "knows" enough about the programming constructs in the language to handle indentation automatically. It places the cursor at the correct position for entering the next line each time you press the Return key. In addition, you can press the Tab key any time and the editor correctly reformats everything in the window.

A side benefit of this capability is that when you press the Tab key, the last line in the portion of the script you are working on, the handler is moved flush with the left border of the editing window. If you press the Tab key and the last line of the handler is anywhere but flush with the left border, you know there's something syntactically wrong with your script.

▶ The script editor's menus

When you open the script editor in HyperCard 2.0 and later, you'll see a new set of menus on the menu bar (see Figure 5-4). These menus give you full editing control over your script.

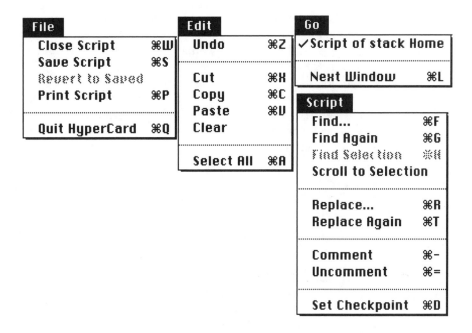

Figure 5-4. Find dialog in script-editing window

The File menu

In the File menu, you can save and close scripts. You can also revert to the most recently saved version of your script if you save it, edit it, and then wish not to save the changes you made since the last time you saved it. You can also print either the full script or, if you select some portion of it (for example, a single handler you may be debugging), just the selected portion. In the latter case, the menu option labeled "Print Script" in Figure 5-4 changes to "Print Selection."

From this menu you can also directly quit HyperCard without having to return to the stack itself.

The Edit menu

HyperCard's script editor's Edit menu is identical to most Edit menus with which you've worked on the Macintosh.

The Go menu

You can have more than one script open at a time in HyperCard (starting with Version 2.0). This menu gives you the means of either accessing other open stacks to edit scripts they contain or moving around among multiple open scripts.

If you have more than one script open at a time (see Figure 5-5), the top portion of the Go menu contains the names of all open scripts. The last item on the menu is always "Next Window." By selecting this you can rotate among the various open scripts and stacks. As with the same command in HyperCard's main Go menu, the Shift key brings the rearmost window to the front.

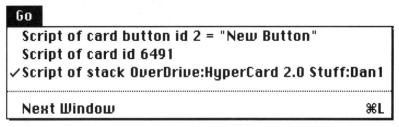

Figure 5-5. Script Editor's Go Menu with multiple scripts open

The Script window

You will do most of your work with an individual script in the Script menu. As you can see from Figure 5-4, this menu allows you to perform find-and-replace operations, comment or uncomment sections of code, or set a checkpoint for debugging purposes.

Finding and replacing are familiar operations to most Macintosh users, and they work in much the same way in the HyperCard script editor. Two options that you may not have seen before are "Find Selection" and "Scroll to Selection." The first lets you double-click on a word or drag-select a phrase in the script and then ask the editor to find the next occurrence of that word or phrase. This option can save you a great deal of typing when you are working through a script. "Scroll to Selection" will move the scroll bars of the script-editing window to make the currently selected text visible. You may need to do this if you select some text and then scroll around in the window looking for something and forget where you are in the window.

The editor includes the ability to select a segment of a script — part or all of a handler or multiple handlers, or even the entire script — and convert it to a HyperTalk comment or from a comment to executable code. You'll find this is quite handy when you are debugging your scripts.

We'll talk more about the "Set Checkpoint" option on this menu in Chapter 19 when we talk about debugging HyperTalk scripts.

▶ Long lines

Because a single command line in HyperTalk can be any arbitrary length, lines can and often do extend past the right edge of the editing window. Although this does no harm (the scripts still execute), debugging and reading these lines can become difficult. Fortunately, HyperTalk has a way to deal with this problem.

If you are entering a line of HyperTalk code into a script-editing window and want to break the line in the middle for readability, simply press Option-Return or Option-L-Return. This places a special symbol (¬) at that point in the text. This symbol is simply a way of notifying HyperTalk that you haven't finished the line. You can use this technique as many times in a single HyperTalk command line as you like. Don't use it in the middle of a text string enclosed in quotation marks, however, or errors will result.

▶ Syntax checking

The HyperTalk editor does not check syntax when you click the OK button. Syntax and logic errors only show up when you run the script. Other than using the Tab key to confirm that you have matched up beginnings and endings of portions of the handlers correctly, the only way to confirm that a script is correct is to execute it.

We'll see in Chapter 19 how we can debug scripts with syntax errors.

▶ Comments

Even though HyperTalk is one of the most inherently readable programming languages yet devised for computers, comments are still in order. You can put a comment anywhere in a script, manually or via the Script menu in the script editor. Comments start with two hyphens (--) and HyperTalk ignores everything that appears to the right of the hyphens. Comments can appear alone on one or more lines or at the end of the line they describe:

```
--This comment is the only thing on this line
put It -- This comment is on the same line as the command.
-- If a comment requires more than one line, each line of
-- the comment must begin with two hyphens.
```

▶ Handlers

Each HyperTalk script consists of one or more *handlers*. A handler is a programming construct that begins with the key word **on** or **function** and ends with the key word **end**. Both key words are followed by the name of the message to which these handlers are designed to respond. The button script template supplied by HyperTalk when you open a button's script window for the first time shows this pattern. It begins with the line **on mouseUp** and ends with **end mouseUp**. The **mouseUp** message is a system message (discussed in Chapter 6) sent whenever the user releases the mouse button.

Commands between the **on** and **end** key words are carried out whenever the object receives the message whose name follows them. This portion of the script handles the particular message for which the script is designed, which is why they are called handlers.

Any HyperTalk script can contain one or more handlers depending on the messages, or events, to which each object responds. These messages can be HyperCard system messages or messages you create just for your scripts.

The key idea to grasp is simply that HyperTalk scripts do one fundamental thing: They respond to messages. Messages are the actions to which a script must respond. Handlers are the intelligent vehicles for responding to the messages.

▶ Where messages originate

We have been talking about messages as if they were all user-generated. Most of the messages for which you will write handlers are a result of the user taking some action. As a result, they handle system messages (see Chapter 6) and have names that identify them as system message handlers. But you can also define your own messages, which then function much as subroutines in BASIC or Pascal. In this case, one handler generates a message that is dealt with by another handler.

This design feature means that you can put frequently needed activities in a single handler and then call that handler from other handlers. For example, you might have a number of handlers that need to ask users if they really want to quit doing some operation. If you define a handler to do this and call it quitOK, you can then call it from inside another handler like this:

```
on mouseUp
   -- some processing
   quitOK
end mouseUp
```

▶ A second type of handler

Sometimes, you need to define a type of message that can return an answer your script can use. This need is met by the ability to define a **function** handler. A **function** handler is identical to a message handler in form except that it always includes a special **return** statement that sends a result back to your handler. For example, you might need to find out the cube of a number in several different handlers. But you need the answer to be returned to you, not just left in the handler that carries out the calculation. The handler to calculate the cube might look like this:

```
function cube num
   return num * num * num
end cube num
```

To use this handler from inside another handler, you would simply write a line like this:

```
put cube(5) into answer
```

You can then take the answer in the container *answer* and operate on it any way you want.

▶ Messages

Without messages, most handlers are irrelevant. Messages are like notices passed from one part of the Macintosh system to another. When the user presses the mouse, a message called **mouseDown** is generated by HyperCard. When the user releases the mouse button, a **mouseUp** message is generated. These messages are sent along a pipeline, to be intercepted and handled by the first object that has a handler with the same name as the message.

▶ Message hierarchy

At first blush, it might appear that a message such as **mouseUp** would be sent to the object in which the pointer was located when the event took place. Most of the time, that's how HyperTalk scripts work. But it is not necessary that they work that way. For example, if a **mouseUp** message occurs on a card, the card may not be designed to respond to such a message at all. But the stack itself might want to do something in response to the user's release of the mouse button anywhere on the card outside of a button. In that case, the card would not have a **mouseUp** handler but the stack would.

So that HyperTalk will know where to route messages as they arise, the language includes a predefined hierarchy through which messages are passed. That hierarchy is depicted in Figure 5-6, an expanded version of the hierarchy described in Chapter 2.

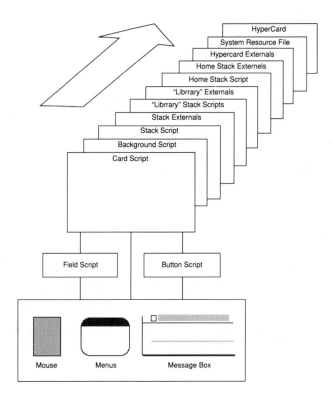

Figure 5-6. The message hierarchy

The three M's — mouse, menu, and Message box — are the primary sources of user-supplied messages. (The keyboard can also be a source of such messages but it generally acts only as a special case of one of the other sources.) Messages originating from the user's interaction with the menu bar or the Message box go directly to the script associated with the active card. This is because almost all such messages have an effect broader than a single field or button.

Mouse messages are the most complex of the three basic types of message. A mouse message — **mouseUp**, **mouseDown**, or **mouseStillDown** — can be sent to a button (the usual case), a field (provided the field contains locked text), or directly to the card. If the mouse message is generated by mouse activity within the confines of a field containing only locked text, the message is sent to that field first. If it occurs within the borders of a button, that button's script gets first crack at the message. If it occurs anywhere outside a field or a button, the card's mouse-message handler (if it has one) is given control.

Note ▶ There is a way to override explicitly the normal hierarchy for sending messages between HyperCard objects. The **pass** and **send** commands serve this purpose. For the moment, though, ignore this possibility and assume that only the natural order of message passing is possible in HyperTalk.

If the first object to receive a message has a handler with that message's name, it handles the message by following the instructions you put into that part of the script. Once this processing is complete, the message that started it all is "swallowed up" by HyperCard and goes no farther unless you force it to do so. But if the object does *not* have a handler for it, HyperCard simply passes the message up the hierarchy to the next level. This process continues until HyperCard either runs out of levels or finds a handler.

Example ▶ If a **mouseUp** message is generated in a locked-text field and that field's script does not have a handler beginning with the key phrase **on mouseUp**, HyperCard passes the **mouseUp** message to the currently active card. If the card doesn't have an **on mouseUp** handler, it passes the message to the background of the current card. This process continues until some object along the way *does* have a handler for this message or HyperCard itself is reached. (HyperCard is also an object in this sense; it is the default destination for all messages.)

The reason a field can only receive a mouse message if it has locked text may be apparent but is worth stating. If the text in a field is not locked, then a mouse click anywhere in the field is the way users show HyperCard where to put the next text they type or paste. This mouse-click is not designed to be intercepted, so no handler can be devised to do so.

In Figure 5-6, you'll notice references to stack externals, Home Stack externals, and HyperCard externals. These refer to HyperTalk's ability to have its language *extended* by the addition of commands and functions. Externals are new commands and functions written in Pascal, C, and other programming languages and added to HyperTalk. External command use is the subject of Chapter 21. Do not be concerned about them at the moment except to note where they are in the hierarchy of Figure 5-6.

▶ User-defined inheritance

Beginning with HyperCard Version 2.0, you can modify the default message-passing hierarchy in an interesting way. With the **start using** command, you can insert up to ten different HyperCard stacks into the normal hierarchy between your stack and Home. Any message — including, of course, system messages generated by HyperCard — that is not handled in your stack will go to the stack scripts in these intermediate stacks before being passed to Home and then to HyperCard itself.

You can use the commands associated with the user-defined hierarchy definition to build libraries of scripts that are useful in certain circumstances. For example, you might have a stack that contains all the scripts (and other things like icons, sounds, and external routines) that relate to a special high-speed data-locating operation that you need to perform in more than one stack. Then any time you needed this functionality available, you would simply **start using** it. When you no longer need that functionality available, issue a **stop using** command. In both cases, you supply the name of the stack to be inserted into or removed from the message-passing hierarchy.

▶ Variables

As with most programming languages, HyperTalk has two types of variables: local and global. Unless you specifically declare a variable to be global, HyperTalk assumes it is local. In this case, local means local to the handler in which the variable is used, not local to the script in which the handler appears. We'll see in a moment how to declare and use global variables.

▶ Naming variables

There are really only three rules about naming HyperTalk variables.

- Variable names must not exactly duplicate HyperTalk reserved words (see Appendix A for a list of the vocabulary of the language).
- Variable names must not begin with a number or special symbol.
- Variable names may not include spaces.

Here are some valid HyperTalk variable names:

```
variable1
temp1
thisIsALongerVariableName
yetAnotherVariable
x
Y
VARIABLE3
```

The HyperCard convention of using uppercase letters in the middle of long strings to show where English words would begin is often a good approach to naming variables. Also, case does not matter in variable names. Three variables named This, this, and ThIs are all the same variable as far as HyperTalk is concerned.

Because variable names cannot include spaces, quotation marks are never needed around the names of variables. You refer to a variable simply by using its name.

▶ Using variables

In keeping with its flexible, forgiving approach to programming language definition, HyperTalk is "relaxed" about the way you declare and use variables. A variable becomes known to the system the first time you use it. No prior preparation is required. If in the middle of a handler you suddenly need to put some value into a variable, just do it:

```
put "Beethoven" into composerName
```

The variable called *composerName* is now known to HyperTalk and can be used later in the same handler by just typing its name.

▶ The special variable, It

HyperTalk, in an effort to make scripting more English-like, includes a highly versatile variable called **It** that is shared by your scripts and HyperCard. This variable lets you write natural-sounding script commands such as the following two-line combination that retrieves the user level and puts the resulting value into the field called *Authorization Code*:

```
get userLevel
put It into field "Authorization Code"
```

Several HyperTalk commands put their results into the **It** variable, so you have to remember to be careful when using **It** in your scripts. Typically, you will use this special variable when few, if any, commands appear between the time you put a value into the variable and the time you need that variable. The following HyperTalk commands place their results into **It** by default. (You can almost always supply an alternate destination to avoid overwriting the contents of **It** if you need to do so.)

```
answer
ask
ask password
convert
get
read from file
```

Don't put a value into **It** and then use one of these commands before you have used the original value of **It**.

▶ Displaying variables

To display the contents of a variable so the user can see them, use the **put** command. This is one of the most frequently used commands in HyperTalk. In its simplest useful form, the command's syntax is

```
put expression
```

where the argument is either a simple source or an expression of arbitrary complexity. In either case, the source or the result of evaluating the expression must produce a string or a number. In this simple form, HyperCard places the expression into the Message box. If the Message box is not visible, HyperCard automatically makes it visible. The HyperTalk command line

```
put "This is a test"
```

will result in the Message box appearing (if it is invisible) and displaying the words *This is a test*.

▶ Assigning values to variables

Another use for the **put** command is the assignment of a value to a variable. In conventional programming languages such as BASIC and Pascal, we use special operators (the equal sign in most versions of BASIC and the := symbol in Pascal) to give a variable a value. In HyperTalk, we use the **put** command in a more complex form than the one we use simply to display a variable's contents. The form of the **put** command for variable assignment looks like this:

```
put expression into variable
```

The **into** preposition causes HyperCard to replace the current contents of the target variable, if it has any, with the value of the expression. The following assignment statements are valid in HyperTalk:

```
put 23 into age
put "This is a test" into testMessage
put 27 * 2 into x
```

The expression assigned to a variable may itself be a variable. After assigning 23 to the variable *age* in the previous example, we could carry out a command like this:

```
put age + 10 into olderAge
```

The **put** statement can use the target variable as part of its expression and as the assignment destination:

```
put age + 10 into age
```

The **put** statement can be used with two other prepositions: **before** and **after**. These are generally, though not always, used with fields of information on HyperCard cards. This use of **put** is described later in this chapter when we discuss HyperCard containers.

▶ Placing a variable's value into It

Because the special local variable **It** is so useful, there are times when you'd like to place the current value of some variable into **It** rather than into the Message box, where a simple **put** statement routes it. To accomplish this, HyperTalk includes a **get** command.

Note ▶	The **get** command, like many other HyperTalk instructions, has multiple uses. One primary use is with the properties of HyperCard objects. That subject, along with the role of **get** in that environment, is discussed in Chapter 17.

To use the **get** command, just supply an expression as an argument. HyperTalk will evaluate the expression and put the result into **It**. Here's an example:

```
get age
```

If you carried out this command just after the last use of the *age* variable above, **It** would contain the value 33.

▶ Global variables

Most of the time, variables are by nature useful locally. But when you need to carry information from one handler to another, HyperTalk includes the ability to define variables as global in scope. The **global** declaration must take place before the variable is used the first time, and it must be made in each handler that uses the global variable.

For example, if you want to store the user's age in a variable and then check the age in another button's **mouseUp** handler to determine if a certain action should be taken, the declarations in the two handlers would look something like this (note that these are both incomplete script fragments):

```
on mouseUp -- Button No. 1's handler
   global age
   put userAge into age
end mouseUp

on mouseUp -- Button No. 2's handler
   global age
   if age > 18 then
   ...
end mouseUp
```

Both handlers declare the *age* variable to be global in scope. Both handlers therefore "know about" this variable and share its value. Note that if you declared *age* to be global in Button No. 1's handler but failed to do so in Button No. 2, the second handler would be working with a different *age* variable than the first handler.

▶ Containers

A HyperTalk variable is a special case of a larger class of objects called *containers*. The inventors of HyperCard had to create a new word for this kind of object because nobody had previously come up with a design that encompassed so many places to put things. Here's a working definition of a container in HyperTalk.

Definition ▶	A container is any place a value can be stored.

Other containers in HyperCard, in addition to defined variables, include several special containers defined by the system. These include **It** (previously discussed), **me, target,** and special containers related to selected text, the current selection, the Message box, and fields.

▶ Using me and target as containers

Prior to the release of HyperCard Version 1.2, two special names that found frequent use in scripts were **me** and **the target**. Both always referred to the objects themselves and not to the contents of those objects, even when the object was a field. With Version 1.2, Apple modified the use of these two special values so that now they can be used as containers.

Generally, **me** refers to the object whose script is now executing, and **the target** refers to the object that received the message now being processed. Most often, these are the same object, but sometimes that is not the case. For example, when a message is passed by one object to another, **the target** continues to refer to the original object that received the message, whereas **me** becomes the designator of the object that is now processing the message.

If **me** or **the target** refers to a field, you can use **put** to alter the contents of the field in conjunction with one of these containers:

```
put "testing 1-2-3" into me
put "where are you?" into target
```

Note ▶	In dealing with this issue in Version 1.2, Apple created a certain amount of confusion. The phrase **the target** continues to refer only to the object itself, not its contents. Without the word **the**, the word **target** refers to the contents of **the target** when it is a field. That means, among other things, that you may not **put** values into **the target** but only into **target**.

▶ Selection as container

Text appearing in a field can be the source or destination for **put** and **get** commands. If the user has highlighted some text in the field, the highlighted text can be referenced as **the selection**. If no text is selected, **the selection** is still recognized by HyperTalk but is empty.

In either case, you can **put** text before or after the selection or replace the selection with other text. All you have to do is change the preposition. Figure 5-7 depicts the effects of the **put** command with its three associated prepositions on the same selected text. In all three cases the text being **put** is *chosen and*. You can see the results of each use of **put** with a different preposition.

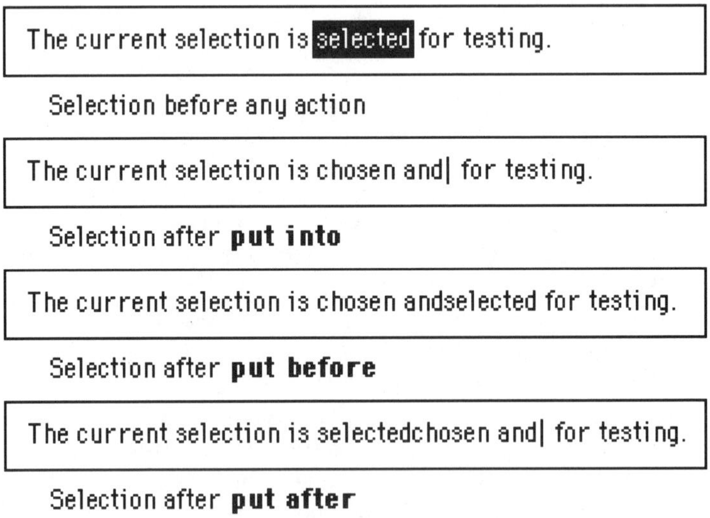

> The current selection is selected for testing.

Selection before any action

> The current selection is chosen and| for testing.

Selection after **put into**

> The current selection is chosen andselected for testing.

Selection after **put before**

> The current selection is selectedchosen and| for testing.

Selection after **put after**

Figure 5-7. The put command and the selection

You can also **get** the selection, in which case its contents are placed into the special local variable **It**. If you want to store the selection, you can use **put** with a different container as the destination.

| Note ▶ | Do not confuse the selection explicitly made by the user or your script with text located using a **find** command. Text found with a **find** command can be accessed (in HyperCard versions beginning with 1.2) via several functions that *act* like containers. These are discussed in Chapter 10. |

▶ Message box as container

The Message box is also a container. You already know that it is the default destination for the **put** command. But the Message box can serve as a place to display information to the user or to send messages directly to objects or to HyperCard itself.

Like many other HyperCard objects, the Message box has a number of aliases. It can be referred to by any of the following names:

- the Message box
- Message box
- msg box
- the msg box
- the Message window
- Message window
- the msg window
- message
- the message
- msg
- the msg

If you use a **put** command with any of these aliases for the Message box as the destination, HyperCard opens the Message box if it isn't already on the screen and visible. Your program needs to manage the Message box's visibility only in very unusual circumstances.

▶ Field as container

We have already seen how the currently selected text in a field can become **the target** for a **put** command. Fields can hold two different types of text data: editable text and locked text. If the field holds editable text, the cursor changes to an I-beam when it enters the field, even if the field's boundaries are hidden because it is transparent. Text in an editable field can be the target of a **put** command.

Fields can have names assigned to them when they are created or any time after they are first generated. (We'll have more to say about addressing fields in a few moments.) Suppose we have a field called Author. Our script has just pulled from another stack the information that Asimov is the author of this particular book. Because we've discovered the information somewhat automatically, we don't want to require the user to type it into the Author field. We need a slick way of handling this situation. The following command will do nicely:

```
put "Asimov" into field "Author"
```

The **into** preposition results in the previous contents of the field, if any, being completely replaced with the new data.

Later we find that Asimov's first name is Isaac, and we want to add that information to our growing bits of wisdom. Simple:

```
put "Isaac" before field "Author"
```

As you would expect, the **before** preposition places the expression or source data at the beginning of the field named in the command. Similarly, **after** places its expression or source data at the end of the field named in the command.

▶ Addressing a Field's Contents

Any container, but particularly a field, can hold many words or lines of information. We often want to access specific portions of the contents of such containers. In this area HyperTalk really shines. It permits us to view a container as consisting of data broken down into items, characters, words, and lines. Furthermore, it permits us to *nest* addresses so that we can refine the focus of our action as much as we want.

The concept of "chunking," mentioned in Chapter 4, is at work here. Each subfield we deal with in this discussion is a chunk.

Although this discussion could also pertain to variables, we will use the term *field* to identify the container type in these examples. This is because fields are the most common places to use these addressing techniques and because doing so simplifies the presentation.

▶ Items in a field

An *item* in a field is defined as any string of text found between commas. If only one comma appears in a field, everything to its left is called *item 1* and everything to its right is *item 2*. In a field without commas, only one item exists. Table 5-1 depicts how items are defined and located in a HyperCard field.

▶ Lines in a field

In many HyperCard fields, text occupies more than one line. Sometimes text "runs over" from one line to the next in a field that's really intended to hold just one piece of information (albeit a large one). For example, a field designed to hold your notes about a book in a bibliographic file might occupy several hundred lines of text, but from your perspective, it's one long field.

Table 5-1. Fields and their item components

Field 1	Item address	Returned value
This is a test	item 1 of field 1	This is a test
A, list, with, commas	item 2 of field 1	list
A, list, with, commas	item 4 of field 1	commas
Everyone is, a comedian	item 1 of field 1	Everyone is
Everyone is, a comedian	item 2 of field 1	a comedian
Everyone is, a comedian	item 3 of field 1	[empty string]

On the other hand, we often break fields into subfields. For example, a field called Address might hold the street address, city, state, and zip code of people in your address book. If you set the cards up so that the person's street address is on the first line of the field Address, city on the second, state on the third, and zip code on the fourth line, you have created something similar to an array in other programming languages.

But how would you access the city in such a field? Because no commas are used to separate things, using the **item** method discussed in the previous section won't have the desired effect. In this case, you need to focus on a **line** of information; HyperTalk permits you to do just that.

To get at the city in the Address field, you would simply write a line like this:

```
get line 2 of field "Address"
```

Similarly, you can place information into a field with the **put** command using the same kind of addressing scheme:

```
put "Kalamazoo" into line 2 of field "Address"
```

▶ Characters and words in addresses

If HyperTalk didn't let you do any more than access data in a single field by its item and line, it would have more powerful data retrieval capabilities than many full-blown data processing programs. But it goes two steps farther.

You can access a word or individual characters within a line or field. And you can use the key word **to** to retrieve ranges of words or characters. To access words, you use the key word **word** (oddly enough). To access characters, you can spell out the word **character** or use the shorthand **char**. Let's look at an example, and you will see what we mean about the power in this flexibility of data access.

Suppose you have a field called Grades. Stored in each line of that field are the last name, first name, and test scores for students in a class on (what else?) Macintosh programming using HyperTalk. Figure 5-8 shows a portion of the field, starting with the first line.

```
Bill Adams    93  100   89  77
Cindy North   99  100   99  98
Cal Morrison  72   0    81  62
Heather Hunton  100  90  90  88
```

Figure 5-8. Field containing student information

A **word** can contain letters, numbers, or some combination of characters. If you are used to other programming languages, you must keep this fact in mind. There is no need to define a particular chunk of a field or variable as consisting of a particular type of data.

Extracting a student's last name is as easy as:

```
get word 2 of line 2 of field "Grades"
```

Similarly, getting the grade made by Heather Hunton on the third test requires only that you code a line like this one:

```
get word 5 of line 4 of field "Grades"
```

What if you want to look at the score made by Bill Adams on the third exam to see if it falls in the A grade range? You can extract just the first digit of the grade with a command like this:

```
get char 1 of word 5 of line 1 of field "Grades"
```

Then you could run a check to see if this first digit is a 9 or a 1, in which case an A is probably indicated (assuming nobody scored under 20 on the exam).

Let's change examples. Now we're working with an inventory stack. (A consultant has to be flexible, after all!) You've designed the stack so that the part number is stored as a single string of characters in a field called "Part No." on each card. The company's part number design defines the supplier in the first three characters, the part number in the next seven characters, and the next major subassembly of which this part is a member in the last four characters. You can break this part number into its component parts with some lines of HyperTalk code that look something like this:

```
put char 1 to 3 of word 1 of field "Part No." into supplier
put char 4 to 10 of word 1 of field "Part No." into part
put char 11 to 14 of word 1 of field "Part No." into subAssembly
```

(As we'll see in a moment, there are some shorthand ways of doing even this powerful addressing. But for now, focus on the use of the **to** key word to select a range of characters.)

You may combine and nest these addressing schemes to as great an extent as makes sense for the data you are managing with your HyperCard stacks. In general, it makes the best sense to move from the smallest unit (*char*) up to the largest (*field*). Very complex data retrieval is eased greatly with this ability to combine such commands. Take a look at this one:

```
put It into char 3 to 5 of word 2 of item 3 of line 4 ¬
 of field "LargeField"
```

We discuss the use of **put** and **get** with these complex data retrieval schemes in greater depth in Chapter 10.

▶ Ordinal numbers in addressing schemes

The next topic we want to cover in this chapter is the availability of *ordinal numbers*, which expand shorthand addressing techniques. HyperCard makes available built-in labels so that we can access items, lines, words, and characters more naturally than using constructs like "word 1 of line 3." Instead, we can write:

```
first word of third line
```

HyperCard defines ordinals for the numbers one through ten (first through tenth), as well as the following special ordinals:

- last
- mid or middle
- any (one picked at random)

We find **last** particularly useful. In an address field, for example, we might not know how many names precede the person's last name (depending on things such as whether a title is used and how many middle names or initials the person has). That would drive some database programs insane. But with HyperTalk, we simply code something like this:

```
get last word of line 1 of field "Address"
```

We *know* that the last name is the last word on the line, regardless of how many words precede it.

Remember, too, that all we have said about addressing fields of data applies equally to variables, **It**, the Message box, and **the selection**.

▶ Debugging

Beginning with Version 2.0, HyperCard includes reasonably extensive debugging capabilities. It also supports the substitution of a third-party debugger (such as Icom Simulations' HyperTMON product) quite easily.

HyperCard's built-in debugger includes facilities that permit you to

- set and clear checkpoints (places in your script at which execution will halt while you examine intermediate results and from which you can continue easily)

- single-step execution through your handler and into handlers used by your handler

- trace execution of your handler and handlers it uses

- keep an eye on the values of one or more variables as your script executes

- monitor the passing of messages as your script executes

We will cover the Debugger and its related tools in detail in Chapter 19.

▶ Summary

This chapter has provided a practical framework and beginning point for your study of HyperTalk, the built-in HyperCard programming language. You have learned that scripts are associated with HyperCard objects and that editing them is relatively straightforward. You have become acquainted with the concept of handlers as the building blocks of HyperTalk scripts.

You saw the hierarchy of message passing built into HyperTalk. You spent considerable time looking at variables and at a larger class, containers. You also learned to address individual components of a field or container with ease. Finally, you looked at HyperCard's debugging capabilities.

Chapter 6 describes all the system messages for which your scripts may want to provide handlers.

6 ▶ System Messages

In this chapter, you'll learn

- what a system message is
- how to choose the destinations for system messages
- how to use all the system messages generated by HyperTalk
- how to transfer messages from their default destinations to other target objects in the HyperCard environment

▶ Messages Galore!

There is always something going on in HyperCard. Even when it doesn't *look* like there's anything happening, HyperCard is sending a constant stream of messages to objects in its environment. If a script isn't active and sending messages of its own and if the user isn't doing something to generate a specific message, HyperCard sends out a continuous stream of messages to let the objects in its hierarchy know that nothing special is happening.

The Macintosh, quite apart from HyperCard, is an event-driven environment. The HyperTalk equivalent of an event is a message. There are only two sources of messages in HyperCard: a script running as part of a stack and HyperCard itself. Messages originating with HyperCard are called *system messages*. In this chapter, we look at all the system messages HyperCard generates. A large percentage of your HyperTalk programming is devoted to responding to or monitoring these messages. Before you read this chapter, make sure you thoroughly understand the concepts of messages and handlers, as discussed in Chapter 5.

▶ Who Gets the Message?

One of the most important ideas to grasp early in our discussion of system messages is that every system message has a *default destination* to which it is automatically sent. As we cover each system message in this chapter, you will see the logic of choosing the default destination for each such message. HyperCard routes some messages to the object in which the event with which they are associated takes place. Others are sent to different HyperCard objects depending on the state of the system. Still otmers have default destinations that are not dependent on any outside factor.

Every default destination can be overridden in your scripts. If HyperCard sends a message by default to the stack, for example, and you want to override the stack's handling of that message in some circumstances, simply design a handler with the same name in your script and intercept the system message.

▶ Using send to direct a message

You can also override HyperTalk's normal message-passing hierarchy by using the **send** command. The basic syntax of this command is:

```
send <message> to <object>
```

For example, if you want to simulate the user clicking a mouse on a particular button, you can do something like this:

```
send mouseUp to button "Test"
```

▶ Using pass to avoid message disappearance

As we pointed out in Chapter 5, whenever a message traveling along the HyperTalk message-passing hierarchy encounters a handler of the same name, it executes that handler and then disappears from the message stream. This is not always desirable.

For example, if you write a handler to intercept a system message and you want to do some special processing of that message but then permit Hyper-Card to add its own standard functionality as well, you need to make sure HyperCard ultimately gets the message. To do this, use the **pass** command. Its syntax is simple:

```
pass <message>
```

The message being passed must be the one the handler is processing. In other words, you can't pass a **mouseUp** message from an **openCard** handler. Here's what a **doMenu** handler might look like if you needed to process some menu activities within a custom handler but wanted HyperTalk to deal with all other menu processing:

```
on doMenu what
    if what is "New Card" then
    ... -- special processing for your handler
    end if
    pass doMenu
end doMenu
```

Note ▶ You should be cautious about writing handlers to intercept and manage system messages. If you do so, you assume all the responsibility for making sure the system reacts appropriately to the message. In some cases, this involves understanding HyperCard at a very deep level. Potential problems will be pointed out in the text.

As we pointed out in Chapter 5, you can modify not only the default destination for a message but also the inheritance hierarchy through which the message will pass.

▶ An Overview of System Messages

System messages usually contain information about the status of some portion of the Macintosh system at the time the messages are generated. In general, they result from the user taking some action that leads directly or indirectly to them being generated. System messages can be divided into the following broad categories:

- mouse messages
- keyboard messages
- action-taking messages
- a menu message
- a help-management message
- window-related messages
- the "non-event" message called **idle**

▶ Mouse messages

HyperCard generates six mouse messages. Three are actually button messages because they report the status of the mouse button. The other three are location messages that tell your script where the mouse is with regard to specific objects. (There are several built-in functions in HyperTalk to help you pinpoint the exact coordinates of the mouse without regard to objects. These are discussed in Chapter 7.)

Mouse-button messages are among the most frequently used in HyperTalk scripts because it is often important to know when and where the user has activated the button. The mouse button is the user's primary means of interacting with a HyperCard stack.

▶ Keyboard messages

Another group of messages reports the pressing of keys on the keyboard, including special keys. One of these messages lets you intercept and deal with any key the user presses. Four other messages permit you to detect when the Return key, Enter key, Tab key, or Command key has been pressed. Yet another message informs your script if an arrow key has been pressed (on those Macintosh keyboards that include arrow keys) and, if so, which of the four arrow keys has been used. If your script is run on a Macintosh with the Apple Extended Keyboard, another system message tells you which function key has been pressed. (In addition to these system messages, there are some properties that you can use to determine the state of keyboard activity. These are discussed in Chapter 17.)

▶ Action-taking messages

There are two subcategories of action-taking messages: those dealing with objects within a stack and those dealing with the state of HyperCard itself. If the user creates or deletes an object, or opens or closes an object, HyperCard sends a system message to inform your script (and the rest of the system) of the event.

A system message is also generated when HyperCard first starts, when the user or a script chooses to leave the environment, and when the user or a script suspends HyperCard temporarily while another application is run. Beginning with HyperCard 2.0, there are also system messages generated when a stack is activated or deactivated after having been previously opened.

▶ Menu message

One system message relates to menu activity. It is a very powerful message — if your script intercepts it, your script becomes responsible for all menu activity from that time until it relinquishes control. By intercepting and handling this message, however, your script gains total control over what happens when the user selects items from the pull-down menus in Hyper-Card or your stack.

Beginning with HyperCard 2.0, you have complete script control over the menu bar and the user's interaction with it. You can tell HyperTalk which menu item in which specific menu on the menu bar to activate, and you can assign a handler to execute when that menu option is chosen by the user.

▶ Help-management message

One message can be discussed under the rubric of housekeeping. It permits you to intercept the user's menu-driven request for help.

▶ Window-related messages

When HyperCard 2.0 appeared and added the ability to resize and move the currently active card through its window, HyperTalk was expanded to include two new system messages. One of these is sent when the user resizes the window and the other when the user moves it.

▶ The idle message

When there is apparently nothing going on in a stack, HyperCard sends the **idle** message.

▶ Handling Mouse Messages

We will first look at mouse-button messages, which form such a major part of any HyperTalk script. Then we'll examine mouse-location messages, which are used less frequently but with which you should be familiar.

▶ Mouse-button messages

When you click the mouse on a button in any Macintosh application, whether it is written in HyperTalk or a more conventional programming language, you probably think of the task as consisting of one or two steps. Most users think of it as one action called *clicking* the mouse button. An astute observer might point out that there are actually two events taking place: pressing the mouse button and releasing it.

HyperTalk views this mouse action as consisting of three separate events, and it generates a system message for each. These events and their associated system messages are

- the pressing of the mouse button, which generates a **mouseDown** message
- the continued holding down of the mouse button, however briefly, which generates a **mouseStillDown** message
- the release of the mouse button, which generates a **mouseUp** message

Usually, the user's mouse-button activities are of interest only when they take place inside buttons. That is why most **mouseUp** handlers occur in button scripts and why all button scripts open with an empty handler for this message. But you can supply handlers for any of these messages in a field with locked text or even in a card.

There are some important rules to remember about how HyperCard processes mouse clicks. First, the **mouseDown** message is sent to the object in which the pointer is located when the button is pressed. Second, all subsequent **mouseStillDown** messages are sent to the *same object that received the mouseDown message* even if the mouse moves outside that object while the button is depressed. Finally, a **mouseUp** message is sent by HyperCard only if the mouse button is released within the confines of the last object to receive a **mouseDown** message. If the user presses the mouse button in, for example, a button labeled OK, and then drags the mouse outside that area and releases the mouse button, no **mouseUp** message is generated. This design is in keeping with traditional Macintosh button use, which permits users to change their minds any time before releasing the mouse button.

You will seldom, if ever, write handlers for **mouseDown** or **mouseStillDown**. But **mouseUp** handlers are among the most common in HyperTalk scripts. Virtually every button has such a handler.

To demonstrate how these three commands relate to one another, let's create our Laboratory stack. We will use this stack repeatedly through the book. Start with a simple, blank stack. Add a new button to the first card. Now we'll put a handler for each type of message into this button's script.

Three mouse-button handlers

Here are step-by-step instructions for this experiment in button scripting:

1. Open the button's script window.

2. Type in the following script, which consists of three handlers. When you've entered and proofread it, click the OK button in the scripting dialog.

```
on mouseDown
    put "Down" into Message
    wait 40
    put 0 into Message
end mouseDown

on mouseStillDown
    add 10 to Message
end mouseStillDown

on mouseUp
    beep 3
    wait 20
    put "Done!" into Message
end mouseUp
```

3. Put the pointer over the button and press the mouse button. The Message box appears (if it was previously invisible) with the message "Down." Hold the button down for a few moments and the word "Down" is replaced by a series of rapidly increasing numbers.

4. Release the button. In a moment, the word "Done!" appears in the Message box.

5. Repeat step 3 but after you press the mouse button inside the HyperCard button, drag the pointer outside the button area. Notice that the numbers keep increasing, indicating that the **mouseStillDown** handler in the button's script is still receiving messages. Now release the button outside the button's area. The counting stops but no "Done!" message appears and no beeps are heard. The system message **mouseUp** was not sent because you released the button in an area outside the confines of the object in which the mouse button was pressed.

▶ Mouse-location messages

Three messages define where the mouse is when the mouse uutton is not being pressed. They relate the position of the mouse to objects such as buttons and fields. The three messages and their meanings are

- **mouseEnter**, indicating that the mouse pointer has entered the boundaries of a button or field
- **mouseLeave**, indicating that the mouse pointer was in the boundaries of a button or field but has now moved outside those boundaries
- **mouseWithin**, indicating that the mouse pointer has entered the area and remains there

HyperCard interleaves the **mouseWithin** message with the **idle** message any time the pointer is located inside a button or field. Mouse-location messages are handled exactly like the mouse-button messages described in the preceding section.

Mouse-location handlers

One interesting use for mouse-location messages is the creation of "pop-up" fields that appear when the user simply moves the mouse pointer to a certain area of the screen. Such a handler might be quite useful, for example, in an educational script. You could provide a picture of a part of the human body with no visible labels. When the user points the mouse at a specific location, a previously hidden field appears, showing the user the label for that location. When the user moves away from that area, the field goes away. The user can scan the entire set of labels with the mouse easily, without ever pushing the mouse button.

Although developing such an application is beyond the scope of simply learning about these handlers, we can give you something of the flavor of such a script with the following laboratory experiment. Open the Laboratory stack again if it isn't already open.

1. If the card does not have a field you want to use for this experiment, create one. Its location is not important. Give it the name Test Field and define it as Transparent. Then put some arbitrary text into it in Browse mode.

2. Create a new button or use an existing one. Enter the following script into its script-editing window:

```
on mouseEnter
    show card field "Test Field"
end mouseEnter
```

```
on mouseLeave
    hide card field "Test Field"
end mouseLeave
```

3. Be sure the field Test Field is not showing — open the Message box and type the following command if the field is visible before this experiment begins:

```
hide card field "Test Field"
```

4. Before the experiment starts, the laboratory card should look similar to Figure 6-1. Move the mouse pointer over the button to which you've added the script. (We've called our button, unimaginatively enough, Test Button.) The field should suddenly appear, as shown in Figure 6-2. As you move the pointer outside the button, the field disappears again.

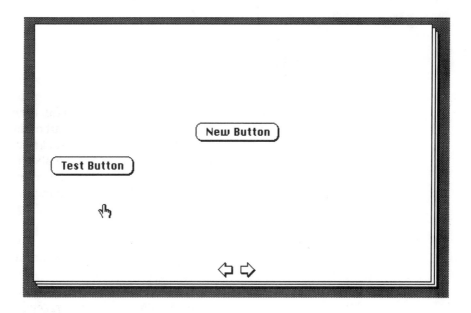

Figure 6-1. Mouse-location test before pointer moves

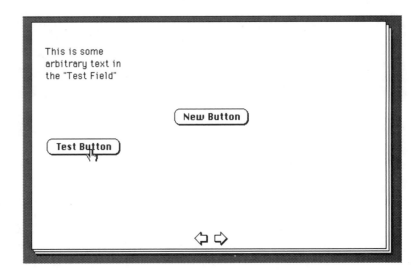

Figure 6-2. Mouse-location test with pointer over test button

▶ Keyboard Messages

Beginning with HyperCard 2.0, you can trap the user's interaction with the keyboard with the **keyDown** message. This message is generated when the user types any alphabetic or numeric key without the Command key being held down at the same time. The message is accompanied by the name of the key being pressed and may also be trapped. Here, for example, is a handler that will display in the Message box each key the user types, replacing the Message box's previous contents as it does so:

```
on keyDown key
    put key
end keyDown
```

The Tab, Return, Enter, and Command keys on the Macintosh Plus and Apple Standard keyboards and the fifteen function keys on the Apple Extended Keyboard generate their own messages when they are pressed anywhere except in a text field. The function keys produce their messages even inside a text field, but the first four function keys have specific reserved meanings in editable fields. To avoid conflict, HyperTalk simply does not generate the first four function-key messages when they take place inside an editable text field. The arrow keys on the Macintosh Plus and subsequent Apple-manufactured keyboards also generate messages.

The possible uses for handlers for these messages are not as clear as the uses for mouse messages discussed in the previous section. But some potential uses are hinted at in this discussion.

The system messages are related to special keys:

- **tabKey**
- **returnKey**
- **enterKey**
- **functionKey** number
- **arrowKey** direction
- **controlKey** number
- **commandKeyDown** key

These are the first messages we've encountered that have parameters. The number that follows the **functionKey** message is a digit between 1 and 15 that indicates which function key was pressed. By convention, function keys 1 through 4 are reserved for editing operations (1=Undo, 2=Cut, 3=Copy, 4=Paste). The direction label associated with the **arrowKey** message is one of the four direction words *up, down, right,* or *left.* The **controlKey** message always carries with it the ASCII code of the key held down with the Control key. If the Control key is held down with no accompanying key, no message is generated. The **commandKeyDown** message always carries with it the key that is pressed while the Command key is being held down. If no key is being held down, pressing the Command key does not generate a message.

All these messages are sent by default to the current card. Among other things, this handler can pass the keyboard-generated message to another object lower in the hierarchy.

Key-button equivalents

One interesting use for message handlers for the Return and Enter keys is to provide a keyboard equivalent for some button selections. Let us assume we have a card with two buttons, one marked OK and one marked Stop. Let's further assume that in documentation or in an onscreen help window (or, better yet, in both places) we have told users that they can press the Return key instead of clicking the OK button and that pressing the Enter key is the same as clicking the Stop button. All we need is a card script that passes these messages to the appropriate button targets when they are received.

Note ▶ | We will use the **send** command in these examples, even though this command is not discussed until later in the chapter. Its use in this experiment is relatively self-evident, but if you simply can't wait to find out what it does, feel free to read ahead and then come back to this experiment.

Here are the step-by-step instructions for this laboratory experiment in using the **returnKey** and **enterKey** system messages to create keyboard equivalents to button-clicks.

1. It is more efficient to create a new card in the laboratory, though you can go through the process of cleaning all the leftover buttons and fields from the present card if you like. We will not be returning to the previous examples, so choose the alternative you prefer. In any event, it is a good idea to begin this experiment with a clean slate with no handlers or objects.

2. Create two buttons. Size, type, and location are immaterial. Select the Show Name option in the Button Information dialog. Name one button OK and the other Stop.

3. Enter the following script into the script-editing window for the OK button:

```
on mouseUp
    put "OK box selected"
end mouseUp
```

4. Enter the following script into the script-editing window for the Stop button:

```
on mouseUp
    put "Stop box selected"
end mouseUp
```

5. From the Objects menu, select Card Info... while holding down the Shift key. (Alternatively, select Card Info... and then click the Script button. The result is the same.) Enter the following two handlers into the card's script:

```
on returnKey
    send mouseUp to button "OK"
end returnKey

on enterKey
    send mouseUp to button "Stop"
end enterKey
```

6. Return to Browse mode. Click on the OK button and confirm that the appropriate message appears in the Message box. Then try the Stop button.

7. Press the Return key. The message "OK button selected" appears in the Message box. Now press the Enter key. The message "Stop button selected" appears in the Message box.

Notice that we did not send the **returnKey** and **enterKey** messages to the buttons. Rather, we sent messages that the buttons already had in their scripts. This is not only permissible, it is the most efficient way of handling the task as long as the actions are the same when the user pushes the button with the mouse pointer or uses the keyboard equivalent. You can, however, send the keyboard message on to another object directly. If, for example, you want to highlight the OK button when users press the Return key but not if they use the mouse, you need a handler in the OK button script for the **returnKey** message. You could then simply pass the **returnKey** message to the button from the card script. The other keys operate in an analogous manner.

▶ Special field-related keyboard messages

When the user presses the Enter or Return key inside an editable (that is, unlocked) field, HyperCard generates the **enterInField** or **returnInField** message, respectively. These messages, added with Version 1.2 of Hyper-Card, enable you to treat these keys as something other than simple carriage returns to be entered into the field. We'll have more to say about using these system messages in Chapter 10 when we discuss managing text and data in HyperCard fields.

▶ Uses for keyboard messages

We have already discussed how keyboard messages can be made to work as keyboard equivalents of button presses. The same technique can be used for other actions that have keyboard equivalents.

The arrow keys lend themselves particularly well to a different usage. Because they are usually seen by the Macintosh user as navigation keys, you can intercept these keys to control navigation in ways that make the user's interaction with the stack more understandable. For example, the right arrow key (message **arrowKey right**) can be intercepted at the background or stack level and interpreted to mean "go to the next card with the same background as this card." In multiple-background stacks, this can be quite helpful.

You should never assume that your script will be used on a Macintosh with the extended keyboard. But you can provide handlers for function key messages so that those who do have such keyboards can use the function keys. Users without function key setups will not notice any difference. As with other keyboard messages, **functionKey** messages should be handled at the card level or higher, then transmitted with the **send** command as needed elsewhere in the HyperCard environment.

The **keyDown** message can be used to create interfaces in which the user need only press a single key to indicate a desire to do something or an answer to a question. This might come in particularly handy in creating educational stacks for young users for whom the mouse might require too much fine-motor skill.

You can use the **commandKeyDown** message to intercept user attempts to bypass your control of menu interaction by pressing the Command key and a keyboard equivalent (for example, Command-Q for Quit). In that case, you probably want to use the **pass** command to make sure that any Command-key combinations for which you do not wish to trap are handled in the way the user expects them to be handled.

▶ **Action-Taking Messages**

As mentioned, action-taking messages fall into two categories. The first group, deals with the management of specific objects in the HyperCard environment. The second is related specifically to HyperCard's own operation.

▶ Object-related action messages

There are typically four things users can do to objects in HyperCard. They can open, close, create, or delete objects. Each of these actions can also be performed by a script. Whether the actions occur as a result of the user's instructions or a script's execution, your script may want to intercept the actions by providing handlers for the appropriate messages.

Fields, stacks, cards, and backgrounds can be the recipients of all these messages. Buttons can be created and deleted but not opened or closed. By combining the first part of the message name — the action to be taken — and the second part — the type of object to be affected — we come up with a matrix like Table 6-1, which lists all these system messages by function.

Table 6-1. Action-taking system messages

Action to Take	Button	Field	Card	Background	Stack
Create object	newButton	newField	newCard	newBackground	newStack
Delete object	deleteButton	deleteField	deleteCard	deleteBackground	deleteStack
Open object	N/A	openField	openCard	openBackground	openStack
Close object	N/A	closeField	closeCard	closeBackground	closeStack

As a general rule, your scripts will not contain message handlers to create or delete buttons or fields because this is part of the design process and not usually something you want to do dynamically. (There is, however, nothing in HyperTalk to prevent you from doing so. You may have a specialized application where you need to do just that. In that case, by all means do so.)

| Note ▶ | It is important to note that HyperCard only sends these messages *after* it has taken the action they indicate. In other words, the **newCard** message is only sent after HyperCard has created a new card. So you can't use these messages to prevent the creation of new cards, though you can achieve a similar effect by sending a **deleteCard** message to the newly created card after it has been generated. This also means that you generally have to place the handler for such messages one level higher in the hierarchy than might seem evident. A **newCard** message handler, for example, will not function as expected if it is in a card script. When the new card is created, it doesn't have any scripts. So you have to put handlers for the **newCard** message in the stack's script, not in a card's script. |

It is easy to become confused about the role of messages versus the role of commands in the case of these action-taking messages. A **closeField** message is generated when the user presses the Tab key in an editable text field after making some changes and then moves to the next such field (if any) on the making some changes and then moves to the next such field (if any) on the card. This message is also generated if the user modifies the text in a nonscrolling field whose Auto Tab feature is true and then presses the Return key from the last line of that field. Your script can intercept and handle this message, as discussed in the next section. But if you want to order a field closed, you would use the **send** command discussed earlier something like this:

```
on someMessage -- defined by your script
   send closeField to card field 1
end someMessage
```

Beginning with HyperCard 2.0, you can also have a script that executes when the user leaves a field without having changed its contents. This overcomes what many people saw as a serious shortcoming in earlier versions of the program. The newly added message is **exitField**, and it is issued whenever the user closes a field without having made any content changes to it.

Typically, your scripts will intercept messages that result from the user taking actions that generate object-oriented action messages and will change the usual manner in which HyperCard processes them. Also typically, your scripts will work with the opening and closing of objects.

Handling a newCard

In this experiment, we set up a script that automatically inserts information into any new card created by the user. It's a good idea to start with a new card in the laboratory.

1. Create a background field in the upper-left corner of the card. Define it to be a rectangle and give it the name Today. Give it any other nonconflicting characteristics you wish.

2. Open the stack's script by holding down the Shift key and selecting Stack Info... from the Objects menu or by opening the Stack Info... option from the Objects menu and then clicking on the Script button.

3. Enter the following script for the stack:

```
on newCard
   put the date into field "Today"
   beep 3
end newCard
```

The function called **the date** simply returns today's date in short format.

4. Return to Browse mode. Select New Card from the Edit menu or hold down the Command-N keys. Add a few more cards if you like (keeping track of how many there are so you can undo the work later) and confirm that each displays today's date when it is created.

5. Delete the cards you created and the new background you generated to avoid confusion with future laboratory experiments. If you want to keep them, make a copy of the stack using the Save a Copy... option from the File menu and then delete the new background and cards.

▶ Another idea

When HyperCard opens an existing card, it generally does not place the pointer anywhere. The same is true when it creates a new card. Quite often, though, stacks are used in applications when the user simply wants to begin entering data when the card appears. To avoid requiring the user to click the mouse explicitly in a field to begin entering data, you can provide a handler for the **openCard** message that would open a specific field. The simplest way to do this (with what you already know about messages and handlers) is to have the **openCard** handler send a **tabKey** message to the card. This opens the first field on the card and automatically selects all of its text. If you want to tab to the second field, send two **tabKey** messages.

A handler to accomplish this task is associated with the stack and looks something like this:

```
on openCard
    send tabKey
end openCard
```

As you gain more experience with HyperTalk scripting, you'll find many occasions for the use of these object-related messages.

▶ HyperCard messages

Six system messages HyperCard generates are related to the status of the HyperCard application itself and of individual open stacks. These six messages and their meaning are

- **startUp**, which is sent when HyperCard is first started
- **quit**, which is sent when the user or a script quits HyperCard
- **suspend**, which is sent when the user or a script runs an external program from within HyperCard and plans to return to HyperCard when the other application has finished executing

- **resume**, which is sent when the external program for which HyperCard has been suspended finishes executing and control is returned to HyperCard
- **suspendStack**, which is sent when the user chooses a stack in a different window
- **resumeStack**, which is sent when the user chooses a stack in a window

An example of a **startUp** message handler is in the Home stack supplied with HyperCard. That handler simply looks to see if there is an external command called **startUp** to which it is to respond. (We have more to say about external commands near the end of this book.) The **startUp** message goes to the Home stack if you start HyperCard by double-clicking the application's icon on the desktop. But if you double-click a stack's icon, the **startUp** message goes to the first card of that stack.

If you want your script to perform a set of actions when the user first opens HyperCard, you may want these same (or a substantially similar set of) instructions followed when the user returns to your stack or HyperCard after running an external application. If so, be sure to put a command in the **resume** handler that carries out those actions because the **startUp** handler is not called when operation of HyperCard resumes after a **suspend** message.

▶ The doMenu Message

When the user chooses a menu item or invokes it with its keyboard equivalent, HyperCard sends a message called **doMenu** followed by the name of the menu item, exactly as it appears in the menu bar (complete with the three dots, or ellipsis, that follow many menu choices). Your script can check for the occurrence of any menu item(s) and react accordingly.

This technique can be used to disable menu items to protect your stack scripts or the stack information base itself. You simply intercept the message, check to see if it's an item you want to disable, and do something like **beep** if it is or pass the message to the next level if it isn't a menu option you care about.

An example of the use of the **doMenu** command involves displaying a special card with a message such as "See you later" when the user decides to leave your stack by going Home or quitting HyperCard completely. (There are other ways to leave your stack; the technique would be the same regardless of the method.) To handle such a situation, you attach the following kind of message handler to your stack's script:

```
on doMenu choice
   if choice is "Home"
   then
      go last card
      wait 20
   end if
   if choice is "Quit Hypercard"
   then
      go last card
      wait 20
   end if
   pass doMenu
end doMenu
```

We discuss the **if-then** construction in Chapter 8. For the moment, just accept our word that this handler performs as advertised.

Beginning with HyperCard 2.0, the **doMenu** message has an optional second parameter that names the menu on which the item to be executed appears. This gives you more direct control over the menu interface and allows you to have multiple items with the same item name appearing on different menus. In earlier versions of HyperCard, you could not create custom menus (see Chapter 12), so this inability to use duplicate names never became a serious problem. With the advent of custom menus, however, it became important to be able to differentiate among two or more identically named menu items. The addition of a second parameter to the **doMenu** message fills this bill nicely.

For example, assume you had a custom menu called "Database" that had a **Next** command in it that the user could choose to move to the next record in an external database being navigated with HyperCard. You could then use a handler like this one to deal with the database **Next** command while leaving the normal HyperCard navigational operations alone:

```
on doMenu item,menu
   if item = "Next" and menu = "Database" then
      -- undertake database processing
   else
      pass doMenu -- to carry out normal processing
   end if
end doMenu
```

▶ The help Message

The **help** message is created and sent to the currently open card when the user chooses Help from the Go menu or types Command-? to invoke help.

The **help** message can be intercepted by your script to route the user's request for assistance to a special stack (or part of a stack) where the user can get customized help or specific references to other sources of assistance. For example, if you have a card called Special Help that contains hints for using your stack, you can send the user there when he or she asks for help. The handler would look something like this:

```
on help
    go to card "Special Help"
end help
```

(In reality, the handler would be a bit more complex because it would involve making sure HyperCard returns to this point when it finishes furnishing the specialized help. The techniques for doing that are covered in Chapter 9.)

▶ Window-Related Messages

When the user or a script moves a card window, HyperCard sends the active card a **MoveWindow** message. When the window is resized, the active card receives the system message **SizeWindow**. Both of these messages were added to HyperCard Version 2.0.

▶ The idle Message

We have perhaps said enough about the **idle** message. It is interleaved with a **mouseWithin** message if the pointer is located over an object. The two alternate during times that HyperCard is simply waiting for the user to do something to generate an event and a related message.

A handler for the **idle** message lends itself well to such activities as putting the current time into a field. The Home Card furnished by Apple Computer has such a handler. It looks like this:

```
on idle
    put the time into card field "Time"
    pass idle
end idle
```

Be careful of putting too many commands in an **idle** handler. Each executes often and you can greatly slow down your stacks by injudicious use of **idle** handlers.

▶ Summary

In this chapter, you saw how to deal with messages. You then became acquainted with all the messages the HyperCard system itself generates. You saw how to handle mouse-related messages, keyboard messages, and action-taking messages. You saw the power and the pitfalls in trapping menu choices to make applications written in HyperTalk more individualized.

You learned there are always messages being passed around the Hyper-Card environment. And you learned that although there is a definite hierarchy to message passing based on the individual message, you can use the **send** and **pass** commands to bypass or accommodate the hierarchy.

Chapter 7 discusses input and output in HyperTalk using the mouse, keyboard, disk drive, and printer.

7 ▶ Mouse, Keyboard, and File I/O

In this chapter, you'll learn how to

- handle several messages that involve knowing where the mouse is and what it is doing
- simulate in a script the user clicking the mouse
- determine the status of the Command, Option, and Shift keys
- examine the keys being pressed by the user
- perform routine file operations on external (non-HyperCard) files containing only text

▶ Monitoring the Mouse

In the last chapter, we learned about several system messages that report on the status of the mouse and its location in relation to objects. Because of the overriding importance of the mouse in any Macintosh application, Hyper-Card includes a number of other mouse-monitoring routines. Three of these functions — **the mouseLoc**, **the mouseH**, and **the mouseV** — report on the screen coordinate location of the mouse at the time the function is called. Two — **the mouse** and **the mouseClick** — determine the status of the mouse button at the time they are used in your script. (The word *the* in each of these names is essential. Without it, HyperTalk does not recognize the function.)

The uses for four of these functions—all but **the mouseClick**—are pretty esoteric. We have seldom seen a need in a HyperTalk script to detect where the mouse is when it is not being clicked except in relation to some object. (Recall our laboratory experiment in Chapter 6 with the field that appears when the user positions the mouse over a button but does not click on it.) This is not to say that you will never use these functions; you may find many uses for them. But they are not among the most often-used functions in HyperTalk.

One reason this is true is the object-oriented way HyperTalk works. We are usually interested in monitoring the location of the mouse and its actions with respect to objects in the HyperCard environment rather than with respect to the abstract screen position it occupies. Another reason for the infrequent use of these functions in most HyperTalk scripts is that the location they report can change before it is reported. These functions report the location of the mouse *at the time they are called*. But a fast mouser—and there are many such users out there in the world of Macintosh afficionados—may well have moved the mouse out of the relevant screen location before your script can react to its presence.

The lone exception to this rule in this batch of HyperTalk functions is **the mouseClick**. This function tests to see if the mouse button has been clicked since the last time it was checked. If so, it returns a value of true; otherwise, it returns a value of false. The returned value can then be used in a logical operation, usually within a loop, to control the actions of your handler. The implementation of logical operations and loops is discussed in Chapter 8.

Screen coordinates

Before you can use the three mouse-location functions we are discussing, you must understand how HyperCard views and addresses locations on the screen. We could present this information with a few paragraphs and diagrams. But because HyperTalk lends itself so well to exploration, we're going to set up a script in our laboratory to explore the screen, then summarize what we learn.

You can use an existing Laboratory stack card for this experiment or create a new one with nothing on it. Once you have opened the card you want to use, follow these steps.

(Note that in the following discussion we assume you are working with the original nine-inch Macintosh screen size. The bottom-right corner of the screen on a larger monitor will, of course, have a different set of values associated with it than those shown in the text.)

1. Open the card's script in one of the usual ways.

2. Type the following script into the script-editing window and click on the OK button when you're done:

```
on openCard
   repeat until the mouseClick
      put the mouseLoc
   end repeat
end openCard
```

Don't worry if you have no idea what the strange group of lines that begin and end with the word **repeat** are all about. We'll explain this programming technique in Chapter 8.

3. Return to Browse mode.

4. Go to a previous card in the stack and then return fo this one so that the card is opened and the handler can take effect. As soon as you do, the Message box appears with two numbers separated by a comma (see Figure 7-1). Move the mouse around without clicking the button and watch the numbers in the Message box change. As you roll the mouse to the right, the first number gets larger until the pointer reaches the right edge of the screen and the number reaches 512. Similarly, as you roll the mouse down the screen, the second number increases until it reaches 342.

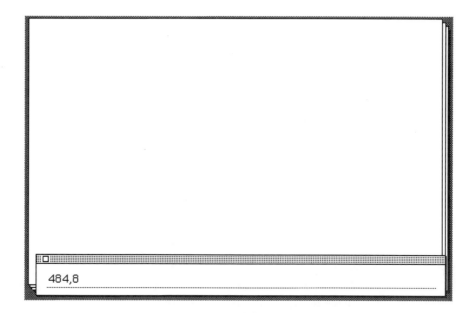

Figure 7-1. Tracking the mouse in the Message box

5. Put the pointer in the upper-left corner of the screen. You should be able to get the two numbers to reach 0,0. The bottom of the menu bar is at the point where the second number is 20.

6. Click the mouse. Notice that as you roll the mouse around now, the numbers don't change. That's because you've exited **the openCard** handler with **the mouseClick**, so the mouse position is no longer being tracked and reported.

From this experiment, you can probably conclude that the screen is laid out as a gridwork of addresses, with horizontal positions reported in the first part of **the mouseLoc** value and vertical positions in the second part of that value. You can probably also conclude that the screen addresses go from 0,0 in the upper-left corner of the screen to 512,342 in the lower-right corner of the screen. Figure 7-2 depicts this addressing scheme.

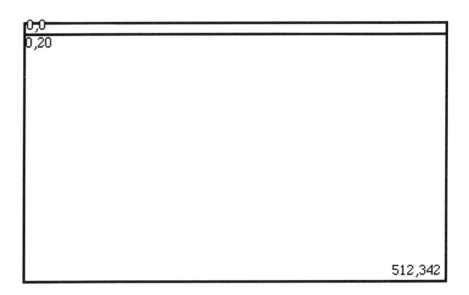

Figure 7-2. The Macintosh screen-addressing scheme

Each screen location, called a *pixel* (shorthand for picture element), has a unique address. You can see how finely a HyperTalk script can examine and manage screen locations when there are more than 175,000 discrete locations on the original nine-inch Macintosh screen alone.

▶ One coordinate at a time

Using the same technique we just explored in the Laboratory stack, you can find out that the function **the mouseH** returns only the horizontal location of the mouse and **the mouseV** returns only its vertical position. Just change **the mouseLoc** in the script to one of these functions and observe the results.

▶ Ending repeated commands

You probably noticed in the **openCard** handler in the last laboratory experiment that we used a **repeat until the mouseClick** statement. We'll be discussing such groups of statements in Chapter 8. For the moment, you should note that **the mouseClick** is one of the most useful HyperCard functions for terminating repeating activities because it monitors users and reacts when they click the mouse anywhere within HyperCard's boundaries.

▶ What's with the mouse?

The last of this group of functions is simply called **the mouse**. It returns the value *down* if the mouse button is being pressed when the function is called, *up* if it is not. In some ways, its functions duplicate those of the **stillDown** system message we discussed in Chapter 6.

A key difference is that **stillDown** is a message that can form the argument to the **on** portion of a handler, but **the mouse** is a function that returns a value and is used inside a handler. In other words, **the mouse** gives us a way to perform some steps inside a handler while the mouse is down.

Is user holding down button?

Let's do a little experimenting, without being concerned about what all the commands mean or do. You can use any existing card with a button whose script you don't need or you can create a new card for this experiment. Then follow these steps:

1. Open the button's script in one of the usual ways.

2. Type in the following script and press the OK button when you're done:

```
on mouseDown
    repeat while the mouse is Down
        put empty
        wait 20
        put "Working..."
        wait 20
    end repeat
    beep 3
end mouseDown
```

3. Return to Browse mode.

4. Click on the button and hold the mouse button down. Notice that the Message box slowly flashes the message "Working..." as long as you hold down the mouse button.

5. Release the mouse button and note that the system beeps three times.

6. You can also use a **mouseUp** handler in this script to put a message into the Message box when you release the button. For example:

```
on mouseUp
    put "Whew! I'm glad that's over!"
end mouseUp
```

Obviously, you wouldn't write such a handler this way just to beep the speaker three times. But if you had more complex processing to take care of that you didn't want to carry out while the user was pressing the mouse button, this approach would work fine.

▶ Clicking the Mouse for the User

Sometimes in HyperTalk scripts you want to put the user in a particular location for some field entry work. Or you may need to simulate mouse clicking that you would normally expect from the user in a demonstration script where you want the user simply to watch what's going on. For these and similar situations, HyperTalk includes the **click** command. Its syntax looks like this:

```
click at location [with modifier key]
```

The location must be an explicit screen address, given as a pair of coordinates like those we have just finished learning about or an expression or variable that evaluates to such an address. If you want to simulate a mouse click as if the Shift, Command, or Option key were being held down, you can add the key name and the **with** connector. Here is an example of an Option-click command:

```
click at 100,235 with optionKey
```

Modifier key additions are particularly useful when you are using the **click** command while working with one of HyperCard's paint tools.

As with other HyperTalk commands we've looked at, **click** is most useful when viewed with a HyperCard object. Every object has a screen location associated with it. You can find this address with the **location** property, which may be abbreviated **loc**. We have more to say about the **loc** property in Chapter 17 when we discuss the properties associated with HyperCard objects. But for the moment you need only know that this property contains the screen coordinates of the center point of the object referred to.

If you have a screen button called Button One, you can activate it exactly as if the user had clicked on it by writing a line of HyperTalk code like this:

```
click at loc of card button "Button One"
```

Of course, you can also produce this effect with the **send** command:

```
send mouseUp to card button "Button One"
```

There are a number of ways to accomplish many HyperTalk tasks. This is not the last time we will see such alternatives.

(Actually, **click** and **send mouseUp** differ in one way. When you use the **click** command, HyperTalk generates both a **mouseDown** and a **mouseUp** message, exactly as when the user clicks the button physically. Sending the

mouseUp message, on the other hand, generates only that message and no **mouseDown**. This distinction is probably safe to ignore most of the time but if you are dealing with HyperTalk activity at a message-passing level, it could become important.)

HyperCard includes three functions to help you determine where the mouse was clicked by the user (or, for that matter, by your script). The **clickLoc** returns the location of the click as a point (two numbers separated by a comma). If you want just the vertical position of the mouse click, you can use **the mouseV** and, if you want only the horizontal position of the click, use **the mouseH**.

▶ Is That Key Down?

Having seen that we can use the Command, Option, and Shift keys with the **click** command, it will come as no surprise that we can also check the status of these keys to find out if they are up or down at the time the script checks them. Like **mouse**, the functions that monitor the keys return *up* if the key is not being pressed, *down* if it is. You can use these values in testing and branching operations in HyperTalk.

In fact, you can actually check not only on these keys but also on the **enterKey**, the **returnKey**, the **controlKey**, and the **functionKeys**. These last two are not implemented on all Macintosh systems, but they are part of the extended keyboard design. The same *up* and *down* logic that applies to the other keys we've been discussing also applies to these keys, with the exception of the **functionKey** message. When a function key is pressed, the message sent in HyperCard includes the number of the key. The resulting handler portion looks like this:

```
on functionKey keyNo
   if keyNo = 5 then
   -- do some processing
   -- etc.
end functionKey
```

Don't use function keys 1-4 for HyperCard activities because most Mac word processors and text editors use these keys for editing operations predefined by Apple Computer.

Don't confuse the process of checking whether the **commandKey** is **down** using this approach with the use of the **commandKeyDown** message we discussed in Chapter 6. You can use the **commandKey** function inside a handler that processes some other system message. The **commandKeyDown** system message, on the other hand, must be intercepted in a handler named after the message.

Keypresses modify results

For this experiment, you can use an existing button whose script you no longer need, or you can create a new button on either a new or existing Laboratory stack card. After you have prepared the button, follow these steps:

1. Open the button's script-editing window using one of the usual methods.

2. Type the following script into the window:

```
on mouseDown
    put "Mouse is down "
    repeat while the mouse is down
        if the optionKey is down then
            put "with the Option Key" after Message
            exit repeat
        end if
        if the commandKey is down then
            put "with the Command Key" after Message
            exit repeat
        end if
        if the shiftKey is down then
            put "with the Shift Key" after Message
            exit repeat
        end if
    end repeat
end mouseDown
```

3. Press the mouse button in the button you are using. The message "Mouse is down " immediately appears in the Message box. Now press the Shift, Command, or Option key. Notice that the Message box adds information after its previous contents about which key you pressed. Confirm that the handler has been executed by continuing to hold down the mouse button and trying the other keys.

4. Release the mouse button. Now repeat the instructions in step 3 for all the special keys. Try holding down two of the special keys simultaneously. Notice that only one of them is acknowledged.

Even though this handler is longer than ones we've dealt with before, it is not very mysterious. The main body of instructions execute as long as the mouse is held down or until one of the special keys is pressed. When one of the keys we are monitoring is pressed, the handler adds some words to the end of the current contents of the Message box indicating which key was pressed. Then it leaves the loop and the handler ends.

▶ Checking for two-key combinations

You can link two key conditions together with the **and** logical operator and check for key combinations. We discuss the **and** operator in detail in Chapter 8. To look for the Shift-Command key combination, for example, you could perform a check like this:

```
if the shiftKey is down and the commandKey is down
```

▶ Saving the key's condition

Given the rapidity with which HyperCard applications execute and the speed with which many people use the Macintosh, it is sometimes useful to store the state of a key and then check later to see if it was pressed when the user made the last selection or took the last action. This is particularly helpful when you write handlers that permit a single button to have more than one effect depending on whether a special key was held down while the button was activated.

Because these operations are functions that return a result, we can put that result into a container. Here is the skeleton for a **mouseUp** message handler that reacts differently to the message depending on whether the Shift, Option, or Command key is held down while the button is activated:

```
on mouseUp
    put the optionKey into optionStatus
    put the commandKey into commandStatus
    put the shiftKey into shiftStatus
    -- some other actions that don't depend on
    -- the keys' status take place here; these
    -- might be commands that are common to all
    -- variations of the button's theme
    if optionStatus is down then
        -- carry out the optionKey version
    end if
    if commandStatus is down then
        -- carry out the commandKey version
    end if
    if shiftStatus is down then
        -- carry out the shiftKey version
    end if
end mouseUp
```

▶ Watching User Keystrokes

There are times in constructing a HyperCard stack when you would like to be able to watch what the user types at the keyboard and react instantly to an unexpected or incorrect keystroke. Beginning with HyperCard 2.0, that became possible with the addition of the keyDown system message. This message was discussed in Chapter 6 in the context of describing all of HyperCard's system messages. Now let's take a closer look at how you could make practical use of this message in dealing with keyboard I/O.

Assume that you'd like to be sure that the user types only numeric values into a field you've created on a card. By intercepting the keystrokes as the user types them and rejecting any keystroke that doesn't meet the criteria you set up in the **keyDown** handler, you can achieve this result. Here is a handler that will screen out all but numbers and related punctuation from a field:

```
on keyDown key
   if key is not in "0123456789$.," then
      beep
      exit keyDown
   else
      put key after card field 1
   end if
end keyDown
```

This handler is not completely usable as it is because it should also allow other keystrokes that it will now reject. For example, you want the user to be able to tab from this field, possibly use the Return key to mean he or she is done entering data, press the Backspace key to delete an entry, and maybe use other keys as well. Expanding the handler to deal with those needs would not be difficult and you might enjoy trying that as an exercise.

You would also want, in a real-world application of this type, to be sure the field was empty before all of the new data was entered into it (or otherwise set up for data entry). This could be handled easily in an openCard handler, for example.

▶ Text File Operations

HyperTalk's vocabulary includes four commands that permit HyperCard to work with text-only files outside its environment. Data can be read from text-only files and used in stacks. Information from stacks can be exported to text-only files for use by word processors, report generators, spelling checkers, and other similar programs.

Whether you are importing or exporting data, the process is fundamentally quite similar. You use the **open file** command to open the file so you can put information into it or take information out of it. Then you use the **read** or **write** command to perform the actual data transfer. Finally, when you're done, you use **close file** to end the processing. Let's look at these commands in the order in which we just listed them.

▶ Open file

There is nothing mysterious or difficult about the **open file** command. Supply the name of the file — either explicitly as a string or implicitly in a container —and HyperTalk establishes a communications channel between your script and the disk file, creating it if it doesn't already exist.

For example, to open a file called Test File, you could simply write this command:

```
open file "Test File"
```

HyperCard looks in the root level directory of the currently active disk drive. If it finds a file called Test File, it opens it. If not, it creates a new file called Test File at the topmost level of the current disk volume.

▶ A word about path names

If you have set any of the Preferences card options in HyperCard's Home stack, you have already gained at least a nodding acquaintance with path names. The path name of a file is a map that helps the Macintosh File Manager (part of the operating system) locate a file on the disk. To make HyperCard look anywhere but the root level of the currently active disk for files you want to open or create, you must supply a path name.

Definition ▶	A *path name* starts with the name of the disk (also called the volume) on which the file is located and then lists each folder in turn to which a file belongs. If you omit the volume name, you can begin the path name with a colon, and HyperCard assumes you mean the currently active volume.

Look at Figure 7-3. It depicts a document called Vendors stored inside a folder called Lists. That folder in turn is found inside another folder called Documents, which is at the top level of the hard disk volume called A Hard Place. HyperTalk can access the Vendors document in an **open file** command by either of the following two lines:

```
open file "A Hard Place:Documents:Lists:Vendors"
open file ":Documents:Lists:Vendors"
```

Figure 7-3. A document in a hierarchy of storage

You can also use the **ask file** command discussed in detail in Chapter 11 to display a standard Macintosh file dialog box in which the user simply points to the file to be read. This command produces a full path name for the file to be used.

▶ Reading from a text file

The full name of the command that reads data from text files is **read from file**. It has two alternative forms. The first, which follows, reads all the data from a file until it reaches a defined *delimiter character*. Generally, two delimiter characters are used in text-only files. Tabs separate individual fields, and carriage returns mark the ends of records:

```
read from file filename until delimiter character
```

The file name must be placed in quotation marks. The delimiter character must be one of HyperTalk's standard constant characters (tab, return, lineFeed, or formFeed) or another character you define using ASCII values or a single-character string. (In case the term ASCII is unfamiliar, it is a standard way of representing characters in computers.) If you supply more than one character as the delimiter, HyperTalk uses only the first character of this string and will stop reading when it encounters the first instance of that character.

Using the form of the **read** command just cited, a script would have to perform two checks. It would read individual files with a command like this:

```
read from file "Test" until Tab
```

Then it would check as each field was read in to see if it was a return:

```
if it is Return then
   -- follow with appropriate processing
```

Depending on the file's structure, you might also need a check for an empty field to recognize that the end of the file had been reached:

```
if it is empty then
   -- follow with appropriate processing
```

The second method of reading a text-only file in HyperCard is to know in advance how many bytes of information you want to read. This approach usually works only for small files because larger ones are hard to manipulate into field formats after you bring them into HyperCard through your script. The format of this version of the **read** command is:

```
read from file name for number of bytes
```

HyperCard has a 16,384-character buffer limit when performing either type of **read** operation. When the **read** process stops, you may want to check to ensure that you have read to the point you wanted to reach. If the last character of the text stream is the one on which you wanted to stop, you can be confident that the **read** did not overflow the buffer. If it is not the desired character, then you have probably read 16,384 bytes of data without encountering the character you specified.

▶ Writing to a text file

If you need to export text from a stack to a text-only field so that a word processor, a database manager, or some other program can use it, you will find the **write** command quite powerful and flexible. Its form is:

```
write content to file file name
```

The content that is written to the file can be either the name of a variable, a text string inside quotation marks, or, more commonly, some file name identifier.

If a field is being written out to the file, you can supply either its assigned name or its field or unique ID number.

The field name can be either the field's assigned name or its field or unique ID number. Locally assigned field numbers are often more useful than names or IDs in **write** scripts because using numbers permits you to loop through all the fields on a card in a small amount of code. The file name must, as usual, be in quotation marks. The comments about locating the file and its path name made in discussing the **read** command apply equally to the **write** command. The **answer file** command (see Chapter 11) will allow the user to name the file to be written, including the path name, using the standard Macintosh file dialog box.

You must insert delimiter characters into your outgoing text. If the program on the receiving end of your output expects a tab-delimited file, add a tab after each field is written to the file. One form of the portion of your script that handles this assignment is:

```
repeat for the number of cards
   repeat with x=1 to the number of fields
      write field i to file "Test"
      write tab to file "Test"
   end repeat
   go next card
end repeat
```

▶ Summary

In this chapter, you saw how to use several messages about the mouse's location. You also examined the **click** command, which permits you to simulate the user's mouse-clicking actions.

You looked at several messages that let you determine whether the Command, Option, or Shift keys were held down the last time the user clicked the mouse. You learned how they worked, and saw a possible application of this approach in a script. You also saw how to monitor the keyboard and react to specific keystrokes. Finally, you learned how to open and close text-only files and how to get information out of such files into HyperCard and vice versa.

In Chapter 8, we take our long-promised look at control structures and their related logical operators.

8 ▶ Control Structures and Logical Operators

In this chapter, you will learn

- how control structures are used in HyperTalk scripts to execute groups of instructions repeatedly or conditionally

- what logical operators and related functions are available in HyperTalk

- how to use special HyperTalk commands to gain better control over loops

- how HyperTalk compares with Pascal and other traditional procedural languages in the way it handles control structures

▶ Loops and Conditions: Background

If you have programming experience in Pascal, C, BASIC, or another traditional programming language, feel free to skip this discussion and move to the next section, "If-Then Processing." But if HyperTalk is your first programming language or you're a bit rusty in the fundamentals, reading this section will make the rest of this chapter more understandable.

Most computer programs — and HyperTalk handlers are no exception — execute linearly, starting with the first instruction, then executing the second, then the third, and so on until they come to some kind of logical end. Along the way, procedural programming languages often include branching instructions that send the program to some other part of the code semipermanently (as with the BASIC GOTO statement) or temporarily (for example, GOSUB in BASIC). These languages also generally include instructions to execute one or more commands conditionally (that is, only if a certain condition is met) or repeatedly (that is, until some condition arises, as long as some condition is true, or a specific number of times).

In all cases, these constructs give programmers great flexibility in the way their programs manage data and interact with the user. It can be argued — and often is — that no interesting or useful programs can be written without such conditional processing and looping constructs. Avoiding that philosophical issue, it is clear that meaningful programs are often more difficult and time-consuming to design and write without such constructs.

HyperTalk includes no commands equivalent to BASIC's GOTO and GOSUB commands. It does, however, offer conditional execution and looping constructs, which are the focus of this chapter.

(We should perhaps be a little clearer at the outset. In HyperTalk, it is possible to call procedures from within procedures. In some ways, this resembles calling the BASIC GOTO and GOSUB statements just described. But there is no inherent, built-in command for such branching.)

▶ If-Then Processing

The first control structure we will discuss is the **if-then-else** construct, which in one form or another is part of most major programming languages.

Many of the decisions we make in our lives can be expressed as if-then decisions. *If* it is Sunday, *then* I won't get up early and go to work. *If* it is 95 degrees outside *and* the sky is azure blue, *then* I won't take a raincoat with me when I leave this morning. In each case, notice that we have the conditional "flag" in the word *If*, a word a wag once declared to be the biggest little word in the English language. This word is followed by a description of a state of affairs or sequence of events that is either true or false. If it is true (that is, if it really *is* Sunday), the second part of the statement is carried out (that is, I don't get up early to go to work).

If-then-else decisions in HyperTalk are similar to such decisions in our daily lives.

▶ General format and use

To undertake some conditional processing in HyperTalk, you have a choice of two related approaches. The first has one set of conditionally executed commands that are carried out only if some condition is true. Its general form looks like this:

```
if <condition> then
    <series of commands>
end if
```

This format can be abbreviated if there is only one command to be executed. In that event, the **end if** statement is not required. The conditionally executed command can be on the same line as the **if-then**

```
if <condition> then <command>
```

or on the next line

```
if <condition>
then <command>
```

The second approach to conditional program processing provides two sets of alternative commands: One is carried out if the condition is true and the other is carried out if it is false. This approach is known as the **if-then-else** approach, which is familiar if you have any experience programming in conventional languages such as Pascal or BASIC. The formatting of this approach is identical to the first one mentioned. The general format looks like this:

```
if <condition> then
    <series of commands>
else
    <alternate series of commands>
end if
```

The simplest form of the **if-then-else** construct is:

```
if <condition> then ≤command_1> else <command_2>
```

Formatting, which is generally not an issue in HyperTalk programming, becomes important in dealing with the **if** command and its variations. The issue centers around when you must supply the **end if** statement. Many HyperTalk programmers have had difficulty sorting out this question. If you run into situations where HyperTalk's script editor refuses to indent your **if-then-else** loops correctly and you can't figure out why, ask yourself these questions:

1. How many **else** clauses are there? (Note that if you put the key word **else** on a separate line from the command to be executed with it, HyperTalk sees this as two clauses, not one.) If you have only one line in the **else**

clause, you should not include the **end if** statement. In fact, it is wrong to do so. If you have two or more lines in the **else** clause, the **end if** is *required*. If you have no **else** clause, then go to the next question.

2. How many **then** clauses are there? (Again, HyperTalk sees the word **then** on a line by itself as a **then** clause line.) If you have only one line in the **then** clause, you should not include the **end if** statement. Otherwise, it is required.

You must, of course, separate clauses into lines; you cannot combine commands in one HyperTalk line inside an **if** statement any more than you can anywhere else in HyperTalk.

It is, of course, possible to set up multiple conditions in the **if** clause of an **if-then** or **if-then-else** construct. In the event you need such multiple conditions, you will find it necessary to connect them with the key words **and** or **or**. We'll see some examples of this usage later in the chapter.

Note ▶ There are some anomalies in the way HyperTalk formats and treats **if** clauses. If you use such clauses in a script that seem not to execute properly, try reformatting the **if-then-else** clauses. This will quite often erase apparent errors.

▶ Nesting if statements

You can nest **if-then** and **if-then-else** statements. In other words, commands executed conditionally can themselves be a set of conditionally processed commands. This ability lends itself to powerful — but potentially complex — programming structures.

Here is an example of a nested set of **if-then-else** statements:

```
on mouseUp
   if the optionKey is down then
      if the shiftKey is down then beep 5
      else beep 3
   else beep 1
end mouseUp
```

The button this script is attached to beeps once when it is clicked, unless the Option key is held down at the same time, in which case it beeps three times. If the Shift and Option keys are held down together when the button is pressed, HyperCard beeps five times. Notice that each **if-then-else** includes only one command in the **else** portion, so no **end if** statements are required.

Nested if statements

Let's go back to the Laboratory stack. Pick any card with a button whose script is no longer needed, or create your own. Then follow these instructions:

1. Open the script-editing window for the button.

2. Type the following script into the window and click OK when you are done and the handler is syntactically correct:

```
on mouseUp
   if the optionKey is down then
      if the shiftKey is down then
         beep 5
         put "Shift-Option Combination" into Message
      else
         beep 3
         put "Option Key Alone" into Message
      end if
   end if
end mouseUp
```

3. Return to Browse mode.

4. Click on the button, first with the Option key held down, then with the Shift-Option keys held down, and finally with no keyboard keys held down. Notice not only the different beep combinations, but also the changing notices in the Message box.

This is the same basic handler script as the one we just looked at in much simpler form. It works the same, but this time we've added multiple statements after each **else**, requiring that each **if** clause be ended with an **end if**. Although this script is simplistic and doesn't do anything to write home about, it does demonstrate the flexibility of multiple nested **if-then-else** statements. A single handler responds to an event that can be sent in three ways: alone, with the Option key, or with the Shift-Option keys.

▶ Conditional Operators and Calculations

Now that we've seen how **if-then** and **if-then-else** combinations work, let's see how we create their conditions.

▶ True or false tests

All conditions in conditional processing must ultimately lead to a true or false situation. Any question that can be answered "yes" or "no" can be used to formulate a condition for an **if** clause in HyperTalk.

You can set up tests for equality (**if** x = 3 then...) or inequality (**if** not x = 3 then...) but generally not for mathematical formulas (**if** x*4 then...) or other expressions that don't produce a true or false, yes or no, 1 or 0 result. Functions and expressions that do return such results are referred to as logical operations or Boolean functions.

Sometimes, you will test the value of a container or variable without using explicit equality or inequality comparisons. A statement such as **if** x **then**... is an acceptable and logical HyperTalk statement if x contains the value true or false or the number 1 (which means true) or 0 (which means false).

In HyperTalk you will frequently test many things in the condition portions of **if** statements. We can divide these tests more conveniently into determinations of

- **equality** of two elements
- **inclusion** of one element in another
- **status** of a particular aspect of the system
- **type** of a particular container or value
- **existence** of a specific object

Let's look at each kind of test.

▶ Equality conditions

The test condition you will undoubtedly use most often in HyperTalk scripts is the **is** command. Actually, **is** is a synonym for *equals*. But most HyperTalk scripters use **is** to keep their scripts readable.

The following examples of equality conditions using **is** are similar to those you will frequently encounter in programming HyperTalk scripts:

```
if field "Name" is empty
if the optionKey is down
if x is 5
```

```
if it is "excited"
```

These are identical in effect to:

```
if field "Name" = empty
if the optionKey = down
if x = 5
if it = "excited"
```

You can use **is** and = interchangeably, but your scripts are easier to read if you confine your use of = to numeric comparisons and use **is** for all other comparisons.

As you might expect from a language as English-like and flexible as HyperTalk, **is** has an opposite just as = does. The opposite of the equal sign is written as either < > or ≠ and the opposite of **is**, logically enough, is **is not**. In many cases, HyperTalk has values that make the use of **is not** and other inequality operators unnecessary. For example, you hardly need to write

```
if the optionKey is not down
```

when the shorter and clearer

```
if the optionKey is up
```

is available. But in other cases, the inequality operator is exactly what's needed:

```
if field "Name" is not empty
if x ≠ 5
if it is not "excited"
```

▶ Comparison operators

Sometimes, it is not enough to know that an item is not equal to another. You need to know if it is greater than or less than the other object. For these situations, HyperTalk includes the usual programming language complement of comparison operators. These operators are summarized in Table 8-1.

Table 8-1. Comparison operators

Operator	Interpretation	Example
<	Less than	15 < 53 returns true
<= or ≤	Less than or equal to	15 <= 53 returns true
		33 ≤ 33 returns true
>	Greater than	15 > 53 returns false
>= or ≥	Greater than or equal to	15>= 53 returns false
		33 ≥ 33 returns true

▶ Inclusion

Besides equality and inequality, your HyperTalk scripts can test for the presence of a sequence of characters in a field or text container. You can use either **is in** or **contains**. Both operators perform text matches that are not case sensitive. They look at one text string — the container — and see if another text string is located anywhere within it.

The syntax for these two commands is as follows:

```
if <source string> is in <container>
if <container> contains <source string>
```

As you can see, the only syntactical difference between the two commands is that **is in** places the string to be searched for first, but **contains** puts it last.

Testing for inclusion

Use either an existing Laboratory stack card with a reusable field or create a new field on either an existing card or a new card. Size doesn't matter; leave the field set at the default size HyperCard creates when it brings up the new field. But define it as a rectangle or shadow so its outlines are visible (this makes things easier when you're testing and come back to the field later).

1. Click into the field. Type in the following text with capitals exactly as shown:

```
This is a dumb TEsT
```

2. Now open the Message box if it isn't already open, or click in the Message box if it is open. Make sure the box is empty.

3. Type:

```
card field 1 contains "test"
```

and press Return. The Message box displays "True." Clearly, HyperTalk has found the string and ignored the case differences. Try the same thing with other combinations of uppercase and lowercase if you like.

4. Type:

```
"dumb " is in card field 1
```

Be sure to include the space after the word *dumb*. Again, the Message box displays "True." You can use this approach to find any combination of characters or spaces in the text of a field.

▶ Status

We have already seen in Chapter 7 how to test the state of the Shift, Option, or Command keys and react accordingly. As we will see in Chapter 17, all HyperCard objects have *properties* associated with them. These properties enable us to find out basic information about the objects other than their contents. For example, using property management commands we can find out if a field is presently visible, the user level for the person accessing the stack, an object's name, how many cards, buttons, fields, or backgrounds are in a stack, and dozens of other useful pieces of information.

Although we defer the discussion of specific properties until Chapter 17, you should be aware that testing the condition of these properties is one of the most frequent kinds of conditional processing you'll do in HyperTalk. The general form for using these properties as conditions is straightforward:

```
if <property name> is <value>
```

To give you an idea of what kinds of things you might test for, here are some sample lines:

```
if card field 1 is visible
if field "Test Field" is empty
if the number of cards > 53
if lockScreen is true
```

Not all properties that can be attributed to HyperCard objects are subject to **if-then** testing or could logically be used in conditional processing statements. In Chapter 17 we make clearer which of the many properties do lend themselves to this treatment.

▶ Type

Beginning with HyperCard 2.0, you can test a particular container's contents or an explicit value to determine if it is one of the following types of HyperCard entities:

- number
- integer
- point
- rectangle
- date
- logical expression

This test is handled by means of an extension to the **is** command we discussed earlier in this chapter. For example, to determine whether a card field contains a valid date or not, you can use a test like this:

```
if cd fld 1 is a date then
    -- do some processing
```

You can use either "a" or "an" as the article preceding the type of value for which you wish to test, or you can omit it entirely.

If you want to determine if a field contains a number or an integer, you must use the **value** function (discussed in Chapter 15) to extract the value of the field before testing its type. This is not necessary if you are testing a variable's type, however.

For the purposes of this operator, HyperTalk defines a point as any two values separated by a comma, whether or not they are numeric. Similarly, a rectangle is defined as any four values separated by commas, regardless of the types of the individual elements of the list. While this makes it possible to determine whether a particular expression could define a point or rectangle, it doesn't really tell you if the expression is a valid point or rectangle.

▶ Existence

Beginning with HyperCard 2.0, you can test for the existence of certain types of entities in the Macintosh or HyperCard environment. This is a welcome addition for scripters who have found themselves trying to find ways to be sure that, for example, a particular field existed before sending it a message or trying to put some information into it.

Using the **there is** operator, you can test for the existence of

- windows
- menus
- menu items
- files
- cards
- backgrounds
- buttons
- fields
- stacks

In all cases but windows, you simply supply an expression that identifies the object for which you wish to test. For example, to find out if there is a background field 1 on the current card, you would use this statement:

```
if there is background field 1 then
    -- some processing
```

To test for a window, you must precede the expression with the key word *window*, as in:

```
if there is a window "Test Stack" then
    -- some processing
```

You can supply path names to point to specific stacks and files that you want to confirm exist or don't exist.

▶ Using the constants true and false

When you do conditional processing programming in HyperTalk, you can use the built-in constants **true** and **false**. These constants are not often used with most of the conditional processing situations we've discussed in this chapter because the true or false nature of the condition is apparent. A button is either up or down. Writing a line such as

```
if the optionKey is down is true
```

is superfluous.

But sometimes the built-in logical constants are handy. Perhaps the most obvious case is the process of setting flags. In complex programs, we often want to keep track of a condition in the system. For example, we may want to know if the user has clicked on Button 1 because if so, certain processing won't be necessary. So we set up a "flag" variable — call it *pressed* in this example — to keep track of that value. Then we can test it at the appropriate time. The framework for the example we just described is:

```
on someEvent
   set pressed to false
   . . .
   if pressed is false then
   . . .
end someEvent
```

▶ Logical connectors

One final topic should be covered to complete our discussion of conditional processing. Oftentimes, a combination of conditions must be tested before a script can proceed with processing. Staying with our by-now-familiar special key checking, for example, we might want to know only if any of the special keys has been pressed. We could get that information by programming a construct such as:

```
on mouseUp
   if the optionKey is down then put "Special key down"
   if the shiftKey is down then put "Special key down"
   if the commandKey is down then put "Special key down"
end mouseUp
```

Pressing any combination of these special keys when the mouse button is clicked puts the message "Special key down" into the Message box. (We should note that if more than one special key is used, the message is actually placed in the Message box as many times as there are special keys pressed. But the effect is all but unnoticeable to the user, so it is not significant in this context.)

But this is more code than we need. If we want to display the message if any special key is being pressed, we can use the **or** connector. This connector links logical conditions so that if any one of the conditions connected by **or** is true, the condition succeeds. Thus, the previous handler can be reduced to this:

```
on mouseUp
   if the optionKey is down or the shiftKey is down or ¬
      the commandKey is down then put "Special key down"
end mouseUp
```

Similarly, if we want to display a special message only if all the keys are down, we use the **and** logical connector. Conditions hooked together with **and** only succeed if all the conditions are true.

The third logical connector in HyperTalk is **not**. It is used to negate or reverse logic. It can be applied to any equality condition check to make it a check for inequality. It can also be combined with **and** and **or** to create complex criteria in control constructs.

Using and

Go to your Laboratory stack again. Use the same button you've been using for these special key combination tests or create a new one. Then follow these steps:

1. Open the button's scripting window by one of the usual methods.

2. Enter the following script into the window:

```
on mouseUp
    if the shiftKey is down and the commandKey is down
         then
         beep 3
         put "Two keys down"
    end if
end mouseUp
```

3. Return to Browse mode.

4. Try pressing the mouse button with the cursor over the button whose script you just created or modified. Notice that something happens only when you hold down the Shift and Command keys together.

Note ▶ We cannot test for all three keys being pressed at once, not because of limitations of the **and** connector but because pressing the Command-Option key combination results in HyperCard suspending operation and highlighting all the buttons on the card. This interrupts script processing. (If, however, you set the **cantPeek** property of a stack to true (see Chapter 17), then you can test for all three keys simultaneously. Try it out!)

▶ Looping Commands

Besides conditionally executing instructions in a handler, we might want to execute some particular step or steps more than once. The repeated execution of commands in HyperTalk is accomplished with an instruction that is named, appropriately enough, **repeat**.

This instruction should properly be looked at as four separate instructions. These variations on the **repeat** theme are

- **repeat for**
- **repeat with**
- **repeat while**
- **repeat until**

As we will see, these commands correspond to similar constructs in Pascal, C, and BASIC. HyperTalk, however, includes something most other programming languages lack: two ways to "escape" from an executing loop without finishing some or all of its instructions.

▶ Basic looping concepts

All **repeat** structures in HyperTalk work similarly. They all start with the word **repeat** and end with the phrase **end repeat**. They all execute the commands contained between those key words zero or more times. And they all end when the circumstances under which they are expected to execute are no longer valid, unless they are interrupted sooner by an **exit repeat** command.

Inside a loop, all the rules of program execution apply exactly as they do in a complete handler. Any conditional statement groups involving **if-then** combinations are evaluated and executed as if they were the only statements in the group. Local and global variables known to the handler can be used anywhere inside the **repeat** loop.

Quite often, a handler consists entirely or nearly entirely of a single **repeat** loop. We saw one such loop in Chapter 7 when we performed a Laboratory exercise to track the coordinate position of the mouse pointer in a card. You may recall that the loop executed until you clicked the mouse.

The most crucial idea in writing loops in any programming language, including HyperTalk, is to make sure there is an escape route. There are two ways to create such routes in HyperTalk:

- by including an **exit repeat** condition that explicitly leaves the loop when some event occurs

- by ensuring that the condition under which the **repeat** command is executed eventually changes to a condition under which it will stop

Failure to do one of these results in a dreaded construct called an *infinite loop*, one of the most common mistakes in programming.

▶ Basic repeat conditions

Whether we are talking about HyperTalk or a conventional programming language, there are two general categories of conditions under which loops can be programmed to execute:

- for a specific number of times
- as long as some condition remains true

In the first category of **repeat** loops, it is the reaching of some specific value in a variable or an upper limit on the number of iterations set as a condition. In the second category, the circumstance that causes the loop to stop is the changing of a condition.

▶ Using object-counting in repeat conditions

One of the most useful things you can find out in HyperCard for use in **repeat** loops is the number of some kind of object with which you wish the loop to deal. For example, if you want to zip through a stack and look at each card individually, you want to know when you're done looking at all the cards. If you want to perform some operation or test on all the card buttons on a given card, you want to know how many buttons you have to deal with. Although you can "hard-code" such information, this is practically never a good idea; any future changes to the stack design might not get picked up in the scripts affected by those designs. All manner of confusion can result.

You can have HyperCard supply you with the number of buttons or fields on the current background or card, the number of backgrounds in the stack, the number of cards in the stack, or even, beginning with HyperCard 1.2, the number of cards sharing the current background.

It then becomes easy to write loops such as this one:

```
repeat for the number of cards
   if field "Accepted" contains "Yes" then add 1 to total
   go to next card
end repeat
```

You will find frequent need for such repeat-loop counter controls that involve knowing the number of some particular kind of object with which the handler must be concerned.

▶ The repeat for command

The **repeat for** command is the most straightforward of the looping constructs in HyperTalk. It simply tells HyperCard how many times to execute a loop. In the absence of an **exit repeat** command inside the loop, the instructions execute exactly the specified number of times, and then the handler proceeds with the rest of its processing.

In Pascal, BASIC, or another conventional language, you implement this same kind of loop with a FOR-NEXT construction, starting with the counter value set to 1 and the upper limit set to the number of times you want to execute the loop.

Here is the syntax for the **repeat for** construct:

```
repeat [for] <number> [times]
   <statements>
end repeat
```

Notice that there are two optional words in the command: **for** and **times**. This permits you to make your **repeat** loops as abbreviated as you want or to opt for maximum readability. The following opening lines of **repeat** loops are equivalent:

```
repeat for 11 times
repeat for 11
repeat 11 times
repeat 11
```

The number argument need not be an explicitly supplied numeric value. It can be a container that holds a number. For example, you might ask users how many times they want some action to occur, store the answer in the variable *numberOfTimes*, and then set up a **repeat** loop like this:

```
repeat numberOfTimes times
   . . .
end repeat
```

You will find this approach to the **repeat** loop most useful when you are performing some process repeatedly but want to insert a wait command to slow things down a bit. (The wait command is discussed in detail in Chapter 16. For now, just remember that it delays the number of ticks, or 60ths of a second, supplied as an argument.) You have undoubtedly noticed, for example, that when we use commands such as

```
beep 3
```

in our scripts, the three beeps take place in such close proximity that the effect isn't always what we intended. By putting the **beep** command inside a **repeat** loop, we can separate the sounds by some silence, achieving the desired effect:

```
repeat 3 times
   beep
   wait 4
end repeat
```

Experiment with the value supplied as the time to wait to convey the audio message you want.

You will also frequently use the **repeat for** approach to looping when you are scanning through all the fields or cards to look for something or to change the data. For example, you might have a client-billing stack that includes on each card a field with the billing rate for that attorney. If the partners decide to increase billing rates by 10 percent, you could write a small **repeat for** loop like this:

```
repeat number of cards times
   put field "Rate" * 1.1 into field "Rate"
   go next card
end repeat
```

▶ The repeat with command

The **repeat with** command adds another level of complexity to the condition. In the **repeat with** approach, you use a special variable, called a counter, that you increase or decrease by 1 during each cycle through the loop until it reaches a predetermined value. Then the loop stops executing.

This command is HyperTalk's equivalent of the FOR-NEXT loop in Pascal and BASIC. The only difference is that you cannot specify an increment or decrement value in HyperTalk. The variable is always increased or decreased by 1.

The syntax for the **repeat with** command looks like this:

```
repeat with <counter> = <start> [down]to <end>
   <commands>
end repeat
```

If the value for *start* is 1, **repeat with** is the same as **repeat for**. In other words, this **repeat** loop

```
repeat with x = 1 to 10
   <commands>
end repeat
```

does the same thing as this one

```
repeat 10 times
   <commands>
end repeat
```

There is an important exception to this equality. If you need to use the number of times through the loop as a value, only the **repeat with** approach will work.

Returning to our time-billing example, suppose each attorney's card contained several billing rates and the fields were called (for purposes of simplicity) Field 1, Field 2, and so on. You could update all the fields on a single card with a single **repeat** loop like this:

```
repeat with x = 1 to number of card fields
   put card Field x * 1.1 into card Field x
end repeat
```

But if billing rates start with Field 7 and are the last fields on the card, a simple modification handles that case as well:

```
repeat with x = 7 to number of card fields
   put card Field x * 1.1 into card Field x
end repeat
```

In this last example, it would be difficult, if not impossible, to use the **repeat for** loop to solve the problem.

▶ The repeat while command

You use the **repeat while** command to carry out a set of instructions as long as a condition is true. As soon as the condition is false, the loop stops executing.

The syntax for the **repeat while** command looks like this:

```
repeat while <condition>
   <commands>
end repeat
```

The *condition* here is identical in use and form to those we discussed with **if** processing previously in this chapter. It must evaluate to a true or false value, and it can use any of HyperCard's built-in functions to do so. If the *condition* is false the first time HyperCard encounters the loop, the loop never executes.

Using the repeat while command

Open the Laboratory stack again. We need a card with a button and a field whose contents you can reuse. Find an old card with this combination of objects or create a new one. The field must be Field 1, or you must make appropriate changes to the following script:

1. Open the button's script-editing window in one of the usual ways.

2. Type the following script into the window and click OK when you're done:

```
on mouseUp
    repeat while card Field 1 < 64
        put card Field 1 * 2 into card Field 1
    end repeat
    beep
end mouseUp
```

3. Return to Browse mode.

4. Enter the number 2 in the field.

5. Press the button. A series of numbers appear in the window, until the value 64 appears. Then the loop stops, your Mac beeps, and the handler ends. Your screen looks similar to Figure 8-1.

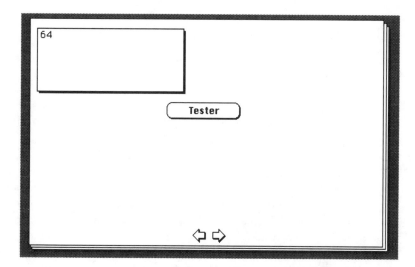

Figure 8-1. The repeat while loop experiment ends

6. Put the number 75 (or any number higher than 64) into the window and notice what happens. The **repeat** loop is never executed. Instead, you get the expected beep sound and the handler ends. The first time the **repeat** loop was entered, the value of the field was greater than 64, so the loop was never carried out.

▶ The repeat until command

The last of the four regular **repeat** forms we will examine is the **repeat until** command. It is easy to understand because it is the flip side of the **repeat while** command we have just examined. The commands within its boundaries execute as long as the condition remains false. As soon as the condition turns true, the loop stops. This generally requires a reversal of the logic of the **repeat while** loop's condition.

Here's the syntax for **repeat until:**

```
repeat until <condition>
   <commands>
end repeat
```

To execute the example in our previous Laboratory exercise the same way using a **repeat until** loop, we have to reverse the logic of the condition. Instead of checking for the field's value to be greater than 64, we check for it being less than or equal to 64:

```
on mouseUp
   repeat until card Field 1 >= 64
      put card Field 1 * 2 into card Field 1
   end repeat
   beep
end mouseUp
```

If you want to experiment with this script, simply edit the **repeat** line of the script from our last Laboratory experiment and run the handler.

Note ▶ We use the condition "greater than or equal to 64" rather than "equal to 64" in the previous example for an important reason. If you use only an equal condition (that is, Field 1=64) and if Field 1's value never gets to exactly 64, the loop could become an infinite one. For example, if the user puts a 3 instead of a 2 into Field 1 at the start, doubling the value each time results in answers of 6, 12, 24, 48, 96, 192, and so on. Because 64 never appears, the loop just keeps executing. In the Laboratory example, we were sure that the value 64 would eventually appear. But unless you can guarantee the ceiling value will be reached, use conditions that are met without an infinite loop.

▶ The naked repeat command

You will occasionally encounter one last form of the **repeat** command in scripts: the naked **repeat**. With no *for*, *with*, *while*, or *until*, the **repeat** command means **repeat forever**. (You can even add the word **forever** if you want to make it clearer.)

In 99 percent of all cases where you use the **repeat** command alone, you will supply a means of exiting the loop using the technique described later in this chapter. And you probably could design the loop as a more conventional **repeat** loop using one of the other ending conditions we've been studying.

But in some limited circumstances, you want to keep all or a major portion of your script's processing in an intentionally infinite loop. Such loops can give the programmer more control over the user's interaction with the program, a decidedly unMac-like thing to do. Because the user can always leave your script by using one of the menu navigation commands to go to a different stack or card, though, you are not really *trapping* the user in an infinite loop. Still, use the concept sparingly. Always ask yourself if there isn't a more straightforward way to deal with the loop requirement.

▶ Control Within Repeat Loops

HyperTalk includes two powerful commands to change the course of action within **repeat** loops. One, **next repeat**, cuts short the execution of part of a collection of repeated statements while continuing the loop at the next iteration. The other, **exit repeat**, causes the loop to stop executing and the script to begin processing at the first statement after the **end repeat** line.

▶ The next repeat command

Although most programming languages do not have a command equivalent to the **next repeat** command, it has some handy uses. Within any **repeat** loop, you can use a command such as

```
if <condition> then [<commands>] [end if] else next repeat
   [<commands>]
```

to make the program go back to the top of the **repeat** loop, without executing any statements between the **next repeat** command and either another **next repeat** command or the **end repeat** command. If any commands appear between **then** and **next repeat**, the **end if** statement is also required, as you will recall from our previous discussion of **if-then** combinations.

Here is a generic example of the use of the **next repeat** command:

```
repeat with x = 10 to 50
   <statement1>
   <statement2>
   if <condition2> then
      beep 3
      next repeat
   end if
   <statement3>
end repeat
```

This loop executes 41 times, once for each value of x from 10 to 50, inclusive, unless the condition specified in *condition2* becomes true before that time. In that event, the system beeps three times and *statement3* is not executed. But *statement1* and *statement2* continue to execute until the loop ends normally. If *condition2* is never changed, *statement3* is not executed again because each time through the loop, the **if** command catches the execution, finds the condition to be true, and returns to the top of the loop.

Again using our time-billing example, assume the partners want to not only increase all billing rates by 10 percent, but also make sure no billing rate is lower than $125. The following loop handles that task:

```
repeat with x = 1 to number of card fields
   put card Field 1 * 1.1 into card Field 1
   if card Field 1 >= 125 then next repeat
   put 125 into card Field 1
end repeat
```

There are more ways to handle this problem, but this solution works, is efficient, and demonstrates the use of the **next repeat** command nicely.

▶ Counting backwards with down to

When you need to count down from a higher number to a lower one rather than in the more common ascending order, you can substitute **down to** for **to** in the **repeat with** loop structure:

```
repeat with x = 10 down to 1
   put x
   beep x
end repeat
```

▶ Defining a different increment

As mentioned, **repeat** loops in HyperTalk that use values with the **with** and **for** approaches do not allow you to increment or decrement the value of the counter by any value other than 1. Sometimes you want to increment a value by another value. In those cases, you can use the **next repeat** function with the **mod** operator to change the increment. (The **mod** operator finds the remainder in a division problem. For example, the result of 6 **mod** 3 is 0 because 6/3=2 with no remainder. But 39 **mod** 2 is 1 because 39/2=19 with a remainder of 1. The **mod** operator is fully discussed in Chapter 15.)

Here, for example, is a loop that effectively increments the counter by 2 each time through the loop:

```
repeat with x = 1 to 100
   if x mod 2 ≠ 0 then next repeat
   put x
end repeat
```

You can confirm that this loop works by attaching it to a button in a Laboratory card. The numbers 2, 4, 6, and so on up to 100 are displayed in the Message box, though you may have to build in a **wait** instruction to see each value displayed. Note that all the usual rules about using **if-then** constructs, described previously in this chapter, apply to **next repeat** commands.

▶ The exit repeat command

The **exit repeat** command is straightforward. It is almost always used with an **if-then** construct. The **exit repeat** command causes the loop to terminate immediately.

The syntax for this command is:

```
if <condition> then exit repeat
```

As with other **if-then** constructions, this command can incorporate other commands between **then** and **exit repeat**. If other commands are included, an **end if** is needed.

Continuing with our time-billing example, the fickle partners have now decided to increase everyone's fees by 10 percent in the first three categories (fields) but to bump only the partners' fees by 25 percent in all remaining categories. The following loop handles the assignment neatly:

```
repeat with x = 1 to number of card fields
   put card Field x * 1.1 into card Field x
   if card Field "Status" is not "Partner" then exit repeat
   if x > 3 then put card Field x * 1.25 into card Field x
end repeat
```

This loop would be part of a larger loop so that when the **exit repeat** command is encountered, the next card is examined and this **repeat** loop executes again.

▶ Summary

In this chapter, you learned about two of the most important programming techniques in HyperTalk (or any other programming language): conditional commands and loops.

You saw that the **if-then** and **if-then-else** command groups permit you to execute instructions in a handler selectively. You learned that there are a wide range of conditions you can check to determine if a command or sequence of commands should be carried out or not.

When instructions need to be carried out multiple times, you learned to use the various forms of the **repeat** command. You saw that each command in a **repeat** loop can be executed a specific number of times or until some condition is true or false.

Finally, you noted that HyperTalk, unlike most programming languages, offers powerful ways to alter the course of a loop's execution, adding another dimension of control.

In the next chapter, we will examine some commands, functions, and operators for controlling the stack and card environments.

9 ▶ Card and Stack Management Methods

In this chapter, you'll learn how to use HyperTalk commands to

- navigate among cards and stacks
- **find and mark** cards in a stack based on their contents
- manage multiple open stacks and their associated windows
- enable the user to return quickly to some predetermined point in the stack
- show or print one or more cards in a stack

▶ Navigation Commands

In a typical stackware application, the user spends a lot of time moving among cards. The user generally controls this movement with buttons you've designed and connected to arrows and icons. But there are times when you want to control which cards the user accesses and in what order. Sometimes this need is temporary, and other times it is an integral part of the stack's design. When you do want to control the navigation process, you can use one of HyperTalk's built-in commands, possibly with one of the language's constants.

Basically two HyperTalk commands are used for navigation: **go** and find. You use **go** to send the user to a specific card that can be named or referred to relative to the user's present position in the stack. The **go** command can also be used to change stacks. The **find** command is used to send the user to a card based on its content.

▶ Using go in a Script

You have probably had the experience of typing **go** commands into the Message box. This command **can be used to move** from your present position in the HyperCard world to any card in the current stack or to any addressable card in any other stack. Using the **go** command in a script is not substantially different from using it in the Message box.

The basic syntax of the command is simplicity itself:

```
go [to] <destination>
```

Notice that you can use the optional word **to** for more English-like syntax. The destination can be a card or a stack. You cannot go to a field or any other object.

▶ Addressing a destination

As you may know, any card can be addressed by name, sequence number, or unique ID number. If the seventh card in the current stack is named Directions and HyperCard has assigned it the unique ID 14238, all of the following commands will take you to the card:

```
go to card "Directions"
go to card 7
go to card ID 14238
```

The argument to the **go** command can be stored in a container so that the addressing is indirect. If the container helpPlace contains the value Directions, this command takes you to the same card as the previous three commands:

```
go to card helpPlace
```

If you want to **go** to a different stack from the current one, simply supply the name of the stack in quotation marks as an argument to the **go** command. In the absence of instructions to the contrary, HyperCard goes to the first card in that stack:

```
go to "My Appointments"
```

You may or may not need the quotation marks in your command, depending on the circumstances. If you include the word **stack** in your command, then you must put quotation marks around the stack only if its name consists of more than one word. If you omit the word **stack**, you must always put the name of the stack in quotation marks. If you place the name or other identifier of the destination stack into a HyperTalk container, of course, then you need not use quotation marks at all; in fact, to do so would be an error. Note that to **go** to a stack, you need not use the word **stack** (though you may do so for readability). HyperCard assumes you want it to change stacks when you issue the **go** command and only needs clarification if you want to go to a card in the current stack.

You can combine these methods of navigation to take the user to a specific card in a stack:

```
go to card 78 of stack "Employees"
go to card ID 41233 of "Help"
```

Beginning with HyperCard 2.0, you can specify that the destination stack is to be opened in a new window, leaving the current stack(s) open rather than closing them, as was automatically the case in earlier versions of the program. The syntax for this command is

```
go to [stack] <stackIdentifier> in a new window
```

We will have more to say about HyperTalk scripting techniques involving multiple open stacks later in this chapter.

Another major enhancement to HyperTalk in HyperCard 2.0 allows you to specify that if HyperCard cannot find the named stack, it will not prompt the user to help locate it. Instead, it will simply fail to find the stack; to the user, the outcome is transparent. To accomplish this, you add the parameter string **without dialog** to your command. Your script can examine the value of the global variable **the result** and determine if a problem occurred, as in the following example script:

```
on mouseUp
  go to stack "Test Stack 3" in a new window without dialog
  if the result is not empty then play "boing"
  -- see text explanation
end mouseUp
```

In this script, the user clicks on a button and the handler attempts to find a stack called "Test Stack 3" in the current search path. If it finds the stack, it opens it in a new window, as previously described. If HyperCard can't locate the stack, it will place the message "no such card" into the global variable **the result**. If **the result** is empty, then no error message has been placed into it and the operation was successful.

▶ Cards with special addresses

Several groups or classes of cards in any stack with special addresses can be used to make navigation easier and more readable. These special addresses include

- positional addresses like first, third, or last
- relative addresses like back, recent, or next

HyperCard includes special constants to address these specific cards.

The *positional* constants include the ordinal numbers 1-10 (**first, second, third,** and so on) as well as the random card address **any** and the address of the last card in any stack, **last**. The middle card in the current stack can also be addressed specially, as **mid** or **middle**, should you come up with a need to do so. All these special addresses are also used to address components of containers. Their use in that context is more fully discussed in Chapter 10. All of the following, then, are valid **go** commands:

```
go to seventh card -- same as "go card 7"
go to last card -- go to the last card in this stack
go to the third card in "Ideas"
go to last card in "Ideas"
go to any card -- pick a card at random and go there
go to mid -- go to the middle card in the current stack
```

Notice that you can use the key word **the** in conjunction with these special card names. It is optional but if you find it makes your script more readable, feel free to use it.

The *relative* constants include **next, previous** (also abbreviated **prev**), **forth, back,** and **recent.** For all practical purposes, the last two are identical. The first two — **next** and **previous** — affect the user's position within the current stack relative to the present position. Thus, if the user is at the fourteenth card in the stack and a script executes the **go previous** command, the user is shown the thirteenth card in the stack even if the fourteenth card was reached without going through the thirteenth card. In other words, **next** and **previous** are not related to the route by which the user arrives at any given point.

On the other hand, **back** and **recent** are both path-related. If the user has been taken or has "driven" through a path like that shown in Figure 9-1, each use of one of these commands backs up the path one step. The **forth** indicator is also path-related. It points at the next card in the Recent stack. If the current card is the last card in the Recent stack, the command

```
go forth
```

takes the user to the Home stack.

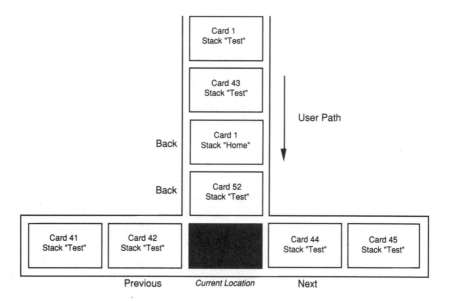

Figure 9-1. The back, next, and previous commands

As you can see in Figure 9-1, the user started at Card 1 of the stack called Test and followed the indicated path to reach Card 43 of the same stack. Now, a **go prev** command takes the user to Card 42 of that stack. A **go next** command takes the user to Card 44 of the stack. But a **go back** command (or a **go recent card**) takes the user to Card 52 of the stack, and another execution of that command moves the user to Card 1 of the Home stack.

▶ Nonexistent cards

If a **go** command attempts to access a nonexistent card, the message "not found" will be returned in a function called **the result**. Good error-trapping strategy dictates that you check for this condition:

```
go to card id 1437
if the result is empty then
   -- some processing
else
   -- error-handling
```

Beginning with HyperCard 2.0, you can use the **there is** operator to determine in advance whether a particular card exists. See the discussion of this command in Chapter 8.

▶ Using the navigation palette

In HyperCard 2.0 Apple added the ability to create and use palettes in your stacks. The general subject of palettes is covered in Chapter 21, but it is appropriate here to discuss briefly the navigational palette built into HyperCard 2.0. You can display a palette that the user can use for basic navigation by using the script command:

```
palette navigator
```

Optionally, you can also pre-position the palette by providing as an argument a string or container name that holds two comma-delimited values for the x-y coordinates of the desired position of the palette on the screen. If you use this version of the command and the navigation palette is already visible, HyperCard will move it to the position indicated. This command, for example, will open the palette navigator if it is not already open and position it near the center of the screen on a standard nine-inch Macintosh monitor:

```
palette navigator, "200,150"
```

When you use this command, a small palette (see Figure 9-2) appears at the indicated or default position. This palette contains icons representing the first ten commands on the Go menu and the last (twelfth) one (that is, all of the Go menu commands except the "Scroll" option). Because it is a palette (also referred to as a "windoid"), it stays visible atop all open stacks and operates with the currently active stack.

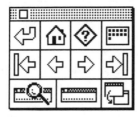

Figure 9-2. Navigation Palette

You can close the navigational palette by sending it a **close** message:

```
send "close" to window "Navigator"
```

▶ Finding Cards by Content

Sometimes, you don't know the specific card you want to steer the user to, but you do **know that it contains some ke**y word or words. In those cases, use the **find** command to locate the desired card.

This command is not mysterious. Almost from the time you began using HyperCard, probably before you were aware that HyperTalk existed, you were using **find** commands to move to cards when you wanted to locate an individual in your Address stack or an appointment in your Datebook stack.

Used within a HyperTalk script, the **find** command is identical, though you may use it with slightly more arguments and sophistication than you were aware was available to you in the Message box. The simplest form of the command is:

```
find "<text>"
```

When it is used this way, the **find** command searches through all fields of each card in the stack, beginning with the currently visible one, and locates the first occurrence of the word or words supplied as an argument.

You can add two types of qualifiers to the **find** command. The first type defines the nature of the search; the second confines the search to a specific field. You use both kinds of qualifiers extensively in scripting. Without these qualifiers, HyperCard locates the text anywhere it occurs, even if it's split over two fields on the same card, as long as the target string is the beginning of a word. Thus, it would find *an* in answer and antidote, but not in *banana* or *Alexander*.

▶ What kind of match to find?

You can add four qualifiers to the **find** command to tell HyperCard what constitutes a "hit":

- whole
- string
- word
- chars

Each of these qualifiers results in a slightly different approach to the **find** command. They may not be used in combination with one another.

We take a look at each of these qualifiers in turn, then we examine an example that clarifies how the qualifiers differ from one another.

The command **find whole** is the most targeted of these commands. Its rules for declaring a combination of characters as a "hit" are as follows:

1. The word or phrase found must match exactly the argument supplied with the command.

2. Spaces are significant.

3. Order is significant.

4. All of the word or phrase must appear in the same field on a card.

This option was added to HyperCard 1.2 to overcome what many users and designers saw as a limitation in earlier releases of the program. Those limitations become clearer when we study an example of the various **find** commands later in this section.

Also added in HyperCard 1.2 was the **find string** command. This command is essentially the same as the **find chars** command, except that when its argument has one or more spaces in it, HyperCard uses its fastest search algorithm. This addition significantly improves the peformance of complex searches but does not add functionality to HyperCard.

If you want to limit the search to the whole word or words supplied as the search text, use the **find word** form:

```
find word "end"
```

This command only finds the word *end* as a whole word. The words *blender*, *ending,* and *weekend* are not located.

Finally, if you want HyperCard to find the target string even if it occurs mid-word, use the **find chars** form of the command:

```
find chars "end"
```

This command finds *blender, ending,* and *weekend.*

Specifying the search

1. Create a new Laboratory stack using the "New Stack" option from the File Menu; leave "Copy **Current Background**" selected in the resulting dialog.

2. Create two background fields for this new stack.

3. On Card 1, type in field 1 the word "*Irving*" and in field 2 the word "*Glotzbach*".

4. On Card 2, type in field 1 the words "*Irving Glotzbach*" and in field 2 the words "*lives here*".

5. On Card 3, type in field 1 the words "*Ingemar Johansen*" and in field 2 the words "*lived here*".

6. Go to Card 1.

7. In the Message box, type:

```
find "Irving Glotzbach"
```

8. After it finds the string on Card 1 (notice that it appears split across two fields), press the **Return** key. Notice that it finds the string on Card 2 as well. Press **Return** again and HyperCard returns to Card 1.

9. Now try typing:

```
find word "Irving Glotzbach"
```

10. Notice that the results match those we encountered in Steps 7 and 8.

11. Change the Message box so that it reads:

```
find whole "Irving Glotzbach"
```

12. Notice that now HyperCard only finds Card 2. This is the only card where the target string, "*Irving Glotzbach*", exists exactly as provided in the argument to the **find** command and entirely in one field.

13. Now type the following line into the Message box:

```
find whole "live"
```

14. Notice that HyperCard simply beeps at you; it cannot find the word "live" as a complete, stand-alone word. (You can achieve the same result with the **find word** variation in this case.)

15. Return to the Message box and type:

```
find chars "ing"
```

16. Now HyperCard finds all three cards, because all of them have the string *ing* somewhere in one of their fields, though not necessarily at the beginning of a word.

17. Let's change the Message box to read:

```
find "ing"
```

18. Now HyperCard only finds Card 3, because that's the only place that the string "ing" begins a word (in this case, *Ingemar*).

▶ ## Narrowing the search

When you design stacks, each field will probably have a specific purpose. Each card on which the field appears will store the same kind of information in that field. On an inventory stack's cards, for example, you might store the part number in Field 1, the quantity on hand in Field 2, the price per unit in Field 3, and the date last ordered in Field 4. If you want to find all parts with a 5 in the number, you can write:

```
find "5"
```

But HyperCard would find every card where the quantity on hand was 5 or 15 or 500, any part that cost $49.95, any date that included a 5 — in short, it would find every 5 in every card of the stack. That's not what you wanted. So you might narrow the search to Field 1 like this:

```
find "5" in field 1
```

HyperCard would ignore the contents of all other fields and concentrate its search for 5s only in Field 1. If the 5 were a stand-alone part of the part number so that it qualifies as a word in HyperCard, then you could even use:

```
find word "5" in field 1
```

This is a little more specific, but it will still find any 5 surrounded by spaces anywhere in Field 1.

In HyperCard Version 2.0 and later, you can further confine the extent of a search undertaken by HyperTalk in response to a **find** command. Every card and background has a property called **dontSearch**. (Properties are discussed in greater detail in Chapter 17.) By setting this property's value to *true* for a particular card or background, you can cause HyperCard not to search the fields in this card or background when a **find** command is issued.

Since this property can be set and reset (to its default value of *false*) from your script, you can selectively turn searching on or off for particular cards and backgrounds quite easily.

Beginning with HyperCard Version 2.0, you can also confine your **find** operations so that it operates only on cards that have been previously marked. The syntax for this version of the **find** command is as follows:

```
find <whatToFind> [in field <fieldIdentifier>]
of marked cards
```

In a large stack, you may be able to make finding specific information far more efficient by combining the process of marking only those cards that are candidates for a successful **find** operation and then carrying out the **find** itself.

▶ Limitations on find

Unfortunately, the **find** command cannot be forced to confine itself to only a specific component of the field. You may know that the 5 you are interested in is always the third digit, but that's not going to help you with the **find** command. In that case, design a customized search routine that looks at the third character of the field and does something if it's a 5.

When you execute the **find** command within a script, the user cannot continue the search with a simple Return key, though you can design the script to make this possible.

▶ The found card

When the **find** command is successful, it makes the card on which it locates the match the current card. You can then use property-retrieval techniques (see Chapter 17) to find out that card's ID, or examine other fields or parts of the same field to qualify the card before continuing processing. If the **find** command fails, it leaves the current card unchanged.

Once a **find** operation has located a "hit," you can use functions described in Chapter 10 to retrieve the text and/or the surrounding information.

If the **find** command fails, a message indicating the approximate reason for the failure will be returned in the built-in function **the result**. The specific error is not usually important, so merely checking to see if **the result** has anything in it is sufficient to deal with error conditions.

```
if the result is empty then step1 else step2
```

▶ Marking Cards for Later Use

A close cousin of the **find** command is the **mark** command. Both of these commands can **be used to locate information in** a card or stack by its content, as explained in the preceding section. The major difference between the two operations is that **find** stops on any card where it finds the target text while **mark** notes that a particular card contains the desired text and goes on searching the rest of the stack. When it has found all the cards with "hits," it stops. You can then work with all of the marked cards as a group in several interesting ways.

▶ Criteria for card marking

You can use any logical expression (see Chapter 8 for a discussion of logical expressions in HyperTalk) as a criterion for marking cards. This means you can use such text-locating operators as **is, is in,** and **contains,** among others, to mark a group of cards with related data. You can also mark cards based on criteria unrelated to the contents of their fields.

For example, let's say you have a stack of cards containing information about the compact discs in your prized collection of jazz music. You want to look through all the CDs that you've described in a field called "mood" as being "upbeat." You can use a command like this to accomplish the purpose:

```
mark cards where field "mood" contains "upbeat"
```

You can use logical connectors **and, or,** and **not** in describing the criteria for marking cards. For example, assume that you only want to listen to relatively recent upbeat jazz CDs tonight. Then you could write a line like this:

```
mark cards where field "mood" contains "upbeat" and field
   "year" > 1968
```

You can also use the power of the **find** command to aid you in marking cards in your stack. The syntax for this variation of the **mark** command looks like this:

```
mark <cardIdentifier> by finding <text>
```

This is useful when you are less concerned with where information appears in a card (as you must be able to specify with the **mark where** variation) than with its existence on a card somewhere.

In addition to marking cards, you can also **unmark** them. The most obvious use of this capability arises when you want to clean up after yourself when you close a stack and want to be ready to mark cards the next time the user runs your application. In that case, just put the following line into an appropriate handler:

```
unmark all cards
```

Another way to use this ability is to narrow the collection of cards marked by a command. For example, let's assume that you've carried out the second of the **mark** commands previously cited and discover that you still have too many CDs on your list to play tonight. But you're not particularly in a mood to hear violins tonight. With the existing set of marked cards, you can carry out this kind of operation:

```
unmark cards where field instrument contains "violin"
```

Now the only marked cards will be those where all three criteria are met:

- mood is upbeat
- year of release is later than 1968
- there are no violins on the CD

▶ What to do with marked cards

Once you've marked a group of cards, you can modify several frequently used HyperTalk commands to work on only the marked cards. For example, all navigational commands can be modified so that you see only marked cards:

```
go to next marked card
go to last marked card
```

Because we can find out how many cards are marked, we can set up **repeat** loops to operate only on those cards:

```
on mouseUp
   repeat number of marked cards times
      put 1.1 * field "Salary" into field "Salary"
      go next marked card
   end repeat
end mouseUp
```

The other operations that you can perform on marked cards as a group include

- show marked cards
- print marked cards

▶ Stack Management and Windows

Beginning with HyperCard 2.0, the user can have more than one stack open at a time. **Each stack can only be open once**, and when it is opened it can either replace a previously opened stack or open in a new window and add to the open windows on the screen.

Your scripts must take this multistack situation into account. For example, they must manage the issue of whether a stack opened under script control will open in a new window or replace the current stack.

A new function, **the stack**, can be used to assist you in this process. It returns a return-delimited list of all currently open stacks.

You may also want to set or read two key properties of open windows so that you can help the user manage the potential screen clutter that can arise from having many stacks open at once. These two properties are **the rectangle** and **the scroll**. Because they are properties rather than commands, and because they therefore follow the rules associated with the dozens of other properties in HyperTalk, we discuss them in Chapter 17 rather than here. But you should be aware that you sometimes need to manage these properties as part of assisting the user in managing his or her HyperCard environment.

There are also two system messages — **moveWindow** and **sizeWindow** — available to help you manage situations where multiple stacks may be opened. These messages are sent even if only the window being moved or resized is open, but they may come in particularly handy when more than one stack is open. See Chapter 6 for a discussion of these window messages.

In addition, you can use the **hide** and **show** commands to change the visibility of any card window. A function added in HyperCard Version 2.0, **the windows**, returns a return-delimited list of all system windows (whether open or not) as well as all open card windows (where the stack name is the window name).

▶ Using pop and push in Scripts

In complex scripts with lots of card movement, you often want to mark a card as one **to return to after some explora**tion is complete. Rather than requiring you to keep track of how many **go back** commands it will take to get there, HyperTalk includes the **pop** and **push** commands. In essence, **push** marks a card for later instant retrieval with the **pop** command.

The **push** command does not require any parameters. (You may, for the usual reason of readability, write the command to **push** the current card as **push card**, but that is not necessary.) If you want to mark the current card, simply use the command by itself. If you want to push the most recent card (that is, the card from which the user got to the current card), you need to add a parameter:

```
push recent card
```

The **pop card** command indicates that you want to return the user to the card to which you most recently applied a **push** command. The **card** parameter is required. The only other use of **pop** is explained later when we describe multiple **push** statements.

▶ The stack created by push

You can think of the **push** command as moving the card to which it applies to a special location that in traditional programming terms would be called a *stack*. Only this is not a HyperCard stack. Rather, it is a kind of single-file line in which cards that are pushed stand until they are called again. In such a situation, only the top card can be affected by a **pop** command. It must "get out of the way" before you can release any of the cards placed there earlier.

This kind of special location is called, in computer terms, a LIFO stack. LIFO is an acronym for "last in, first out." The last card pushed into this line is the first one popped out of it. Most of the time, your scripts will not push more than one card at a time. Only very complex applications ever need to handle multiple-card special stacks.

▶ Using pop without showing the card

But if you do have an application that uses multiple-card pushes and you want to **pop** a card other than the top one into view, you will need to use the technique of popping the card into a container.

The syntax for this technique is:

```
pop card into <container>
```

When you **pop** a card into a container, the card's ID and stack location are placed in the container and the card is removed from the special stack location without being shown to the user. Later, you can use the information in the container, along with a **go** command, to show the card that was popped into the container.

For example, assume you have executed two **pop** commands. The first one operated on Card 6 of the current stack and the second operated on Card 157. Now you want to take the user to the card that was popped first. The basic handler segment looks like this:

```
pop card into card field 1 of holder
pop card
```

Now the card identifying information for Card 157 is stored in the container called *holder*, in Card Field 1. If you want to show that card, use a command like this:

```
go to card field 1 of holder
```

Notice that this does not take the user to the field but rather to the card whose identifier is stored in the field.

Using push and pop

For this experiment, let's create a new stack that uses the background of the Laboratory stack. **After you've done t**hat, follow these directions:

1. Get into Edit Background mode.

2. Add a rectangular field to the background. You don't need to name it because we'll refer to it by its field number. The card should look similar to Figure 9-3.

3. Return to Browse mode.

4. Create six new cards for the stack so that the stack has seven cards. Name the cards Test 1, Test 2, and so forth, in the Card Info… dialog.

5. Label each card Card 1, Card 2, and so forth, in the field you've created. These are used as visual cues as we go through the experiment.

6. Go to Card 1 and create a new scrolling field. Name it Tracker. Put it anywhere on the card. Card 1 should now look similar to Figure 9-4.

7. Open the Message box. Type the following commands, in the order shown:

```
go to card "Test 1" -- Card 1 should appear
push card
go to card "Test 3"
go to card "Test 4"
pop card -- Card 1 should reappear
```

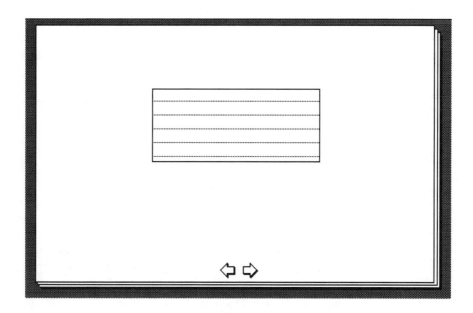

Figure 9-3. New Laboratory stack card

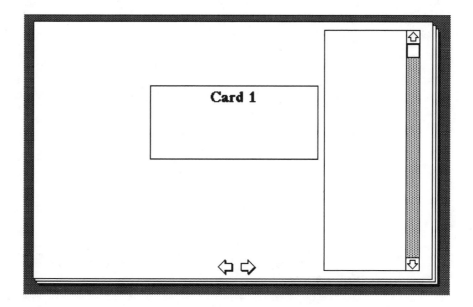

Figure 9-4. Card 1 with Tracker field added

8. Now we'll try a multiple-push experiment. Type the following commands, in the order shown:

```
go to card "Test 1" -- Card 1 should appear
push card
go to card "Test 3"
push card
go to card "Test 5"
push card
go to card "Test 6"
pop card into card field "Tracker" of Card "Test 1"
pop card after card field "Tracker" of Card "Test 1"
pop card -- Card 1 should reappear with text in Holder
```

9. Your screen should look similar to Figure 9-5. Notice that identification information, complete with path, is now stored in the Tracker field of Card 1. These are the IDs of the two cards that were pushed onto the stack after Card 1 and then popped into this container. To confirm this, go to those cards and choose Card Info… from the Objects menu. Note the card ID numbers shown there.

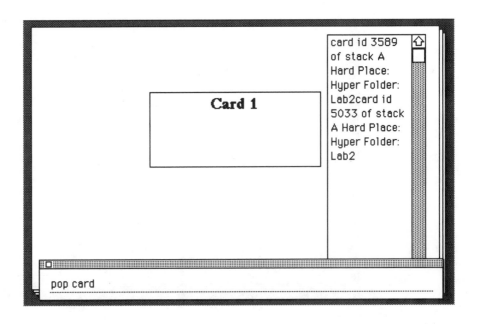

Figure 9-5. Card identification in Tracker field

▶ Using push and pop between objects

It is not necessary that balanced **push** and **pop** commands work with the same object or one of the same level. It is not only possible but often useful to **push** a card as a result of the user having pressed a button and later to **pop** the card from a card script.

You'll find that judicious use of **push** and **pop** can save you a great deal of unnecessary navigation.

▶ Showing and Printing Cards

You've undoubtedly noticed the icon on many HyperCard stacks that is used to zoom through the stack looking for a specific card. Such an icon is included in the Address stack, for example, and is shown in Figure 9-6 (the second icon from the bottom of the panel of icons along the left side of the Address card). Open this button's script in one of the usual ways. It should look like this (assuming it has not been modified):

```
on mouseUp
    show all cards
end mouseUp
```

Figure 9-6. Address stack card with "show cards" icon

This **show** command lets the browser skim through a stack. It shows cards until it has shown all the cards it has been asked to display or until the user clicks the mouse, whichever happens first. The first card shown is the one after the one showing when the command is issued. You can use it to let the user flip through all the cards in a stack or just through a specific number of cards. In the latter case, the command syntax is:

```
show <number> cards
```

If you ask HyperCard to show more cards than are in the stack, it simply recycles through the stack until it has shown the requested number of cards. The principles that apply to **show** also pertain to the **print card** command. This command has three forms:

```
print card
print card "Test 3"
print 5 cards
```

The first form prints the current card. The second prints any identified card. The last prints a specific number of cards, beginning with the currently visible one, and may use the word **all** in place of a number.

As we have stated earlier, you can also confine both card printing and the **show** command to those cards that have been previously identified by the **mark** command. In that case, these commands look like:

```
show marked cards
print marked cards
```

▶ Summary

In this chapter, you saw how to use script commands to move the user through a stack with variations of **the** go **comm**and. You also saw how to save one or more cards for quick return and retrieval using combinations of **push** and **pop**. Finally, you learned to use **show** and **print** to display and produce printed copies of cards in various ways. In Chapter 10 you explore a wide range of commands that involve managing information in HyperCard stacks.

10 ▶ Managing Text and Data

In this chapter, you'll learn how to

- read the contents of fields
- get information about data in fields
- find and select field contents
- modify the contents of fields
- work with styled text in fields
- use fields to simulate arrays and tables of data
- sort cards by the contents of fields
- use text in fields to create hypertext applications
- deal with date and time data as a special class of information
- trap the use of the Return and Enter keys in a field

▶ HyperCard as an Information Base

When HyperCard was first announced, many people, in a sincere attempt to describe what was clearly a new class of product, compared it to conventional database management systems. This turned out to be an oversimplification for at least two reasons:

- HyperCard does much more than manage data, which is what database management systems do.
- Database management systems have other capabilities for data manipulation that exceed those of HyperCard.

Nonetheless, HyperCard does manage data. Its management of information through hypertext features (the links between cards and stacks that make authoring without HyperTalk more powerful than many kinds of programming) and HyperTalk scripts is its most important feature. In HyperCard, before the release of Version 1.2, the ability to find data and to position the cursor correctly in a data entry field were quite difficult to implement. In Version 1.2, HyperCard added a great deal of functionality to make the **find** command more useful as well as providing a new **select** command. Used together, these two instruction groups significantly improved the data-management capabilities of HyperCard.

HyperCard Version 2.0 significantly improved its hypertext functionality. It added a new text style called **grouped** that permits you to join multiword phrases into what, for many purposes, can be treated as a single word. It also added three new functions that let you quickly decode the user's mouse-clicks into the words over which they occur. We'll discuss these enhancements later in the chapter.

In this chapter, we examine HyperTalk commands that manage information. This data is stored in fields on cards because fields are the only places changeable data can be stored and still be visible to the user.

▶ Reading Information in a Field

When information is stored in a card field or background field, it can be obtained by the **get** command. This command is not new to us. We've used it in several Laboratory experiments and in other discussions. But now we will take a close look at how it works and gain more insight into its use.

We can also use the **put** command to retrieve data, even though the action of retrieval sounds contrary to what we usually think of when we use the word *put*. We can use **put** to copy information from a field to another field or a container. The **put** command also serves as the means for permanently modifying information in a field. We'll talk about the **put** command several times from several different perspectives in this chapter.

▶ The get command

As you may recall, **get** retrieves data and puts the result into the special *It* variable. From there, your script can access *It* and do whatever it wants, including

- test the contents of *It* and use the test result in an **if** construct
- use **put** to move data into another temporary container or field
- modify data in *It* and then perform another function

Generally, if your plan for the data after it is retrieved involves moving it from *It* to any other container or field, it is better to use **put** (discussed next) to move it directly. This is true for two reasons:

- This approach requires fewer keystrokes and is a more efficient use of memory.
- The *It* variable is used extensively by HyperCard, so minimizing its use in your scripts is a good idea.

▶ Addressing reminder

As you may recall from our previous discussions, particularly in Chapter 5, data in fields can be addressed in many ways to gain access to very specific information chunks. In the remainder of this discussion, we frequently use the **item, line, word,** and **char** operators to focus on the information we want to retrieve.

One major use of the **get** command is to obtain information in HyperCard fields. You can retrieve all of a field's contents or the contents of some chunk of a field with commands like these:

```
get field 1
get field 3 of card "Test 2"
get first word of line 2 of field 1 of card "Test 2"
get char 3 to 6 of word 2 of line 2 of field 1 of card "Test 2"
```

In each of these cases, when the **get** command has been executed, the contents of the respective field or chunk expression is stored in the special global variable *It*. You can then use this variable's contents in whatever way is appropriate.

To see these retrieved values, you will have to use the **put it** command or type **it** in the Message box.

If the argument that precedes a **to** expression is larger than the value that follows the **to**, you will only extract a single element of the object. For example, a statement like

```
get char 7 to 0 of word 2 of line 2 of field 1
```

will return only the seventh character of the second word on the second line of the field called field 1.

The other major use of the **get** command is obtaining values associated with certain characteristics of HyperCard objects. These characteristics, called *properties*, are discussed in Chapter 17.

The **get** command is also used to retrieve the values of certain functions such as the time and date. This use of the command is explored later in this chapter.

▶ Using put commands to read data

Because the **get** command always puts its results into the special *It* variable, we need an alternate way of retrieving information from a card field. The **put** command is used for this purpose.

You may recall from our discussion of this command in Chapter 5 that it has two basic forms:

- With only a source argument, **put** places the source into the Message box.

- With both a source and a destination argument, **put** places the contents of the source at a specified point in the destination container.

▶ Typical uses for put

In general, you can think of **put** as having two fundamental uses, corresponding to its basic forms.

First, it can be used to display the contents of containers so the user can see them. The contents of these containers can be put into the Message box, in which case the destination may be omitted (though it is probably best to include it for readability), or into visible fields. Sometimes the source argument to the **put** command is an expression, and the result of its evaluation is placed in the destination. Here are some examples:

```
put "Hello, world" into card field 1
put 3.14*23.2 into card field "circumference"
put return & "new line of text" after field "tracking"
```

The second use of **put** is to alter the contents of variables and/or invisible containers (fields). In this case, the purpose of the command is not to let the user see the result of an operation but to place the result into a temporary or semipermanent storage area.

▶ How Many Characters in the Field?

The **length** function can tell you how many characters are in any string, including any addressable component of a field. This is often useful in reports, in using the **offset** function (described in the next section), and in ensuring that user-entered data meets any length limits your script must impose.

The **length** function has two forms. The first spells out the command in full, readable English:

```
the length of line 1 of field 1 of card "Test 2"
```

The second form uses an abbreviated approach (similar to Pascal or C commands):

```
length(line 1 of field 1 of card "Test 2")
```

The two forms are interchangeable. Your choice of which to use will be governed by your experience and the need for script readability.

In either case, you should know that if you apply the **length** function to a full line in a field, the function does not count the carriage return at the end. This becomes particularly important when you use the **offset** function, because that function does count the carriage return.

▶ Finding and Selecting Text

Starting with HyperCard Version 1.2, the designer's ability to extract and manipulate data based on field contents was significantly increased. Not only was the **find** command enhanced (see the discusion in Chapter 9) with the addition of the new **whole** and **string** parameters, but two new capabilites were included:

- the ability to determine precisely where the text was found by the **find** command
- the ability to select text based on the results of a **find** operation or on the text's location in a field, or even to position the cursor in a field before or after a particular location

▶ Where did the find take place?

Let's look first at the use of several functions to determine where a particular piece of text for which we have searched has been found. When a **find** operation is successful, HyperCard notes the location of the found text in four special functions:

- **the foundText**, which returns the characters enclosed in the box after the **find** command has located the text
- **the foundField**, which returns the identification of the field in which the text was located
- **the foundLine**, which returns the number of the line in the field in which the text was found
- **the foundChunk**, which returns the complete chunking expression to indicate where the text was found

For example, if we had a field such as that shown in Figure 10-1 and we performed a **find** operation such as

```
find "ran"
```

the foundText would contain the word *range* (because with the unadorned **find** command HyperCard locates the first occurrence of the string at the *beginning* of a word, then makes the entire word the found text). On the other hand, **the foundChunk** would contain the value char 5 to 9 of card field 1, whereas **the foundField** would point to card Field 1 and **the foundLine** to Line 1 of card Field 1.

```
The range of the radar can be
set by the operator.
```

Figure 10-1. Sample field to demonstrate find options

If we were to change the search from *find "ran"* to *find whole "range of"*, we would see different results. Because of the use of the **whole** qualifier, HyperCard would put *"range of"* into **the foundText** and appropriate values into the other functions. (Strictly speaking, HyperCard actually does not put these values into these functions. Rather, the use of the function returns these values. For this discussion, that is a distinction without a difference.)

▶ Using select to pick up found text

Once we've found some text and know where it is located, we quite often want to manipulate it. But we can't manipulate **the foundText** directly. Remember, it's not a container but a function result. So we use HyperCard's **select** command to accomplish the task.

In essence, the **select** command puts whatever text it is pointed to into **the selection**, a container we discussed briefly in Chapter 5. Once that text is in this special container, we can manipulate it. For example, we can copy it, cut it, or put something new into the container.

Returning to our small field example, once we've found the text *range of*, we can easily turn it into text with which we can work:

```
select the foundChunk
-- puts the located text into the selection
doMenu "Cut Text"
tabKey
doMenu "Paste Text"
```

This little program fragment assumes a **find** has just taken place. It deletes the found text from one field, tabs to the next field in sequence, and pastes the found text into the new field, replacing the contents of the destination field (because the **tabKey** command highlights the entire contents of the destination field and the Paste Text command then replaces that selection).

We used **the foundChunk** rather than **the foundText** here because it makes no sense to tell HyperCard to select words; the **select** command expects an address as its argument.

▶ Using select without the find

Of course, you don't have to use **select** only with a **find** operation. You can select any arbitrary text that you can address. Both of the following operations, for example, select the words "range of" in Figure 10-1:

```
select word 2 to 3 of line 1 of card field 1
select char 4 to 12 of card field 1
```

▶ Using select to position the cursor

Besides selecting text, you can use the **select** command to place the cursor precisely where you want it in a field. This means you can put the user in the right location to enter the next piece of information. You accomplish this with the **select before** and **select after** combinations. They can be followed by any chunking expression. Here are some examples:

```
select after last line of card field 1
-- puts cursor at end of field
select before first line of card field 1
-- puts cursor at start of field
select after word 3 of line 2 of card field 1
select before char 5 of word 3 of line 2 of card field 1
```

▶ Selecting everything and nothing

You can also use the **select** command with the **text of** parameter to put the entire contents of a field into the selection. For example, the line

```
select text of field "testing"
```

would select all of the contents of the background field called "testing" and put them into **the selection**.

The final form of the **select** command removes any existing selection. To do this, type:

```
select empty
```

▶ Combining select and find for data management

You should realize by now that the intelligent use of combinations of the enhanced **find** command and the **select** command in HyperCard after Version 1.2 can lead to powerful data management operations in HyperCard.

By using the proper qualifiers on the **find** command, you can narrow the search. With the functions that return the precise location of a successful search, you can locate the targeted text with ease. Then you can select that text and copy it, move it around, replace it, and otherwise manipulate it.

Some more advanced functions can be performed with combinations of these commands and the **do** command described in detail in Chapter 16.

▶ Locating a sub-string's position

As you may recall from our discussion of the **find** command in Chapter 9, locating a card that contains a given string of text in a specific field or anywhere on the card is straightforward. But sometimes we need to know where a particular text string is located in a field by its relation to other known characters or strings. This is quite often useful in decoding formatted product codes and numbers, for example.

To carry out this assignment, HyperTalk includes the **offset** function. This function takes two strings as arguments and returns a number indicating the character position of the beginning of the first string in the second string. The syntax is:

```
offset (<string1>,<string2>)
```

Either argument (or both) can be a string enclosed in quotation marks or the address or name of a container that holds a string.

If Field 1 contains the string "Blue Rondo a la Turk" and the variable *lookFor* contains the string "Rondo," then

```
offset("Rondo",field 1)
```

or

```
offset(lookFor,field 1)
```

return the same answer: 6. This identifies the starting position of the source string (string1) in the target string (string2). (Of course, you must *do* something with the returned value of the **offset** function. Normally, you will either **put** it somewhere or test it with an **if** clause group.)

▶ Using the offset function

A use for the **offset** function may not be immediately evident. Let's look at an example using our inventory stack analogy. After you work through this example, you will undoubtedly see many places in your stackware that you can use the **offset** command to great advantage.

Assume that the part number field in your inventory stack consists of two or more characters, followed by a hyphen, followed by three to ten additional characters. The first segment of the code, up to the hyphen, is the Vendor Code, which tells you who sells you the part. The second portion of the part number, from the character to the right of the hyphen to the end of the code, is your company's internal part number. There are many places where you want to separate those two segments of the part code and use them independently. Let's do a short Laboratory exercise to see how to do this.

Using offset for field decomposition

Open the original Laboratory stack and create a new card for it. Name the card Inventory 1. Now follow these directions:

1. Create a new field for this card. Make it a rectangular or shadow field so you can see its outline. Call it Part Number. We will use only one line of it, so you can narrow its height to one line if you like.

2. Get into Browse mode.

3. Type into the Part Number field the following text:

   ```
   AB23-00984
   ```

4. Create a new button for the card if it doesn't already have one. If it already has a button, you can use it unless you want to save its script.

5. Open the button's script-editing window by one of the usual methods.

6. Type in the following handler:

```
on mouseUp
    global vendor, part
    put length(line 1 of card field "Part Number") into len
    put line 1 of card field "Part Number" into temp
    put offset("-",temp) into divider
    put char 1 to divider-1 of temp into vendor
    put char divider+1 to len of temp into part
end mouseUp
```

 Note ► You may be wondering why we put global declarations in this handler when we have never done this before. Because we will want to examine the contents of these variables in the Message box and because the Message box is outside the scope of the handler, the variables must be declared global. Otherwise, HyperCard will complain that it "never heard of" the variable when you type its name into the Message box.

7. Get back into Browse mode. Press the button to which the new script is attached.

8. Open the Message box if it isn't already visible.

9. Type *vendor* and press Return. The Message box contains AB23. (See Figure 10-2.)

9. Type *vendor* and press Return. The Message box contains AB23. (See Figure 10-2.)

10. Type *part* and press Return. The Message box now contains 00984.

11. Change the contents of the Part Number field so that a different number of characters appear before and after the hyphen. Then retry the button until you are comfortable with how this process works.

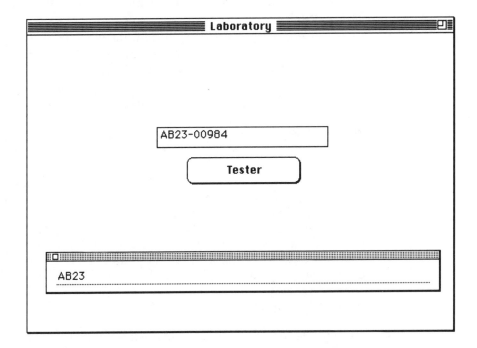

Figure 10-2. Vendor code portion of part number

▶ Modifying the Contents of Fields

It will come as no surprise that the primary command for changing the contents of a field is **put**. This versatile command — arguably the most often used in HyperTalk — can replace the contents of all or part of a field or place new information at any addressable place in a field.

But **put** is not the only command that modifies the contents of fields. Two others, less often used but occasionally helpful, are **type** and **delete**. We've already described the **put** command, so this discussion will focus on the other two field-modifying commands.

▶ The type command

The **type** command works very much like the **put** command, with two key exceptions:

- The **type** command does not include the ability to address a container as part of its structure. There is no equivalent of the **put into** command (or **before** or **after**, for that matter) for the **type** command.

- The **put** command places data into the field as a single block of text, but **type** places data into the field as if it were being entered by a fast typist.

These limitations make the **type** command less than a critically important tool in your HyperTalk vocabulary. But there are two occasions when it can prove useful.

First, if you are creating a self-running demonstration of a stack and want to simulate for the user the manual entry of text into a field, the **type** command works exactly as desired. To put text into a field, you must be sure the cursor is *in* the field before you type anything into it. This can be accomplished with the **click** command or with the **select before, select after,** or **select empty** commands discussed elsewhere in this chapter. This makes it impossible to experiment with **type** from inside the Message box. If, for example, you type,

```
type "Hello, there, world!"
```

into the Message box, the contents of the Message box are immediately replaced by the typed message.

Second, the **type** command is a convenient way of sending certain characters to a field from within a script. For example, you can write a background or stack script that types a Tab character each time a card opens. As a result, each time the user opens a card, the cursor is placed in the first field on the card and the current contents of that field are selected. The next character typed from the keyboard or the script then replaces everything in the field.

▶ The delete command

One of the most powerful commands in HyperTalk is the version of the **delete** command that removes text from a field. The command can be used in a similar way to remove text from any other container. You can erase any addressable component — characters, words, items, or lines — of text in a field on any card with this command. The deleted text is not placed into the Clipboard. To save the text for later, use a **doMenu** command and select the Cut option, as explained in Chapter 12.

If you use **delete** to cut an entire line of text from a field, HyperCard removes the line and its accompanying carriage return, moving any lines below the deleted line up in the field. If you delete individual words, even the last one on a line, however, HyperTalk does not alter the carriage return. If you delete all the words on a line one at a time, the carriage return remains in place unless you explicitly delete it as well.

Using delete

For our first experiment with the **delete** command, let's use the Message box and a variable. Open the Message box if it is not already visible (it doesn't matter what card you are on) and then follow these directions:

1. Type the following line of text into the Message box

```
put "one two three four five" into temp
```

and press the Return key.

2. Now type this text into the Message box

```
delete second word of temp
```

and press Return. To confirm that the deletion worked as expected, type *temp* into the Message box. The display should contain: *one three four five.*

Now let's set up a more elaborate experiment. This time we'll use scripting rather than the Message box. Pick any Laboratory card with a field and at least one button. If you don't have a card with those objects with scripts you are ready to erase, create a new card. In the example, we'll refer to the card field as TD1 (for Test Delete 1) to reduce the amount of typing.

1. Open the button's script-editing window in one of the usual ways.
2. Type in the following script and click the OK button when you're done:

```
on mouseUp
    delete second word of line 1 of card field "TD1"
    put "First deletion complete"
    wait 1 seconds
    delete third item of line 2 of card field "TD1"
    put "Second deletion complete"
```

```
        wait 1 seconds
        delete char 3 to 7 of line 3 of card field "TD1"
        put "Final deletion complete"
    end mouseUp
```

3. Get into Browse mode.

4. Type the following three lines of text into the field:

```
This is is a test
Do,you,see,see,how,it,works?
That onis is a test
```

5. Select all the text in the field, and use the Copy Text option from the Edit menu to save it in the Clipboard. Then de-select the text. The screen now looks like Figure 10-3.

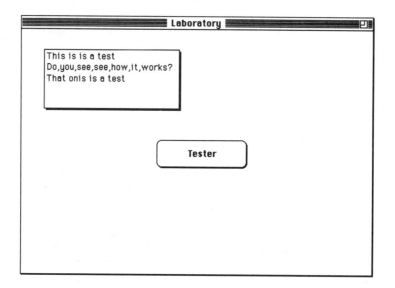

Figure 10-3. Second delete experiment ready to run

6. Press the button and watch the Message box closely. At each deletion, the script displays a message pointing out that the deletion was made and pauses so you can examine the effect.

7. If you want to repeat the experiment to watch it more closely, select all the text in the field, use the Backspace key to delete it (don't Cut it or the preexperiment version of the text will disappear from the Clipboard), choose Paste Text from the Edit menu, and press the button again. Repeat

this process as many times as you like. You can also modify the script between runs, perhaps increasing the amount of time the script pauses or deleting different components of the field.

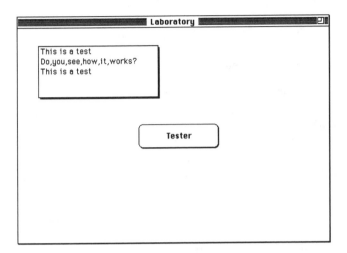

Figure 10-4. Second delete experiment completed

▶ Changing Fields by Concatenation

HyperCard has some of the most powerful text concatenation capabilities of any microcomputer programming language. Using these facilities, you can combine the contents of various containers, components of fields, and string or character constants to modify the contents of fields or other containers.

There are two text concatenation operators: **&** and **&&**. The only difference between them is that the latter adds a space between the concatenated objects and the former concatenates them exactly as it finds them. Thus

```
put "test" & "ing"
```

displays the word "testing" in the Message box, and

```
put "test" && "ing"
```

displays "test ing", with a space between the two strings, in the Message box.

The items to be joined by concatenation can be any combination of addressable field components, actual strings, or containers of text. The resulting concatenated text can be placed into a field or into a variable using the **put** command. Or it can be displayed, tested, or manipulated in the same ways as any text field. There is no difference between a field created by user entry and one synthesized by concatenation.

▶ Uses for concatenation

There are dozens of places in scripts where it is useful to join two or more pieces of text. Three such possible uses are discussed here for illustration.

Recall our inventory example with the part number divided into two components separated by a hyphen. If you think about it for a moment, you might have the user enter the vendor code separately from the internal part code. In fact, it may be essential to do it that way given the normal operation of business. The user might know the internal part code but have no idea who the product is purchased from without checking another source of information during data entry.

To accommodate this need, assign two global variables, for example, *Ven* and *IPN* (for Internal Part Number). After the user enters those values for a new part being added to inventory, your script would have a command like this one:

```
put Ven & "-" & IPN into Field "Part Number"
```

The result is the concatenation of the vendor code (for example, AYS29), a hyphen, and the internal part number (for example, 90087) so that the Part Number field contains the full part number: AYS29-90087.

Another use for concatenation is personalizing a card in a stack that is used by several people. Suppose three different people use your stack and all have personalized information stored in it. The cards are named in such a way that the person's last name forms the first part of the card name and the card type forms the second part. Thus, Yeats's expense card might be named YeatsExp. At the beginning of a session or when the user changes, your script asks the user for his or her name and saves the last name in a variable called *User*.

Now when a button is clicked to take the user to his or her expense account card, the script does a simple concatenation to get the name of the card:

```
go card User & "Exp"
```

Each user may be unaware that other people using the stack have similar cards to theirs. Yet this is far more efficient than creating separate stacks for everyone.

The last example involves the extraction and display of information from several different fields or even several different cards in such a way that the user only sees the result, not the work that goes into it. For example, a button called Summary on a card might indicate that a manager wants to see the employee's name, hire date, salary, and last review date. The stack's only job is to get those fields and put them into the Message box. Using concatenation, it can do so with one simple **put** command:

```
put field "Name" && field "Hire Date" && field "Salary" && field ¬
   "Last Review" of card "Evaluations"
```

▶ Special constants for concatenation

In addition to text containers, fields, and strings, concatenation can also include built-in HyperTalk constants that represent special characters frequently needed in text streams. These special constants are

- **quote**
- **return**
- **space**
- **tab**
- **formFeed**
- **lineFeed**

You can insert these special constants anywhere in a stream of text being concatenated. You probably won't have a lot of use for the **space** constant in view of the double-ampersand concatenation and the ability to place spaces inside literal strings. But the others will come in handy at one time or another.

The **quote** constant is particularly useful when you want to place a quotation mark into a field but are frustrated in your attempt to do so because HyperTalk sees the quotation mark as marking the end of a string. Simply embed the **quote** constant in the stream of text:

```
put "The" && quote & "boss" & quote && "is here."
   -- Message box shows:  The "boss" is here.
```

Inserting carriage returns to mark the end of one line and the beginning of another in a field is another good use for concatenating with special constants. The **formFeed** and **lineFeed** characters, as well as **tab**, are useful in telecommunications and the design and printing of script-managed reports.

▶ Working with Styled Text

Beginning with HyperCard Version 2.0, fields can mix type fonts and styles. Each field has a default font and style, which can be set manually from the Field Info Dialog when or after the field is created. It is also possible to use any of several field properties (discussed in detail in Chapter 17) to set or change this default text style information.

Any text entered into a field by any means — whether typed in manually by the user or placed into a field by a put command, for example — will have the default style and font information applied to it. You can, however, use chunking expressions to select a run of connected text and then change the style attributes of that particular selection. Again, this process involves setting properties that are covered in detail in Chapter 17.

The specific field properties involved in setting and changing the text style information for a particular field or any of its contents are

- **textFont**
- **textStyle**
- **textSize**
- **textHeight**
- **textAlign**

For example, to change the default font used in a particular field, you can use a line like this:

```
set the textFont of card field "parts" to "Helvetica"
```

When you do this, any text that held the previous default font for the field is automatically changed to the new font. Any text whose font has been explicitly altered, on the other hand, is unchanged by this command.

One of the styles you can set is called "grouped." This style is new with HyperCard Version 2.0 and can be applied to a run of text to cause HyperTalk to treat a multiword string as if it were a single word for some specific purposes. (We'll take a look at the hypertext use of this style later in the chapter.) To do this, just apply this **textStyle** to a string of two or more words, as in this example:

```
set the textStyle of words 3 to 7 of card field 1 to "grouped"
```

Notice that because of its purpose — which is to override HyperCard's normal treatment of a word as being delimited by certain punctuation or white space — this style is only meaningful when applied to groups of two or more words.

▶ Treating Fields as Arrays and Tables

Card and background fields, beyond their usefulness as flexible, addressable containers for text, can be used in your stacks exactly as if they were two-dimensional arrays or tables in other programming languages. HyperTalk does not specifically define a variable type that can contain a two-dimensional array of data. Many experienced programmers, before they examine the language closely, decide this omission is a fatal flaw. But it turns out that using the text field in HyperTalk as such an array is relatively trivial.

By setting up the contents of a field carefully, you can create the same effect as a two-dimensional array. Here is part of such an array. We will use it in a Laboratory exercise in a few moments, uut for now just examine it as we discuss it.

```
Record,LastName,FirstName,Employee#,HireDate,Salary
1,William,Genevieve,3904,2/10/79,49575
2,St.  Germaine,Elmer,4001,7/11/79,36099
3,Butler,Karl,8977,3/14/82,46230
4,Yeats,Stephanie,9998,5/1/82,28900
```

There are two noteworthy aspects of this collection of data.

First, the first line is different from the others. It contains some labels that describe the contents of each field in the table. This line is not required in HyperTalk, but we have found it quite useful in helping to keep track of exactly what is where in a table several months after we've written a script.

Second, notice that all items in each line are separated by commas. This permits us to address them as individual objects (*items* in HyperTalk parlance), which means we can retrieve any single piece of information in the field discretely from the others.

Having set up the field this way, we can make flexible use of its contents. In fact, proper use of fields as arrays can lead to some database-like applications of HyperCard.

Setting up an array

Open your Laboratory stack and add a new card with only the direction-arrow buttons and no other objects. Because we will stay with this card during our experiments, you need not give it a name, though in practice you would probably append a card name or identifier to many of our sample commands.

Now follow these instructions:

1. Create a new scrolling field nearly as wide as the card and occupying about 3/4 of the card's height, as shown in Figure 10-5. Choose a suitably small font to allow lots of information to be placed in the field. Name the field Table 1.

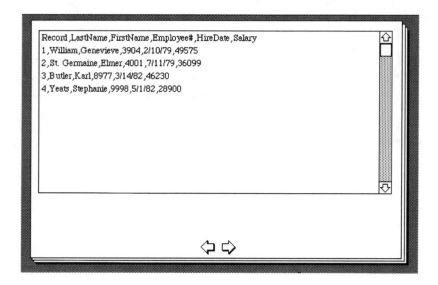

Record,LastName,FirstName,Employee#,HireDate,Salary
1,William,Genevieve,3904,2/10/79,49575
2,St. Germaine,Elmer,4001,7/11/79,36099
3,Butler,Karl,8977,3/14/82,46230
4,Yeats,Stephanie,9998,5/1/82,28900

Figure 10-5. New field for array exercise

2. Get into Browse mode.

Note ▶ The **number of** function we are using is quite significant when dealing with fields as arrays. We'll have more to say about it soon.

3. Enter the text in the small employee table, as shown in the previous listing. Proofread after you're done.

4. Open the Message box and type the following line into it:

```
put number of items in line 1 of card¬
field "Table 1"
```

5. Make sure the answer is 6. If it isn't, you've made a typing error. Find and correct it.

6. Repeat step 4 for the other lines in the field, ensuring in each case that the answer is 6.

7. Type the following command lines into the Message box and observe the results. After each line, the contents of the Message box should be as indicated beneath each line:

```
put item 2 of line 3 of card field "Table 1"
   -- Message box should read "St. Germaine"
put item 4 of line 3 of card field "Table 1"¬
&& item 4 of line 4 of card field "Table 1"
   -- Message box should read 4001 8977
```

▶ Loops and the number of Function

When your script deals with arrays of data, it will probably execute one or more loops (see the discussion of control structures in Chapter 8) as it scans through data looking for some information or accumulating answers in a container. Before it can begin such loops, however, it has to know how many lines or items it must examine. Obtaining this information is the job of **the number of**, a HyperTalk function with many uses.

In fact, **the number of** can be used to find out how many characters (**chars**), words, lines, or items are in a field or in an addressable component of a field.

Generally, you'll **put** the results of **the number of** function into a local variable and then use that variable to control the looping process. Let's go back to the Laboratory stack and run an example to demonstrate what we mean.

Looping for data retrieval from arrays

Return to the same card we used in the last exercise. Close the Message box if it is still visible. Now follow these instructions:

1. Create a new button and name it Total Salary. Make it whatever shape you want, but be sure the Show Name check box in the button definition dialog is checked. Position the button outside the field Table 1. Figure 10-6 gives you an idea of how it should look.

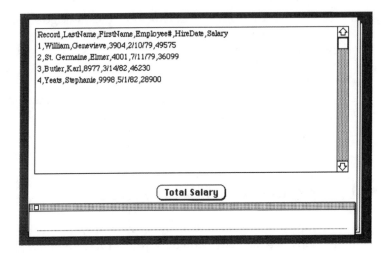

Figure 10-6. Adding a Total Salary button

2. Open the script-editing window for the Total Salary button in one of the usual ways.

3. Type in the following script, proofread it, and confirm it is syntactically correct by pressing the Tab key. Then click the OK button to return to the card.

```
on mouseUp
    put number of lines of card field "Table 1" into
        maxLines
    put empty into totSal
    repeat with count = 2 to maxLines
        put totSal + item 6 of line count of card field
            "Table 1" into totSal
    end repeat
    put "Total salaries =" && totSal
end mouseUp
```

4. Return to Browse mode.

5. Press the Total Salary button. After a moment, the screen looks similar to Figure 10-7. Notice the use of the local variable *maxLines* to control the loop and the use of another local variable, *count*, to determine which line to read. This is a common looping technique when dealing with arrays of data in any programming language.

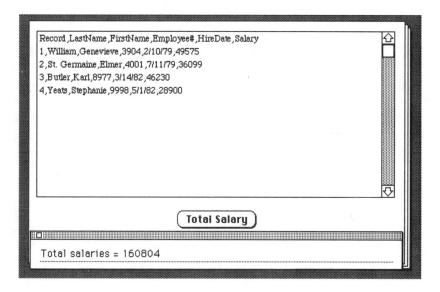

Figure 10-7. Array experiment concluded

▶ Sorting Stacks

Given the flexibility of the HyperText approach to data management, which is the very essence of HyperCard, it may seem a little out of character to include a sort capability in HyperTalk. But in two situations, sorting may be important to your stack's users: flipping through the stack one card at a time and expecting to find the cards in some particular order, and producing reports where the cards appear in some particular order.

To accommodate either need, use the HyperTalk **sort** command. Although this is one of the easiest commands to use in HyperTalk, it offers a large array of possible arguments, or parameters. In its simplest form, the **sort** command looks like this:

```
sort by <expression>
```

Alternatively, beginning with HyperCard 2.0, you can add some "throwaway" words between the **sort** command and the *by* keyword to make your statements more readable. The effect of all these variations is the same; the only difference is in how they read:

```
sort cards by <expression>
sort stack by <expression>
sort cards of stack by <expression>
sort cards of this stack by <expression>
```

The *expression* argument must be a text expression. In other words, it must either *be* text or *evaluate to* text. This expression can be as complex a field component address as is needed. If each record in our employee database example is stored on a separate card, with the information still in one field called Employee Data, you could sort the stack by employee last name with a command like this:

```
sort by item 2 of card field "Employee Data"
```

Beyond this simple use of **sort**, there are two other sets of parameters that can be added to the command. The first set concerns the sort direction, and the second concerns the data type of the sort expression.

▶ Selecting the sort direction

By default, any **sort** ordered in HyperCard is assumed to be in ascending order. But you can override this assumption with the word **descending**. Thus, to sort the employees (assuming, again, that they are on separate cards) according to salary, with the highest-paid employee at the top of the list, you would write a command statement like this:

```
sort descending by item 6 of card field "Employee Data"
```

▶ Defining the data type

From HyperTalk's perspective, four different types of data can be sorted:

- text (the default and most often used)
- numeric
- dateTime
- international

If you don't supply a second parameter, HyperTalk treats the sort expression as text. This results in a straight ASCII sort sequence.

Numbers don't fall in numeric order in the ASCII sort sequence. If you want HyperCard to treat the sort expression as numeric, you must tell it so by supplying the **numeric** parameter to the sort command.

As you will see in the concluding section of this chapter, HyperTalk treats date and time data differently from other types of information. This leads to some very powerful applications. But if you want HyperTalk to treat a particular sort expression as a date or time data type, you must use the **dateTime** sort parameter.

You will probably never have occasion to use the **international** parameter. It is only necessary if you are sorting data that contains special characters called *ligatures* or *umlauts*. English has neither of these special types of characters, so **text** is adequate for most applications involving alphanumeric data.

▶ Naming the sort field

In most cases, you will either supply the name of a background field explicitly or program a container name with the name of the field in it. It is possible to sort by the contents of a card field but that is not often done since fields that appear on multiple cards are almost always designed as background fields.

You must be careful about one thing in naming the field by which to sort. If you supply a variable that has not been initialized or if you use a string with no *field* identifier preceding it, HyperTalk appears to complete the sort but the order of the cards isn't changed. For example, the line

```
sort by "Date"
```

appears to work but does not. You must explicitly tell HyperTalk that the word Date refers to a field.

▶ Confining the sort to a background

Beginning with HyperCard 2.0, you can confine your sort to a specific background. Only cards sharing the indicated background will be sorted; the rest of the stack's sequence remains unchanged.

The syntax for this form of the **sort** command is identical to that for stacks except that you substitute a background identifier for the stack identifier:

```
sort <background Identifier>by <sort criteria>
```

▶ Confining the sort to marked cards

You can instruct HyperCard to sort only those cards that have been previously marked. This feature was added with HyperCard Version 2.0 when the notion of marking cards was introduced. The basic syntax for this form of the **sort** command is as follows:

```
sort marked cards [of <background Identifier>] by <con-
tainer> [<sort criteria>]
```

Notice that you can even tell HyperCard to sort only marked cards belonging to a specific background.

▶ Sorting by function

In addition to being able to sort stacks and fields by their explicit contents, you can also use HyperTalk and user-defined functions as sort criteria. For example, you can move all of the marked cards in a stack together by the statement:

```
sort by (marked of this card)
```

You might even define a function that handles a sort in a non-standard way (for example, skipping some cards based on contents of fields that are not involved in the sort) and then use a statement like the one below to use that function to sort the stack:

```
sort by mySortFunction
```

▶ Some complex sorts

The following examples are self-explanatory and straightforward, but they show how the **sort** command can become quite complex and specific:

```
sort dateTime by card field "Hire Date"
sort descending numeric by item 3 of card field "Table 3"
sort descending dateTime by chars 1 to 5 of line 4 ¬
of field 1
```

▶ Sorting within fields

Beginning with HyperCard 2.0, you can sort information contained within a single field. You can sort all of the contents of a field by line or by item, or you can select specific groups of lines or items to sort.

To sort all of the lines in a particular container, you use a syntax like this:

```
sort lines of <container> <parameters>
```

where the *parameters* are the same as for sorting cards (i.e., type of sort and direction) and have the same defaults (i.e., text and ascending). Similarly, to sort a container's items, you would use a command with this syntax:

```
sort items of <container> <parameters>
```

If you want to sort only part of a container, you can specify that as well. For example, to sort only the first 10 lines of a field, you could use a command like this:

```
sort line 1 to 10 of cd field "Scores"
```

You can use a similar syntax to sort only specified items of a field.

If you don't specify either lines or items but you tell HyperTalk to **sort** a container, it will sort the lines in that container.

Note ▶	When you sort the contents of a field whose text is styled, the styles are lost when the sort is completed. When the text is redrawn in sorted order, the field's text style defaults are applied to the contents.

▶ Hypertext Techniques

From its inception, HyperCard was designed to permit hypertext-style applications to be constructed easily by nonprogramming end users. To a great extent, Version 1.2 of the program succeeded in making such power available. But with the release of Version 2.0, Apple Computer made hypertext even more flexible and accessible. We have already seen how the new **textStyle** called "grouped" enables you to treat a multiword string as if it were one word. Now we're going to see how to take advantage of that fact in combination with three functions — **the clickChunk, the clickLine,** and **the clickText** — to create extremely usable hypertext-style interfaces and interactions.

Hypertext experiment

We'll conduct a brief experiment that will enable you to see how flexible and useful hypertext connections can be in HyperCard beginning with Version 2.0. For the purposes of this experiment, you can create a new stack with a single card and a single card field or add a card with a card field to your existing Laboratory stack. With that done, follow these steps to examine the capabilities of hypertext features in HyperCard:

1. Type the following text into the field, with a carriage return at the end of the string "2.0." This creates a two-line entry in the field. Use the Font and Style menus to set up the text to be whatever size and font you wish.

2. Select the words "click stuff in Version 2.0." with your mouse.

3. From the Style menu, cooose "Group".

4. Lock the text in the field.

5. Open the field's script-editing window in one of the usual ways and enter the following script:

```
on mouseUp
   put "clickChunk = " & the clickChunk
   wait until the mouseClick
   put "clickLine = " & the clickLine
   wait until the mouseClick
   put "clickText = " & the clickText
   wait until the mouseClick
end mouseUp
```

6. Click on the first word in the field, "This." The Message window will show, in succession, the following results, waiting after displaying each one until you click the mouse:

```
clickChunk = char 1 to 4 of card field 1
clickLine = line 1 of card field 1
clickText = This
```

7. Now click on any of the words in the run of text to which you applied the "Group" style at Steps 2 and 3. In the Message box, you'll see the following results; as in Step 6, you must click the mouse after each message is displayed.

```
clickChunk = char 27 to 52 of card field 1
clickLine = line 1 of card field 1
clickText = click stuff in Version 2.0.
```

8. Finally, click on the word "the" in the second line of the field. The Message box results will look like this:

```
clickChunk = char 65 to 67 of card field 1
clickLine = line 2 of card field 1
clickText = the
```

As you can see, these new functions allow you to examine the precise contents of the text in a locked field where the user clicks. You can then do a great many things with the results of the click, particularly with **the clickText**. You could, for example, perform a **find** operation with **the clickText** as a parameter to create a hypertext link to occurrences of the word or phrase in the stack. Or you might go to a card named after the text on which the click occurred. These are just two ideas for uses of this information.

▶ Date and Time: Special Data Types

We will conclude our discussion of HyperTalk data management techniques and commands by turning our attention to the use of dates and times as special data types. As we just saw, data that is intended to be sorted as if it were a date or time must be pointed out to HyperTalk as part of the **sort** command. Other considerations must also be watched when you deal with such data.

Five functions are involved in managing date and time data, and most of them have several versions. The five basic functions are

- **date**
- **time**
- **seconds**
- **ticks**
- **convert**

We will discuss each of these in the order shown.

▶ The date function

In its simplest form, **the date** simply returns the current date in what is called *short format*. This format is the one you are probably most accustomed to writing: mm/dd/yy. Thus, January 15, 1988, appears as 1/15/88.

The next simplest form of the command is **the abbreviated date**. This command can be written out completely or shortened to **the abbrev date** or even **the abbr date**. A date retrieved in this form includes the day of the week and the month (both abbreviated) and the year. Neither abbreviation includes a period. January 15, 1988, written in an abbreviated HyperCard form is Fri, Jan 15, 1988.

Finally, there is **the long date** function. This command spells out all of the date's components: Friday, January 15, 1988.

Usually, you will put the date, or some portion of it, into a field on a card in an **openCard** or **openStack** script. There are, of course, many other uses for this function.

You can extract the individual items in either **the abbreviated** or **the long date**. For example, to pull out the day of the week and put it into a card, you would write something like this:

```
put item 1 of the long date into card field "Day of Week"
```

If you use **the abbreviated date** rather than **the long date**, the abbreviation for the day of the week is retrieved and **put** where you direct it to be placed. Individual items cannot be extracted from the short form of the date, which exists entirely as one item. When you extract such information from a date field, it must then be treated as text and not as a date on which special mathematical operations can be performed.

▶ The time function

There are two forms of time functions. The first function, **the time**, has no qualifiers and returns the current time in hours and minutes. The second is written **the long time** and adds the seconds to the end of the time. In all other respects, they are identical.

How the time is displayed — for example, as 5:15 P.M. or as 1715 — is determined by the settings in your Control Panel and may not be altered in HyperTalk. Individual components of the time functions' return values may not be retrieved.

▶ The seconds function

The seconds function can be written as either **the seconds** or **the secs**. In either form, it returns **the number of** seconds that have elapsed since January 1, 1904. This is the date Apple Computer used as the basis for its internal clock. Because of that, **the seconds** returns incredibly large numbers; billions of seconds have passed since January 1, 1904.

One useful application for this function is in stacks where you want to time user responses or document usage. Simply store the value of this function when a process begins, and then store its value when the function ends. A simple calculation reveals how much time has elapsed between steps.

▶ The ticks function

Every time you turn on your Macintosh, it begins keeping track of how long the system is turned on using a special unit of measure called a *tick*. A tick is 1/60 of a second. You can use the special function **the ticks** to obtain the current value of this counter. The function has no arguments and returns a number — generally a very large number — that you can use like any other number.

Like **the seconds** functions, **the ticks** can be used to time the distance between two events. It is 60 times as fine a measurement as **the seconds**, so it can be used when you need very accurate timing. One such situation is programming the Macintosh double-click mechanism. Much of what takes place in HyperCard uses only single clicks, but many Macintosh users are accustomed to double-clicking on items. Because HyperCard doesn't penalize the user for double-clicking (it simply ignores the second click), the usefulness of a double-click mechanism is marginal.

▶ Using convert to reformat dates

We have seen date and time information in HyperCard in six formats:

- seconds
- long date
- short date
- abbreviated date
- long time
- short time

All of these represent the time elapsed since the Macintosh base date and time of January 1, 1904, at 00:00:00. Sometimes you will want to **convert** a date stored in one format into a more readable or usable format. To perform such a task, HyperTalk includes the **convert** command. Its syntax looks like this:

```
convert <container> to <format>
```

The container must contain data in a date or time format. The **convert** command converts this information into the form specified by the format argument. The converted result replaces the contents of the container, so you will usually want to do conversions of dates and times in variables rather than in fields on the screen. Imagine the consternation of the uninitiated user who sees a nice, readable date such as Jan 15, 1988, suddenly turn into the staggering number 2652048000!

We haven't looked at one of the most useful conversions in HyperTalk. The **dateItems** format is a special form of the date that can be used easily in arithmetic. When you convert a date to this format, HyperTalk returns a comma-separated list of seven items, beginning with the year, continuing down to seconds, and ending with a number indicating the day of the week. The day of the week assigns Sunday as 1, so Monday is 2, Tuesday is 3, and so forth.

To see the **dateItems** conversion work, go to any card and stack in Hyper-Card and open the Message window. Type in these three lines:

```
put "1/15/88" into date1
convert date1 to dateItems
date1
    -- Message box shows 1988,1,15,0,0,0,6
```

Notice that because we didn't store a time in the field, HyperTalk simply substitutes zeros for the three time fields. You may be surprised to see that happen if you've worked with more stringent programming languages that return an error if you try to convert something without enough data in the original value. The number 6 at the end of the **dateItems** list tells us that January 15, 1988, is a Friday.

The real value of the **dateItems** format is that you can perform math on any item in the list. Want to know the date 45 days from now? Type the following lines into the Message box and see the answer. (We used January 15, 1990, for our current date.)

```
put the date into date1
convert date1 to dateItems
put item 3 of date1 + 45 into item 3 of date1
convert date1 to date
date1
   -- Message box contains February 29, 1990
```

If you are curious about how this works, go through the same process, but after you perform the addition (the third line of code) and before you restore it to a readable format, type *date1* into the Message box. Look at the third item. Don't be surprised if it is larger than the number of days in any month! Yet when you perform the conversion back to a readable date format, HyperTalk takes care of this discrepancy and produces a logical answer.

▶ Trapping the Return and Enter Keys

During data entry into a card with more than one field, the experienced Macintosh user expects to be able to press the Return key or the Enter key to move from one field to another. In versions of HyperCard prior to 1.2, this was not possible; HyperCard reacted to either key being pressed in an editable field by simply placing a carriage return in the field. But beginning with Version 1.2, HyperTalk has two field-specific system messages to enable you to create real-world data entry environments. (System messages are discussed more broadly in Chapter 6.)

The two messages are **returnInField** and **enterInField**. The first message is sent whenever the user presses the Return key while typing in an editable field. The other is sent in response to the user pressing the Enter key in an editable field. You can write handlers to respond to these messages so that you can customize how your stack responds to these commonly used keys. For example, if you want to simulate a word processor's reaction to the Return key so that HyperTalk adds a second carriage return and "tab" five spaces, you could write a handler like this:

```
on returnInField
   put return & return & " " after me
   select after text of me
end returnInField
```

If you wanted the Return key to be used to move from one field to another, write a handler like this at the card level or higher:

```
on returnInField
    send tabKey
end returnInField
```

This moves the cursor to the next field and selects all of the text of that field. (You could accomplish this without programming by simply checking the "auto Tab" box in the Field Info dialog for this field.) But if you wanted instead to position the cursor at the end of that field, you could improve on this handler substantially. Assuming that you want to move the user around the card in field-sequence order (for example, field 1 to field 2 to field 3...,), a handler like this at the card level or higher does the trick:

```
on returnInField
    put the number of the target into holder1
    -- the target is the field receiving the message
    if holder1 = 6
    -- or whatever the highest-numbered field is
    then
        go to next card
        exit returnInField
    end if
    select after text of field (holder1 + 1)
end returnInField
```

You could as easily change the last line before the end of the handler to

```
select before text of field (holder1 + 1)
```

and place the cursor at the beginning of the next field. It should not be too difficult to see how you could use combinations of the **returnInField** message and the **select** command to do very sophisticated data-entry management in HyperTalk.

Everything we have said about **returnInField** is equally true of **enterInField**.

▶ Summary

This has been a full chapter. You learned many tasks that make it possible to use HyperCard as a competent database management system. You learned more than a dozen new commands and functions and gained additional insight into the use of commands and functions that we discussed earlier.

You now know how to use **get** and **put** to read and alter the contents of fields in stacks. You know how to use the **length** and **offset** functions together to track down strings inside fields and set them up for recovery or modification.

You have seen how to combine the powerful **find** and **select** commands to perform data management tasks, such as locating and manipulating textual information in fields.

You have seen how to establish and change the font, style, and other characteristics of the text displayed in HyperCard fields when you are using Version 2.0 or later of the program.

You saw that even though HyperTalk does not include an explicit data type that handles two-dimensional arrays (tables), you can easily use fields to mimic such a data type. You not only learned how to set up fields for such use but also saw a complex, real-life example of how to get data from a table in HyperTalk.

You learned to use the **sort** command to rearrange the order in which cards are stored in HyperCard stacks for the times when the user wants to go through a stack in some predetermined order rather than use the HyperText techniques that are the heart and soul of HyperCard.

You have also seen how to take advantage of some additions to the HyperTalk language in Version 2.0 to create true hypertext applications.

Finally, you learned to deal with dates and times: how to obtain them, how to convert them to usable forms, and how to use the special **dateItems** format to perform useful arithmetic on date and time fields.

Chapter 11 continues the process of examining techniques that make HyperCard stacks usable as applications. We also look at how to implement the classic Macintosh-style dialog box in HyperTalk.

11 ▶ Dialog Boxes

In this chapter, you will learn to use several new HyperTalk commands

- **answer**, for dialog boxes requiring only that the user press a button to give your script some information
- **ask**, for dialog boxes requiring that the user type something to give your script some information
- **answer file** and **ask file**, for dialog boxes that help the user find or name external files and stacks
- **ask password**, for a special type of **ask** dialog box

▶ Dialogs and HyperCard

As anyone who has spent more than five minutes with a Macintosh knows, dialog boxes are a crucial component of designing good applications. Dozens, perhaps hundreds, of kinds of dialog boxes have appeared in Macintosh applications over the time the system has been available. Some are standard, built-in dialogs (as dialog boxes are often called) such as those you see when you want to open a file (Figure 11-1) or print a document (Figure 11-2). Others are specific to the application, such as Microsoft Word's character-formatting dialog (Figure 11-3).

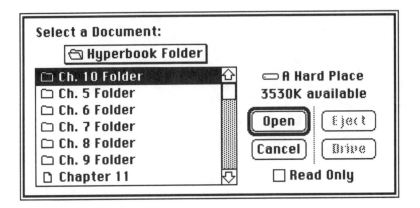

Figure 11-1. Standard open file dialog

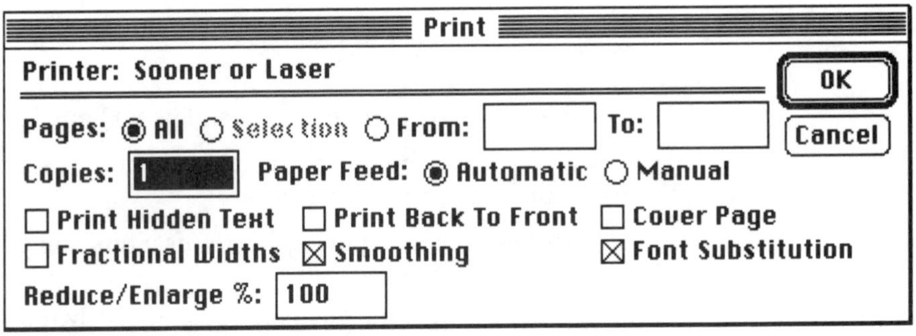

Figure 11-2. Standard print dialog

Few Macintosh applications, if any, operate without dialogs. But in our exploration of HyperCard so far, we have not seen any way to obtain information directly from a user in an interactive way. We learned in Chapter 10 how to read information the user had placed in fields. And we know the Message box can be used as a type of mini-dialog where we display a request for information and read the user's response. But the Message box only works for HyperTalk commands, so its use is limited.

Fortunately, HyperTalk includes the ability to produce several basic kinds of dialogs. Two have limitations that don't exist in more conventional approaches to Macintosh dialogs. Nevertheless, they give us a way to ask users for information and all but force them to give us a reply we can use in our scripts.

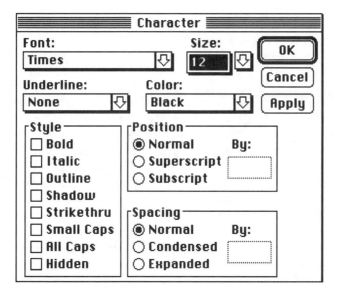

Figure 11-3. Microsoft Word's character-formatting dialog

▶ Three kinds of Mac dialogs

In the world of the Macintosh, there are three types of dialogs. There are *alert* dialog boxes, which are generally used for error messages. These frequent Mac screen visitors (see Figure 11-4) usually have an icon that lets us determine the seriousness of the error or message and a single OK button we can click in to remove them from the screen.

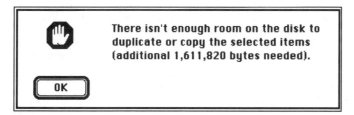

Figure 11-4. Typical alert box

Second, the Macintosh displays *modal* dialog boxes, so named because they put the Macintosh into a mode in which only the dialog box responds to user input. Modal dialogs do not have a close box, so users can't simply dismiss them — they must respond to their presence. Alerts are a special category of modal dialogs.

Finally, there are *modeless* dialogs designed to assist the user in some types of processing. These boxes are more like document windows on the Macintosh. A modeless dialog generally has a close box, and the user can make it inactive by clicking in another window to make a different window the active one. A common example of a modeless dialog is the Find box in most Macintosh word processors. If you bring up a modeless dialog and then click in another window, the modeless dialog doesn't get put away; it simply goes behind the newly active window. You can prove this by opening a document window in your favorite word processor and collapsing it so that it occupies only part of the screen. Then call up the Find dialog and click in the document window. You will see that the Find dialog is still on the screen, but it's not the topmost (active) window.

All HyperCard dialogs are modal. The user must respond to them before continuing any processing. They have no close boxes. Clicking anywhere outside the dialog results only in a Macintosh system beep. Palettes, on the other hand, are by nature modeless.

▶ Four modal dialogs in HyperCard

There are four styles of modal dialogs in HyperTalk. One, like that shown in Figure 11-5, poses a question to the user and displays one, two, or three labeled buttons to use as a reply. This is the dialog created using the **answer** command. The second, like that shown in Figure 11-6, is generated with the **ask** command and allows the user to enter text in a small text-editing rectangle before accepting the entry.

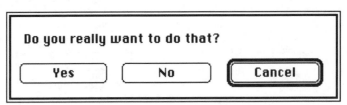

Figure 11-5. An answer dialog

Figure 11-6. An ask dialog

The other two modal dialogs made their debut in HyperCard 2.0. They are the standard file dialogs that are part of almost all Macintosh programs. The **ask file** command produces the standard file-saving or file-creating dialog, complete with an optional prompt and an optional default file name. The **answer file** command produces the standard file-opening dialog, with an optional prompt.

▶ Using Dialogs in HyperTalk

When your script executes an **ask, answer, ask file,** or **answer file** command, the user's response is placed into the special *It* variable. You can then store the response, test it for conditional processing, or do anything else with it that you like. (Remember our frequent cautions about the use of the *It* variable. Don't keep things in *It* any longer than necessary.)

The **answer** dialog can also act much like a standard Macintosh alert, though without the usual icons that give users a visual clue as to the type of warning they are being given.

▶ The answer Dialog

The syntax for the **answer** dialog looks like this:

```
answer "<question>" [with "<reply>" [or "<reply>" [or "<reply>"]]]
```

As you can see, **answer** requires only one parameter: the question to be posed to the user. If you supply only the question and no possible responses in the form of **with** parameters, HyperTalk displays a dialog with only one default response: OK.

You can display dialogs from within the Message box. Let's see what a one-answer dialog looks like. Open the Message box in any card or stack and type the following line:

```
answer "This makes no sense!"
```

When you press Return, the dialog shown in Figure 11-7 appears immediately. You can see why this is very much like a Macintosh alert box. It has only one response the user can make, so its job is obviously to inform the user of something, make sure the user has noticed it, and then slip quietly away into the nether reaches of the program.

Just out of curiosity, you might want to click in the OK box and then type *It* in the Message box. The OK response is stored there.

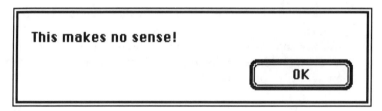

Figure 11-7. One-answer answer dialog

▶ Some rules about answer dialogs

Now let's create an **answer** dialog with two responses in it. In the Message box, type:

```
answer "This makes more sense!" with "OK" or "Oh yeah?"
```

The result looks like Figure 11-8. Notice that the OK button is listed first in the **answer** command line but shows up in the middle of the dialog, not at the right where we expect to find OK buttons. Also notice that the "Oh yeah?" button is highlighted. These two observations come about because of two basic rules in **answer** dialogs:

1. The options fill in the dialog box as if they were being inserted into the dialog box from the right and pushing existing options to the left. If you put in all three options, as we will in a moment, the one listed first in the command line ends up in the first, or leftmost, spot.

2. HyperCard always highlights the rightmost button, which is the last one listed.

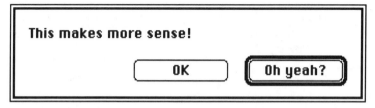

Figure 11-8. Two-answer answer dialog

So if you want the dialog in Figure 11-8 to look like other Macintosh dialogs, you have to write:

```
answer "This makes more sense!" with "Oh yeah?" or "OK"
```

▶ Text in answer dialogs

In designing *answer* dialogs, it is important to consider the limitations on the size of text fields for the question and the responses. HyperCard uses the standard but space-hungry Chicago 12-point font for all text in its dialogs. Beginning with HyperCard 2.0, these dialogs resize dynamically to accommodate a reasonably large amount of text. You can place up to 240 characters in the prompt for an **ask** or **answer** dialog and HyperCard will size the containing dialog appropriately. This is a big improvement over earlier versions, which limited prompts to one line (essentially about 40 characters).

All of the modal dialogs created with variations on the **ask** and **answer** commands resize themselves dynamically to accommodate up to 240 characters of text in their prompts.

Similarly, the buttons are intended to hold very short replies. Ideally, buttons should contain one word or two short words. Keeping the button text to 10 to 14 characters works best. Also, remember that the Mac centers text in these buttons.

▶ Tailoring text in a single answer dialog

The question displayed in an **answer** dialog is a text field like any other in HyperCard. Thus, you can use concatenation to tailor the text in an **answer** dialog without having to create a separate dialog for each possible event. For example, suppose you need an alert to notify the user that a problem exists in a file. You can simply create a standard format for a dialog and have it add the file name when it is displayed:

```
answer "Error in file " & filename
```

Figure 11-9 shows such a dialog when the file name is Words.

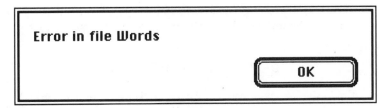

Figure 11-9. Tailored answer dialog

▶ Macintosh design consideration

There is a final point to make about these HyperCard dialogs. Most Mac users are accustomed to being able to cancel all but alert dialogs. So it is very important that your script include a Cancel button as one of the options in an **answer** dialog. (You need not concern yourself with this issue in **ask** dialogs because HyperCard automatically furnishes such a button in those dialogs.)

▶ The ask Dialog

Aside from the fact that users type an answer in response to an **ask** dialog rather than press a button to select a reply from among those you've offered, the **ask** dialog is similar to the **answer** dialog. In fact, everything we've said about **answer** dialogs can be applied to **ask** dialogs except for the issue of how buttons fill in the dialog. There are two predetermined buttons in an **ask** dialog, and you have no control over what they say or where they are placed.

Syntactically, the **ask** dialog command differs only in that it permits only one optional **with** argument:

```
ask "<question>" [with "<reply>"]
```

Generally, you will not use the **with** option when you write **ask** dialogs. But if you do supply a **with** argument, the text it contains becomes the *default* text in the dialog's text-editing rectangle when the dialog appears. The text you supply is selected, as is the case with standard Macintosh dialogs of this type, so if the user types any key except Return, the typing replaces the text you supply as the default. Users can also edit the text your script places in the rectangle. First they must click somewhere in the text field to remove the selection. Thereafter, they can use any standard Macintosh editing technique to modify the text.

As usual, pressing the Return key or the OK button accepts the text, storing it in the *It* container. From there, you can process the text.

▶ Example of the ask command

Open the Message box any place in HyperCard and type the following line. The resulting dialog looks like Figure 11-10.

```
ask "Which computer has the best stuff?" with "Macintosh!"
```

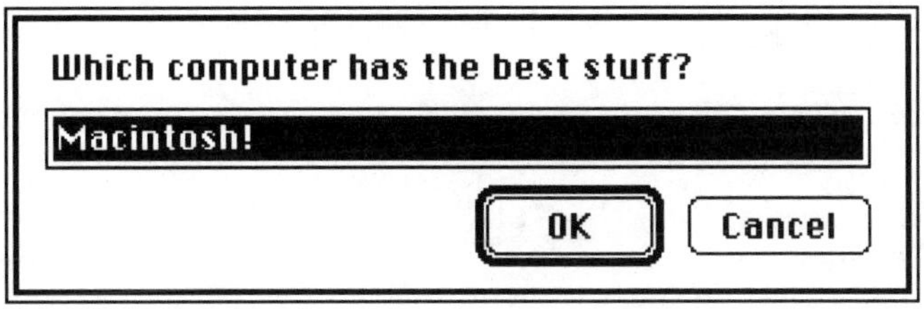

```
Which computer has the best stuff?
Macintosh!
                              OK      Cancel
```

Figure 11-10. Typical ask dialog

▶ Standard file dialogs in HyperCard

To create a standard Macintosh file-saving or file-creating dialog (referred to in Mac programming parlance as an SFPutFile dialog) in HyperTalk, you will use the **ask file** command. Its syntax is:

```
ask file "<prompt>" [with <defaultName>]
```

The user's response is stored in the special global variable *It*. You can then use this response to open, write information to, and close the designated file. Here is a small example of the use of the **ask file** command:

```
on closeCard
   ask file "Where should I save the text?" with "Temp"
   if it is empty then exit closeCard
   open it
   write card field "Data" to file it
   close it
end closeCard
```

The user's response — and therefore the variable *It* — will be empty if the user clicks the Cancel button in the file dialog.

To open an existing file via a standard file-opening dialog — whose technical name is the SFGetFile dialog — you will use the **answer file** command. Its syntax is:

```
answer file "<prompt>" [of type <string | fileTypeExpression>]
```

If you supply an *of type* parameter, you can furnish up to four file types, using either their 4-character names or HyperTalk equivalents. Table 11-1 shows the correspondence between file types (referred to as *fileTypeExpression* descriptors) and file types in HyperTalk.

Table 11-1. File Types in HyperTalk 2.0

HyperTalk Literal	*File Type*
stack	'STAK'
text	'TEXT'
application	'APPL'
picture	'PICT'
paint	'PNTG'

The following two lines are equivalent:

```
answer file "Open which file?" of type stack or text
answer file "Open which file?" of type "STAK" or "TEXT"
```

If you use the file types, they must be all capital letters or HyperTalk will not recognize them. You can supply up to four file types in the argument list to the **answer file** command.

▶ The ask password variation

There are two differences between **ask** and **ask password**. The first lies in what happens to the user's answer. Before HyperCard places the response into *It*, the program converts the reply to an integer value and then encrypts it. This encrypted integer can then be compared with a previously stored encrypted integer to see if the person has used the proper password to gain access to the script or some portion of it.

The second difference between the plain **ask** command and the **ask password** command lies in the fact that the user's answer to an **ask password** command is not displayed in readable text. Instead, a bullet takes the place of each character the user types. This prevents people who may be watching the user enter a private password from seeing what that password is.

For example, suppose that the first time a new user runs a script, the user is asked for a password of his or her own creation. After the user enters the password, you store the encrypted integer HyperCard places in *It* in a card field called Protect. The next time the same person uses the stack and reaches the password point, he or she enters a password. Your script then simply examines the password value entered this time against the one stored previously. If they are equal, all is fine and the user can proceed. If not, you may want to give the user more chances to enter the correct password or take some other action.

▶ Summary

In this chapter, you learned to post dialog boxes during HyperTalk script execution as a way of obtaining information from the user. You saw that the language has four different modal dialogs. The one created with the **answer** command presents users with one or more options in the form of buttons they can press to supply an answer. The one generated using **ask** or its variation **ask password** permits the user to type a response. The **ask file** and **answer file** commands generate standard Macintosh file dialogs.

Chapter 12 explains how to manage menus and access the other tools available in HyperCard.

12 ▶ Managing Menus and Using Tools

In this chapter, you'll learn how to

- use the **doMenu** command to carry out from within a script any action that can be taken with a menu selection in HyperCard

- add your own custom menus to a stack

- manage the entire menu bar, including both the standard HyperCard menus and your custom menus, by deleting items, changing their style, connecting HyperTalk handlers to them, and turning menu options on or off

- use the **choose** command to switch among the various tools used in authoring HyperTalk scripts

▶ Running Menus from Scripts

Like most well-designed Macintosh applications, HyperCard invests a lot of its power in menus from which the user can choose functions. But unlike most Mac programs, HyperCard gives you the ability to carry out menu-driven operations from scripts. Any function that can be performed from a menu can be performed from within a script.

The command that allows you this flexibility and power is the **doMenu** command. It takes only one argument, the exact name of the menu choice as it appears on the pull-down menu. Among other things, the requirement for an exact match means that menu choices that end with an ellipsis (three periods), indicating that a dialog box of choices is displayed when it is chosen, must have those three dots included in the **doMenu** command. The **doMenu** command is not, however, case-sensitive.

Figure 12-1 is a menu map of HyperCard with all its menu choices (unless a particular stack adds menus of its own). Not all of these menus are on the menu bar at one time, of course. Sometimes you have to be in a particular mode (for example, painting mode) for a specific menu or menu item to be available.

If the stack with which you are working is write-protected (see Chapter 3) against changes, the following menu choices are not available. An attempt to invoke them with a **doMenu** command produces an error.

- on the File Menu, the "Compact Stack," and "Delete Stack..." options

- on the Edit Menu, the "New Card," "Delete Card," "Cut Card," "Copy Card," and "Paste Card" options

- on the Objects Menu, the "Bring Closer," "Send Farther," "New Button," "New Field," and "New Background" options

- on the Options Menu, "Edit Pattern..."

In addition, neither the script nor the user may rename a stack, change any scripts in the stack, or sort the stack if it is write-protected. Additionally, any editing changes the user or a script makes are lost when a card movement takes place.

You can use **doMenu** in a script even if you've turned off menus in your stack. (This might give you a clue about how to access menus when they are hidden in a stack designed by someone else. Because **doMenu** can be executed from the Message box, you can invoke menu access even when direct use of menus is disabled.)

To prove this, open the Message box anywhere in HyperCard and type:

```
hide menubar
```

Then press the Return key. The menu bar at the top of the display disappears. Now type the following in the Message box:

```
doMenu "Open Stack..."
```

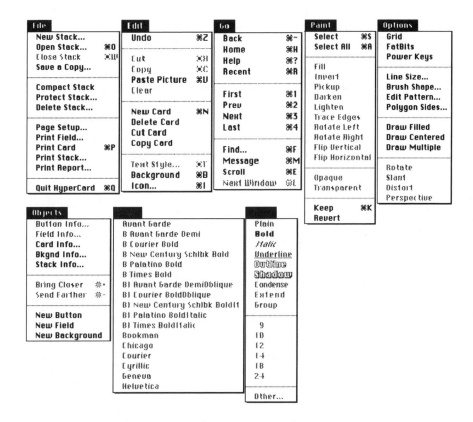

Figure 12-1. Complete menu map of HyperCard

The usual file opening dialog appears. Press Cancel, because you really don't want to open a stack at this point. To redisplay the menu bar, type

```
show menubar
```

You can also open desk accessories with the **doMenu** command. From the Message box, type

```
doMenu "Control Panel"
```

and watch as the standard Macintosh control panel appears on the screen.

| Note ► | At this point, you are facing one of the most disconcerting dilemmas in HyperTalk scripting. You can enable the user to open a desk accessory but you cannot cause HyperCard to do anything at this point. You can't click in the Control Panel somewhere to change a value (for example, the blinking rate for the cursor). You can't even get rid of the Control Panel. The user is in charge and HyperCard is essentially sitting back waiting for control to return to it. You must be very mindful of this problem, particularly when designing stacks for people who are not Macintosh-proficient. |

► Using doMenu in Scripts

You are not likely to encounter many places where the **doMenu** command is useful in your HyperTalk scripts. Virtually everything that can be done from the menus is in one of two categories:

- actions that are done only or primarily during script authoring rather than script execution

- actions that are available as HyperTalk commands and for which **doMenu** is therefore a redundant and less efficient way of accomplishing a task

But four tasks are occasionally useful, not accessible from HyperTalk commands, and therefore good candidates for the **doMenu** command. These tasks are: compacting the stack, protecting the stack, adding a new card, and deleting a card.

| Note ► | Starting with HyperCard Version 2.0, you can avoid the appearance of dialog boxes with menu commands that normally ask the user to intervene and supply some information or approve an action. You do this by adding the parameter *without dialog* to the end of an appropriate **doMenu** command. For example, if you attempt to cut a background field, HyperCard always asks you to confirm that you wish to delete the field and its contents from all cards on which it appears. You can avoid this problem with the line:
`    doMenu "Cut Field" without dialog` |

Obviously, you'd execute this statement after having selected the desired field. In this case, HyperCard would simply delete the selected field without asking the user to approve the action. There are many menu-based commands that normally produce a dialog; you can process all of them without dialog intervention using this technique.

▶ Compacting the stack

As the user works with a stack, adding and deleting cards can cause free space to develop. If this free space becomes excessive, it can slow down the execution of a script and the movement among cards in a stack. The Compact Stack option on the File menu eliminates this free space. As a result, stacks run more efficiently.

You can check the amount of free space in a stack by using the **freeSize** property. (HyperCard properties are discussed fully in Chapter 17.) If the **freeSize** property has a value greater than zero, free space can be recovered from a stack. That doesn't mean you should compact the stack any time this value is more than zero. But you may want to keep an eye on the situation, particularly if the stack is prone to become quite large.

Some successful stack designers report that if they check the amount of free space that has accumulated in a stack and find that it exceeds 20 percent of the stack's current size (which can be obtained as the stack's **size** property), they either compact the stack or advise the user to do so. A partial script to handle this task — probably best included in a **closeStack** handler — might look like this:

```
put size of this stack into stacksize
put freeSize of this stack into freespace
if freespace > .2 * stacksize then doMenu "Compact Stack"
```

▶ Protecting the stack

Most of the time, you will protect a stack before you make it available to end users, if you protect it at all. By *protect*, HyperCard means not to prevent copying, but just to control access. But sometimes users of your stack may create a new stack (perhaps a copy of the one you've furnished or one generated by the operation of your stack) that they want protected or that your design requires to be protected. In that case, you can use the **doMenu** command to force stack protection. In fact, **doMenu** is the only way to accomplish this objective other than relying on the user to handle it.

When users encounter a script that carries out a **doMenu** command to set up script protection, they will see a dialog box like that shown in Figure 12-2. If the user then clicks on the Set Password button, a new dialog appears (see Figure 12-3).

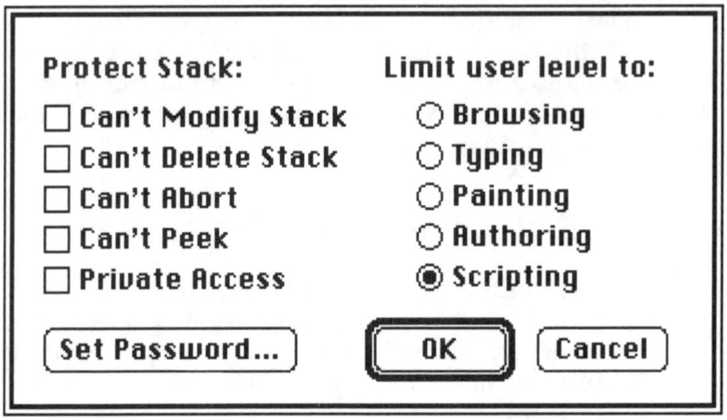

Figure 12-2. The Protect Stack... menu dialog

Figure 12-3. Setting a password

Besides setting a password, the user can also protect the stack from deletion, modification, or termination of scripts, peeking at the location of objects, or any combination by selecting the appropriate check boxes in the dialog shown in Figure 12-2. (The "Can't Modify" option is available only in HyperCard 1.2 and later versions. The "Can't Abort" and "Can't Peek" options are available only in HyperCard 2.0 and later.) If the user or the designer specifies a stack as not subject to deletion, the stack cannot be deleted, even with a proper password. The same is true of modification. Password protection applies only to accessing the stack.

If the "Can't Modify Stack" check box is selected as part of stack protection, the "Can't Delete Stack" check box is also selected automatically by HyperCard.

Any attempt to modify a stack that has been protected against modification is met with an alert dialog. Menu items for deleting the stack and compacting it are dimmed on the File menu if the stack is protected. (You can use scripting techniques to allow temporary modification of protected stacks. See Chapter 17.)

You can also handle stack protection in your scripts without user intervention by setting an appropriate property for the stack. Properties are discussed fully in Chapter 17.

If the "Can't Abort" check box is checked for a stack, the user cannot interrupt processing of a script by pressing the Command and Period keys simultaneously, as he or she normally can. If the "Can't Peek" check box is turned on, the user cannot use the Command-Option key combination (with the Shift key if fields are involved) to see where all the buttons and fields (even the invisible ones) are located. As a side effect, the user also cannot examine or modify the script of any button or field if this check box is checked for a particular stack.

Note ▶	Password protection only goes into effect in the next HyperCard session. If you (or the user) check the "Private Access" check box and supply a password as requested, you can still do anything for which you have the appropriate user level during the present HyperCard session. This is true even if you leave the stack and come back to it. But the next time you launch HyperCard, this password protection will be in effect.

▶ Adding and removing cards

In the extensible, flexible world of HyperCard, it is not unusual for a stack user to be increasing and decreasing the size of a stack routinely. Most HyperCard users know how to add a new card or delete one. But what if you want the menu bar hidden or you want to do something out of the ordinary when new cards are created or old ones deleted?

As you know from our earlier discussions, particularly those in Chapter 6, you can intercept the user's interaction with menus to carry out peculiar processing needs. But sometimes you need to allow the user to use stack buttons that have an effect similar or identical to using menu commands.

For example, you might have a project-planning stack that works on the basis of weeks. If the user clicks on a button labeled New Card, Extend Stack, or some similar text, your script might need to create seven new cards, perhaps with different backgrounds. The only way to accomplish this is with a script, part of which looks something like this:

```
repeat with count = 1 to 7
   doMenu "New Card"
end repeat
```

Another possible use for the "New Card" menu command arises if your stack creates a card to store information temporarily while your stack's script is being executed. This can be a very efficient way to store information that might otherwise be in variables, where confusion among names and uses might arise.

But if you create new cards during execution of the script, particularly if you do so without the user's knowledge, you should get rid of them later so the stack is returned to its original state. To do this, you can use the **doMenu** command with the "Delete Card" option from the Edit menu. This **doMenu** option is also useful when your script deletes cards on its own or because of a user request. For example, a calendar stack might have a Purge Appts. button that goes through the stack, finds appointments older than some set number of days, and deletes them.

▶ User level and doMenu

As mentioned, before a **doMenu** command can be issued for a particular menu option, that menu option must be available to the user. In part, this is a function of whether the user is using the right tool (the subject of a later section of this chapter). But it is also related to the user's level when the menu command is needed. If, for example, the user is limited to the browse level and you want to carry out in your script a menu command that requires a higher level of access than the user's, you must modify the user level. You can do this with a script fragment like this:

```
put the userLevel into currentLevel
-- save current level for later
set the userLevel to 5
-- execute doMenu and other commands here
set the userLevel to currentLevel
-- restore former level
```

▶ Custom Menus

Beginning with HyperCard 2.0, you can customize the menu bar used in your HyperCard stacks. This includes the ability to

- create new menus
- add specific items to standard or custom menus

- activate and deactivate any menu item
- modify the appearance of any menu item
- change the name of any menu or menu item
- return the menu bar to its original, unmodified condition

We'll discuss just how to handle each of these tasks in a moment. First, let's be sure we understand the terminology related to menus on the Macintosh.

▶ Basic menu terminology

On the Macintosh, regardless of the application being used, there are three basic terms that describe the elements of the menu subsystem.

The menu bar (sometimes written as one word, *menubar*) refers to the area at the top of the screen where all of the menus appear. It always means the entire area and all of the menus that appear there.

Before the user interacts with the menu bar in any way, it appears to consist of a series of short labels. These are referred to as menus. Thus, in HyperCard we can talk about the Objects menu.

As the user opens a particular menu by pressing the mouse button over the menu's name, it "drops down" to reveal one or more individual choices. These are referred to as menu items (again, sometimes written as one word, *menuitems* or *menuItems*).

Figure 12-4 shows a typical HyperCard menu with all three parts labeled.

▶ Adding menus to the menu bar

You can add a menu to the menu bar with the **create menu** command. Its syntax is simple:

```
create menu <menuName>
```

The argument *menuName* must be either a single word (in which case no quotation marks are needed), the name of a HyperTalk variable or other container that stores the name of the menu (in which case quotation marks are incorrect), or a multiple-word phrase (in which case quotation marks are required).

When HyperTalk executes this command, it immediately puts a new menu on the menu bar with the name you furnish. At that point, the menu has no menu items associated with it.

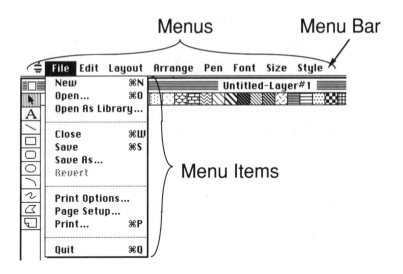

Figure 12-4. The three parts of a typical HyperCard menu

▶ Adding menu items to a menu

Obviously, a menu without a menu item is not very useful. To add menu items to any existing menu, you use a variation of the widely used **put** command with the following syntax:

```
put <itemName> {before | after | into} {menu | menuItem}
<identifier> [of menu <identifier2] [with menuMsg <command>]
```

In this command, *itemName* is the name of the menu item you wish to add to an existing menu. The usual rules about quotation marks apply. The prepositions **before**, **after**, and **into** have their usual meaning. You can place a new menu item anywhere in the list of menu items attached to a menu, so you can designate either the menu name or the name of the menu item to which the position of the new item is to be related. If you use a menu item in this position, you must then tell HyperTalk which menu you mean. This approach means that you can have the same menu item name on more than one menu.

Finally, you use the "with menuMsg" option when you want to tell HyperTalk which handler or command to execute when the user selects this menu item. In this context, *command* can be either the name of a handler or function or it can be a HyperTalk command, with or without parameters, and enclosed in quotation marks if necessary.

Creating and Using Custom Menus

For this Laboratory exercise, you can use an existing Laboratory stack or create a new one. In either case, follow these directions:

1. Go to the first card of your stack, open the card script (which should be empty; if it's not, you should remove at least any **openCard** handler you find there), and enter the following script:

```
on openCard
    create menu "Testing"
    put "Once" after menu "Testing" with menuMsg "beep 1"
    put "Twice" after menu "Testing" with menuMsg "beep 2"
    put "Four times" after menu "Testing" with menuMsg
        "beep 4"
    put "Three times" before menuItem "Four times" of menu
            "Testing" with menuMsg "beep 3"
end openCard
```

2. Close the script-editing window.

3. Move to a previous card in the stack (or, if this is a one-card stack, just close the stack by going to another one and then return here).

4. Return to the card we just programmed.

5. There will be a brief delay while HyperCard 2.0 displays the custom menu.

6. Select the various menu items and confirm that they perform as expected.

7. Keep this card around for a few minutes; we'll use it again shortly.

There is one special case of this use of the **put** command to generate custom menus. If the first character of the string you instruct HyperTalk to add to an existing menu is a hyphen, HyperTalk will place a divider line across the width of the menu at the indicated position. HyperTalk ignores any characters to the right of the hyphen. The inserted line becomes a menu item in the numbering scheme as well.

► Deleting menus and menu items

You can delete a specific item from a menu or an entire menu with the **delete** command. To delete a single item, you will use this syntax:

```
delete <menuItemDescriptor> from menu <menuIdentifier>
```

To remove an entire menu from the menu bar at once, use this syntax:

```
delete menu <menuIdentifier>
```

You can designate a menu item to be deleted any of several ways:

- by its name
- by its numbered position on the menu (that is, menuItem 3)
- by its ordinal position on the menu (that is, third menuItem)

Similarly, you can designate a menu by its name or by its numbered or ordinal position although as a practical matter you will almost always use its name for clarity.

Delete a Custom Menu

Back in the Laboratory, let's use the same card as in the previous exercise.

1. Open the card script of the same card you used to create the menu earlier.
2. Add a new handler to the script as follows:

```
on closeCard
    delete menu "Testing"
end closeCard
```

3. Close the editing window.
4. Change to a different card in the stack or close the stack. Notice that the menu disappears.
5. Create a new button on this card. Call it "Delete Menu Items" and attach to it the following handler:

```
on mouseUp
    delete item 3 of menu "Testing"
end mouseUp
```

6. Click on that button. Now look at the menu "Testing" and note that the third item is gone.
7. Close the card and then reopen it. Now look at the menu; the third item is restored because the **openCard** handler puts up a new version of the menu.

▶ Activating and deactivating menus and menu items

You have already had some experience with menu items that are inactive during certain times. For example, if you protect the stack, the "Compact Stack" option on the File menu becomes dimmed. Selecting it has no effect.

This kind of dynamic menu management is a key part of a well-designed Macintosh program. Any operation that you don't want the user to be able to perform under some circumstances and that is represented by a menu item must be disabled when those circumstances arise. Otherwise, users get frustrated trying to figure out when they can do certain things and when they can't.

In HyperTalk you use the **enable** and **disable** commands to handle this processing. The syntax for the commands is identical:

```
enable [menuItem <itemDescriptor> of] menu <menuDescriptor>
disable [menuItem <itemDescriptor> of] menu <menuDescriptor>
```

When a menu or menu item is disabled, its label is dimmed. Any attempt to select it via the mouse or keyboard (or a Command-key equivalent if it has one) or in a script will be unsuccessful. However, the **doMenu** command will still carry out HyperCard's built-in menu commands even when the menu or menu item has been deleted via a handler.

▶ Changing the appearance of a menu item

You can control the style (but not the font) of text used in a menu item. To italicize a menu item, for example, you can write a line of HyperTalk code like this:

```
set the textStyle of menuItem "Labels" of menu "Print" ¬
  to italic
```

You have probably seen Macintosh applications that used a checkmark or some other symbol in front of a menu item to indicate that it is the current selection in a group of related options. With custom HyperCard menus, you can define both the character to be used to create the checkmark and whether the checkmark is on or off for a particular menu item.

The syntax for determining the character to be used for a menu item's checkmark indicator is:

```
set the markChar of menuItem <itemIdentifier> of menu  ¬
    <menuIdentifier> to <char>
```

If you don't change it for a particular menu item, the default checkmark for all menu items is the checkmark (√).

To turn the checkmark on or off for a particular menu item, use the following syntax:

```
set the checkMark of menuItem<itemIdentifier> to ¬
    {true | false}
```

One appearance change you can make that also has functional implications is to attach to a menu item a Command-key equivalent. The most frequently used menu commands in well-designed Macintosh applications generally have a method of invoking them via the keyboard. By holding down the Command key and the letter "O" in HyperCard, for example, you invoke the "Open" menu item from the File menu. To give your menus the same functionality, you can use a command with syntax like this:

```
set the cmdChar of menuItem<itemIdentifier> of menu ¬
    <menuIdentifier> to "<char>"
```

You should be careful not to use the same Command-key equivalent for one of your custom menus as one used for a standard HyperCard built-in menu. If you do, the standard menu keyboard equivalent will not function. For example, if you write a line like the one below, then the Command-O key combination will no longer bring up the dialog for opening a file but instead will execute your custom menu's menuMsg:

```
set the cmdKey of menuItem "Orange" of menu "Colors" to "O"
```

▶ Changing the name of a menu or menu item

Some menu items act like toggles. For example, you might have a menu item called "Hide Detail." When the user has selected that item, it is no longer possible to hide the detail (since it is already hidden), so you need a new menu item called "Show Detail." You can do that in HyperTalk 2.0's custom menu routines by setting the menu item's name. The syntax for this command looks like this:

```
set the name of menuItem "Hide Detail" of menu "Options" ¬
to  "Show Detail"
```

Changing the menuMsg associated with a menu item

Some menus are context-sensitive, that is, their actions are dependent on the state of the system or some other factor rather than being fixed. You can dynamically alter the menuMsg sent when a menu item (custom or standard) is selected by changing it as if it were a property. The syntax for this command is:

```
set the menuMsg of menuItem <menuItem> to <message>
```

Using our earlier example, where we had a menu item called "Once," we could use this statement to change its function so that it put the word "once" into the message box:

```
set the menuMsg of menuItem "Once" of menu "Testing" to ¬
   "put once"
```

Activating a custom menu item

Like HyperCard's standard menu items, custom menu items can be invoked in any of three ways:

- by the user selecting a menu and an associated item with the mouse
- by the user typing a Command key equivalent if one is defined for a particular menu item
- from your script with the **doMenu** command

Modifying standard menus and menu items

You have complete control over the menus in HyperCard beginning with Version 2.0. This control includes the ability to delete, disable, or change the behavior of all of HyperCard's standard menus and menu items. The following principles apply both to standard and custom menus and menu items unless otherwise indicated.

If you delete a standard menu from the menubar, its menu items remain accessible via your scripts. If you delete a custom menu, you can no longer access its items by means of scripting commands. The menu does not appear on the menu bar and therefore doesn't exist as far as your scripts are concerned. But commands that affect the menu itself (for example, **enable** or **disable**) will not work for a deleted menu regardless of whether the menu is custom or standard.

Similarly, if you disable a menu or a menu item, you can still invoke any item on that menu or an individually disabled menu item with the **doMenu** command from your scripts even though neither of the normal methods of menu operation (mouse selection and Command key equivalent) will work.

You can use the **set** command to change the menuMsg associated with a standard HyperCard menu item. This means you can not only control whether the user can access a particular menu item or not, but what will happen when the user does invoke a particular menu item.

It is perfectly permissible for you to create a menu item with the same name as a standard HyperCard menu item. If you do this, its behavior will be identical to that of its namesake except that HyperCard will not automatically check, uncheck, enable, or disable such menu items as it does for the corresponding standard menu items. You can also create a menu item with the same name as a standard HyperCard menu item and associate it with a menuMsg that gives it different behavior, but if you leave both menu items enabled at the same time, the user could become quite confused trying to deal with your interface.

Relationship between doMenu and menuMsg

Whenever a menu item is selected or invoked, HyperTalk looks first for a **doMenu** handler which responds to the associated menu. If it doesn't find one, then it looks for a menuMsg attached to that menu item and executes it if it locates such a menuMsg.

This means you can use a menuMsg to override standard behavior of a standard or custom menu item and a **doMenu** handler to override both standard behavior and special behavior contained in a menuMsg.

▶ Restoring the menu bar

After you've customized the menus for your stack and you are returning the user to standard HyperCard operations, you can undo all your customization with a single command:

```
reset menuBar
```

This command will remove all of your custom menus, cause all HyperCard menus to reappear in their normal state and with their normal operations, and enable and disable all appropriate menu items.

▶ Using choose to Select HyperCard Tools

Many tools are available to the HyperTalk programmer and the HyperCard user at the authoring level and above. You may be wondering what we could possibly mean by *many*, given that there are only three basic tools: the browse tool, the button tool, and the field tool. During the creation of stacks, you use these tools frequently.

But from HyperCard's perspective, fifteen other tools are available. These are all painting tools. Figure 12-5 shows all of them, as they are arranged in the Tools tear-off menu, along with the name(s) by which each tool is called in a HyperTalk script.

The syntax for the **choose** command is:

```
choose <tool name> tool
```

The word *tool* is mandatory. The tool name must be spelled correctly according to the names shown in Figure 12-5.

▶ Duplicating tool use and menu calls

Sometimes you will want to do something that requires one of the general tools — the button tool or field tool — and you will assume the program should look something like this:

```
choose button tool
doMenu "New Button"
```

But that is not necessary. The **doMenu** command automatically selects the appropriate tool for its execution. So in this example you essentially end up selecting the button tool twice, which is inefficient.

▶ Using select to choose a tool and an object

In HyperCard versions above 1.2, a new command is included. Use the **select** command to pick a button or a field and simultaneously choose the appropriate tool. This command comes in handy if your script is designed to perform operations on specific objects. For example, to select a button named "Choose" for copying, you could either use the "old" approach

```
Choose button tool
click at the loc of button "Choose"
doMenu "Copy Button"
```

or the new approach

```
select button "Choose"
doMenu "Copy Button"
```

Either approach works, but the latter is much faster to program and execute.

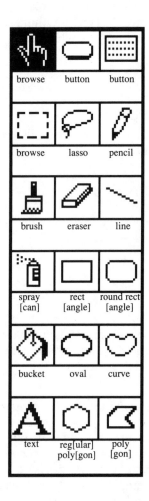

Figure 12-5. HyperCard tools and their HyperTalk names

▶ Returning to the browse tool

It is very important to return users to the browse tool after you have changed the current tool in your script. If you forget to do so, you may end up with frustrated users who suddenly find themselves unable to click buttons, activate fields, or type into the Message box. If your script, or someone else's script that you are using, should leave a tool other than the browse tool selected, press Command-Tab to return to the browse tool so you can correct the mistake.

▶ Using a container to name the tool

You can store the name of the tool you want to use in a HyperTalk container and then use the contents of the container to **choose** the desired tool. For example, suppose your script has a variable called **useTool**. Based on any number of events taking place in the stack, you might put any of several values into this container. Then one command can use the appropriate tool:

```
choose useTool tool
```

▶ Summary

In this chapter, you learned to access tools from inside HyperTalk scripts. You saw how to use the **doMenu** command. Then you looked at how to create and manipulate custom menus from within your HyperTalk scripts. Finally, you saw how to choose and use painting tools using the **choose** command.

In Chapter 13, you put these techniques and others to work in creating graphic and visual effects from within your scripts.

13 ▶ Graphic Commands, Pictures, and Visual Effects

In this chapter, you will learn

- how to program visual effects in a script
- when to use each visual effect
- how to create artistic paint effects in a script, including setting various painting properties
- how to animate objects on a card
- how to display PICT files as part of your stacks
- how to manage card- and background-level pictures

▶ A Graphic Computer

You've heard it a million times. The Macintosh is an all-graphics computer. Everything that appears on its screen, regardless of how much it looks like text, is graphics.

With that formality out of the way, let us say that HyperCard offers the casual user and application programmer more graphic capability and control than almost any other Macintosh program. If you've run through a few good stacks, you've seen these effects. They resemble television production techniques, which is no accident. If you don't know the names of these effects, get ready to learn about wipes and dissolves, barn doors and irises.

Beyond the visual effects HyperCard can use any time it moves from one card to another, HyperTalk programmers also have complete access to the paint tools and techniques that are such an integral part of HyperCard. As we saw in Chapter 12, you can choose different tools from the menu bar, and you can use the **doMenu** command to carry out any menu function. These techniques become particularly important as we turn our attention to the graphics power of HyperCard.

▶ Programming Visual Effects

Perhaps the most noticeable thing about a stack as compared to many other Macintosh applications and environments is the smooth transition from one card to another using sophisticated visual effects. Those visual effects can only be placed into a stack by writing HyperTalk handlers, so users, even at the authoring level, miss out on these capabilities. The command to cause these effects is **visual**, usually written in its full-name variation, **visual effect**. Its syntax is:

```
visual [effect] <effect name> [<speed>] ¬
[to black | white | gray |inverse |card]
```

We will explore each parameter to the **visual effect** command shortly. First, you need to understand some rules about its use and operation.

▶ Basic rules for the visual effect command

When HyperTalk encounters a **visual effect** command in a handler, it stores that effect and uses it the next time a card switch takes place. You also can, with HyperCard Version 1.2 and later, encapsulate visual effects within an **unlock screen** command, in which case the visual effect is executed immediately.

Generally, a card switch is dictated by a **go, find,** or **pop card** command that results in a different card being displayed. However, you can create a visual effect using a **go** command that goes to the same card in which the command is executed. In other words, if you have two lines like this

```
visual effect dissolve
go to this card
```

HyperCard displays the visual effect without the card changing. You seldom need to do this, however, particularly with HyperCard Version 1.2 and later, where you can create visual effects that seem to apply only to selected objects on a card.

To alter the visual effect HyperCard uses in the transition from card to card, you must include the **visual effect** command in your script before the next **go** or **find** command appears. Many HyperTalk programmers keep the **visual effect** command immediately before the card switching command whenever possible so that it is easier to find the effects later if they need modification.

During idle time — when HyperCard is between handlers and messages — any visual effect is forgotten. As a result, it is a good idea to include an initial **visual effect** for your stacks in a **stack open** handler.

If you are working with HyperCard Version 1.2 or later, you can also attach a visual effect to a specific object or group of objects by locking the screen, hiding or showing objects to which you want the visual effect to apply, then unlocking the screen with the visual effect as an argument. We see an example of this process later in this chapter.

Beginning with HyperCard Version 2.0, you can add visual effects to a stack without programming. The Button Info dialog contains a new button that allows you to define a visual effect to be associated with the activation of that button. Use of this option modifies the button's script.

▶ Effects you can program

The first parameter you must supply to the **visual effect** command is the name of the effect to be used. There are eleven basic effects, seven of which are associated with two or more directional descriptors. The eleven basic effects are

- **wipe**
- **scroll**
- **zoom**
- **iris**
- **barn door**
- **stretch**
- **shrink**
- **dissolve**
- **checkerboard**
- **venetian blinds**
- **plain**

The first seven effects in this list require that you define the direction of their animation. Both **wipe** and **scroll** have four directional descriptions: *up*, *down*, *left*, and *right*. The next three — **zoom, iris,** and **barn door** — permit you to instruct them to **open** or **close**. In the **zoom** effect, you can substitute **in** for **open** and **out** for **close**. *In* and *out* are television production terms that are often used in audio-visual circles to describe the **zoom** effect, so HyperCard permits you to use either the internally consistent **open** and **close** or the TV standards **in** and **out**. The **stretch** and **shrink** effects both allow you to specify that they operate to or from the top, bottom, or center of the screen.

The **plain** visual effect cancels any special effects and returns to normal card-to-card transitions. We discuss the visual impact of the other effects shortly.

▶ Varying the speed

Some effects can be made more dramatic or interesting by varying the speed with which they occur. HyperTalk recognizes four speed commands

- **very slow** (or **very slowly**)
- **slow** (or **slowly**)
- **fast**
- **very fast**

You probably won't notice much difference between **fast** and **very fast** except on a Macintosh II system.

▶ Changing the image

If you include the last parameter associated with the **visual effect** command, it is preceded by the key word **to** and followed by one of these words:

- **white**
- **gray**
- **black**
- **card**
- **inverse**

Most of the special effects you can program in HyperTalk do not benefit much from this parameter, but the use of black and gray as the image to which to make the transition can have a nice impact with the **dissolve** approach.

HyperCard moves through one of these intervening images as it moves to the next card. Thus, if you insert a command such as

```
visual effect dissolve to black
```

in a handler, the next card transition results in a totally black screen appearing for a moment, followed by the image of the next card.

▶ Chaining effects

For extra-special visual effects, you can chain these commands in a handler. HyperCard simply accumulates them and then executes them one at a time at each card transition. A fairly soft transition can be achieved by this combination:

```
visual effect dissolve to black
visual effect dissolve to white
```

This combination gives the impression of an image fading slowly and then reappearing in a new form.

▶ Flashing a card

One more effect occurs not on the next card transition but immediately when it is executed. The **flash** command inverts the Macintosh screen area occupied by HyperCard and then returns it to its original state. The command takes an optional numeric argument that tells it how many times to go through the flashing process.

The visual effect command in card switches

Open the Laboratory stack and create two new cards. Each should have a button approximately in the middle of the card. Then use the HyperCard paint tools to create some different shapes and patterns on each card. Fill a substantial part of the card with these patterns and be sure they are sufficiently different from one another to make it obvious which card you are looking at. (You don't need to get artistic. The idea is simply to have contrasting cards so that when you perform visual effects you can see clear transitions between cards.)

Next, follow these instructions:

1. Open the script-editing window of the card that has the lower number in the stack sequence. (If you're not sure which one this is, use the "Card Info..." option from the Objects menu.)

2. Type the following script into this editing window:

```
on mouseUp
    ask "What visual effect?"
    put it into request
    do "visual effect" && request
    go next
end mouseUp
```

3. Click on the OK button for that script, move to the next card, and open the script-editing window for its button.

4. Type the following script into this editing window (it is the same except for the **go** line, so you can use copy-and-paste methods to edit it):

```
on mouseUp
    ask "What visual effect?"
    put it into request
    do "visual effect" && request
    go prev
end mouseUp
```

5. Close the script-editing window by clicking OK. Use the left arrow at the bottom of the card (or any other method) to return to the first card.

6. Press the button. An **ask** dialog like that shown in Figure 13-1 appears.

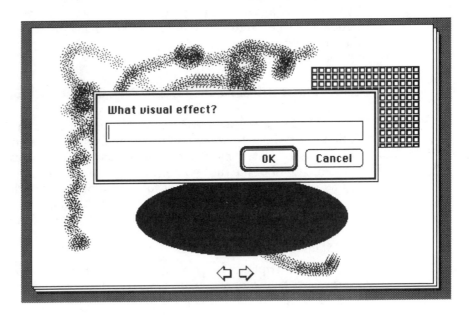

Figure 13-1. Visual effect testing ask dialog

7. Type in the following line in response to the query:

```
dissolve
```

8. Watch as the card dissolves into the next. Press the button on this card. Another dialog box appears. Enter into that dialog box:

```
zoom in slowly
```

9. You can repeat this sequence as many times as you like. If you enter a **visual effect** command that HyperTalk doesn't understand, it greets you with an error-alert box like that shown in Figure 13-2. Just click the Cancel button and go on.

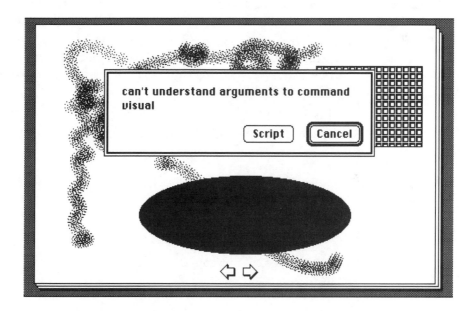

Figure 13-2. Error message during visual effect testing

▶ Using visual effect on objects

As we indicated earlier, you can cause HyperCard to use visual effects as it hides and shows various objects (buttons, fields, and pictures). The framework for the portion of a handler that would accomplish this task looks like this:

```
lock screen
-- hide or show one or more objects
unlock screen with visual effect dissolve
-- or other visual effect
```

All of the objects you hide or show while the **lock screen** command is in effect — that is, until the **unlock screen with visual effect** command is encountered — appear and disappear at the same time, using the single visual effect called for in the **unlock screen** command. You can include only one visual effect in this case. You cannot stack them as you can card-switch visual effects.

The visual effect command with objects

Open the Laboratory stack to any card with three or more card buttons on it. If you don't have such a card, create one. Resize two of the buttons so that they are large enough to be visible when the transitions take place.

1. Be sure that the buttons are numbered card button 1, 2, and 3 and that you use card buttons 2 and 3 as the buttons to hide and show. If necessary, use the **send farther** and **bring closer** menu items from the Objects menu to set up this alignment or create a new card.

2. Open the script window of card button 1.

3. Type the folowing script into this editing window:

```
on mouseUp
    lock screen
    hide card button 2
    wait 15
    unlock screen with visual effect dissolve
    lock screen
    hide card button 3
    show card button 2
    wait 15
    unlock screen with venetian blinds
    lock screen
    show card button 3
    wait 15
    unlock screen with checkerboard
end mouseUp
```

3. Click the OK button of the script-editing window.

4. Return to the browse tool if necessary.

5. Click card button 1.

▶ Choosing Visual Effects

With such a variety of visual effects, how do you decide which to use? The answer is complex. Many psychologists and media experts have spent years studying the issue of special effects and how they affect people. At the same time, much of the answer is quite subjective: What works for you may leave others cold, bewildered, or unfocused.

There are, however, some basic guidelines you can follow with some assurance that they will be successful, thanks in large part to research in this area. In the next few sections, we focus on the more traditional visual effects — scrolls, wipes, dissolves, irises, and zooms — and some tips about their usage. The others are more "gimmicky" effects. (We're not using the term *gimmicky effects* to demean them or to suggest they shouldn't be used. It is just a way to categorize them.) You should use them sparingly and primarily for variety.

▶ Scrolls

If you've experimented with scrolls — and if you haven't, you should go to the Laboratory and work through the previous experiment with some scrolls, especially at slow speeds — you probably had the feeling that the new card was shoving the old one out of the way. Scrolls are particularly effective when you want to make the browser feel that a change in content or emphasis has taken place with the transition, that the old is being bumped aside for the new topic. Scrolls are also effective in slide show presentation stacks, because the scroll is similar to a slide projector as it moves from slide to slide.

▶ Wipes

When you carry out a wipe, the browser's impression is of a card sliding into place over another card, rather than bumping another out of the way and replacing it (as with scrolls). As a result, wipes usually work best when you want transitions between cards that are less abrupt than those signaled by a scroll effect.

When the subject matter remains the same and you're providing additional content at about the same level of depth as the previous card, the wipe is a good effect to choose. Browsers feel like they are on the same level as before and that a new card has simply shuffled into view.

▶ Dissolves

The dissolve is one of the most artistic effects in HyperTalk and, as a result, is one of the most often used. It is also, unfortunately, one of the most abused.

You should consider a dissolve as representing a gradual transition in material or content between cards. In that respect, it is midway between wipes and scrolls. It gives the browser the feeling of one thing metamorphosing into another without any "rough edges" or clear borders.

Unlike most other effects, dissolves work best when there is either a great graphic contrast between cards or when only one small part of a design changes from one card to another.

▶ Irises and zooms

We'll discuss irises and zooms together because they are quite similar. The only difference is that a **zoom out** begins its "telescoping" where the mouse is clicked to activate the effect, and **iris open** always focuses on the center of the card.

Note ▶	Even though some documentation on the **zoom in** effect says that it returns to a point other than the center, that is not the case. A **zoom out** emanates from the point where the command is activated, but **zoom in**, like **iris close**, always goes to the center of the card.

An **iris open** and a **zoom out** give browsers the sense of going deeper into something. They are quite useful when browsers click on a button that takes them to a card displaying more detailed or focused information. The sensation is of a door opening as you walk through it. An **iris close** and a **zoom in** reverse that effect. If you use a series of **zoom in** or **iris close** effects to take browsers several levels into a stack, use a corresponding number of **zoom out** or **iris open** effects to bring them out.

The **zoom out** and **iris open** effects are also useful if you want to give the illusion of magnifying a small part of a card by moving to a card with a more detailed, close-up look at that portion.

▶ A general observation

None of these principles is hard and fast, of course. Occasionally there are good reasons to disregard them and do something out of the ordinary. Sometimes it is a good idea to have a graphic artist — particularly one with experience in film or TV — look at your stack and give you some advice.

If you think about the effect you want to create and the feeling you want the browser to have, and if you concentrate on keeping the effects simple and clean, you'll have no trouble designing interesting stacks that furnish your browser with visual cues as to what is going on.

▶ Painting from a Script

HyperCard's designer, Bill Atkinson, built in some very powerful painting capabilities. This is no surprise because Atkinson also wrote Apple's popular and widely emulated MacPaint program, the first software to show off the real power of bit-mapped graphics and the Macintosh interface.

All painting techniques available to the user at and above the painting level can also be accessed through HyperTalk commands in scripts. If your stack could benefit from animation on a single card, use the painting tools.

▶ Why paint in a script?

Most painting and artistic design takes place within the realm of stack development rather than stack use. By the time a user gets to the stack, the painting and drawing are done. In fact, of the dozens of scripts we have built and examined during the preparation of this book, not one undertook any artwork while the stack was executing. But in at least three circumstances, script-generated artwork may be a useful feature of HyperCard.

First, if you are designing a stack and are a better mathematician and programmer than an artist, you might want to write scripts that generate some of the graphics in your stack. This is particularly true if precision in the graphic is important. For example, if you need to draw a series of equidistant rectangles, writing a small script to do so is easier than creating a single rectangle, duplicating it, and moving it into the proper position.

Second, if one of the purposes of the stack is to enable the user to design something that requires graphics, you want to access the paint properties and tools we discuss in the rest of this chapter.

Finally, if the animation of objects on a single card has some value in your stack, you may want to be able to select and move an object within some constraints you establish.

▶ Choosing painting tools

Recall that in Chapter 12 we discussed the **choose tool** command. In that discussion, we pointed out that each painting tool has a distinct name by which it can be invoked and used. To refresh your memory, Figure 13-3 lists the tools as they appear in the tool palette, along with the HyperTalk names for each.

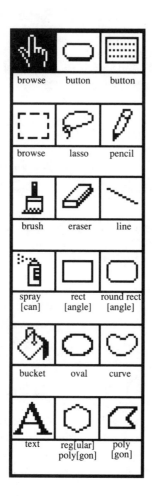

Figure 13-3. Paint tools and their HyperTalk names

To choose the paint brush, for example, just write a line like this in your script:

```
choose brush tool
```

Until you change the tool explicitly, the script will use the brush tool. You generally perform three basic functions with paint tools:

- **get** and/or **set** properties
- **click at** card locations with the tool
- **drag** the tool to card locations

▶ Paint properties

As you know from our discussion in Chapter 4, an important idea in Hyper-Card is *properties*. Many objects that make up the HyperCard world have properties associated with them. We take an in-depth look at properties and their management in Chapter 17. But for the moment, we will quickly examine the use of properties to carry out painting tasks in HyperTalk scripts.

Each property in HyperCard can assume a range of values. You can discover the current setting of a property with the **get** command:

```
get brush
```

You can change the current setting of a property with the **set** command, which generally takes the form:

```
set <property> value
```

For example, if you want to change the brush shape, just insert a HyperTalk command like this:

```
set the brush to 12
```

Table 13-1 summarizes all properties associated with painting tasks in HyperTalk and the range of values each can assume.

Table 13-1. Paint properties and their ranges

Property Name	Values
brush	1-32
centered	true or false
filled	true or false
grid	true or false
lineSize	1, 2, 3, 4, 6, or 8
multiple	true or false
multiSpace	1-9
pattern	1-40
polySides	number larger than 2
textAlign	left, right, center
textFont	font name
textHeight	numeric value
textSize	numeric value
textStyle	any combination of bold, italic, underline, outline, shadow, condense, extend, and plain

Most of these properties are self-explanatory, particularly if you've used the Options menu in HyperCard. Some, however, require further explanation.

The **brush** property can have any of 32 shapes. The shapes are numbered in the order in which the brush shapes are listed in the mini-palette that appears when you select Brush Shapes... from the Options menu or double-click on the brush tool. The brush shapes and their corresponding numbers are shown in Figure 13-4.

■	●	╱	╲	|	—	╱	⋮
1	5	9	13	17	21	25	29
■	●	╱	╲	|	—	╱	⋯
2	6	10	14	18	22	26	30
■	●	╱	╲	|	—	╱	⋰
3	7	11	15	19	23	27	31
■	•	╱	╲	|	—	·	▪
4	8	12	16	20	24	28	32

Figure 13-4. Brush shapes and their values

Line widths are set with the **lineSize** property, which can have a value of 1, 2, 3, 4, 6, or 8, corresponding to the line weights shown in Figure 13-5.

Figure 13-5. Line widths and their values

Similarly, **pattern** properties are numbered in a matrix that matches the pattern palette that appears under the Pattern menu and which may be torn off to be available during paint operations. Pattern numbering begins in the upper left-corner with the number 1 and continues down the first row to 10. It then resumes numbering at 11 with the top pattern in the second column, and so forth. Figure 13-6 depicts the standard paint patterns and their numbering scheme.

Figure 13-6. Patterns and their values

The **multiSpace** property determines how many pixels to leave between each copy of a shape generated as the tool used to create it is dragged through a drawing area when **multiple** is set to true.

The **polySides** property determines the shape of the regular polygon to be drawn when that tool is selected. The property may have any numeric value larger than 3. The higher the number, the more nearly the shape approaches that of a circle.

Finally, the **textStyle** property sets combinations of characteristics for text as follows:

```
set textStyle to bold,italic,underline
```

One more property is not strictly a paint property, but its use is primarily confined to painting activities. It is referred to as a global property and is a member of a group of properties discussed in Chapter 17. Its name is **dragSpeed** and it can take any numeric value you like, though experience shows that values larger than 144 cannot be distinguished by most people. When used with the **multiple** and **multiSpace** properties, **dragSpeed** can determine how regularly spaced your drawings look when you use multiple images.

Properties, then, determine the characteristics of drawings produced with basic paint commands. After you set the properties and select the tool, drawing is a matter of clicking, dragging, or both, depending on what you want to accomplish.

▶ Clicking and coordinates

The standard nine-inch Macintosh screen consists of a collection of addresses 512 pixels wide and 342 pixels deep. Each position on the screen is addressed by a two-part number. The first part is the horizontal location, or coordinate, and the second is the vertical. They are separated by a comma. The upper-left corner of the screen is address 0,0, and the lower-right corner is 512,342.

In Chapter 7, we saw how the **click** command could be used with a set of coordinates to simulate button-pressing. You can also use the **click** command to select a location on a card that does not contain a button or a field. You can then execute a painting command, using the clicked-at location as the starting point.

Most of the time, you will only use **click** to draw with tools that do not work by dragging. The text tool and the bucket tool do not work by dragging.

▶ Painting special effects

In HyperCard 2.0, Apple Computer added four special effects to the arsenal of paint tools available. These special effects are

- Rotate

- Slant

- Distort

- Perspective

You can invoke these special effects in your scripts by following this step-by-step process:

1. Choose an appropriate shape tool.

2. Use the **drag** command to draw the shape.

3. Choose the *select* tool.

4. Drag a region large enough to encompass the entire shape you've drawn.

5. Use the **doMenu** command to choose the right special effect.

6. Use the **drag** command to cause the special effect to be created.

7. Don't forget to return to the browse tool when you're done.

Here's a sample script that draws a small rectangle and then rotates it counter-clockwise:

```
on mouseUp
   choose rectangle tool
   drag from 50,50 to 100,200
   choose select tool
   drag from 40,40 to 110,210 -- note larger rectangle
   doMenu "Rotate"
   drag from 110,210 to 70,70
   choose browse tool
end mouseUp
```

Dumping paint and drawing text

We'll use the Message box for our next experiment, though you can also create a button script for it. In the Laboratory stack, create a new, blank card containing only the background arrows. Open the Message box if it isn't already visible and type the following sequence of instructions, observing what happens after each:

```
choose rectangle tool
drag from 150,150 to 300,200
choose bucket tool
set pattern to 6
click at 151,151
```

The result should look like Figure 13-7. The bucket tool, as you probably know, simply spreads its associated pattern from the point where it is clicked to the borders of the area in which it is clicked.

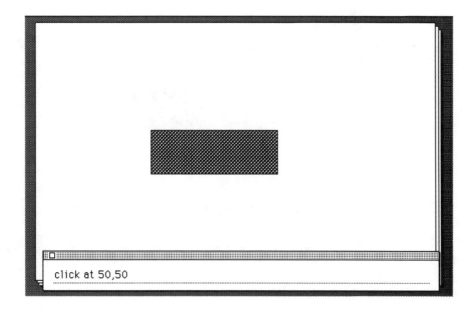

Figure 13-7. Using the bucket tool and the click command

Stay in the same Laboratory stack, with the same card showing, and type the following commands in the Message box, observing what happens after each:

1. choose text tool

2. set textFont to "Times" — use a font you have installed

3. set textSize to 18

4. set textStyle to bold,italic

5. click at 50,50

At this point, the cursor should be flashing near the upper-left corner of the card. Anything you type at this point is displayed on the card using the text characteristics you set with instructions 2-4.

Figure 13-8 shows what happens when you type the words *this is a demonstration of painting text*.

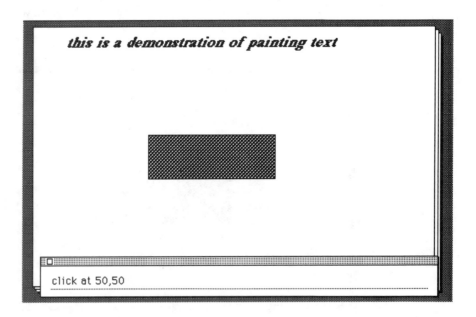

Figure 13-8. Using commands to add painted text to a card

To return control to the Message box, you have to click in it because anything you type at this point is displayed on the card.

▶ Dragging tools for effect

All painting tools, except the text and bucket tools, are used by dragging them from one location to another. Depending on whether the **centered** property is true or not, painting tools draw a shape that starts at the first set of coordinates and ends at the second, or they draw a shape centered on the first set of coordinates and extending in one direction to the second set.

We have already seen the rectangle tool used with the **drag** command to create a place to dump paint from the bucket. But just to be sure we understand what's going on with the **drag** command, here is its syntax:

```
drag from <point> to <point> [with <key>[,<key>]]
```

The point parameters are two-number coordinate addresses, with the numbers separated by a comma. You can specify one or more keys that will be simulated as held down during the drag. Here are some examples of the **drag** command:

```
drag from pt1 to pt2 with shiftKey,optionKey
drag from 0,0 to 512,342
drag from 50,50 to 200,275 with commandKey
```

Although a discussion of all the painting techniques in HyperCard is beyond the scope of this book, it might help to refresh your memory about the use of the special keys with paint operations.

If you **drag** with the **shiftKey** parameter, you constrain the movement of the dragging to the 15-, 45-, or 90-degree axis in which it begins movement. The angle of constraint depends on the shape and the tool, but in general you can think of the Shift key as being a constraint key.

Dragging with the **optionKey** parameter makes a copy of the selected item(s) and drags the copy. If you are using the lasso tool to drag with the **optionKey** parameter, lasso operates differently from its normal use. Generally, using the lasso tool on an object selects only the object and not the surrounding white pixels. But if you use the lasso, press the Option key, and then drag to select an area, the white pixels are also selected.

Using the usual selection marquee tool to **drag** with the **commandKey** parameter, the marquee "hugs" the outline of the enclosed item rather than selecting everything inside the marquee. This technique is particularly helpful if you know within a small tolerance the location of a painted item on the card, but need some margin of error.

If you are dragging with drawing tools such as any of the shapes (filled or not), use the **optionKey** parameter to cause the drawing to take place in the currently selected pattern rather than in black. To refresh your memory about the use of special keys with paint tools, refer to the *Macintosh HyperCard User's Guide* from Apple Computer.

Brush painting and drawing with a border

Get a clean Laboratory stack card, open the Message box if it isn't already visible, and type the following commands into the Message box, observing what happens after each:

1. choose brush tool

2. set brush to 5

3. set pattern to 12

4. drag from 60,60 to 350,60

5. drag from 80,60 to 280,60 with commandKey

After step 4, the screen looks like Figure 13-9. After step 5, the screen looks like Figure 13-10. When the Command key is held down while the paint brush is in use, it reverses the pattern and essentially erases what lies under it.

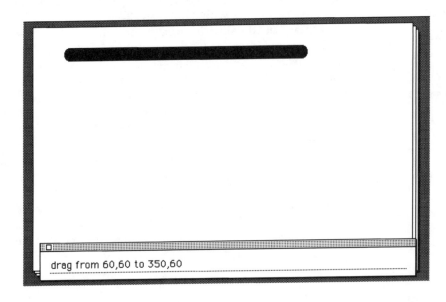

```
drag from 60,60 to 350,60
```

Figure 13-9. Screen after regular paint brush use

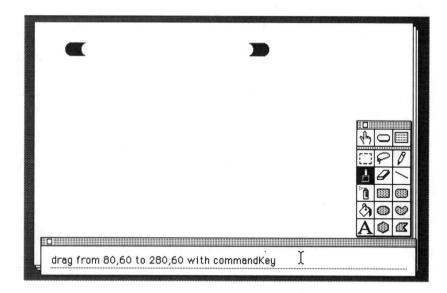

Figure 13-10. Screen after Command-key paint brush use

Stay in the Laboratory stack and either create a new blank card or simply erase the contents of the one you just used. (Remember you can double-click on the eraser tool to erase all the graphics in the current layer.) Now type the following instructions into the Message box and observe what happens after each:

```
set the filled to false
drag from 50,50 to 150,150
drag from 160,50 to 260,150 with optionKey
```

Notice that using the Option key while dragging a drawing tool causes the line to be drawn in the currently selected pattern.

▶ Animation with Selecting and Dragging

The last topic we will cover in this chapter is the use of selection and dragging to make objects in HyperCard appear animated. Generally, the process of animating HyperCard paint objects involves three steps:

1. Select the item(s) to be moved. This sometimes involves a simple process using **doMenu**, but other times it is more complicated.

2. Set the **dragSpeed** to a rate that is appropriate to the effect you want to achieve. You can only really find this value by trial and error. Start with something like 100 and work from there.

3. Use **drag** to move the object.

You may also want to be sure the object reverts to its original position when the animation sequence is finished.

▶ Selecting items to animate

If the object you want to animate is the only paint object on the card or you want to animate all the painted objects, the selection process is greatly simplified. Choose a painting tool, then carry out these two instructions:

```
doMenu "Select All"
doMenu "Select"
```

(The reason for the first menu command selection is that if you haven't de-selected the last object drawn, the **doMenu "Select"** command automates only that object.) A **doMenu "Select All"** command de-selects any object that may be selected. A subsequent **doMenu** call then selects all the painted objects on the screen and prepares them for animated movement.

   If there are multiple objects on the screen and you only want to animate one of them, you must use one of the other selection methods. Use a **choose tool** command to switch to the marquee (select tool) or the lasso. Then **click** and **drag**, using the **optionKey** parameter, to select the object.

▶ Setting dragSpeed

The **dragSpeed** property can take almost any value. If it is set to 0, it is at the fastest speed. At that speed, the movement of objects is not smooth and gradual. Instead, the object disappears from one point and instantly reappears at the other. If that's the effect you want, use a **dragSpeed** of 0.

For the most part, though, you will want a speed between 72 (which is quite slow) and about 400 (which is smooth and fast). You'll have to experiment with various speed settings to decide what works best for a given effect.

After you select a speed, use the **set** command to assign it to the **dragSpeed** property:

```
set dragSpeed to 200
```

▶ Using drag to move objects

We've already covered the **drag** command. When you use the **drag** command in animation, you must make sure your starting point for the dragging motion is within the boundaries of the object you want to move. You will also want to ensure that you don't drag some portion of the image beyond HyperCard's boundaries so that it becomes partially invisible.

Animation experiment

Return to the card you used for the last experiment or create a new one with one or two rectangles near the upper-left corner of the card area. If you create a new object, be sure to choose the Keep option from the Paint menu. This ensures that when you revert to the image, the objects return to this position. Then follow these instructions:

1. Create a new button called Animate it! and position it wherever you like on the card.

2. Open this newly created button's script-editing window by one of the usual methods.

3. Type in the following script:

```
on mouseUp
   choose select tool
   doMenu "Select"
   set dragSpeed to 200
   drag from 100,100 to 300,200
   drag from 300,200 to 350,100
   doMenu "Select All"
   doMenu "Revert"
   choose browse tool
end mouseUp
```

4. Click OK and then activate the button. Watch as the objects move from the upper-left corner to the right-center portion of the card to the upper-right corner, pause for a moment, and then return to their original location.

▶ Managing Pictures on Cards and Backgrounds

Beginning with HyperCard Version 1.2, you have the ability to hide and show all the artwork you have created on a given card or background. All the art you create in Version 1.2 or later, or that is contained on stacks designed using an earlier version, then compacted using Version 1.2 or later, is defined as a single picture for each card or background. In other words, if you create some paint text and graphic shapes on a card, the entirety of that artwork is defined and managed as a card-level picture. The same is true of artwork on a background.

You have no choice in the matter; the artwork is treated as a single unit for the purposes of the commands discussed in this section. You cannot hide and show selective portions of the card or background art with these commands.

If you wish to hide the picture on a card, you can use one of two forms of the **hide** command. To hide the art on the currently visible card, write:

```
hide card picture
```

If the card whose picture you wish to hide is not the currently visible card, you must use the alternate form of the command:

```
hide picture of <card description>
```

For example, to hide the picture on the fourth card in the current stack before going to that card, you could write a command like this:

```
hide picture of card 4
```

The same logic applies to showing a card-level picture. The current card's picture can be shown by the command

```
show card picture
```

but to show the picture on another card you must designate that card with a description:

```
show picture of <card description>
```

Background pictures have their own set of equivalent commands. To hide the art on the current background, write:

```
hide background picture
```

To hide the background picture on a different background, designate that background by a description:

```
hide picture of <background description>
```

Showing background pictures works similarly.

Because a picture is treated in some respects as if it were an object, it can be shown and hidden in concert with visual effects. Earlier in the chapter, we talked about the **lock screen** and **unlock screen with visual effects** commands. You can use those commands with the **hide** and **show** commands discussed in this section to achieve some interesting visual effects without changing cards.

▶ Displaying Picture Files

Beginning with HyperCard 2.0, you can display picture files stored outside HyperCard within a special window using the **picture** command. (In reality, **picture** is an external command, or XCMD, supplied with HyperCard 2.0 rather than an integrated change to the program. But the flexibility of external routines, which we will discuss in the final chapter of this book, enables you as a HyperCard designer to ignore this distinction.) The syntax of the **picture** command is as follows:

```
picture where, [file | clipboard | resource], windowStyle, ¬
  windowPosition, origin, dither
```

The first parameter, *where*, is the name of the file or resource containing the picture you wish to display. Pictures can be of either of the two most popular types of picture formats: PICT (for object drawings such as those produced by most CAD/CAM programs and such products as MacDraw II from Claris Corporation) or PNTG (bitmapped paint files such as those produced by MacPaint from Claris Corporation).

For the second parameter, you describe the location of the file or resource containing the picture. Note that you can have one of three literal parameters in this position.

You next describe the type of window in which you wish the picture to be displayed, choosing from among the following valid types:

- plain
- rect
- zoom
- dialog
- shadow

- roundRect
- windoid

The *windowPos* argument must contain a rectangle (that is, a four-item numeric list with commas separating the items) that describes where you would like to position the window containing the picture. If you define a rectangle that is not on the present screen or if you omit this argument, HyperCard will use a default rectangle. If you are using a multiscreen system, you can even tell HyperCard to position the picture in the most advantageous place by use of one of these parameters in this position:

- *card*, which tells HyperCard to center the picture on the same screen as the card window

- *biggest*, which will center the picture on the screen with the largest area

- *deepest*, which will center the picture on the screen with the greatest depth of color display available

- *main*, which will center the picture on the screen where the menu bar is located

You can choose to show some portion of the picture in a window that has a smaller rectangular area than the picture itself. If you do that, you'll need to tell HyperCard where to position the corner of the window with respect to the picture. The *origin* argument serves this purpose. It is a point, defined in the picture's terms (that is, its upper-left corner is defined as 0,0).

The final argument is useful only if you are running on a system with 32-bit Color QuickDraw installed. It defines whether the display uses a technique called *dithering* to increase the number of apparent colors available to show the picture.

By default, the **picture** command assumes the picture is stored in a file. If you don't supply a name or a location type, it will present a standard file-open dialog for the user to pick the picture file. It also assumes a window style of zoom, an origin of 0,0, and no dithering.

▶ Managing and manipulating picture windows

The window created by the use of the **picture** command is an external window. We discuss the concept and use of external windows in greater depth in Chapter 21; all of that discussion applies to picture windows.

Briefly, you can send messages to picture windows to cause them to zoom, scroll, move, close, and resize, among other things. You can also set properties of these windows much as you can other HyperCard objects.

In addition, there is a special message associated with picture windows called **pictureClick** that lets you intercept user mouse-clicks in the picture window and decode their location. You can thus use pictures as an integral part of the user interface in your HyperCard stack applications. This message has the following parameters:

```
pictureClick (<windowName>, <horizontal>, <vertical>)
```

You must write one or more **on pictureClick** handlers to respond to the mouse-clicks at various locations. For example, in an educational stack you might present the student with a color picture of the heart and ask the student to click on the left ventricle. By decoding the click location, you can determine if the student's response is correct or not and respond accordingly.

▶ Summary

In this chapter, you were introduced to the use of visual effects and graphic commands from within HyperTalk scripts. You saw how to use **visual effect** commands and variations and learned something about when and where they are best used. You also examined the use of graphic tools and their associated commands. In addition, you learned about properties and how they are changed to create specific graphic images. You saw how **click** and **drag** working together with selected objects can be used to animate objects on cards. Finally, you got a brief glimpse at how to use the **picture** command to display painting and drawing files and resources in a special window that you can then manipulate and with which your users can interact.

Chapter 14 explores another area of creativity in HyperTalk, the use of sound and music in scripts.

14 ▶ Sound and Music Basics

In this chapter, you will learn how to use the

- **beep** command
- **play** command
- **sound** function

You will also gain some insight into the appropriate use of sound in Hyper-Card stacks.

▶ Using the beep Command

We have used the **beep** command throughout this book without providing a formal explanation of its use. One is probably not mandatory at this point. But let's note its syntax for the record:

```
beep  [<number>]
```

The number you supply can be a numeric value, an expression that evaluates to a numeric value, or a container that holds a numeric value. If you don't supply a number, HyperCard assumes you want a single beep.

The only "tricky" thing about the **beep** command is that if you want to use multiple beeps to alert the user to different conditions, you may find that HyperCard's timing puts them too close to differentiate them. That's particularly true if you use more than five beeps.

If you need a large number of beep sounds in a script, you should probably put them into a **repeat** loop (see Chapter 8). An example of such a loop might look like this:

```
on mouseUp
   repeat with counter=1 to 15
      beep
      wait 30 -- 30 "ticks", about 1/2 second
   end repeat
end mouseUp
```

The half-second delay in this loop might be too long or short for your purposes. You can supply almost any value for the **wait** command.

The **beep** command has limited application. It can't vary in duration or pitch, so it can't be used for music. But it can be quite useful as an audible device to get the browser's attention when he or she has done something untoward.

▶ Using the play Command

If you've explored many HyperCard stacks, you've probably come across a range of sound effects people have used to make their applications more interesting or fun. HyperCard has one of the most powerful and versatile sound-reproducing capabilities of any programming language we know.

The **play** command is one of the most complex in HyperTalk. It can have as many as five separate sets of arguments, and one of them can contain a large number of individual notes, so the commands tend to be long.

Here is the basic syntax of the **play** command:

```
play "sound" [tempo <speed>] [<notes>]
```

As you can see, the only mandatory parameter to the **play** command is the first one, called "sound." The sound parameters must be enclosed in quotation marks and must match exactly the name of the sound resource to be used (more on sound resources later in this chapter). Let's look briefly at each optional parameter.

▶ Tempo

The **tempo** parameter applies only to a series of at least two sounds. It dictates how quickly the notes are played after one another. If you don't supply a value for the speed, preceded by the key word **tempo**, HyperTalk uses a tempo of 200. This is considered an average tempo, a little faster than a waltz is usually played. Above the value of 800 or so on a Macintosh Plus, the notes simply blend into one another. Increasing the number after that has little or no audible effect.

Unfortunately, there is no relationship between HyperCard's **tempo** settings and any standard musical measurement. In music, the term *tempo* means "beats per minute," but that is not the case with the **tempo** parameter in the **play** command. You'll just have to experiment with ranges of values to see what works for each composition you use.

▶ Notes

You will almost always want to give HyperTalk one or more musical notes to play when you use the **play** command, though it is not mandatory that you do so. If you do not supply a note (that is, if you simply use the **play** command with a sound name), HyperCard uses middle C as the note.

The string of notes you want played must be enclosed in quotation marks. You can have (theoretically) as many notes as you like. Each note has the following syntax:

```
<name>[# | b] [<octave no.>] [<duration>]
```

For the name of the note, use the name of the note on the scale, just as you'd expect. The seven letters a, b, c, d, e, f, and g are used to name the notes of the scale.

Each note name can be optionally followed by an *accidental*. This is a special symbol for a sharp or a flat. A note that has a sharp accidental is played one-half step higher in the scale than the name of the key indicates. A flat note is played one-half step lower than expected. In HyperTalk music notation, the pound sign (#) signifies a sharp, and a lowercase letter *b* signifies a flat.

Using this notation and starting with middle C on the piano keyboard, the next few notes up the scale could be written as follows:

```
c c# d d# e f f# g ab a bb b
```

We have deliberately mixed the use of the sharp (#) and flat (b) signs so you see how they look. All the intermediate notes have two names, one refers to the note below and uses a sharp symbol, and one refers to the note above and uses the flat symbol. This means A-sharp and B-flat are the same note.

The octave number tells HyperCard where along the piano keyboard to play the note. The piano is divided into collections of octaves spanning from one C note to the next and encompassing seven keys. The octave that starts with middle C is referred to as octave 4 because it's the fourth up from the lowest C note on the piano. The octave beginning with the C note that is one octave up from middle C is the first note of octave 5.

If you don't supply an octave number, HyperCard uses octave 4. After you change the octave, however, the change stays in effect until you insert another octave number in the note string.

The duration parameter uses something akin to standard musical notation, allowing you to use the first letter of the spelled-out name of the note duration. Thus, a quarter note is signaled by a *q* and an eighth note by an *e*. You can add a period after any duration to extend its value by 50% (the equivalent of dotted notes).

Table 14-1 shows you several musical notes expressed in HyperTalk notation, their English names, and their musical notation.

Table 14-1. Some musical notes in HyperTalk, English, and music

HyperTalk	English	Music
g#e	G-sharp, octave 4, 8th note	
c5h.	C, octave 5, dotted half note	
aq	A, octave 4, quarter note	
bbt	B-flat, octave 4, 32nd note	

Notes in HyperTalk can also be represented as numeric values, in which case the octave and accidental parameters are not used. Middle C has a numeric value of 60, and each step up or down represents a half-step. Thus, the E above middle C is 64, B-flat is 70, and the C one octave above middle C (the one that starts octave 5) is 72. You still need duration values unless you are happy with HyperTalk's defaults.

One advantage of using numeric values for notes is that you can calculate sounds, enabling you to play scales and other mathematically related musical groups in a loop. You can also set up generic loops that work from a starting numeric value and play major scales, minor scales, and transposed tunes.

Some familiar tunes

For our next exercise, we need a Laboratory stack card with a single field and a single button. **The field can be c**alled Field 1 and the button should be named Play It! (just for variety). Either create a new card or modify an existing one. Make Field 1 big enough to accommodate several lines of typing. Now follow these instructions:

1. Open the script-editing window for the Play It! button in one of the usual ways.

2. Type in the following short script and click OK when you've proofread it:

```
on mouseUp
    do "play" && "Harpsichord" && card field 1
end mouseUp
```

(We use the *harpsichord* sound here because it is one of the built-in sounds in HyperTalk and because it comes the closest of any of those sounds to playing notes that sound like music rather than sound effects.)

3. Return to Browse mode.

4. The melody lines for several well-known musical tunes written in HyperTalk notation follow. Pick one and type it *carefully* into Field 1 of the experiment card.

5. Press the Play It! button.

If all goes well, you will hear the melody line you chose played with HyperCard's harpsichord sound. You can change the instrument or voice by a simple edit of the button's script. (Some of these tunes could stand some tempo improvement. You can easily modify the button script to take care of this if the tempo jars your ears.)

Here are the melody lines:

1. "America, the Beautiful"

```
gq gq. ee eq g gq. de dq e f g a b gh. gq gq. ee eq g gq.
de dq d5 c5# d5 e5 a4 d5h g4q e5q. e5e dq c5q cq. b4e bq
c5 d b4 a g c5h. c5q cq. a4e aq c5q cq. g4e gq g a c5 g4
d5 ch.
```

2. "When the Saints Go Marching In"

cq e f gw gq cq e f gw gq cq e f gh e c e dw dh eq d ch.
cq eh gq g g fw fq eq f gh e c d cw cq e f gw gq cq ef gw
gq cq e f gh e c e dw dh eq d ch. cq eh gq g g fw fq eq f
gh e c d cw

3. "Skip to M'Lou"

bq b g g be b bq d5h a4q a f# f# ae a aq c5h b4q b g g be
b bq d5h a4q be c5e b4q a gh gq

4. "Frère Jacques" (3 rounds)

cq d e c c d e c e f gh eq f gh ge a g f eq c ge a g f eq
c c g3 c4h cq g3 c4h cq d e c c d e c e f gh eq f ghge a
g f eq c ge a g f eq c c g3 c4h cq g3 c4h cq d e c c d e
c e f gh eq f gh ge a g f eq c ge a g f eq c c g3 c4h cq
g3 c4h

▶ The play stop variation

Because the **play** command continues executing while other script commands
are carried out, you can sometimes find sound effects being played at inappropriate times. If you want to control some precise time when the sound
should simply stop playing, use the *stop* parameter. The command **play stop**
immediately stops whatever sound is playing. If no sound is playing, no action
is taken but no error results.

▶ Sound Resources and HyperTalk

When you receive HyperCard from your Apple dealer, it has four built-in
sounds: harpsichord, boing, silence, and dialing tones. You can supply any of
these as the sound name in a **play** command and get a response (though in the
case of the **silence** choice, it will be hard to tell unless you intersperse it with
other sounds). But there are dozens of other sound effects available for
inclusion in stacks. Where do these come from and how are they used?

To answer that question, we need to explain that all sound effects accessed
by **play** commands must be stored as *resources*. (If you don't know what resources are, don't panic. In Chapter 21 we take a close look at them. For now,

just think of them as stored instructions that have a name associated with them.) Each resource that has a type called 'snd ' can be used by HyperTalk as a sound effect. What is actually stored in the sound resource is a waveform pattern that describes the sound to HyperCard.

If you have a sound resource called, for example, *applause*, you can create a command like this:

```
play "applause"
```

HyperTalk finds the resource and plays the sound it finds represented there.

Sound resources can be copied from other stacks, other Macintosh programs, and special files of sound effects that you can obtain from electronic bulletin board systems (BBSs), user groups, and similar places. They are often created by digitizing real sounds using one of several pieces of Mac software.

In Chapter 21 we examine resources and how HyperCard accesses and uses them. We also discuss how you can move a resource from another stack or application into your stack or even the HyperCard Home stack, where more than one stack in your HyperCard environment can access it.

▶ Testing the Sound

When HyperCard encounters a **play** command, it starts the sound and then continues with processing even while the sound continues to play unless you issue the **play stop** command. You can thus have "background music" behind your script as it executes. This is a nice feature of sound effects in HyperCard.

Sometimes you want the sound to be more synchronized with the screen's activity. Controlling the sound's pace to match the screen action can be tricky. To assist in this process, HyperTalk includes a function called **the sound**. Like all HyperTalk functions, it requires no parameters and returns a value. The value it returns is the name of the currently playing sound or the string "done" if no sound is playing.

You can use this function to control a loop as follows:

```
repeat until the sound is "done"
   <statements>
end repeat
```

Alternatively, you can use **the sound** in a conditional processing structure so that nothing happens until the sound is finished playing:

```
repeat
   if the sound is "done" then
      <statements>
   else wait 1 -- or any other reasonable number
end repeat
```

(In this example, the statements should include an **exit repeat** and may consist of only that command depending on what you are trying to accomplish.)

▶ Using Sound Effects Wisely

Like any good thing, sound effects can be overdone. On the Macintosh, with its wonder**ful sound capabilities, it is** an easy thing to do. But you should guard against using sound in a way that confuses the browser.

Unless the stack's primary purpose is to perform music or create or reproduce sound effects, you should only use the **play** command where it will add value to the stack from the browser's viewpoint.

For example, in a stack designed to quiz a child about the letters of the alphabet, playing the well-known "Alphabet Song" at the beginning and end will probably be well received by the young browser. But if you play the song every time he or she gets a question right, you're going to bore the tot.

Associating single sounds with buttons can add dimension to your stacks. browsers become accustomed to hearing a certain sound as they move "down" into a stack for more information and a different sound signaling that they are moving "up" toward the top and the beginning of their browsing experience.

▶ Summary

In this brief chapter, you learned how to use **beep** and **play** commands to create sound effects from the si**mple to the** symphonic. You also saw how to use **the sound** to determine when a sound effect is finished playing so you can proceed with another aspect of your script where the sound is unneeded or unwanted. In Chapter 15, we shift our attention to mathematics.

15 ▶ Math Functions and Operators

In this chapter, you will learn about a host of HyperTalk functions and operators that enable your scripts to perform mathematic operations. These include tools to perform

- simple arithmetic calculations
- number manipulation
- advanced mathematics, including trigonometry
- financial math

▶ An Aside to Mathephobes

Many people put off learning more about computers because computers seem so inherently mathematical. But a majority of computer programs involve no math more complicated than you probably learned in the fourth or fifth grade. Still, *mathephobia* is a sufficiently widespread phenomenon that many high schools and community colleges offer courses in how to overcome it. They report the courses are jammed and the students largely successful.

Let us be clear at the outset about the role of mathematics in programming most HyperTalk applications. First, you don't need to learn any math to program in HyperTalk. If you have an occasional need to perform a simple calculation, you can quickly and easily look up the proper operator or function, use it with minimal understanding, and go on with your life as if math never existed. If you want to skip this chapter, feel free to do so. We promise you won't hurt our feelings.

Second, HyperTalk takes some of the "scary stuff" out of math by making operations more English-like and by reducing the number of special characters (operators) necessary. You might find that learning a little about math using HyperTalk isn't nearly as difficult as you may now think.

▶ How Numbers Are Represented

In the discussions in this chapter, we will deal with numbers. Functions and operators work on numbers, and they produce numbers. A number in HyperTalk is stored as a string of characters, all of which are numeric. A number can be up to 73 characters long, which means it can have 73 digits if it's positive and 72 (to allow for the minus sign) if it's negative. It's not likely you'll need larger numbers than these! If you attempt to calculate a value that exceeds this maximum, HyperTalk returns a question mark as the answer.

Any number used in this chapter can be thought of as being represented in the Macintosh in any of the following ways:

- a number stored as text (for example, 17234511.2)

- a container holding a number stored as text (for example, sumTotal)

- an expression containing numbers and operators that evaluates to a number (for example, 2 + 8, which evaluates to the number 10)

This last case is a special situation. If a field on a card contains an expression such as 2+8, and you really want to put the result of *evaluating* that expression into your math calculations, you must use the HyperTalk **value** function. The **value** function evaluates a string containing numbers and (usually) operators and returns the numeric value. (In a moment, we'll have more to say about the concept of returning a value.)

If card field 3 contains an arithmetic expression such as 2+8, and you want to put its value into a container called *temp1*, you could do so this way:

```
put value(card field 3) into temp1
```

When HyperTalk encounters this command in your script, it looks in card field 1, finds the arithmetic expression there (it must be the only thing in the field if you've addressed the entire field as in the example), carries out its calculations, and does what it's told with the result.

Another aspect of representing numbers follows HyperTalk's pattern of making programs more readable. Instead of using the digits 0, 1, 2, and so forth, you can write out their names: zero, one, two, and so on, up to ten. You can enter expressions like this

```
put three + nine into answer
```

and expect the value of *answer* to be 12. You can even concatenate these numbers to make larger numbers (that is, one and three combine to make 13).

Beginning with HyperCard 2.0, you can also ensure that a container is numeric before you attempt to perform a math operation on it. Use the **is a number** function to test for a numeric value.

We should point out that the way a specific number is represented can be affected by the setting of a global property called **numberFormat**. This value determines the number of decimal points of precision to which the number will be displayed and used in calculations. We discuss this property in more detail in Chapter 17.

▶ Bringing Order to Things Numeric

Mathematicians spend a lot of time dealing with — and designing systems to avoid — ambiguity. An ambiguous situation arises in mathematics when there are two or more ways to evaluate an expression. For example, if we gave the problem 2+4+8*3 to two different students, one might answer 42 and the other might answer 30. The first student added the first three numbers and then multiplied their sum, 14, by 3. The second student decided to multiply 8 and 3 first, then add this result to the other two numbers. Both are reasonable results. But if you put the problem to HyperTalk, it will reply, unequivocally, 30.

That outcome is determined by something mathematicians call *precedence*. The term applies to decisions about what mathematic operations will be carried out in what order. HyperTalk, not unlike many other languages, applies some fairly simple rules of precedence:

1. Operations contained within parentheses are performed before those outside parentheses.

2. Exponentiation (raising a number to a power, which is discussed under "Advanced Math Operations") is the highest-priority math operator.

3. Multiplication and division are the next most important math operators.

4. Addition and subtraction are the least important math operators.

5. When you have operators of equal precedence, perform calculations from left to right.

There are many nonmathematic operators among HyperTalk's total set of rules about precedence, but these are the ones that concern us here. Now you can see why HyperTalk got 30 when it evaluated the expression 2+4+8*3. It scanned the line and found a multiplication, which it determined was the highest-priority operation in the expression. So it performed it first in accordance with rule 3. Then it found it had two addition operations, so it applied rule 5 and did them left to right (although the order in which numbers are added doesn't matter), resulting in the answer, 30.

When you want HyperTalk to alter its normal order of precedence in mathematic calculations, use parentheses and take advantage of rule 1. To force HyperTalk to come up with the answer 42 in the simple example we've been following, you would write it as (2+4+8)*3. Now, rule 1 means that HyperTalk will perform the two additions first because they occur inside parentheses. That reduces the expression to 14*3, which is 42.

You can nest parentheses inside parentheses practically to your heart's content. HyperTalk begins with the innermost set of parentheses and works its way outward until it is left only with expressions outside parentheses. Then it applies rules 2 through 5, as appropriate.

▶ Functional HyperTalk

One final point needs to be made before we begin our first experiment. There are three kinds of actors in HyperTalk, as we have seen. There are commands (such as **put**) that usually require one or more arguments, or parameters. There are **operators** (such as +) that simply perform operations on objects. And there are *functions*. Functions are like special kinds of commands. The difference is that a function provides information about something, and a command changes the state of an object. A function in itself never alters anything in the HyperCard environment. In programming parlance, we say that a function "returns a value" as part of its operation. It determines something we ask it about and provides us with the information.

We've seen a few functions already. All the date-related tasks we worked through in Chapter 10 used a function that looked at the Macintosh clock and calendar and gave us the information stored there.

▶ Building a math lab

If you want to try out any or all of the functions, commands, and operators in this chapter, you can do so in two ways. Because of the many topics covered in this chapter, we won't interrupt the flow of the presentation to suggest that you try each one. But if you're curious about how a function works, what its return value is or how it affects a number or expression, feel free to experiment.

First, you can type the examples given in the text into the Message box. Sometimes this requires you to type **put** commands so you can examine the result. Second, you can follow the instructions in the next section and build a math laboratory card in your Laboratory stack. Then just type numeric expressions into the field on the card, press the button, and the answer appears in the Message box.

A math function tester

Create a new, blank card in your Laboratory stack. Add a field and a button to the card and give the field a rectangle outline. Name the field card field 1. Name the button whatever you like. Then follow these instructions:

1. Open the script-editing window for the button by one of the usual methods.

2. Type in the following short script and press OK when you're satisfied it has been typed in correctly:

```
on mouseUp
    put value(card field 1)
end mouseUp
```

3. Return to Browse mode.

4. Test your script with a simple arithmetic expression. Type something like 3+9 into the field. The Message box appears (if it was invisible) and contains the answer, 12. Figure 15-1 shows how our card looked with this answer returned.

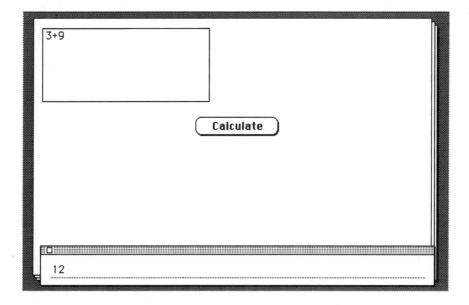

Figure 15-1. Card used to test math functions

▶ Simple Arithmetic Operations

Enough background information. Let's get into some serious calculations! In this section, we'll discuss the simplest arithmetic operators, which carry out addition, subtraction, multiplication, division, modulo, average, minimum, and maximum functions. If some of these terms are mysterious, don't worry. We'll explain the math as we go.

▶ Addition

There are two ways to perform addition in HyperTalk: with the **add** command or with the + operator. They are slightly different in terms of syntax, but both perform basic addition.

The **add** command syntax shows that it involves at least one container:

```
add <number> to <container>
```

When the **add** operation is finished, the container is changed by the value of the number. Notice that the original value stored in the container before the math operation is carried out is lost in this calculation. This is the key difference between **add** and the + operator. With **add**, HyperTalk knows what to do with the answer. With +, it must be told explicitly what to do with the result.

The + operator appears between two numbers, as you've become accustomed to seeing. But an expression such as

```
8 + 45
```

all by itself on a line in a HyperTalk script or in a field makes no sense. It violates a basic rule of HyperCard: everything is done with messages. There is no message here and no receiver. You generally write addition expressions using the **put** command

```
put 8 + 45 into answer1
```

or, if you wish to use the **add** command instead

```
add 8 to variable1 -- assuming variable1 has value 45
put variable1 into answer1
```

This will have the same effect as the previous **put** command using the + operator.

The same logic holds for the other math operators that don't include a destination for the answer.

▶ Subtraction

As with addition, so with subtraction. There are two subtraction methods: one uses the **subtract** command and includes a destination, and one uses the minus sign (-) and does not include a destination.

The syntax for **subtract** is logical enough:

```
subtract <number> from <container>
```

Note, again, HyperTalk's readability. This is exactly how we would say a subtraction problem: "subtract 15 from 38."

If we perform a subtraction with the minus sign, we typically use a **put** command to instruct HyperTalk where to place the result:

```
put temp1-value3 into result4
```

Note ▶ Another use of the minus sign is to perform negation (that is, to make a positive number negative). In that case, there is no number to the left of the minus sign, and the minus sign applies to the number to its right. Thus, 13-(-3) is the same as 13+3 because subtracting a negative number is the same as adding a positive number.

▶ Multiplication

The two ways to multiply in HyperTalk are to use the **multiply** command and the * operator. (The asterisk is the most commonly used character for multiplication on computers. In writing out such problems, we usually use a lowercase letter x. But because that is difficult, if not impossible, to distinguish from an intent to use a real letter, it was discarded as a possible multiplication operator by early system designers.)

The syntax for the **multiply** command again stresses readability:

```
multiply <container> by <number>
```

The asterisk multiplication symbol works with the **put** command:

```
put factor1 * factor2 into product
```

▶ Division

It will come as no surprise to those who struggled with long division through high school that division has some peculiar "wrinkles" that don't apply to the other simple arithmetic operations we've discussed so far. HyperTalk has a total of four operators, commands, and functions for division. Let's dispose of the expected two — **divide** and the slash sign (/). The use of the slash sign for division on computers derives from the difficulty of displaying the usual division sign (÷) on conventional computer keyboards. (The Mac has no problem with this special character. But the slash mark was defined a long time before the Mac was a reality.)

The **divide** command has the same two parameters we've seen in other HyperTalk math commands:

```
divide <container> by <number>
```

The result is what you expect: The original value of the container is replaced by the result of the division of the two numbers.

Using the slash operator usually requires the **put** command so that HyperTalk will know what to do with the answer:

```
put number1 / number 2 into quotient
```

You can use two other operators to carry out division and get different kinds of results. The two operators are **div** and **mod**.

As you may remember from your early days of learning division before decimals made any sense (if they do yet), a division problem can be thought of as producing two answers rather than one. The first answer is the whole number of times one value goes into another. The second is the amount left over after the division is complete. This latter value is called the *remainder*.

There are still times when you'd like to be able to get these answers. In Chapter 8, we saw an example where we wanted to execute a portion of a repeat loop every fifth time through. We used the **mod** operator with the promise that we'd explain it later.

The **div** operator produces the whole-number result of the division, with the remainder ignored. The **mod** operator produces the remainder. The statements

```
put 39 div 7 into temp1
put 39 mod 7 into temp2
```

place the value 5 in the *temp1* container and the value 4 into the *temp2* container, because 39 divided by 7 is 5 with a remainder of 4.

Now you can see how and why we used the **mod** operator in the repeat loop example in Chapter 8. If we want to simulate the STEP operation in BASIC and Pascal so that we execute a loop only when the controlling value changes by 5, we can set up a construct as follows:

```
repeat with counter = 1 to 50
   if counter mod 5 <> 0 then next repeat
   <loop statements>
end repeat
```

The expression *counter mod 5 < >* is 0 only when *counter* is evenly divisible by 5. Any other time, it has a value of 1 through 4 and the *loop statements* are not carried out.

This same technique is often used to determine values when fractions and decimals are not very helpful. For example, if we know how many hours are required to complete some task and want to know how many days are required, we probably don't want the answer to look like 4.125 days. Instead, we want the answer to be 4 days, 3 hours. So we use the **div** and **mod** operators. With *duration* containing the value 99, the following lines produce the answer 4 days, 3 hours:

```
put duration div 24 into numberOfDays
put duration mod 24 into numberOfHours
put "The task took" && numberOfDays && "days," ¬
&& numberOfHours && "hours to complete."
```

▶ Average

If you have your right arm in a bucket of ice and your left arm in a flaming pit, on the average, you're comfortable. That's an old saw about statistics. It describes graphically the meaning of *average*. The average is calculated by adding all members of the list and dividing by the number of members in the list. Thus, the average of 2 and 4 is 3, because 2+4 is 6 and 6 divided by 2 is 3.

HyperTalk, not surprisingly, has an **average** function. It takes an argument — a list of numbers separated by commas — and returns their average value. Its syntax is:

```
average(<number1>,<number2>...<numberN>)
```

If we write a HyperTalk script line such as

```
put average(30,70,20) into ave1
```

the container *ave1* has a value of 40 when the script has executed. Like all functions, note that we must tell HyperTalk where to store or display the result of its efforts.

▶ Maximum and minimum

We will discuss together the last two simple arithmetic operators — maximum and minimum — because they are nearly identical in operation. In programming it is often important to know the largest value in a list of numbers. Similarly, it is sometimes valuable to be able to find the smallest number in a list.

HyperTalk includes the **max** and **min** functions for these purposes. Each function takes a list of numbers, separated by commas, and returns the appropriate value. Their syntax, then, is identical:

```
max(<number1>,<number2>...<numberN>)
min(<number1>,<number2>...<numberN>)
```

The **min** and **max** operators come in handy when you need to find the range of a set of values. The range is frequently used in statistics. Given a list of test scores stored in a container called *Scores*, the following calculates and displays the range of scores:

```
put max(Scores) into top
put min(Scores) into bottom
put "Range of scores is:" && top && "to" && bottom & "."
```

▶ Number Manipulation

HyperTalk includes three functions that change the value of a number, **abs**, **round**, and **trunc**, and one that creates new numbers on demand, **random**.

▶ The abs function

When you need to find out the value of a number, regardless of its sign (positive or negative), use the **abs** function. This function takes a number or numeric expression as an argument and returns the result with a positive sign.

This function is often useful in finding the difference between two numbers when you don't know in advance which is larger or if one or both are negative. For example, suppose you have weather data stored in such a way that yesterday's high temperature is in a container called *dayHigh* and its low temperature is in *dayLow*. If you live someplace where one or both of those temperatures could be below zero, and you want to know the total number of degrees by which they differ, you could write:

```
put abs(dayLow-dayHigh) into dayRange
```

▶ Rounding and truncating numbers

Two functions reduce a number with a decimal part to an integer. The **round** function takes a number or numeric expression as an argument and returns its value rounded to the nearest whole number. If the decimal portion is 0.5 or larger, it rounds the integer up to the next whole number. If the decimal part is less than 0.5, it leaves the integer unchanged. Here are three examples. The comment lines show the value the variable has after the expression is executed.

```
put round(15.7) into t1
   -- t1 = 16
put round(15.5) into t1
   -- t1 = 16
put round(15.3) into t1
   -- t1 = 15
```

Sometimes, we don't want the nearest whole number for a decimal value. Rather, we want the equivalent of its value rounded down regardless of the size of the decimal fraction. For example, if we are trying to determine how many shares of stock to issue to an investment club where the rules require that each member receive whole numbers of shares and the fractions stay in a common pool, we would use HyperTalk's **trunc** function. Its name stands for what it does: it *truncates* a value, or discards the decimal portion. Here are two examples, with the resulting values shown in comment lines:

```
put trunc(15.99999) into t1
   -- t1 = 15
put trunc(15.00001) into t1
   -- t1 = 15
```

▶ Generating random numbers

Occasionally, you may need to create a number at random. This need frequently arises in game programs, but sometimes business and personal applications need a number with which to begin some decision-making. (We know one person who uses a random-number approach to seat people at parties. She reports as much success as her friends who spend hours agonizing over seating charts!)

When you need a random number, use HyperTalk's **the random** function. Its syntax looks like this:

```
[the] random of <number>
```

This function returns a number selected at random between 1 and the value of the number parameter, which may not be larger than 32,767.

▶ Advanced Math Operations

Eleven HyperTalk functions and operators deal with what we call "advanced math." They can be divided into four categories: square root, exponentiation, logarithms, and trigonometric functions. (We use the term "advanced math" somewhat arbitrarily, but it serves to divide arithmetic operations most people know how to do and that they perform with some frequency from those that are more obscure.)

▶ The square root function

To find the square root of a number (that is, the value that, when multiplied by itself, returns the number whose square root is being calculated), use the **sqrt** function. It takes a number or numeric expression as an argument, as do most of the other functions in this chapter.

The numeric argument must be positive. An attempt to find the square root of a negative number leads to an error message that is uncharacteristically cryptic for HyperTalk (see Figure 15-2). This is because in implementing many math functions, HyperTalk relies on the Standard Apple Numerics Envronment (SANE), which has built-in error messages.

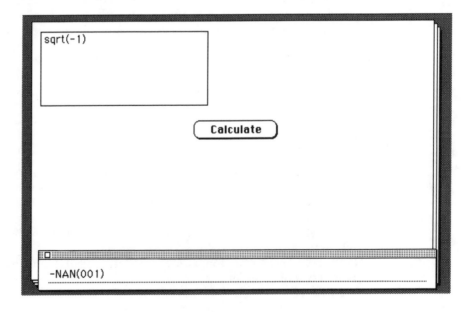

Figure 15-2. Error message for square root of negative number

The error message abbreviation NAN, also sometimes seen as NaN, is SANE shorthand for "not a number." You'll run into it if you try to apply math functions to text arguments, for example. In this case, the square root of a negative number is what mathematicians term an imaginary number and SANE isn't equipped to deal with it. You can guarantee that you won't encounter this error if you use the **abs** function described earlier.

Here are two examples of the use of the **sqrt** function, with the comment lines again indicating the results:

```
put sqrt(900) into temp1
    -- temp1 = 30
put sqrt(abs((182)) into temp1
    -- temp1 = 13.490738
```

▶ Exponentiation functions

Three functions and one operator handle exponentiation in HyperTalk. The operator performs the most common type of exponentiation, where one number is raised to the power indicated by another number. This operator is indicated by the ^ symbol placed between the two numbers.

Raising 3 to the 4th power, for example, is written:

```
3 ^ 4
```

In advanced math, several other types of exponentiation are needed for specialized types of calculations. Two involve something called the natural exponential, also referred to as base-e exponentiation. These calculations are based on the natural number 2.718282. A discussion of the reason for the use of this number as a base for logarithms is beyond the scope of this book, but it is related to the fact that many natural phenomena can be measured as a function of this number. But if you need the *natural exponential* of a number, use HyperTalk's **exp** function. If you need the natural exponential minus 1 (another frequently needed calculation in complex math), use the **exp1** function.

Finally, HyperTalk includes the ability to raise 2 to any power with the **exp2** function. It is faster and easier to write this function using the usual exponentiation with the ^ symbol, though, and you'll rarely need the SANE equivalent. (The **exp2** function is negligibly faster, but if you are writing a routine where there is a great deal of this calculation, the cumulative effect could become significant.)

▶ Logarithms

HyperTalk includes three functions that return logarithms of numbers. A logarithm is the mathematic inverse of an exponent. There is no HyperTalk function for the logarithm of a value to base 10, which is the most commonly used logarithm in math below the very complex. This is undoubtedly because the primary use of logarithms is to assist in speeding calculations, and one doesn't need that help with a computer. In fact, using logarithmic calculations to speed math operations in a computer is counterproductive.

But the SANE library, which is part of HyperTalk's world, includes logarithm functions that correspond exactly to the other three exponentiation functions discussed in the preceding section. The **ln** function returns the natural logarithm of the number supplied as an argument, and **ln1** first adds 1 to the argument and then computes the natural logarithm. The **log2** function returns the power to which the number 2 would be raised to calculate the number supplied as its argument.

▶ Trigonometric functions

Included in HyperTalk are four basic trigonometric functions from which all others can be derived: **atan, tan, sin,** and **cos.** They all operate the same way, taking an argument that is the size of the angle in radians (1 radian = 57.295 degrees) and returning the appropriate trigonometric value for that angle.

▶ The constant pi

The numeric constant *pi* is defined in HyperTalk. It has a value of 3.14159265358979323846. Its precision in a specific calculation can be affected by the setting of the global property **numberFormat**, discussed in Chapter 17.

▶ Financial Math Operations

If the SANE library includes some obscure functions and produces some strange error messages, why was it included in so elegant a programming language as HyperTalk? Aside from the fact that it is a very efficient way of making available some functions that are occasionally needed in higher math, it also includes two handy financial functions that find more everyday use in business stacks. These functions are **annuity** and **compound**.

▶ The annuity function

To calculate the present value of one payment unit into an annuity fund, you would use the annuity function. Its syntax is:

```
annuity(<interest rate>, <periods>)
```

The interest rate must be expressed so that it reflects the rate per period that coincides with the periods. In other words, if you are expressing periods in months, the interest rate must be the monthly rate.

The value calculated by the **annuity** function must be multiplied by the size of a single periodic payment to calculate the net present value of the annuity, which is the most common reason for wanting to carry out this calculation. To figure out today's value of your savings account in 10 years if you save $100 per month at an annual interest rate of 6 percent, for example, enter this line in a HyperTalk script:

```
put  100*annuity(.06/12,120)
```

The answer is 9007.345333, which, rounded off to the nearest cent, means that the present value of this savings plan is $9,007.35.

▶ The compound function

The **compound** function returns the future value of a current periodic payment unit. Future value is a frequently used financial equation. Its syntax is:

```
compound(<interest rate>, <periods>)
```

As with the **annuity** function, you can multiply the answer from **compound** by the amount of each payment to determine the future value of an ordinary investment.

▶ Summary

In this chapter, you have learned how to use about 30 mathematic operators, commands, and functions in HyperTalk. Chapter 16 takes a look at a few action-taking HyperTalk commands that don't fit neatly into any of the niches we've examined to this point.

16 ▶ Action-Taking Commands

In this chapter you will learn about several HyperTalk commands that have only two things in common. First, they take some kind of action in a script (as opposed, for example, to providing information or controlling program flow). Second, they don't fit neatly into any of the categories into which we have divided HyperTalk's other operations. These commands include

- **do**
- **wait**
- **open** (with applications and documents)
- **print** (document)
- **open printing, print,** and **close printing**

▶ The do Command

We have used the **do** command already in our discussion. But it is time to examine it more closely and see when and where it can be used.

The syntax of this command is as follows:

```
do <string>
```

The string is usually the name of a field, though it can also be any other addressable component of a field or a variable containing text. It can even be a simple string, a valid HyperTalk command most likely created using concatenation.

Beginning with HyperCard Version 2.0, you can place even complex, multi-line scripts into these fields or containers and ask HyperTalk to execute them with the **do** command. This is a significant change to the way the command works in versions prior to 2.0, where **do** only works on single-line statements and will not carry out certain commands at all. With the new version, you can even use **do** to execute commands that include **repeat** loops and other **do** commands, which makes this an extremely powerful command.

Using the do command

Open the Laboratory stack. Create a new card with a single button and a single field or use a card you don't mind dismantling from a previous experiment. In the example script, we call the field Field 1. If you change the field's name, be sure to change the name in the script as well. After you have such a card, follow these instructions:

1. Open the button's script-editing window in one of the usual ways.

2. Type the following script into the editing window and click OK after you've proofread it:

```
on mouseUp
   global t1
   do(card field 1)
end mouseUp
```

3. Return to Browse mode.

4. Click in Field 1 and type in the following commands to test your card. After each command is entered into Field 1, press the button. The comment lines describe the commands' actions.

```
doMenu "Open Stack..."
   -- brings up the standard file open dialog. Click Cancel
put 43*3 into t1
   -- nothing visible happens
put t1
   -- Message box appears if it was invisible; 129 is
      shown.
```

```
type "Hello from the Message box."
   -- The text appears in the Message box as if typed.
go previous
   -- Previous card appears. Use usual methods to Go Next.
```

5. Experiment with other commands.

6. This is a good card to have during script design because you can use it to find out quickly which commands execute from a field with the **do** command and which don't.

▶ Why use do?

You might be wondering why you'd ever want to use the **do** command when you can simply execute instructions directly in your handler. The most likely use of the command is when you ask the user a series of questions or gather input from the user or another source without asking questions and then execute a series of instructions based on the responses. Because you can't anticipate the answers or perhaps even the number of answers, coding this kind of process directly into your script is difficult, if not impossible.

Another good use of the **do** command if you're working with HyperCard Version 2.0 or higher is to overcome the limitation on the size of scripts imposed by the program. A script cannot be longer than about 32,000 characters. It is unusual but not unheard of for stack scripts in complex applications to reach that limit without having accomplished all they need to do. If you run up against this design wall, you can simply store up to 32,000 additional characters of script in a hidden field and use the **do** command in the crowded script to execute it.

▶ The wait Command

The **wait** command is another action-taking command we've used without describing it. As you'll see, we've only used this command in its simplest form. Here is its syntax in that form:

```
wait [for] <number> [ticks | seconds]
```

You can use two units of time with the **wait** command. If you don't specify one or the other, HyperTalk assumes you want to use **ticks**, units that are approximately 1/60 of a second. If you want to use seconds, you must provide that key word in the command.

A *tick* is only *approximately* 1/60 of a second. The exact time varies from model to model of the Macintosh. In addition, disk accesses during the handler's execution can alter the timing. Seconds are more accurate and more often used.

In some ways, **wait** is like a loop with nothing going on inside it. The **wait** command has two other forms that resemble the control structures we examined in Chapter 8. The syntax for these two variations is as follows:

```
wait until <true/false>
wait while <true/false>
```

These should be reminiscent of the **repeat until** and **repeat while** loops. They cause HyperCard to go into a holding pattern until the true/false expression is true (in the case of **wait until**) or to stay there only as long as it *is* true (in the case of **wait while**). These commands can be used to wait for the user to do something to trigger the script to continue processing. A common use is to have the script wait for the user to click the mouse as a signal to go to the next card or step:

```
wait until the mouseClick
<next command>
```

▶ Opening Applications and Documents

Many people first used HyperCard to replace the portion of the Finder that most of us use all the time: program launching. This was made possible by variations of HyperTalk's **open** command.

The basic syntax of this command is as follows:

```
open ["<document name>" with] "<program>"
```

As you can see, you can open a specific document and furnish the name of the application that document is designed to run with, or you can simply open the application program without an attached document.

The program name must be identical to the name of the application as it is stored on your Desktop. Special symbols, punctuation, and spacing are all significant, although capitalization is not. If you spell the name of the program incorrectly, HyperCard is unable to locate it. One way to ensure that the name is correct is to go to the Desktop, copy the application's name to the Clipboard, then go to HyperCard and paste the name into the **open** command line. Notice, however, that the name of the application must be enclosed in quotation marks.

▶ A classic new launcher

We couldn't go on with our discussion of the **open** command without a brief mention of one of the best-designed Finder replacement stacks we've seen. It's called *Home Desk*, and it is the creation of Russell A. Lyon. When you first open the stack (Figure 16-1), you find yourself in a dark room with a light switch.

Figure 16-1. Home Desk stack opens on a dark room

Press the switch, and your own rolltop desk is revealed (Figure 16-2). Press the lock on the desk, and it opens to reveal a typical desktop (Figure 16-3).

Buttons include the pencil holder (which activates your word processor), a calculator (which opens a desk accessory calculator if one is available), and more than two dozen other application-suggesting buttons. Some are hidden in drawers. There's even a private safe where you can hide documents, applications, and other items that only a person who knows the combination can browse.

Each of these buttons uses the **open** command. Just studying the script can give you a lot of good ideas for places to use this versatile HyperTalk command. More than any other HyperTalk command, **open** makes it possible for you to consider using HyperCard as the focal point of your Macintosh world.

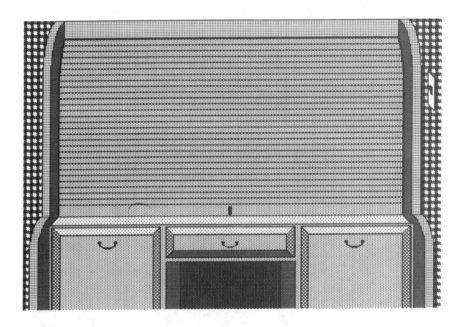

Figure 16-2. Home Desk ready for opening and use

Figure 16-3. Home Desk desktop

▶ What happens when you use open?

When HyperTalk encounters an **open** command in a script running under finder, it sends a special message called **suspend** to the current card. It then notifies your Macintosh System File that when you quit this new external application, control should be returned to HyperCard. Finally, HyperCard clears itself from memory.

After you finish using the application you launch from HyperCard, control returns not just to HyperCard but to the very card that was active when you executed the **open** command.

Note ▶	If you run HyperCard under MultiFinder or with a mini-finder present, the system does not return control to HyperCard when the opened application quits. Instead, control returns to the top level of your system.

▶ Specifying a document to open

If you want to open a specific document by using the application that created it, add the middle parameter to the **open** command along with the key linking word **with**. Here is a typical example (don't type this command into your stack unless you have the same document and application pair):

```
open "Chapter 16" with "Microsoft Word"
```

HyperCard's processing in this case is identical to that described earlier, except when it has opened the application, it loads the document file listed in the first parameter.

▶ Helping HyperCard find files

Before you settle into long-term use of a particular **open** command, be sure you place the full path name where the document and the application can be found into Look for Documents In... and Look for Applications In..., two Home stack cards. If you don't do this, the first time you try to use the **open** button, HyperCard interrupts the processing to ask where the files are located. Thereafter, of course, it will automatically remember the path.

▶ Printing Non-HyperCard Documents

In addition to opening other documents and applications, you can order HyperCard to print a document prepared in another application (using that application) and then return to HyperCard when the printing is complete. The **print** command makes this possible. Its syntax is nearly identical to that of the **open** command:

```
print "<document name>" with "<program name>"
```

The **print** command has no optional parameters. HyperCard must know both the document to print and the name of the application whose print routines are to be used.

All of the caveats we discussed when we explained the **open** command apply equally to **print**, including spelling and setting up the paths correctly.

Printing with the **print** command from a HyperTalk script is akin to printing from the Finder with the Print command from the File menu. The application launches, opens the document, prints it (often pausing for a print dialog in between), and then returns to the Finder or, in this case, to the same card you were using when HyperCard encountered the **print** command. Generally, you cannot do other tasks while the external application is running and before control is returned to HyperCard.

▶ Printing Cards from a Script

Anyone who has used HyperCard for more than a few hours of browsing knows that full-blown reports are not a particular strength of the program. HyperCard was not designed to be a database, so this is not surprising.

But printing is not completely unavailable from within HyperCard. Your scripts can enable users to request that certain cards, or even entire stacks, be printed. The process of printing two or more cards from a script requires that you use a structure similar to the following:

```
open printing
print first card
print card ID 50128
go to card "Report File"
print 23 cards
close printing
```

Notice that there are three separate HyperTalk commands. The first, **open printing**, sets up the printing operation. Its syntax is simple:

```
open printing [with dialog]
```

If you include the **with dialog** argument, the command displays the standard HyperCard printing dialog (see Figure 16-4) before it begins printing, waits for the user's responses, and then initiates printing with the parameters set by the user. If the **with dialog** parameter is *not* included in an **open printing** command, printing proceeds without user intervention and uses the current settings for HyperCard stack printing.

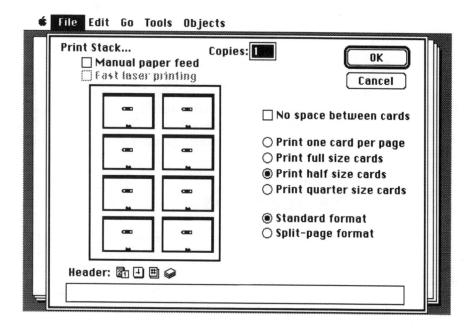

Figure 16-4. Standard HyperCard printing dialog

After printing has been opened, your script executes one or more **print** commands with this syntax:

```
print [all | {<number> | marked} cards | this card]
```

The **print all cards** command is equivalent to **doMenu "Print Stack..."** except that you can bypass the print dialog box with the first approach. You can also supply a number of cards to be printed, starting with the current card. Beginning with HyperCard Version 2.0, you can use the **mark** command to identify cards that meet certain criteria (see Chapter 10). If you do that, you can then tell HyperCard to print only those cards that are marked. Or you can simply instruct HyperCard to **print this card** or, more concisely, **print**, which it interprets the same way.

When you have ordered your last **print**, you must execute a **close printing** command. This not only ends the printing process and returns control to your stack where it left off, but also ensures that no unprinted cards end up in computer hyperspace. If you order the printing of fifteen cards and select to print half-size cards so that eight fit on one page, HyperCard stores each group of cards in a buffer in memory until it has eight cards in a group, and then it prints them. If you don't **close printing**, HyperCard would reach the end of the printing operation with seven cards in a buffer waiting to be printed. They would never print.

▶ More sophisticated printing

Beginning with Version 2.0, HyperCard includes far more sophisticated printing than we've discussed in this chapter. This new capability is embodied in the **open report printing** command and its associated facilities. We'll discuss this command and its use in data management applications in Chapter 19.

▶ The dial Command

There are two ways to dial a telephone with HyperCard: through a special device connected to the Macintosh that uses speaker tones to dial an ordinary telephone or through a modem connected to the modem port on the Mac.

▶ Using dial without a modem

Several devices on the market connect to the Macintosh's speaker jack on one end and a telephone line on the other. They use internally generated dialing tones to place calls. HyperCard can activate these devices with the **dial** command in its simplest form:

```
dial "<phone number>"
```

Although you can supply a telephone number explicitly with the **dial** command, you will probably use the standard containers *It* or *selection*, a variable, a field name, or a component containing the telephone number. If you do supply a telephone number rather than the place the number can be found, be sure HyperCard doesn't think 555-4232 means subtract 4,232 from 555. You can do this one of two ways. First, you can format the number in the usual way with the separating hyphen and enclose the entire phone number in quotation marks. Second, you can supply the phone number with no internal punctuation, such as 5554232.

▶ Using dial with a modem

If you use the **dial** command on a telephone line connected to the Mac serial port through a modem, you must tell HyperCard you are using a modem for the call. You may also want to send some parameters to the modem as part of the dialing process. The syntax for the **dial** command using a modem is as follows:

```
dial "<phone number>" with [modem] ["<modem parameters>"]
```

The presence of the key word **with** tips off HyperCard that you're using a modem. The word **modem** is optional, though if you opt for the usual HyperTalk readability, you will include it. The modem parameters, also optional, consist of a string enclosed in quotation marks. HyperCard sends anything contained in this string to the modem before any attempt is made to dial the phone.

Unless you know what kind of modem the user of your script has, including explicit modem parameters can be a little tricky. Sending the wrong parameters to the modem can result in no connection and can cause the user's blood pressure to rise. If including parameters is important to your script, you can use at least two strategies. First, you can require a modem compatible with standards established in the industry by Hayes Microcomputer Products Co. and tell your users they can only use your script without modification if they are using a Hayes-compatible modem. This includes, by the way, both the Apple Modem 300/1200 and the Apple Personal Modem. Second, you can supply a setup card with a script that obtains parameters from the user and builds the parameter string as a result.

▶ Modem parameters

Although there is some variation among modems as to the kinds of parameters that can be set with commands, a reasonable amount of standardization has developed around the Hayes command set. Even though some modems may use different commands to effect changes, almost all modems permit the user to set with commands such parameters as type of dialing (pulse or tone), baud rate, mode (answer or call), how long to wait for a carrier after dialing (used only in computer-to-computer communications), and loudness of the modem's built-in speaker.

Because HyperTalk's **dial** command is intended for use only with voice calls, most of these parameters do not have much value in scripts. But you will probably want to set at least three as part of the modem dialing process.

First, you will want to be sure the modem is set for tone dialing, not pulse dialing. In a Hayes-compatible modem, this is accomplished with the *DT* (for dial tones) parameter.

Second, you will probably want to reduce the amount of time the modem stays connected to the line after dialing. Normally, the modem stays connected for about 30 seconds after the dialing process is complete. During this time, it degrades the quality of the phone connection and sometimes sends an annoying, ear-splitting signal as it looks for a computer connection on the other end. The command *S7=1* gives the user one second after dialing to pick up the phone before the modem disconnects the line. You can set this to any value; typical values are between 1 and 30.

Finally, you may want to reduce the volume of the modem's built-in speaker, if it has one, by the command *L0* (that's a zero, not the letter *O*). Some modems are quite loud while dialing, and the noise can be aggravating to others (particularly in a work environment) besides jarring the user who is next to the modem.

With a Hayes-compatible modem, all these commands are set with a single set of parameters enclosed in quotation marks. They start with the letters *AT*, which is the way the Mac gets the modem's attention and informs it that what follows is intended for use by the modem directly and not by the software running in the Mac. To dial a number such as 555-1234 with a modem and the previous settings, place the following **dial** command in your script:

```
dial "555-1234" with modem "ATDTS7=1L0"
```

For the most part, modems are forgiving about spaces and the order in which commands are given.

▶ Summary

In this brief chapter, you learned how to use two of the most powerful and versatile HyperTalk commands: **do** and **open**. They make flexible scripting possible and facilitate using HyperCard as the centerpiece of your Macintosh environment. You saw how to print documents outside HyperCard. You also saw how to print cards inside the program and to use HyperCard's **dial** command.

In Chapter 17 we learn a range of special characteristics of HyperCard objects called properties and how to manage them in scripts.

17 ▶ Properties and Their Management

In this chapter, you will learn about

- HyperCard properties and the important role they play in scripts
- the nearly 80 properties besides the painting properties previously discussed that you can manage in your scripts
- the two commands — **get** and **set** — that manipulate those properties

▶ Role of Properties in HyperCard

HyperCard is, as we have said, highly graphic, interactive, and object-centered. All these facts about the program, combined with a desire on the part of its creators and designers to give the script-level user a great deal of flexible control over the environment, lead to the important role of *properties* in HyperTalk.

A property is a characteristic of an object. If your previous programming experience includes Logo or LISP, you understand properties because they play an important part in those languages. As human beings, we have thousands of properties. Genetic engineers are learning how many of those properties are determined and how they can be either predetermined or altered. Human properties include such diverse things as eye color, height, propensity to gain weight, many diseases, and nose shape. Other properties are not part of the genetic process but are shared by all of us: age, physical condition, abundance or absence of hair, place of residence, whether our parents are still alive, and so on.

Put together a sufficient combination of properties and you can identify any individual. The same is true of HyperCard properties. Every window, stack, background, card, field, and button has properties. Identifying each is a much simpler task than identifying a human individual, of course, because each has an ID number that is guaranteed to be unique (this ID is one of its properties). But other properties more fully describe the object.

HyperCard also has *global* properties that apply to all objects for which they are relevant. These can be viewed as analogous to the traits that make us human: our physical makeup as members of the human race, for example.

▶ How important are properties?

Putting aside for the moment global properties (which we will discuss separately) and painting properties (which we discussed in Chapter 13), HyperCard properties by and large describe what the objects to which they are attached look like, rather than how they behave. Behavior is dictated by scripts. Even the famous link capabilities of buttons create script commands. These scripts actually execute the links we create by mouse clicks.

Properties determine whether an object is visible, its location on the card or background, and its appearance to the user. In a graphic environment like HyperCard, this means properties are vitally important. Understanding properties and how to manipulate them will go a long way toward not only streamlining your stack creation but also making your stacks intuitive and useful.

Virtually any value you can determine in an object's dialog box or in the HyperCard Preferences card can also be set from a HyperTalk script.

▶ General usage

In general, you will find yourself using most of the properties available to you in HyperCard in similar ways.

Often, you will want to retrieve the value of the property with the **get** command and then test that value in a conditional **if-then-else** construct (see Chapter 8). Then, based on the value it now has, you may want to change the value with a **set** command. This means much of your property management scripting takes place within a structure like this:

```
. . .
get some property
   if it is what you want it to be
      then proceed with processing
      else set it and proceed with processing
   end if
. . .
```

Alternatively, you may wish to test the property directly, as in:

```
if the visible of card button 1 is false then
        show card button 1
```

▶ Terseness versus readability

Perhaps nowhere else does HyperTalk offer as much flexibility as in naming properties. You can be almost as terse or as verbose as you like. Many of the property names have short and long forms. For example, **rectangle** can be spelled out or abbreviated **rect**. Because the use of **the** is optional with property names in **get** and **set** commands, both of these instructions have the same effect:

```
get the rectangle of the Message box
get rect of Msg
```

▶ Using the in property names

HyperTalk novices are sometimes bewildered by what appears to be a willy-nilly use or omission of the definite article **the** before property names. If you've examined any scripts, you have probably noticed this apparent arbitrariness and wondered about it.

Well, it turns out not to be so mysterious after all. Follow these basic rules to decide when to use **the** with properties:

1. The word **the** is never required in a **get** or **set** statement.

2. If the property has parameters, **the** may be included or omitted.

3. If the property has no parameters and appears in any statement other than a **get** or a **set**, **the** is required.

The easy method is to adopt the convention we use throughout this book. Use **the** in the interest of both safety and readability. It is *never* wrong to include it, and it is wrong to omit it often enough that it causes aggravation when scripting.

▶ Order of discussion of properties

In this chapter, we discuss properties in the following order:

- global properties
- properties common to two or more classes of objects
- unique stack properties
- unique card-window properties
- unique card properties
- unique field properties
- unique button properties
- unique picture properties

There are no properties that are unique to backgrounds.

Table 17-1 summarizes all nonpainting properties in HyperTalk, defining the class or classes to which each belongs and the possible values it can have. Syntax for those with arguments is discussed in the text rather than the table.

▶ **Global Properties**

Global properties, as you can deduce from their name, apply throughout the HyperCard environment. They can be changed almost any time from any script or the Message box (or, in some cases, from the Preferences card in the Home stack), but when you change them, they stay in their changed state until they are changed again, with few exceptions. Whether you change stacks or even quit HyperCard and return later, these values remain the same until they are changed. There are 33 global properties, four of which are related to Preferences settings.

▶ The userLevel property

One global property you may have encountered in your HyperTalk scripting is the **userLevel** property. It determines which of the five levels of access the user has. Each level increase is indicated by an increase of 1 in the value of **userLevel** and represents a step upward in complexity and power. Table 17-2 depicts the five values of **userLevel** and how they relate to the Preferences card settings.

Table 17-1. HyperTalk properties and their values

Property Name	Classes	Legal Values
autoHilite	Bt	true or false
autoTab	F	true or false
blindTyping	G	true or false
bottom	F, Bt, W	numeric
bot[tom]Right	F, Bt, W	two numbers separated by a comma
cantAbort	S	true or false
cantDelete	S, Bk, C	true or false
cantModify	S	true or false
cantPeek	S	true or false
checkMark	MI	true or false
cmdChar	MI	any character
cursor	G	numeric or string (see note 1)
debugger	G	string
dontSearch	Bk, C, F	true or false
dontWrap	F	true or false
dragSpeed	G	numeric
editBkgnd	G	true or false
enabled	M, MI	true or false
fixedLineHeight	F	true or false
freeSize	G	numeric; read-only
height	F, Bt, W	numeric
hilite	Bt	true or false
icon	Bt	numeric or string
id	Bk, C, F, Bt	numeric; read-only
language	G	string (name of language)
left	Bt, F, W	numeric
loc[ation]	F, Bt, W	two numbers separated by a comma
lockMessages	G	true or false
lockRecent	G	true or false
lockScreen	G	true or false
lockText	F	true or false
long Version	G	when applied to HyperCard, one number; when applied to a stack, same as version property (below)
longWindowTitles	G	true or false
markChar	MI	character
marked	C	true or false
menuMsg	MI	string (see note 2)
messageWatcher	G	string
name	S, Bk, C, F, Bt, M, MI	string
number	Bk, C, F, Bt	numeric; read-only
numberFormat	G	see note 3
powerKeys	G	true or false
printMargins	G	four numbers separated by commas
printTextAlign	G	left, center, right
printTextFont	G	string
printTextHeight	G	numeric
printTextSize	G	numeric
printTextStyle	G	one or more strings separated by commas (see note 4)
rect[angle]	F, Bt, W, C	four numbers separated by commas
right	F, Bt, W, C	numeric
screenRect	G	four numbers separated by commas; read-only
script	S, Bk, C, F, Bt	entire script

Table 17-1. HyperTalk properties and their values (continued)

Property Name	Classes	Legal Values
scriptEditor	G	string
scriptTextFont	G	string
scriptTextSize	G	numeric
scriptTextStyle	G	one or more strings separated by commas (see note 4)
scriptWindowRects	G	list of one or more sets of four numbers separated by commas
scroll	W, F	numeric
sharedHilite	Bt	true or false; applicable only to background buttons
sharedText	F	true or false; applicable only to background fields
showLines	F	true or false
showName	Bt	true or false
showPict	P	true or false
size	S	numeric; read-only
stacksInUse	G	string of one or more stack names; read-only
style	F, Bt	see note 5
suspended	G	true or false
textAlign	F	left, center, or right
textArrows	G	true or false
textFont	Bt, F	Valid font name
textHeight	Bt, F	numeric
textSize	Bt, F	numeric
textStyle	MI	one or more strings separated by commas
top	Bt, F, W, C	numeric
topLeft	Bt, F, W, C	two numbers separated by a comma
traceDelay	G	numeric
userLevel	G	numeric, 1-5 (See Table 17-2)
userModify	G	true or false
variableWatcher	G	string
version	G, S	when applied to a stack, five numeric fields separated by commas; when applied to HyperCard, one numeric value
visible	F, Bt, W	true or false
wideMargins	F	true or false
width	F, Bt, W	numeric

Key: Under Classes, the following abbreviations are used:
Bt = Button, G = Global, S = Stack, C = Card, F = Field, Bk = Background, W = Card window,
P = Card/background picture, M = Menu, MI = Menu item

Notes:

1. Eight predefined cursor names are permissible. See text.

2. Must be the name of a handler or an executable HyperTalk code fragment consisting of one uncontinued line.

3. The value of **numberFormat** is described in the text.

4. Any of the **textStyle** properties can mix any of the following values in their lists, in any order: plain (which overrides all others), bold, italic, underline, outline, shadow, condense, extend, or group.

5. The values of the **style** property depend on whether the object is a button or a field. See text.

6. Table excludes properties associated with built-in debugger-related windows in HyperCard 2.0.

Table 17-2. Meanings of userLevel settings

Value	Level
1	browsing
2	typing
3	painting
4	authoring
5	scripting

▶ The powerKeys property

When users are employing the painting power of HyperCard, implying that they have a **userLevel** setting of 3 or higher, they can also enable the use of power keys to accelerate their painting control. Normally, users check the check box in the Preferences card to indicate when they want this feature enabled. But you can use the **powerKeys** property to do so if you wish. This property can be either true or false. The default is taken from the Preferences card in the Home stack.

▶ The blindTyping property

You have probably had the experience of starting to type something into HyperCard with the Message box hidden only to have HyperCard beep. If you check the check box next to Blind Typing on the Preferences card of the Home stack, you can get around this problem. The **blindTyping** property gives you a way of accomplishing the same thing in a script. When it is true, you can type and send messages to HyperCard by typing as if you were entering text into the Message box.

You must be careful in using this feature, however, because syntax errors you produce are not easy to detect if the Message box is hidden. Fortunately, you can always press Command-M and request HyperCard to display the Message box. When you do so, the last message entered into the Message box is available for inspection and editing if necessary.

To **set** the value of **blindTyping**, the **userLevel** must be 5. The property can be either true or false. The default is taken from the Preferences card in the Home stack.

▶ The textArrows property

In Version 1.1 of HyperCard, Apple Computer added the capability of using the arrow keys on the keyboard in one of two ways. They also added a check box to the Preferences card of the Home stack opposite the **Typing** user-level label. By checking this box, the user can decide that the arrow keys on the keyboard will be used to move the cursor inside fields and script-editing windows. By leaving it unchecked, the arrow keys remain as they were permanently set in earlier versions of the program, namely to navigate among cards.

The script version of this process uses the **textArrows** property. It can be either true (equivalent to the check box being checked) or false. If it is set to true, the user can still navigate with the arrow keys by using them with the Option key. The opposite is also true, so that if **textArrows** is false, the user can hold down the Option key with an arrow to use it as a cursor-movement key.

Regardless of the setting, holding down the Command key and the left arrow key moves to the beginning of the stack, and pressing the Command key and the right arrow key moves to the end of the stack. The Command-up arrow combination pops a card, and Command-down arrow pushes the current card.

▶ The cursor property

We move now to global properties that are not equivalent to settings in the Preferences card of the Home stack. The **cursor** property may only be **set**; the **get** command does not work with this property. This is also one property that cannot be usefully **set** from the Message box; the effects of its modification can only be seen within a script. This is because HyperCard reverts to normal cursor settings when the script ends and the system begins to send **idle** messages (see Chapter 6). This means that even though you *could* **set** the cursor from the Message box, it would be difficult to see the effect because the system would begin sending **idle** messages immediately after the Message box message was handled.

When you **set** the cursor, you must use the number or name of a cursor resource that is available in the current stack or in the HyperCard file. (See Chapter 21 for a discussion of resources and HyperCard.)

HyperCard (after Version 1.2) predefines eight cursor shapes, one of which actually consists of a group of shapes repeated in an animated sequence. These eight shapes are called **none, hand, watch, arrow, iBeam, plus, cross,** and **busy.** You may use the **set** command to change the cursor to any of these shapes simply by referring to them by name:

```
set the cursor to watch
set the cursor to iBeam
```

Figure 17-1 depicts six of the eight shapes. The cursor shape called **none** results in an invisible cursor. This was a request made by many early users of HyperCard prior to Version 1.2. In earlier versions, it was not possible within HyperTalk to make the cursor disappear. The cursor **busy** is an animated sequence of several shapes that result in the appearance of a rotating "beach ball," a shape with which most Macintosh users are quite familiar.

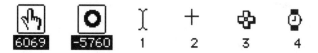

Figure 17-1. Six of HyperCard's predefined cursors

You will probably change the cursor very seldom, if at all. When you do, though, the chances are pretty good that you'll be changing it to the watch (cursor 4 in HyperCard parlance). As you know as a Macintosh user, you don't mind waiting for a process to complete if the watch cursor is showing (for some reasonable period of time), but even relatively brief delays without the watch cursor make you nervous. You wonder if something has gone wrong to hang up the system. So if you're executing something in a script that takes longer than a second or two, you are well advised to change the **cursor** shape to 4 with a **set** command, and then execute the function. Design your scripts so that if you do reset the cursor's shape, the cursor reverts to its normal, idling shape when the handler ends.

▶ The dragSpeed property

We dealt with the **dragSpeed** property in Chapter 13. It is included here only for completeness, because it is a global property, although it is used exclusively by painting operations.

▶ The editBkgnd property

If your script undertakes a painting, button, or field modification that operates on the background rather than the current card, you must **set** the value of **editBkgnd** to true. Otherwise, your changes alter only the current card.

Your script can only access this property if **userLevel** is 3 or higher. The **editBkgnd** property can be either true or false. The default setting is false.

▶ The language property

It is unlikely that you will have any occasion to use the **language** property. Language translators for HyperCard became available beginning with Version 1.1, but unless you either write scripts for multiple languages or are translating scripts, you will have no need for this property.

The **language** property can take the name of any valid language translator as a value. If translators are installed in your version of HyperCard, they appear on the Preferences card in the Home stack. If you attempt to **set the language** to a language for which your version does not have a translator, an error message like that shown in Figure 17-2 results.

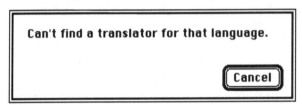

Figure 17-2. Language translator error message

▶ The lockMessages property

There are occasions in advanced scripting when you want to suppress the execution of messages designed to trigger when a card or stack is first opened. By setting the value of **lockMessages** to true, you effectively intercept and bury all messages that deal with opening these objects.

This is sometimes necessary, for example, if you want to write a script that navigates through a stack where cards or backgrounds may have **on open** handlers. If **lockMessages** is false, these scripts will execute even though you don't want them to.

The value of **lockMessages** does not affect any other kind of system or other message. Its value is always set to false at idle time.

▶ The lockRecent property

As you navigate in HyperCard, whether in one stack or among multiple stacks, HyperCard saves the most recent 42 cards you've visited in a special place it knows by the name **recent**. Stored there is a miniature of each of the last 42 cards you've displayed (see Figure 17-3). By clicking on any of these images, you can move directly to that card.

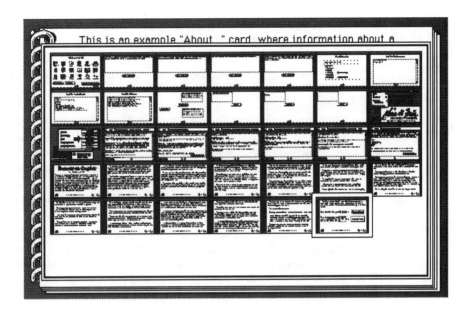

Figure 17-3. The recent display

If you don't want to clutter up the user's **recent** area as you carry out some specialized processing, you can use the **lockRecent** property.

This property can be true or false. The default, of course, is false. If you find it necessary to **set** this property to true, be sure it is returned to its normal false state before returning control to the user. Its value is always reset to false at idle time.

▶ The lockScreen property

You'll find the **lockScreen** property one of the most useful in HyperTalk's repertoire of properties. It can take a value of true or false, with its default being false. When you **set** it to true, any activity you undertake in your script that normally updates the screen becomes invisible to the user.

You can open other cards, read data from them, modify them, even open new stacks, and none of this activity is evident to the user. This approach is often useful to avoid confusing the casual browser. It is also a form of protection from too-easy delving into your scripts and their actions. (Although it is not a very strong form of such protection, it prevents the nontechnical user from being aware anything is happening.)

It may be a good idea to use the **lockScreen** property in conjunction with the **lockMessages** and **lockRecent** properties. It is also a good idea to consider setting the **cursor** to the watch with a **set the cursor to 4** command before you begin processing complex operations with the screen locked. Otherwise, there is almost no way for users to know something is happening, and they may decide the system is "hung" and reset the Macintosh at an inopportune time.

To keep things in balance, you should make sure that your script sets **lockScreen** false for each time it sets it true. In effect, **lockScreen** sets up a value that is decreased by one each time the property is set to false. Only when the value reaches 0 is **lockScreen** set to false. This enables handlers that call other handlers to rely on the status and value of the **lockScreen** parameter not changing unless it is specifically modified by the individual handler.

You can also lock the screen with the **lock screen** command in HyperCard Version 1.2 and later. The effects of **lock screen** and **set the lockScreen to true** are identical. Whether you have used the property or the command, you can use the **unlock screen**, optionally with a visual effect, to unlock the screen (see Chapter 13 for a discussion of the use of the **lock screen** and **unlock screen** commands.) Its value is always reset to false at idle time.

▶ The numberFormat property

The **numberFormat** property controls how numbers are formatted and displayed in HyperCard. Its format is as follows:

```
set the numberFormat to "<format string>"
```

In its default mode, HyperCard formats all numbers with up to six digits to the right of the decimal point and no *required* digits to the left of the decimal point. You can change this by using three pattern characters:

- the number 0, which means HyperCard must put a 0 in that position if it would otherwise be empty

- the decimal point

- the crosshatch, or number sign (#), which is only used to the right of the decimal point to determine maximum precision without regard to trailing zeros

You can use the **set the numberFormat** command to establish any format that makes sense for the numbers you are calculating and displaying in a stack. When the script is finished executing and HyperCard returns to its **idle** state, the system resumes the default pattern. This means you must set the **numberFormat** in a script and not from the Message box.

Table 17-3 presents some typical number formatting patterns and shows how the values 11.9752 and 0.85629371 are displayed in each.

Table 17-3. Typical numeric formatting patterns

Format Pattern	11.9752	0.85629371
"0.00"	11.98	0.86
"0.#########"	11.9752	0.85629371
"0.000000000"	11.975200000	0.856293710
".###"	11.975	0.856

▶ The userModify property

In a locked stack, the user is prevented from making any changes to field contents or to artwork. But there are times when you want to offer the user the *illusion* of being allowed to make changes, or you want to capture information from him or her for some other purpose without modifying the stack. When a stack is used as a "front end" to some other product, for example, it might be useful to allow the user to enter data into a HyperCard stack, capture the information, and place it in another program's storage area. But you might not want the user to be able to make any modifications to the appearance of or content in your front-end stack.

To deal with this problem, HyperCard Version 1.2 and later includes the **userModify** property. In a locked stack, this property is set to false unless your script specifically sets it to true. If it is set to true, the user can make modifications to cards and fields in the stack, but those changes are discarded on leaving the card.

Combining the use of the **userModify** property and a **closeField** or **closeCard** message (see Chapter 6), you can capture information from the user without permitting modification of your stack. The basic approach would look something like this:

1. The user opens your locked stack. An **openStack** handler sets the **userModify** property to true.

2. The user enters some information in one or more fields.

3. In a **closeCard** handler or in individual **closeField** handlers for each field involved, your script uses a **put** command to take the information entered by the user and place it in another stack or write it into an external file.

Here is an example of the salient part of such a script. We assume that users can enter information into two fields and that we are capturing their entries when they indicate they are done by pressing a button that appears to take them to the next card in the stack.

```
on openStack -- this handler goes at the stack level
   set userModify to true
   -- perhaps do other processing as well
end openStack
on closeCard -- this handler goes at the card,
background or stack level
   set lockScreen to true
   put field "Customer Name" into nameEntered
   put field "Amount Due" into dueEntered
   push this card
   go to stack "Updates"
   put nameEntered & return after field "New Names"
   put dueEntered & return after field "New Amounts"
   set lockScreen to false
   -- not required but good form
end closeCard
```

It is not necessary to clear the fields "Customer Name" and "Amount Due" on the entry stack (which could be a one-card stack) because HyperCard automatically discards the user's changes when he or she leaves the card. Thus, a single stack could be essentially reused for hundreds or thousands of data entries, which would then be placed elsewhere for processing later.

► The screenRect property

Beginning with Version 1.2 of HyperCard, you can determine the dimensions of the screen the user has by means of the **screenRect** property. This read-only property returns a rectangle as a value, so it consists of four numbers, separated by commas. The first two numbers are both zero.

For the Macintosh Plus and SE with the standard Macintosh nine-inch monochrome monitor, **screenRect** returns 0,0,512,342. For a Macintosh II with a standard Apple color monitor, the value is 0,0,640,480. Other screens will return different values, of course.

► The version property

Since the introduction of HyperCard Version 1.2, the differences between versions of the product have become significant to the developer. Some functionality peculiar to Version 1.2 and later will cause difficulties if used in stacks running under HyperCard 1.1 and earlier. Similarly, stacks created under versions earlier than 1.2 and then run under later versions need compacting under the new version before they work as expected.

You can determine the version of HyperCard now in use with the **version** and **long Version** properties. Each can take an optional parameter, **of HyperCard**. The **version** property returns a single decimal value with the actual version number (e.g., 1.2). The **long Version** property, on the other hand, returns an 8-character number. For example,

```
put the version
```

places the value "1.2" into the Message box, assuming you are running HyperCard Version 1.2. With the same version, the command

```
put the long Version
```

places the value "01208000" into the Message box. As later versions are released, this number will increase accordingly.

There is also a stack property called **version**, which is discussed later in the chapter. Using its return values and the stack's version information, you can determine when a forced compacting should take place.

▶ Three script-editor properties

Beginning with HyperCard Version 2.0, you can set the style, font, and size of the text used to display scripts in all script-editing windows. The three properties that handle these settings are

- **scriptTextStyle**
- **scriptTextFont**
- **scriptTextSize**

You can both **get** and **set** these properties.

For the **scriptTextStyle** property, you can combine any of the legal values for a text style (see note 4 to Table 17-1) in a comma-separated list, as in

```
set the scriptTextStyle to bold,italic,underline
```

The only argument required by the **scriptTextFont** property is a string containing the name of a valid font (or, alternatively, the name of a HyperTalk container that holds such a value). Here's an example:

```
set the scriptTextFont to "New York"
```

As you can probably deduce, the **scriptTextSize** property requires a numeric value that represents the point size you wish to use, as in

```
set the scriptTextSize to 14
```

The parameter must be a whole number; using a decimal value like 14.5 will produce a HyperTalk error, "Expected integer here."

▶ Six printing-related properties

As printing in HyperCard Version 2.0 became more sophisticated, six new global properties to describe the default output appearance of reports printed from within HyperCard, whether by menu or script command, were added. The first three of these properties are nearly identical, except in name, to their namesakes discussed in the preceding section when we talked about the script editor. The others are discussed in detail below. These printing-related properties are

- **printTextFont**
- **printTextStyle**
- **printTextSize**
- **printTextAlign**
- **printTextHeight**
- **printMargins**

The **printTextAlign** property can take one of three arguments: *left*, *right*, or *center*.

You can supply any whole number as a value to the **printTextHeight** property. Be sure that this number is at least one unit larger than the value of **printTextSize** for best results.

The value for **printMargins** is a rectangle (that is, four comma-separated numeric values). Taken together, they define a rectangle on the page within which printing will take place. But they define this rectangle somewhat indirectly. The default value for the **printMargins** property is 0,0,0,0, which instructs HyperCard to use all of the available page area for printing. (The available page area is defined in part by the printer you are using.) Setting this property to 20,20,20,20, for example, would move the margins toward the center by 20 pixels in all four directions. We'll have more to say about the judicious use of this property in Chapter 19, when we talk about printing reports from within HyperTalk.

▶ Five debugging-related properties

HyperCard Version 2.0 adds significant debugging power for the scripter. In the process, it adds five global properties that relate to the debugging process:

- **scriptEditor**
- **debugger**
- **messageWatcher**
- **variableWatcher**
- **traceDelay**

The first four of these properties allow you to use an editor, debugger, message-watching window, or variable-monitoring window that is different from the one supplied with HyperCard. At this writing, there is only one commercially available third-party debugger, HyperTMON from Icom Simulations. We expect more to be made available since HyperCard has provided developers with a straightforward way to permit users to choose any tool they like.

All of these first four properties take strings as arguments. These strings must point to the name of an application or external routine that you wish to use in the indicated capacities.

The fifth of these properties takes a numeric parameter; that tells HyperTalk how long to delay between lines of a script when executing while you have turned tracing on. The default value is 0 (that is, no delay).

▶ The stacksInUse property

Beginning with HyperCard Version 2.0, your scripts can modify the standard message-passing hierarchy used by the system. The **stacksInUse** property is a read-only property that takes no arguments and returns a list of all the stacks you've placed into the message-passing path. It is read-only. Items in the list are separated from others by a carriage return.

▶ The longWindowTitles property

This property, which was added with HyperCard Version 2.0, can be set to either true or false. If it is true, then the title in the title bar of all windows will consist of the entire path name of the stack. Otherwise, it contains only the name of the stack. The default value of this property is false.

▶ Shared Properties

Eighteen properties are shared by two or more classes of HyperCard objects. Rather than duplicating the discussion of each of these properties by dividing the chapter by object type, we present these common ones before we discuss those that are unique to each type of object.

▶ The id property

All backgrounds, cards, fields, and buttons have associated with them a number that is guaranteed to be unique for a particular object type in a particular domain of a stack. This means no two backgrounds in a stack are assigned the same ID number. Two background fields also do not share the same ID number, though there could be a background field and a card field with the same ID. This guarantee makes IDs a very safe way to address these objects.

You can only **get** an **id** property of an object. It can never be **set**. It is assigned automatically when the object is created and is never changed. Even if the card or other object is deleted, the unique ID number is never used again in that stack for another object of the same type in the same domain.

Don't confuse the ID number of an object with its *sequence number*, which determines its relative position within a card or stack. Sequence numbers can be changed by the Bring Closer and Send Farther selections in the Objects menu.

▶ The location property

All fields, buttons, and card windows have a specific **location** (also abbreviated **loc**) that describes their relative position on the screen. Recall that HyperCard views the Macintosh's nine-inch display (built in on all but the Macintosh II) as beginning at the location 0,0 in the upper-left corner and extending to the location 512,342 in the lower-right corner. The **location** property uses this addressing scheme.

If you **get the location** of any of these objects, HyperCard returns two numbers separated by a comma, for example, 100,250. These numbers give the horizontal and vertical offset, respectively, of the *center* of the object. This location can be useful for clicking and dragging operations. Or you can relocate an object with the **set the location** command. For example, Figure 17-4 shows one of our familiar Laboratory stack cards after the **set the loc** command shown in the Message box has been executed. The button, formerly near the center of the card, has shifted 100 pixels to the right.

This method of relocating buttons, fields, and card windows is faster and more efficient than changing the tool and dragging the object. It does not, however, work with painted objects. They must be moved as described in Chapter 13.

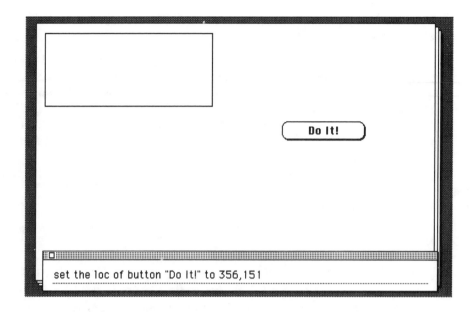

Figure 17-4. Moving a button by altering its location property

▶ The name property

You can find out or change the name of the current stack, background, or card or of an identified menu, menu item, field, or button by examining and altering its **name** property.

You define the name of a stack, background, card, field, or button any time after you create it, and you can always alter it. HyperCard leaves the names of these items blank unless you supply a name. It does not insist that these objects even have names.

There are two forms of the **name** property. One is called **the long name** and the other, **the short name**. If you don't specify which you want to use, HyperTalk generally (but not always) assumes that you want to see **the long name**. These modifiers do not apply to menu and menu item names.

Example overleaf shows 3 forms!

Looking at names

Go to any card in the Laboratory stack with a button and a field. Find out the sequence numbers of each object you want to experiment with so you can address them correctly. In the example, we assume that you have a button and a field and that each is the only object of its kind on the card. We also assume the field is named Test Field and the button is named Do It! Now type the following lines into the Message box and examine the results:

1. `put the name of card field 1`

   `-- Message box displays card field "Test Field"`

2. `put the short name of card field 1`

   `-- Message box displays Test Field (no quotation marks)`

3. `put the long name of card field 1`

   `-- Message box displays card field "Test Field" of card`
   `-- id 6001 of stack "A Hard Place:Hyper Folder:Laboratory"`

4. Repeat the previous steps with the button field.

As you can see, if you ask for **the name** of an object, HyperCard returns the entire name, including the type and domain (card field, background button, and so on). But if you specify **the short name**, HyperCard returns only the name as it appears in the Info dialog box.

▶ The number property

To find out the sequence number of a background, card, field, or button, you can use the **get** command to return the **number** of that item. The sequence number is the one the system assigns in the order in which objects are created and should not be confused with the ID number discussed earlier (see "The **id** property").

As with the **id** property, the **number** property cannot be changed in a script. Only the Bring Closer and Send Farther options in the Objects menu alter this value.

▶ The rectangle property

The **rectangle** property is closely related to the **location** property described earlier. The difference is the **rectangle** property describes the upper-left and lower-right corners of the rectangle enclosing a field, button, or card window; the **location** property only defines the center point of those objects.

You can move an object using the **rectangle** property just as you can with the **location** property. With **rectangle**, however, you can also resize the object. If you use the **set** command to change the **rectangle** property of an object and if you modify the proportional distances between the corners, you will resize and perhaps reshape the object. You can, of course, do this without relocating the object. Another use of the **rectangle** property is with the **drag** command using the appropriate tool to resize the object.

The **rectangle** property has four numeric values, separated by commas. The first two define the horizontal and vertical position, respectively, of the upper-left corner. The last two define the horizontal and vertical position, respectively, of the lower-right corner. Both sets of coordinates are essentially offsets because the upper-left corner of a HyperCard screen is at 0,0.

A very important use of this property involves clicking in a field. If you use the **location** property, you will find yourself clicking in the center of the field, which results in the cursor appearing either in the center of a line in the center of the field or at the left margin but centered vertically. If you want to click in the upper-left corner of the field, use the **rectangle** property, then use **delete** to remove items 3 and 4 (or, alternatively, use **put** to extract items 1 and 2) of the address group. Then you can use **click at** with those two values to place the cursor in the upper-left corner of the field.

▶ Other location and size properties

Beginning with Version 1.2, HyperTalk added eight new properties related to the location and size of HyperCard objects. These properties allow you to access specific portions of the information returned by the **rectangle** property for a given object. These properties are

- **left**
- **top**
- **right**
- **bottom**
- **topLeft**
- **bottomRight** (may be abbreviated to **botRight**)
- **width**
- **height**

Each of these properties, as with all other properties related to objects, is followed with the key word **of** and then with the identifier that names the object whose property you wish to **set** or **get**. The next Laboratory exercise makes this clear.

Using size and location properties

For the next experiment, you'll need a Laboratory stack card with at least one button and one field. Create a new one or find one whose script you don't mind overwriting. Then follow these instructions:

1. Open the script-editing window of a button in one of the usual ways.

2. Type the following handler into the script-editing window. Click OK when you have proofread the script.

```
on mouseUp
    put the rectangle of card field 1 into r1
    put third item of r1 -1 into corner
    put "," & fourth item of r1 -1 after corner
    choose field tool
    put "Click the mouse where you want the corner."
    wait until the mouseClick
    drag from corner to the mouseLoc
    choose browse tool
end mouseUp
```

3. Return to browse mode.

4. Click on the button. The Message box appears (if it was invisible) and requests that you click the mouse where you want the lower-right corner of the field to be located.

5. Click the mouse where the field won't cover up the button. The corner moves immediately there. Experiment with different screen positions. If you move the mouse inside the field and click, the field gets smaller.

6. When you've experimented enough with the **rectangle** property, create a card field and name it "Where." Make it a scrolling field so that if the information we're going to put into it gets lengthy, you'll be able to see it.

7. Either create a second button or overwrite the script of the existing button with the following script:

```
on mouseUp
    put "Left edge =" && left of card field 1¬
    & return into card field "Where"
    put "Top edge = " & top of card field 1¬
    & return after card field "Where"
    put "Right edge = " & right of card field 1¬
```

```
    & return after card field "Where"
    put "Bottom edge = " & bottom of card field 1¬
    & return after card field "Where"
    put "Top left corner = " & topLeft of card¬
    field 1 & return after card field "Where"
    put "Bottom right corner = " & botRight of¬
    card field 1 & return after card field "Where"
    put "Width = " & width of card field 1 &¬
    return after card field "Where"
    put "Height = " & height of card field 1 &¬
    return after card field "Where"
  end mouseUp
```

8. Compare the results of these printouts with the **rectangle** of the field as reported in your last run of the previous handler to satisfy yourself that the two handlers essentially produce the same information in different forms.

Notice in the script that we use the **rectangle** function, extract the third and fourth items of it (which point to the lower-right corner), and put them into their own local variable. This makes later command lines more efficient to write than spelling out "item 3 of the rectangle of card field 1." (We subtract 1 from each value to place the drag point inside the rectangle rather than exactly at the corner. This is necessary because of the way coordinates relate to the screen position to which they correspond.) Also notice that we've used the **mouseLoc** function rather than the **clickLoc** function as we advised you to do in Chapter 7. This was done to accommodate an apparent anomaly in HyperTalk: It remembers the mouse-click location at the button used to activate the script rather than the one from the new mouse-click executed at the script's request while the script is executing. Because there are no instructions between the positioning of the **mouseLoc** and the **drag** command that uses it, this approach works fine and is probably a little quicker than the more usual method of using **clickLoc**.

► The script property

One of the most powerful features of HyperTalk is the ability to use the **script** property to modify scripts. This self-modification feature is an advanced idea with origins in symbolic processing and AI languages like LISP. Used properly, it can lead to highly personalized HyperCard applications that appear to be quite intelligent about their users.

You can both **get** and **set** the script of any object capable of holding a script. You can access individual elements in the script by placing it into a variable and then treating the script as an ordinary container of text (which it is). The process (which you can experiment with in the next Laboratory exercise) involves a framework like this:

```
put the script of card button 1 into scripter
-- use put to modify one or more words or lines
set the script of card button 1 to scripter
```

You may also simply delete the script by using a command like:

```
set the script of this card to empty
```

This might come in handy if you build one or more temporary scripts during execution of an application, and you don't want them hanging around the next time the application runs.

By the way, the object whose script is being modified can easily be the object currently being accessed (for example, a button script can modify itself).

A self-modifying script

All you really need for this experiment is a card with a single button. The experiment is more rewarding and easier to follow, however, if you use one of our now-famous one-button, one-field card designs in the Laboratory stack. Again, you can use an existing card or create a new one. After you have such a card, follow these instructions:

1. Open the script-editing window of a button in one of the usual ways.

2. Type the following handler into the script-editing window. Click OK when you have proofread the script.

```
on mouseUp
   beep 2
   put the script of card button 1 into card field 1
   get word 2 of line 2 of card field 1
   -- use a variable name if you don't have a field
   add 1 to it
   put it into word 2 of line 2 of card field 1
   set the script of card button 1 to card field 1
end mouseUp
```

3. Return to browse mode.

4. Click on the button. Notice that the system produces two short beeps in rapid succession. If you have card field 1 showing, you can see the script appear in the field. But the number on line 2 will become 3. Click the mouse on the button again. This time you hear three beeps and the number in the script changes to 4. This will go on almost forever if we let it!

▶ The visible property

The **visible** property is another shared property. You can both **set** and **get** it. To check whether an object is presently visible, you can use a construct like:

```
get the visible of card field 2
```

Then, if *It* is false, you can make the field visible as follows:

```
set the visible of card field 2 to true
```

There is little or no penalty in HyperCard for making a visible field visible or making an invisible one invisible.

There are other commands for making a field visible or invisible. You can use the **hide** command to the same effect as setting an object's **visible** property to false. Similarly, you can use the **show** command rather than setting the **visible** property to true.

▶ The cantDelete property

Beginning with Version 1.2, HyperCard enables you to protect stacks, backgrounds, and cards from deletion "on the fly." You can set the **cantDelete** property of any object of these types to true to prohibit deletion and to false to permit it.

Changing the value of this property changes the setting of the check box in the Info dialog for that property. Therefore, if a card's "Can't Delete Card" box is checked and you set the **cantDelete** property to false, you can delete the card. If you forget to change back the value of this property before closing the stack, the user always is able to delete the card.

▶ The dontSearch property

Backgrounds, cards, and fields can have their **dontSearch** properties set to true or false beginning with HyperCard Version 2.0. When any of these objects has its **dontSearch** property set to true, any search operation initiated by the **find** command either from the menu or from a script will simply ignore that object's contents.

You can turn this property on and off as needed to focus searching operations, though with the significantly more sophisticated **find** capabilities in HyperCard Version 2.0 and higher, you may not find this necessary.

▶ The scroll property

Both fields and card windows have a **scroll** property beginning with Hyper-Card Version 2.0. However, in a real sense this property is not shared in the same way the others we have been discussing are shared because its behavior is so different between the two types of objects. Therefore, we'll discuss this property with each individual object type rather than here. We have listed it in this section only for completeness.

▶ Unique Stack Properties

Six HyperCard properties pertain to stacks alone: **size, freeSize, cantModify, cantPeek, cantAbort**, and **version.**

▶ The size property

You can determine the size in bytes of a stack by using the **get** command with the **size** property. It cannot be **set**. You must tell HyperCard the name of the stack you want to check. If you want the size of the current stack, you must use the key word **this**, as in

```
get the size of this stack
```

▶ The freeSize property

When cards are deleted from a stack or when other stack changes, such as adding or removing scripts or objects takes place, the space they vacate is left open rather than "collapsed" so that all cards are stored contiguously in the file. During stack construction, many events can also cause holes to appear in the stack. If you have ever opened a Stack Info... dialog (see Figure 17-5), you have probably noticed the Free in Stack indicator. This number tells you how many bytes of space are vacant in the stack and thus occupying unnecessary disk space.

You can find the value of the free space in a stack with the **freeSize** property. You cannot **set** its value, however. The only way to modify it is to compact the stack using the "Compact Stack" option in the File menu. When compaction is complete, the stack's **freeSize** is 0.

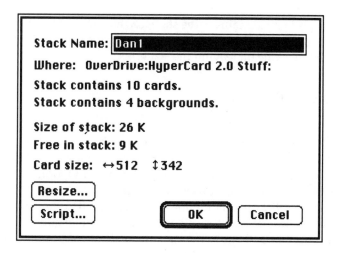

Figure 17-5. Stack Info... dialog box showing free space

Experience shows that when the **freeSize** of a stack exceeds about 15 percent of the stack's total size as given by the **size** property, compaction results in more efficient stack usage as well as freeing disk space. In your stacks, you might want to check for this condition in a handler as follows:

```
on closeStack
   if the freeSize of this stack > 0.15 *¬
   the size of this stack then answer¬
   "You should compact this stack!"
end closeStack
```

You may, of course, choose to put up the watch cursor and perform the compaction yourself with this command:

```
doMenu "Compact Stack"
```

▶ The cantModify property

This property was added with the release of HyperCard Version 1.2. It can be set to true or false. It has no effect on a locked stack. But if it is set to true, the user is prohibited from making any modifications to the stack, including deleting or compacting it.

When the property is true, a padlock symbol appears at the end of the menu bar and the menu options for compacting and deleting the stack are dimmed in the File Menu.

The property remains in the state to which it is set when the stack is closed, so if you intend a change to be temporary in the value of this property, be sure to reset its value on leaving the stack.

▶ The cantPeek property

Beginning with HyperCard Version 2.0, you can make it impossible for the user to use the Command-Option key combination to find out where all the buttons on a card are located. The same technique also makes it impossible for the user to find fields with the Shift-Command-Option key combination.

Setting the **cantPeek** property to true will make these key combinations inoperative. If the user holds down the Option and Command keys, for example, and then clicks on a button rather than opening that button's script, the button will simply be activated. The default condition of this property is false.

▶ The cantAbort property

There are times when it would be dangerous or potentially damaging to data for the user to interrupt execution of your scripts by pressing the Command-Period key combination. Prior to HyperCard Version 2.0, there was no way to prevent the user from doing this. However, starting with that version, you can now set the **cantAbort** property of a stack to true and thus disable the Command-Period key combination.

Generally speaking, it's a good idea to use the true setting of this property somewhat sparingly. The reason is that it removes the user from control, and if an inadvertent loop should be entered or a user orders the beginning of what could be a long series of processing steps and then legitimately wishes to change his or her mind, he or she will be unable to do so. You should therefore avoid the temptation to use this approach, in conjunction with a true setting for the **cantPeek** property, as a means of protecting your stack from inspection.

▶ The version property

You can use the **version** property to obtain useful information about the versions associated with a stack's creation and modification history. The property is read-only and has two forms. The **version** property returns a single number, like "2.0," that is the version in use. Applied to a stack or, without a stack by adding the word "long" before "version," it returns five 8-character numbers separated by commas. They are, in order of appearance in a **put** statement:

1. the version of HyperCard used to create the stack

2. the version of HyperCard last used to compact the stack

3. the oldest version of HyperCard used to modify the stack since its last compaction

4. the version of HyperCard that last changed the stack

5. the most recent modification date and time, in seconds, of the stack

If any of the stack values — that is, items 1–4 of the list returned by the **version** property — is less than 1.2, its value in this list will be "00000000."

The fifth value is only updated when the stack is closed, not each time a change is made.

▶ Unique Card-Window Property

When Apple Computer made it possible, with the introduction of HyperCard Version 2.0, to have multiple windows open at one time (one window per stack), it enhanced the concept of a card window. In earlier versions, there was such a thing as a card window but it was almost of purely academic interest. With multiple windows open, card windows took on a new significance.

There are actually two properties of card windows that were added or changed as a result of this introduction. One of them is not, however, unique.

The **rectangle** property of a card window, which was a read-only property in versions of HyperCard prior to Version 2.0, is now read-write. You can **set** its value and thereby move and/or resize the card window.

The other property of a card window is the **scroll** property. It is not unique in name (there is a **scroll** property associated with scrolling fields as well), but its use with a card window is completely different from its use with a scrolling field. The most obvious difference is that the **scroll** of a field is a single value in pixels while the **scroll** of a card window is a two-number, comma-separated value. This is because the scrolled position of the card within a card window is a point, which is always defined with two integers separated by a comma.

When the upper-left corner of the card coincides with the upper-left corner of the card window, then the **scroll** of that card window is 0,0. The first value is the horizontal location of the card within the card window and the second is its vertical location. Thus, if you write a command like the one below, you will move the horizontal position of the card 100 pixels to the right of the origin (upper-left corner) horizontally while leaving its vertical position at the origin:

```
set the scroll of card window to 100,0
```

► Unique Card Property

Beginning with HyperCard Version 2.0, cards have a single unique property, **marked**, that can have a value of true or false. If a card has been previously identified as matching some criterion with the **mark cards** command (see Chapter 9), then that card's **marked** property is true; otherwise, it is false.

A number of HyperTalk built-in functions and commands (for example, **print** and **show**) take advantage of the **marked** property to make themselves more useful.

► Unique Field Properties

HyperTalk includes eight properties that apply exclusively or uniquely to fields. Seven — **scroll, wideMargins, lockText, autoTab, fixedLineHeight, dontWrap,** and **Shared Text** — apply only to fields. The eighth, **style**, is common to both fields and buttons but has markedly different values for each.

We should point out, too, that fields have five text properties associated with them: **textAlign, textFont, textSize, textStyle,** and **textHeight.** But these are identical in operation to the same properties as they relate to HyperCard's painting environment, which is discussed in detail in Chapter 13. We will not repeat the discussion of those five properties here.

► The autoTab property

Beginning with HyperCard Version 1.2, a field may be defined as having an Auto Tab characteristic (see Chapter 4). This property can also be set in a script to be either true or false. If it is true, the Return key acts exactly like the Tab key under some circumstances. If it is false, the Return key always inserts a carriage return in the field.

The **autoTab** property only works with nonscrolling fields. If this property is true for a particular field and the user presses the Return key when he or she is on the last line of this field, HyperCard treats this Return as if it were a Tab. It moves the user to the next field on the card (if there is one) and sends the **closeField** message if text has been changed (see Chapter 6).

► The lockText property

Two types of text can be displayed in a field: editable text and locked text. Generally, when you want to make the text in a field noneditable, you check the Lock Text check box in the Field Info... dialog (see Figure 17-6). But this property can also be changed from within your scripts by modifying the **lockText** property.

The **lockText** property can be true or false. When it is true, it is the same as checking the Lock Text check box in the dialog. This makes the text in the field uneditable. When the pointer moves into a field with locked text, it does not change to the text editing I-beam cursor but remains the browsing pointer. When the **lockText** property is false, the cursor changes to the I-beam when the pointer enters the field, and clicking anywhere in the field makes the text available for editing.

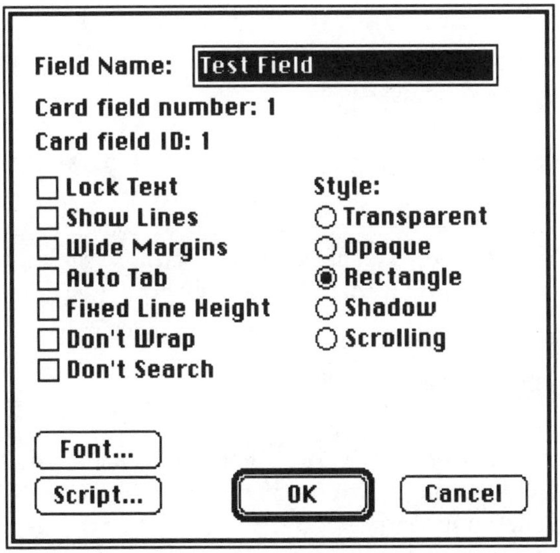

Figure 17-6. Field Info... dialog showing Lock Text

Locked text is used much like painted text, which also cannot be changed by simple editing. But locked text also cannot be changed with paint tools. Standard headings can be placed into locked-text fields. This is particularly useful if part of these headings' contents changes from card to card but you don't want the user to be able to edit them.

▶ The scroll property

The **scroll** property is one of the most interesting properties in HyperCard. Using it in calculations, you can determine how many lines of text have scrolled off the top of a scrolling text field and change the number (and thus the visible contents of the field) in a script. The **scroll** property's value is the number of pixels that have scrolled off the top of the field to which it is attached.

By dividing the value obtained from **get**ting the **scroll** property for a field by the **textHeight** value for that field, you can find out how many lines are in the scrolling field but no longer visible:

```
put the scroll of field 1 / the textHeight of field ¬
    into invis
```

You can then use **set** to change the number of invisible lines to any value you want by a reverse process:

```
set the scroll of field 1 to 3 / the textHeight of field 1
```

This command scrolls the text in the field so that the first three lines are invisible to the browser. The user can still scroll to see those lines using the arrows and other scroll controls. They are not gone, just temporarily invisible.

Manipulating the scroll

This two-phase experiment requires that you create a new Laboratory stack card with a single scrolling text field and a single button. Make the text field relatively small, though large enough to permit two or three lines of text to be visible. When you have things set up, follow these instructions:

1. Open the script-editing window of the button in one of the usual ways.

2. Type the following handler into the script-editing window. Click OK when you have proofread the script.

```
on mouseUp
    put the scroll of card field 1 / the ¬
    textHeight of card field 1 into invis
    put invis
end mouseUp
```

3. Return to browse mode.

4. Type a few lines of text into the scrolling field. Make sure that at least five or six lines of text are in the field. Then use the scrolling arrows to position the first three lines of text so they are hidden at the top of the field.

5. Now click the button. The result should resemble Figure 17-7. The Message box contains a 3 because there are three invisible lines above the top of the scrolling field.

6. Scroll a few more lines off the top of the field with the scrolling arrow. Now press the button again and notice that the value in the Message box changes. Experiment with different field depths and perhaps even different fonts and sizes to see how the calculation is affected.

7. Now for the second phase of our experiment. Add a second button. (We labeled the first one Line Finder and the second one Line Reset so we could tell them apart. Choose your own names or use ours, but label them.)

8. Open the script-editing window of this button in one of the usual ways.

9. Type the following handler into the script-editing window. Click OK when you have proofread the script.

```
on mouseUp
    set the scroll of card field 1 to 0
end mouseUp
```

10. Return to browse mode.

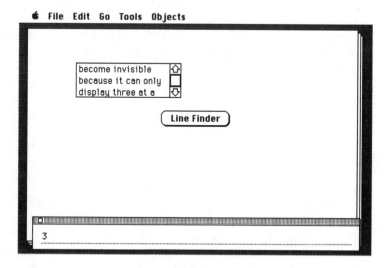

Figure 17-7. Scrolling field test, phase one

11. Make sure at least one line has scrolled off the top of the scrolling field and then click this new button. The result should resemble Figure 17-8. The top line of text is again visible in the field.

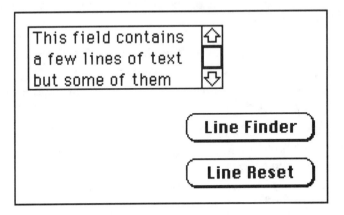

Figure 17-8. Scrolling field test, phase two

▶ The showLines property

Like the **lockText** property, the **showLines** property is normally set from the Field Info… dialog. The **showLines** property can be either true or false. If it is true, the lines under each line of text in the window are displayed. If the **showLines** property is false, which is its default condition, the lines are not shown.

The distance between the lines in the text field when **showLines** is true is the value of **textHeight**.

This property has no effect on scrolling fields.

▶ The style property

Buttons and fields share the **style** property, but the values the property can have associated with it are different between the two types of objects. A field's style, like most other property features we've been discussing, is generally selected from the Field Info… dialog, using the set of radio buttons on the right side of the window. Notice that only one **style** attribute can be set at a time.

The choices for the **style** property in a field are *transparent, opaque, rectangle, shadow,* and *scrolling*. The first two **style** values produce fields with no visible borders. The difference is whether underlying paint objects can be seen (*transparent*) or not (*opaque*). The next two values, *rectangle* and *shadow*, determine the appearance of a border around the field. The last, *scrolling*, defines a field with a border and scroll bars capable of displaying as much as 32K bytes of information. (Although all HyperCard fields can hold 32K bytes of data, all but scrolling fields are limited to displaying as much as will fit into their physical configuration on the card.)

▶ The wideMargins property

The **wideMargins** property is yet another property that is normally set with the Field Info… dialog. It can have a value of true, in which case HyperCard adds some extra space at the left and right margin of each line of text to improve its readability, or false, in which event the full width of the line is used. Figure 17-9 shows you the same field (from our previous Laboratory exercise) with **wideMargins** set to true (on the left side) and in its default state of false (on the right).

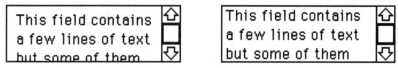

Figure 17-9. Effect of wideMargins settings

▶ The fixedLineHeight property

HyperCard Version 2.0 added a new property for all fields, **fixedLineHeight**. This property is normally false, but if you set it to true, then HyperCard maintains a constant vertical spacing between lines in the field regardless of the size of type entered into it.

The interaction between this property and the properties affecting the size or height of text in a script or field calls for careful consideration. If, for example, you set the **fixedLineHeight** property for a field to true and then put some 14-point text into the field with a **textHeight** property value of 10, the newly entered type will be quite crowded vertically.

▶ The dontWrap property

If you want to force a physical line of text to correspond to a logical line in a field, you can set the **dontWrap** property of a field to true beginning with HyperCard Version 2.0, where this property was added. Normally, this property has a value of false, meaning that text wraps over to the next line automatically when it encounters the edge of the field in which it is displayed.

▶ The sharedText property

In versions of HyperCard prior to the release of Version 2.0, if you wanted the same text to appear on all the cards in a stack or background, the only way to accomplish this was to use the text paint tool and paint the text onto the background. This is because background fields in those earlier versions of HyperCard have card-specific contents, that is, what is in a background field can and often does vary from card to card.

Most of the time, this card-dependent data content is exactly what you want. But when you want, for example, to display a title on all of the cards in a background or stack, the use of paint text has a major disadvantage in that it is not easily manageable from your script and cannot be examined and tested from within the script. The **sharedText** property added with Version 2.0 of HyperCard addresses these needs nicely. If you set a background field's **sharedText** property to true, then all of the cards that share that field will have the same text in the field.

One interesting problem you may encounter involves the inadvertent mixing of card-specific and shared text in a single field. For example, if you were to create a background field, type some text into it on one card, create one or more new cards, and then set the **sharedText** property of this field to true, you would notice that the text you entered into the field before setting this property has disappeared. If, on the other hand, you set **sharedText** back to false, the shared text you entered into the field disappears and the card-specific content reappears. You may be able to come up with some situations in which this somewhat bizarre-looking behavior will be useful.

▶ Unique Button Properties

Six HyperCard properties pertain only to buttons: **autoHilite, hilite, shared-Hilite, icon, showName,** and **style.** In addition, text properties that apply to painting and fields are also pertinent to the text inside buttons.

▶ The autoHilite property

The **autoHilite** property, which can be either true or false, is normally set through the Button Info… dialog (see Figure 17-10) using the Auto hilite check box. It determines whether the button will become momentarily highlighted, or inverted, when it is pressed. The default for the **autoHilite** property is false.

Most experienced HyperTalk programmers we know generally change the **autoHilite** property to true because it is more Mac-like to have the button highlighted when it is activated.

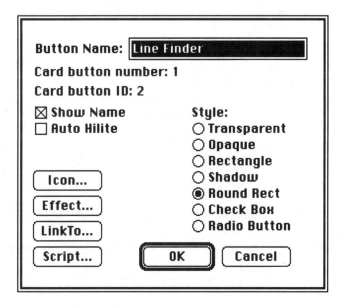

Figure 17-10. Button Info... dialog

▶ The hilite property

The **hilite** property is true if the button is presently highlighted and false if it is not. You can use both **get** and **set** with this property, and it can be used from a script or from the Message box. Figure 17-11 shows what a button looks like when its **hilite** property is set to true from the Message box.

▶ The sharedHilite property

Beginning with HyperCard Version 2.0, you can set the **sharedHilite** property of a background button to true or false. Its normal condition is true. When you set it to false, the highlighted condition of the button is saved automatically as a part of each card. This helps overcome a problem that existed with radio buttons and check boxes in earlier releases of HyperCard. If you had a background radio button, for example, that was turned on on one card and off on another, the state of the button remained the same throughout all of its occurrences in the stack.

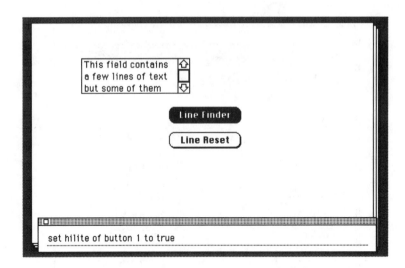

Figure 17-11. Button with hilite set to true

This added property allows you to treat any radio button or check box's status independently of the button's setting on another card without requiring you to write any code to handle it. In earlier versions of HyperCard, you had to write a script to deal with this issue, saving the on/off state of a button or buttons in a hidden field and using those values to be sure the buttons were changed to their proper state on each card. With Version 2.0, this is no longer necessary.

▶ The icon property

Many buttons in HyperCard stacks have an icon associated with them, though they are not required to do so. Each icon is a resource (see Chapter 21) with an associated name and number. HyperCard uses only the number to identify icons in scripts. The **icon** property contains the number of the icon assigned to a button.

Most of the time, you won't use the **icon** property. But there is at least one occasion when you might want to use **set** with the **icon** property to change an icon associated with a button.

Many Macintosh applications, as you know, have icons that invert when they are selected. Others change the icon completely when it is selected. You can achieve these same effects in HyperCard applications by including in an **on mouseUp** handler a command to change the icon of the button to indicate activation. There is no point in using this approach only to cause HyperCard to invert the icon because HyperCard can do that as a matter of design. But when you want to achieve a dramatic effect by changing the icon to indicate that it is selected, you can do so with a command like:

```
set the icon of button 3 to 1048
```

In the last Laboratory exercise, we created a button called Line Reset. It had a simple one-line script. If you modify that script and enlarge the button, it looks like Figure 17-12 when it is selected. Here is the new script:

```
on mouseUp
    set the icon of card button 2 to 27056
    set the hilite of card button 2 to true
    set the scroll of card field 1 to 0
    wait 10 seconds
    set the icon of card button 2 to 0
    set the hilite of card button 2 to false
end mouseUp
```

Icon 27056 is supplied with HyperCard as one of the icons you can select when you click the Icon button in the Button Info... dialog.

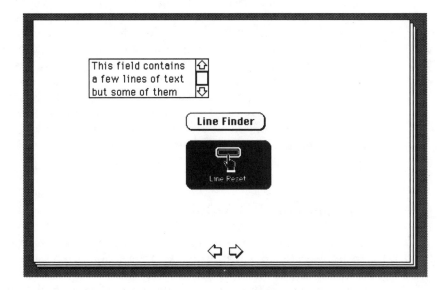

Figure 17-12. Substituting icon when button selected

▶ The showName property

The **showName** property is another property that is generally turned on and off through the Button Info... dialog. When it is true, the name chosen for the button in the text-edit rectangle at the top of the dialog is displayed inside the button. If the button also includes an icon, the name is displayed under the icon in small type. Otherwise, it is displayed in the text pattern set by a script, or the system default (12-point Chicago centered).

With **showName** set to false, only the icon or underlying painted material shows through the button. The icon is always visible, but paint on the card or background is visible only through a button whose style is *transparent*. Button **style** is discussed in the next section.

▶ The style property

Like its field-related counterpart, a button's **style** property is normally set from the Button Info... dialog, using the set of radio buttons on the right side of the window. This property has seven possible values: *transparent, opaque, rectangle, shadow, round rect, check box,* and *radio button*. The first four are identical in effect to their duplicates in a field's **style** property.

The *round rect* style of button is the one that HyperCard uses if you don't tell it to do something else. Like *rectangle* and *shadow*, it affects only the border around the button.

The check box and radio button style buttons are well known to anyone who has used a Macintosh even casually. But if you've programmed the Macintosh in other languages, you should be aware that HyperTalk does *not* handle the management of these button types for you simply because you declare them to be one of these types. If you define a set of radio buttons, your script must manage turning on one and only one at a time. If you use check boxes, you can have more than one in a set selected at one time. That is the fundamental difference, besides shape, between the two types of buttons. We have more to say about handling banks of radio buttons in Chapter 20.

▶ Unique Picture Property

Beginning with Version 1.2 of HyperCard, Apple Computer defined a new quasi object called a **picture**. (See Chapter 13 for a discussion of pictures and their manipulation.) A single property associated with these new types of objects is provided so that you can determine in your script if a particular card or background picture is visible. This property is the **showPict** property.

In effect, this property is a card or background property because each card and background can have only one piece of art, which is treated as a single picture.

As you would expect, the value of the **showPict** property is true if the picture in question is visible, false if it is not.

Your script may **get**, **put**, or **set** this property. For example, to find out whether the picture on the current card is visible, you can use a command like this:

```
if the showPict of this card is true then...
```

The important thing to note is that even though the property applies to a picture, it is addressed as if it were a card or background property.

▶ Summary

In this chapter, you learned about HyperCard properties and how to manage them. You examined every property that wasn't covered when we discussed painting in HyperTalk scripts in Chapter 13. You saw how to use **get** to find out the current value of a property and how to use **set** to change the values of those properties subject to modification.

Chapter 18 examines report printing, a new capability added to HyperCard Version 2.0.

18 ▶ Printing Reports

Beginning with Version 2.0, HyperCard provides significantly enhanced report printing capabilities over earlier versions of the program. From within a script, you can print

- part or all of a card or group of cards
- any HyperCard container — including individual fields and even scrolling fields whose content is not entirely visible on the card
- any of several prestored, formatted reports

These capabilities are all in addition to the basic printing of a single card, marked cards, selected cards, or stacks, as described in Chapter 9. In this chapter, we will focus exclusively on the three report-related printing activities listed above. Before we discuss the processes in detail, however, we will begin with a description of how you can control certain aspects of the printing output when you print containers or preformatted reports.

▶ Controlling the Printed Output

As we indicated in Chapter 17, there are six properties that affect the appearance of printed output in HyperTalk. You can set these properties at any point and they retain those settings until you change or reset them. These properties do not affect the printing of a portion of a card as described in the next section. Nor are they generally used with the printing of formatted reports, since part of the process of creating the template involves making most of these decisions. But you can use these settings with reports to override the basic default formatting.

The six global properties you can set are

- **printTextFont**
- **printTextStyle**
- **printTextSize**
- **printTextAlign**
- **printTextHeight**
- **printMargins**

All of these properties, like all other global properties, have default settings. These defaults are shown in Table 18-1.

Table 18-1. Print Setting Defaults

Global Variable	*Default Value*
printTextFont	Geneva
printTextStyle	plain
printTextSize	10
printTextAlign	left
printTextHeight	13
printMargins	0,0,0,0

When you have changed one or more of these defaults and wish to restore them, you can use the command **reset printing**. This command restores all of these globals to the default values indicated in Table 18-1.

The legal settings for most of these global variables are not surprising if you've had any experience with setting the font and other related printing information within a word processor, for example. For the record, though, let's look at each of these globals and their possible values.

You can choose any currently available font for the value of the **printTextFont** global.

▶ Printing Part of a Card

You can print any portion of a card by specifying the top-left and bottom-right corners of the rectangle to be printed. These coordinates are defined in terms of the window in which the card appears (that is, the upper-left corner of the window is 0,0) rather than the screen coordinates (where the upper-left corner of the display is 0,0).

The basic syntax for this command is as follows:

```
print <printObject> from <startPoint> to <endPoint>
```

This is sometimes useful if a portion of a card contains a drawing, for example.

When HyperTalk executes this command, it prints a bitmap image of everything that appears within the bounds of the described rectangle. This includes buttons, fields, and graphics.

If you supply a printObject that results in the same portion of more than one card being printed, HyperCard uses the same spacing and alignment as it would if you ordered a Print Stack... operation from the File menu.

▶ Printing Containers and Fields

Often, you want to print the contents of one or more fields on a card or on several cards because it is the contents of these fields that is important, not their shape, location on the card, or other details about them. Furthermore, if you want to print all of the contents of a scrolling field some of whose contents are invisible because of the size of the field on the card, you cannot accomplish this task with a **print card** command. In this case, the **print field** command comes in handy.

The syntax for this command is simple:

```
print <fieldExpression>
```

The argument you supply can be the name, number, or ID of a card or background field. Regardless of whether you identify a card or background field, only that field's contents on the current card will be printed. Thus, if you have a stack of fifteen cards and a background field called "Project Description" and you want to print out all the project descriptions, you'll need to use a **repeat** loop to accomplish your purpose, as shown here:

```
on mouseUp
    repeat number of cards times
        print field "Project Description"
        go to next card
    end repeat
end mouseUp
```

As useful as this command is, it is only part of the HyperTalk container printing capability included in HyperCard Version 2.0. You can print selected chunks of a field, as in:

```
print line 3 to 5 of field "contents"
```

More complex containers can also be defined. For example, if you have a data field that contains comma-separated elements (which, as you'll recall, are individually referred to as *items* in HyperTalk), and you needed to list the third element in each line on all the cards in a stack, you could use a construct like this:

```
on mouseUp
   go to card 1
   set lockScreen to true -- optional but a good idea
   repeat number of cards times
      repeat with k = 1 to the number of lines of field "data"
         print item 3 of line k of field "data"
      end repeat
      go to next card
   end repeat
end mouseUp
```

As it turns out, this handler probably doesn't produce what you had in mind. Each **print** statement produces a new page of output, so this handler would turn out a separate page for each line in the field "data" for each card in the stack. If you want to produce a single list, on one or more contiguous pages, you could modify the handler slightly, as shown here:

```
on mouseUp
   go to card 1
   set lockScreen to true -- optional but a good idea
   repeat number of cards times
      repeat with k = 1 to the number of lines of field "data"
         put item 3 of line k of field "data"¬
            & return after listing
      end repeat
      go to next card
   end repeat
   print listing
end mouseUp
```

Here we use the same two **repeat** loops as earlier, only we build up a variable called **listing** and then we print it at the end of the handler. This also shows HyperTalk's ability to print any container's value.

▶ Printing Formatted Reports

In HyperCard Version 2.0, each stack can store up to sixteen different report formats. Each of these report formats must have a name. The formats themselves are created manually by users or stack designers and then stored. Users can then order these reports from the File menu by choosing the "Print Report..." option. In this section, we'll focus on the printing of reports from scripts. We assume you know how to create a report template, in much the same way we assume you know how to create stacks, cards, and backgrounds.

There are three steps to producing a report from a template within a HyperTalk script, the second of which is optional:

1. Use an **open report printing** command to define the template to use (or to indicate that you wish to use the format used during the last report run on this stack) and to initiate the process.

2. Define the cards to be printed.

3. Use a **close printing** command to generate the report in the Macintosh memory and print it.

▶ The open report printing command

The first step uses the **open report printing** command, whose syntax is as follows:

```
open report printing [with {template<templateName> | dialog}]
```

If you omit the **with** portion of the statement, HyperTalk prints the report without the intervening dialog, asking the user to confirm options and using the last report template used in this stack. As you can see, you can use either a template name or the key word **dialog** if you choose the **with** option, but not both. If you use the **with dialog** approach, HyperTalk will allow the user to choose the report template to be used and to change its parameters as well. Deciding which approach to use is at least partly a function of how much control you want to give the user over the report-printing process.

▶ Defining the cards to print

The reason the second step in the report-printing process is optional is that each report template carries with it a specification of which cards in the stack are to be printed when the report is run. The person who creates the template can choose to have HyperCard print either all of the cards in the stack or only those cards that are marked (see Chapter 8 for a discussion of card marking). If your **open report printing** command is not followed by any statements that change this behavior, HyperCard simply uses the setting in the report parameter file.

You may, however, wish to override this default behavior. For example, you may have a report format defined so that it normally prints all the cards in a stack. But in some specific circumstances, you may wish to mark certain cards in advance and then print the same format using only those cards. In that event, you would construct a handler something like this:

```
on mouseUp
    markTheCards -- a user-defined function that marks cards
    open report printing with template "Status Report"
    print marked cards -- overrides normal behavior of all cards
    close printing
end mouseUp
```

▶ Using close printing to start the report

It may feel paradoxical to learn that the statement that actually causes the printing to start on your printer is **close printing**. But if you think of the process as actually involving two steps from the computer's perspective, it will make some sense.

Printing on the Macintosh involves two stages, regardless of the program you use. The first stage is assembling the information you want to print, along with any parameters about the destination of the printout, the format to be followed, and other details. The second stage is the actual printing.

In HyperTalk, then, the **open report printing** and **open printing** commands handle the majority of the first stage of printing, and the **close printing** command handles the second. It is this command that actually sends to the printer the information and parameters generated by the first statement.

If you don't include a **close printing** command in your script and then later you try to start another print run with an **open printing** or **open report printing** command, you will see a dialog box that indicates that the current print job will be canceled if you proceed.

▶ Finding names of available report templates

Each stack in HyperCard, beginning with Version 2.0, has a function called **reportTemplates** that contains a list of all of the report templates stored with that stack. This list is return-delimited. If no report templates have been defined for a stack, then this function returns an empty result.

You may find this valuable if you want to ensure a report template is available before ordering it. A handler like this would be useful in such conditions:

```
on checkTemplateAvailable templateName
    if templateName is in the reportTemplates then
        open printing with templateName
        print all cards
        close printing
        exit checkTemplateAvailable
    else
        play "boing"
        answer "Sorry, template" && templateName && "not available."
    end if
end checkTemplateAvailable
```

▶ Report Combinations

One thing you cannot do simply by opening report printing is to combine a formatted report with other printed information such as the contents of fields that are not included in the report template. Once you write an **open report printing** statement, any **print** statements that appear before the next **close printing** statement affect that report print run. An example will help to clarify what we mean.

Look at the following handler:

```
on mouseUp
    open report printing -- uses last template
    print marked cards
    sort dateTime by field "Activity Date"
    print all cards
    go to card "Title"
    print card field "Main Title Summary"
    close printing
end mouseUp
```

What might you expect to happen if you ran this handler in an appropriately designed stack? As it turns out, you'd get two separate outputs. The first would combine the two reports using the template that are called for by the first two **print** statements. They would be printed without a page break between them, with marked cards duplicated but appearing in their sorted order after the last card in the stack had been printed in the unsorted sequence. The second would be the contents of card field "Main Title Summary" on the card called "Title."

This is probably not what you want. You want the first two reports to be separate documents. The easiest and most efficient way to accomplish this is with two **open report printing** statements, as shown here:

```
on mouseUp
    open report printing -- uses last template
    print marked cards
    close printing
    open report printing
    sort dateTime by field "Activity Date"
    print all cards
    close printing
    go to card "Title"
    print card field "Main Title Summary"
end mouseUp
```

This will produce three separate pieces of output.

What if you want the lone card field "Main Title Summary" included in your report output? There is no way to accomplish that purpose. Report printing is designed to deal with regularly formatted reports where the same information from all printed cards appears in the report. The HyperTalk **print** command, on the other hand, does not format or otherwise attempt to structure the information it prints. The two approaches are completely different from one another.

▶ Summary

In this chapter, you've learned how to work with report printing, a capability added to HyperCard Version 2.0. You've learned how to use various HyperTalk commands to

- print all or a portion of one or more cards
- print the contents of HyperCard containers, including fields
- print formatted reports

In Chapter 19, we turn our attention to debugging and other script-related activities that are aimed primarily at you as a scripter rather than at the users of your stacks.

19 ▶ Script-Related Commands and Debugging

In this chapter, you will learn about

- the **edit script** command and its uses
- the **wait** command
- using and manipulating parameters in HyperTalk scripts
- using new features in HyperCard 2.0 to debug your scripts

▶ Using the edit script Command

If you are designing stacks to be used by technical people, particularly utilities for other stack developers, you may find it useful to know how to use the **edit script** command. When HyperTalk encounters this command, it opens the script-editing window for the object whose identification is supplied as an argument. Here is the command's syntax:

```
edit script of <object>
```

You should be judicious in your use of this command because it gives the user complete access to the script. If you design a stack for a nontechnical user but the script occasionally requires modification or customization, consider using the less intimidating method of **put**ting the script into a variable, modifying the variable, and then **set**ting the script to the contents of the modified variable. This technique is discussed in detail in Chapter 17 where scripts are treated as properties of their associated HyperCard objects.

Although you can enter this command from the Message box, you will probably never do so because it is easier to hold down the Shift key and double-click on a field or button to get at its script. You can use the **edit script** command to edit the script of the present script, card, or background or to edit some other script, card, or background. If you want to edit a script for an object that is not on the screen, this command can be a good shortcut.

Using the **edit script** command is not the only way to access or modify the script of an object. You can also follow a sequence like this:

1. **put** the script of the object into a field or, less likely, a container.

2. Manually edit the script (if you put it into a field) or use scripting techniques such as **put** "a new line of code into line x of field fieldName" to modify the script's contents.

3. **set** the script of the object to the field or container.

▶ The wait Command

We have used the **wait** command quite a few times in the book without explaining it. Its action is quite apparent, but it does have some nuances worth noting.

The command has three forms of syntax:

```
wait [for] <number> [ticks]|seconds
wait until <true/false>
wait while <true/false>
```

Using the first form, the minimal command you can issue looks like this:

```
wait 20
```

This results in the script pausing for 20 ticks, where one tick is 1/60 second. So the pause here would be about 1/3 second. HyperTalk assumes you want to use ticks unless you supply the word *seconds*, as in:

```
wait 3 seconds
```

If you want to use ticks, you need not supply the label, though you may want to do so for readability. You can also put the word *for* after the **wait** command for readability; it is a throw-away word that HyperTalk ignores. HyperCard also recognizes the singular word *second*. This makes the use of one-second delays read more naturally. Seconds may also be abbreviated *secs*, or singularly as *sec*.

The second and third forms of the syntax for the **wait** command use Boolean expressions to determine how long to wait or, more accurately, when to stop waiting. The **wait until** command continues to hold in a waiting state until the expression in the Boolean true/false argument becomes true, then the script continues processing. Conversely, **wait while** continues to wait only as long as the Boolean argument is true, resuming script operation as soon as it becomes false.

An obvious use of the **wait until** command, and one we've used a few times in this book, is to give the user control over when to proceed to the next step in processing. Generally, use the **mouseClick** function to determine when to continue, and let the user know that clicking the mouse ends the pause:

```
wait until the mouseClick
```

▶ Parameters in HyperTalk

Many system messages in HyperCard and some messages you design in your scripts include one or more parameters. When you use a **go** command, for example, you supply one or more parameters naming the destination card, background, or stack:

```
go card "Testing"
go stack "My Contacts"
go first card of stack "My Contacts"
```

When commands and messages involve parameters, you can use built-in HyperTalk functions to find out how many parameters are being sent with the message, place the entire parameter list into a variable or container, or extract and use a specific parameter by its position in the parameter string.

▶ How many parameters?

To determine how many parameters are sent with a message, use **the param-Count**. Because there is only one actively processing message or command at any moment, this function ironically requires no parameters. It simply returns an integer indicating how many parameters were passed with the last message.

You might use this construct, for example, where it is important to your handler that a certain number of parameters be passed before it can carry out its task:

```
on openHandler
    if the paramCount <3 then ask "I need three arguments."
end openHandler
```

▶ Extracting individual parameters

Quite often when a message or command with parameters is sent to a handler you've designed (as opposed to a system message handler), you will need to pull the parameters apart and use them in different ways throughout the script. You can extract any parameter from a string with **the param**. Its syntax looks like this:

```
the param of <integer>
```

To extract the first parameter, you simply code:

```
the param of 1
```

Using this method, you can extract any individual parameter or combination of parameters for later manipulation and analysis in the handler. For example, if you've defined a handler called *grab Words* that receives two parameters, one of which is the number of the first word to be extracted from line 1 of a field and the other of which is the number of the last word to be extracted, you might write something like this (in part):

```
on grabWords
    put the param of 1 into startWord
    put the param of 2 into endWord
    repeat with counter = startWord to endWord
       put word counter of line 1 of field 1 after holder
    end repeat
    --put holder somewhere
end grabWords
```

You can use **the param** to identify the message being sent as well. The message name, which is always one word, is numbered 0 so that extracting it requires a construct like this:

```
put the param of 0 into lastMessageName
```

▶ Storing the parameter string

The third parameter-handling function in HyperTalk lets you manage the entire string of parameters as one entity, typically storing it for later use. The function called **the params** returns a string containing the entire message, including the message name. You can then use the usual chunking methods to extract whatever portions of the string you need. This function does not require any parameters.

Normally, you will probably use **the params** function to store the parameter string for later use in a handler that may be sending or dealing with other messages as it executes.

Remember that all three of these parameter-related functions only deal with the most recent message sent (that is, the one that is being executed or processed at the time).

▶ Debugging Your Scripts

With the release of HyperCard Version 2.0, Apple Computer addressed a shortcoming of earlier versions of the program that had been encountered by many scripters: the difficulty of finding logic and programming errors in scripts. By adding significant new debugging capabilities, HyperCard Version 2.0 makes it much easier to develop complex scripts by enabling you to figure out what went wrong when the result of executing your scripts isn't what you anticipated.

To debug your scripts in HyperCard, you must first enter the built-in debugger or choose a third-party debugger if you're using someone else's tool. Assuming that you use the built-in debugger, you can then walk through the execution of a handler or function one step at a time, including or excluding the other handlers or functions it calls. You can also monitor the values of the variables your script uses as well as the messages it generates.

| Note ▶ | If you wish to use a third-party debugger, variable watcher, and/or message watcher, you can do so simply by setting the global variables **debugger**, **variableWatcher**, and/or **messageWatcher** to the name of the external command file that contains the program you want to use. If you do this and HyperCard can't find the external, it loads the built-in default tool. |

Debugging is clearly a script-specific task. In the sections that follow, we'll examine how to enter and leave the debugger, how to set and clear temporary checkpoints (places where script execution will stop and permit you to do more detailed analysis), and how to use both variable and message watching during debugging. The process of identifying errors and correcting them is a general programming issue that is beyond the scope of this book.

▶ Entering and leaving the debugger

There are essentially three ways you can get into the HyperCard debugger: by creating an error condition as a result of which HyperTalk gives you the option of debugging, by interrupting script execution with a special key combination, or by creating a deliberate entry point to the debugger.

If you encounter a bug in your script or in a built-in script created by someone else that creates an error condition that HyperTalk understands could be subject to debugging, you'll see a dialog box like the one shown in Figure 19-1. Clicking on the "Debug" button will take you to the debugger. (The message in the dialog, of course, will vary depending on the type of error encountered. Also, not all error messages will have a "Debug" option.)

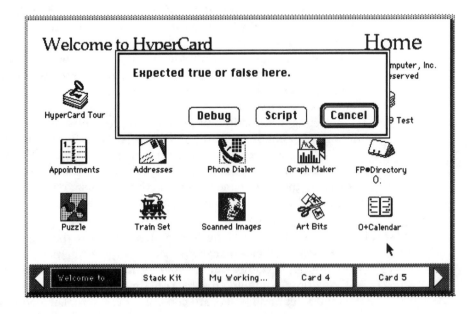

Figure 19-1. Dialog with Debug option

When a script is executing, you can interrupt it and instruct HyperTalk to enter the debugger by pressing the Period key while simultaneously holding down the Command and Option keys. This does not set any checkpoints; it simply places you into the debugger.

You can create a deliberate entry into the debugger with the command **debug checkpoint**. When HyperTalk encounters this command, it will open the debugging environment and halt execution of your script. You are then in position to undertake various debugging approaches outlined later in this discussion.

Once you've identified and fixed the bug(s) in your scripts or analyzed the processing and understood it well enough so that you're ready to proceed with your scripting, you can leave the debugger in any of three ways:

- by selecting the "Abort" option from the debugging menu (characterized by the icon of an insect)

- by choosing the "Go" option from the debugging menu

- by clicking in the debugger's Close box (Command-W does not work in the debugger)

The difference between the first two approaches for leaving the debugger is that the first terminates execution of the script and leaves you in the script editor while the second resumes execution where it was when you stopped your debugging activities.

If you leave the debugger with the variable or message watching window open, closing the debugger will not affect these windows.

▶ Setting and Clearing Checkpoints

A checkpoint in HyperTalk corresponds roughly to a breakpoint in traditional programming language tools. It represents a place at which HyperTalk will stop executing your script and either enter the debugger if it isn't already there or pause to allow you to examine variables, messages, or other aspects of the environment if it is already in the debugger. There are two basic types of checkpoints — permanent and temporary.

You set a permanent checkpoint in a script with the **debug checkpoint** command just referred to. This checkpoint remains in effect until you remove it by deleting or commenting out the command. Every time HyperTalk encounters this command, it will enter the debugger unless it is already there.

Temporary checkpoints are not saved to the disk and are thus active only so long as you don't close the stacks to which they or their associated object belongs. There are two ways to set a temporary checkpoint:

- in the script editor, you can click anywhere in the line where you wish to set the checkpoint while holding down the Option key

- in the debugger, you can select the "Set Checkpoint" option from the Debug menu or use the Command-D keyboard equivalent to set it

In both cases, the operations that set checkpoints are toggles; if you repeat them on a line where a checkpoint has already been set, HyperTalk will clear that checkpoint. HyperTalk puts a checkmark in the left margin next to the line when a checkpoint is set (see Figure 19-2).

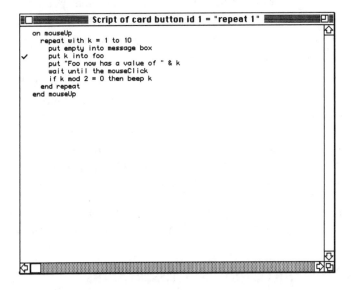

```
on mouseUp
  repeat with k = 1 to 10
    put empty into message box
✓   put k into foo
    put "Foo now has a value of " & k
    wait until the mouseClick
    if k mod 2 = 0 then beep k
  end repeat
end mouseUp
```

Figure 19-2. Checkmark on line indicating checkpoint is set

When HyperTalk encounters a checkpoint, whether it's permanent or temporary, it halts execution of the script and places you into the debugger.

▶ Running Scripts in the Debugger

Once you are in the debugger, you can follow the execution of your handler(s) and function(s) in one of two ways — by stepping or tracing.

If you choose either the "Step" or "Step Into" option from the Debug menu, HyperTalk will execute each line of the handler and pause before continuing. While execution is paused, you can only carry out commands that are available on the debugging menu. This means, among other things, that you can't edit the script of the object while you're debugging. You must first terminate debugging by one of the methods described earlier. If you attempt to select a menu option from any other menu while you're in the debugger, you'll be greeted with a dialog like the one shown in Figure 19-3.

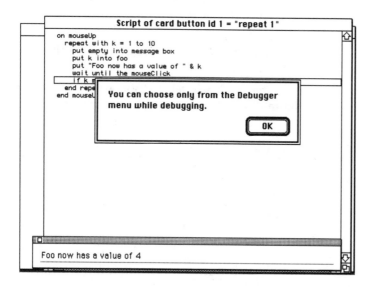

Figure 19-3. Result of choosing nondebugging menu option

The difference between the "Step" and "Step Into" options is important. If you choose "Step" and the handler you are debugging makes a call to another function or handler, HyperTalk will not step through the execution of that function or handler. It will execute it completely and then return to stepping through the current handler. But if you choose the "Step Into" option, then HyperTalk's step-by-step execution carries over to all functions and handlers called from the current handler, directly or indirectly. Even if the handler you are debugging calls a function that in turn calls another handler, all of those script elements will be executed a step at a time as long as you are in "Step Into" mode.

Sometimes, you don't really want to pause execution at each line of HyperTalk code in your handler or function. Instead, you are interested only in certain lines of code. In that case, you set temporary checkpoints on those lines of code in which you are interested and then choose either the "Trace" or the "Trace Into" option from the Debug menu. The difference between the two is the same as for "Step" and "Step Into" as described in the preceding paragraph. When you are tracing rather than single-stepping through a handler or function, HyperTalk only pauses at those lines with checkpoints set. You must then choose to step, trace, or abort debugging or continue script execution exactly as if you had just entered the debugger.

When you are tracing rather than single-stepping, you can instruct HyperTalk to pause between each line of code it executes so that you can observe the progress of the script by watching the rectangle that surrounds the currently executing line. Normally, HyperTalk does not delay at lines where no checkpoint is set. But you can instruct HyperTalk to delay at each line in one of two ways:

- by setting the global property **traceDelay** to some value (in ticks) other than the default value of 0
- by choosing the "Trace Delay..." option from the Debug menu as shown in Figure 19-4 and entering a value other than 0

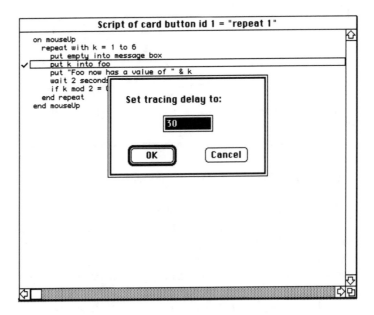

Figure 19-4. Setting trace delay in the debugger

HyperTalk will slow its execution to pause on each line of the handler or function for the specified number of ticks (remember that 1 tick = 1/60 second). You can then observe the rectangle as it highlights each line during script execution. This is often a useful way to gain an overview of what a handler or function is doing, particularly if it contains a number of nested **repeat** or **if** loops.

▶ Watching Messages and Variables

Perhaps the most useful aspects of HyperCard's built-in debugging environment are the Variable Watcher and the Message Watcher. These two windoids allow you to monitor what is going on in the environment in which your scripts are executing. Their contents can quite often help you understand where something is going wrong.

To open these windows, you choose the "Message Watcher" or "Variable Watcher" option from the Debug menu. You can, of course, have both of these windoids open at the same time. Figure 19-5 shows you what the windoids look like. We'll examine them separately and then discuss their use in debugging.

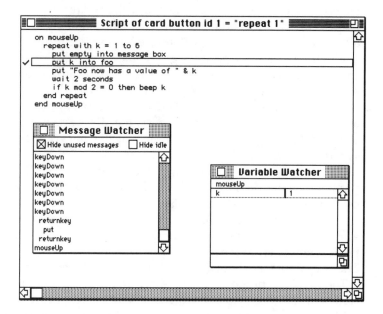

Figure 19-5. Message and Variable Watchers

▶ The Message Watcher

As you can guess from its name, the Message Watcher's function is to permit you to watch the messages being passed around in the HyperCard system during the execution of your scripts. You can cause it to appear in one of two ways:

- by choosing the "Message Watcher" option from the Debug menu
- by typing `show window "message watcher"` or simply `show [the]` `message watcher` either in the Message box or in a script

The latter approach lets you display the Message Watcher without entering the debugger.

When the Message Watcher is visible, it displays the last 150 lines of messages sent. You can scroll through these and even copy and paste the contents of the window so that you can examine the order in which various system messages and user-defined messages are interacting with each other. Since this is a frequent source of scripting errors, this capability is one you'll probably find useful.

In the Message Watcher window, you'll notice two check boxes. The one labeled "Hide Unused," when checked, will display only messages for which HyperCard finds a handler somewhere in the hierarchy. If this is unchecked, all messages are displayed, with unused messages surrounded by parentheses. Figure 19-6 shows the Message Watcher window with the "Hide Unused" check box unchecked as the user moves the mouse into and out of a button that has no **mouseEnter**, **mouseWithin**, or **mouseLeave** handler.

When you uncheck the "Hide Unused" check box, you almost always want to check the "Hide Idle" check box unless the **idle** message is an important part of your debugging needs. The Message Watcher quickly fills up with lines that say "(idle)" if you don't uncheck this check box.

You can also control the settings of these two check boxes by using properties of the Message Watcher called **hideUnused** and **hideIdle**. You can **set** these properties to true or false.

The Message Watcher has four other properties: **nextLine**, **text**, **loc**, and **visible**. The last two are properties with which you should already be familiar since they are shared by numerous other HyperCard objects. We will briefly examine the first two properties in the next few paragraphs.

The **nextLine** property is write-only and permits you to place your own comments into the Message Watcher's scrolling text field. This is sometimes helpful when you want to be able to look at the contents of the Message Watcher later and find out which object(s) the user was entering or leaving, for example. You might have a handler like the following at the card level or higher, for example, to put into the Message Watcher the names of all buttons or fields through which the mouse cursor passes while the Message Watcher is active:

```
on mouseEnter
    put the name of the target into objName
    set nextLine of window "Message Watcher" to "•••" & objName
        & return
end mouseEnter
```

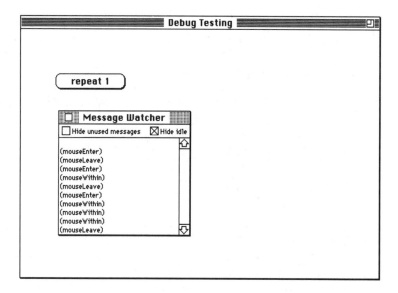

Figure 19-6. Message Watcher with "Hide Unused" Unchecked

The **text** property contains all the contents of the Message Watcher window. You can **set** or **get** this text or even use it in conditional tests in your scripts. To clear the Message Watcher, for example, you can use a line like this:

```
set text of window "Message Watcher" to empty
```

Using the **contains** or **is in** operator (see Chapter 10), you can examine the contents of the Message Watcher window and vary your script's response depending on what the user is doing.

It is interesting to note, too, that even though the Message Watcher is hidden or closed and therefore not monitoring messages, modifying the **nextLine** or **text** property still works. You can therefore treat the Message Watcher window as a repository of dynamic information gathered during script execution and stack usage and then show or use its contents as needed. This can be a very powerful tool for stack analysis as well as debugging.

▶ The Variable Watcher

Compared to the Message Watcher, the Variable Watcher has fewer complexities. But it may turn out to be more useful in debugging your scripts than the Message Watcher, simply because you will find that your scripting errors more often relate to variables than messages.

While the Variable Watcher is in use in the debugger, it keeps track of the current values of all variables it has encountered. As these values change, the Variable Watcher window updates its contents automatically. If you leave the Variable Watcher open when you leave the debugger, it no longer tracks local variables in your scripts; instead, it tracks all global variables, including those established by HyperCard itself. Simply studying this list of global variables may reveal a great deal about what has gone on in the environment as well as about settings in the environment itself. For example, **userName** is a global and if it has a value, it will be shown in the Variable Watcher outside the debugger. Figure 19-7 shows a portion of the Variable Watcher outside the debugger.

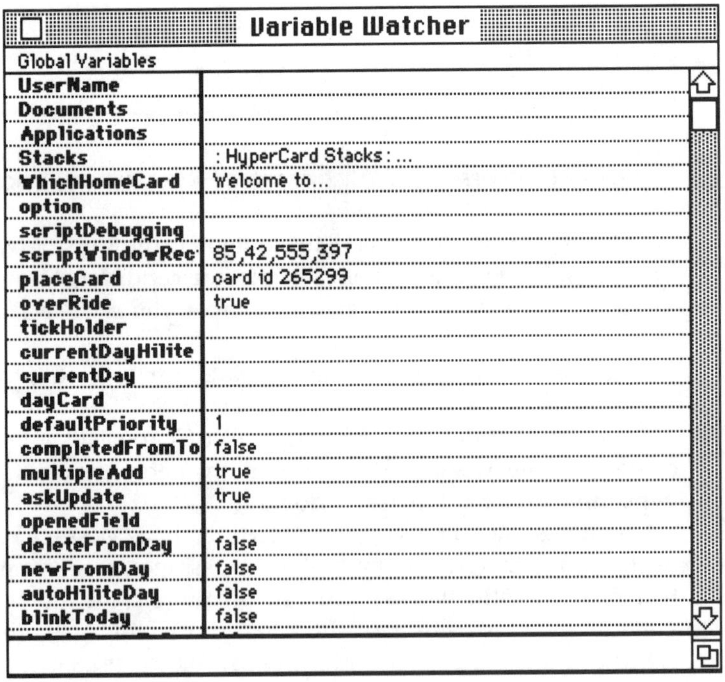

Figure 19-7. Variable Watcher Outside the Debugger

If you double-click on the right-hand portion of the Variable Watcher in a rectangle where some value appears, you can examine the entire contents of that variable in the bottom rectangle, as you can see in Figure 19-8. This is helpful when a variable like **Stacks**, which is set in the Home card of Hyper-Card so that it keeps track of all the places the program should look for stacks before asking the user for help, contains several lines. The horizontal and vertical bars that divide the Variable Watcher can be moved much as they can in a spreadsheet application.

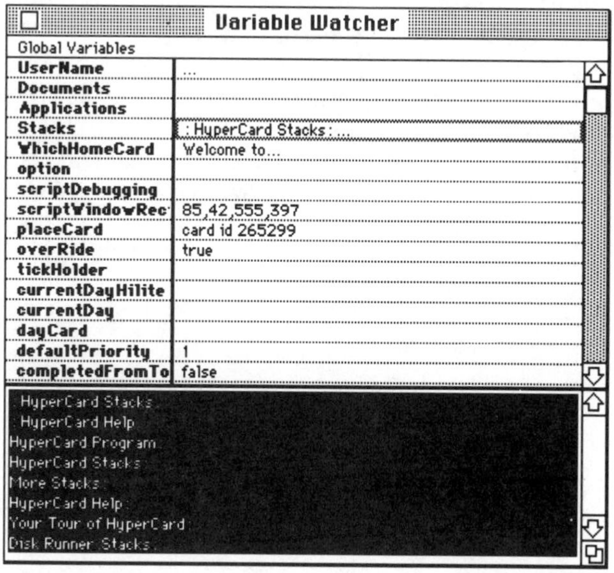

Figure 19-8. Examining a Multiline Variable

You cannot examine or modify the contents of the Variable Watcher in any way. It has five properties:

- **vBarLoc** , which contains the location of the vertical bar in the Variable Watcher window

- **hBarLoc**, which contains the location of the horizontal bar in the Variable Watcher window

- **loc**

- **rect**

- **visible**

▶ Summary

In this chapter, you learned about some useful, though somewhat miscellaneous, commands that deal with script-level issues. You saw how to use the **edit script** command to give technical users easy and immediate access to scripts they want to change in your stack. You learned about the various forms of the **wait** command and its use in scripts.

You also examined the use of parameter-passing operations and the built-in HyperCard functions for manipulating parameter lists. Finally, you learned how to debug your scripts in Version 2.0.

In Chapter 20, we'll look at some techniques that will help you design your stacks to make them as usable and attractive as possible.

20 ▶ Designing Stacks

In this chapter, you will be given a number of tips related to the design of HyperCard stacks. These tips include such topics as

- how the nature of the data your stack will contain relates to its design
- the trade-offs between multiple stacks and multiple- background stacks
- consistency in card and background layout and in stack design
- user-oriented button design
- communicating with the user

▶ Two Caveats

There are two general ideas to keep in mind as you read this chapter. First, suggestions in this chapter are just that — suggestions. They are neither rules nor official guidelines. They are just ideas that grew out of examining hundreds of stacks, creating a hundred or so of our own, and talking to lots of other HyperTalk scripters. They also grew out of our several years' experience using and writing about the Macintosh.

Second, Apple Computer has a book entitled *HyperCard Stack Design Guidelines*, published by Addison-Wesley as part of the Apple Technical Library. Apple has pioneered the issuance of formal guidelines through its Human Interface Group. You should buy a copy of these guidelines, read them, and take them to heart. If what they say conflicts with what's in this chapter, Apple is right.

▶ Before You Begin Stack Construction

Designing a stack is not totally dissimilar from other programming tasks you may have undertaken. At the beginning of any task involving information management, it's a good idea to ask yourself two basic questions:

- Who is the ultimate end user of this program and what does he or she know?
- What approach to the organization and management of this information will best enable the user to find and use it?

In this case, the user's identity is reasonably well known. Your stack's users will almost certainly be people who have used the Macintosh previously. There's also a good chance they will have at least a passing acquaintance with HyperCard. It is possible that your stack will be used by someone to whom both the Mac and HyperCard are new. Helping such users get started in the use of your stack may take a fair amount of effort and perhaps some written documentation or an orientation stack.

Less predictable than the likely end user of your stack is the nature of the data that the stack contains. With HyperCard, you can store data in a single stack or in a group of connected stacks that are closely related, loosely related, or virtually unrelated. If the information is related, you may connect it in any of several ways, including

- linearly (sequentially)
- hierarchically (tree structured)
- nonlinearly (quasirandomly)
- combination of these

Each type of informational relationship can influence the way you organize your stacks. For example, if the data in your stack is linear—if the user is likely to want to view it in sequence most or all of the time — you will use straightforward navigation approaches to movement. This means not much exotic linking is involved and probably very little programming is needed to accomplish navigation-related tasks. Figure 20-1 is a schematic of a sequentially organized stack.

Hierarchically structured data, on the other hand, implies that the browser has multiple options at many points in the navigation process. Figure 20-2 depicts this type of data organization. Quite often, one or more of these multipath cards calls for a different background to differentiate it and to make it operate as expected. In addition, navigation not only requires forward and backward buttons but also links to other points in the stack or in related stacks.

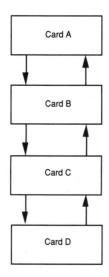

Figure 20-1. Linear stack organization

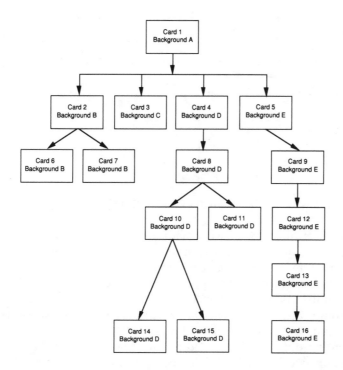

Figure 20-2. Hierarchical stack organization

When data chunks — typically stored as cards in HyperCard — have multiple entry and exit connecting points, the data is organized nonlinearly, as shown in Figure 20-3. In this kind of stack, navigation is ad hoc, and each card probably has no buttons to move to the next card or a previous card but may have many linking buttons. This kind of information requires a sophisticated level of thinking and planning.

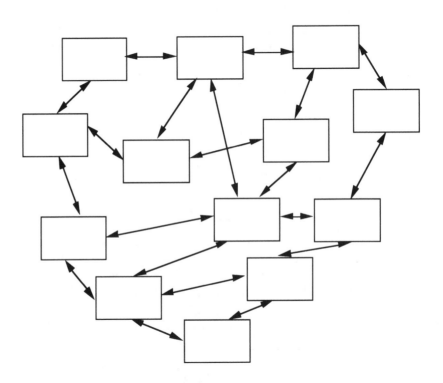

Figure 20-3. Nonlinear stack organization

Much of the data we work with in everyday life, whether it is stored in HyperCard or on 3x5 index cards, is organized by a combination of linear and nonlinear means. Such a structure can be conceptualized as looking like Figure 20-4. The horizontal portion of the structure has a linear organization in the illustration, and the vertical portion is somewhat tree-structured though also quite linear. Yet the overall structure is neither tree-structured nor linear.

If the data you are working with requires a mixed organization, navigation controls require both **back** and **previous** buttons as well as linking buttons. The impact of the type of data organization is not confined to navigational issues, but these are the ones that are most obviously and directly affected as a rule.

▶ Add Stacks or Backgrounds?

When you have data of more than one type in a stack, you typically must decide how to treat the different types of information so that the user understands it and so that the amount of programming, disk space, and execution time is minimized. There are two approaches:

- create separate stacks and link them at appropriate points in the navigation or execution process

- stay with one stack and create separate backgrounds for different types of data

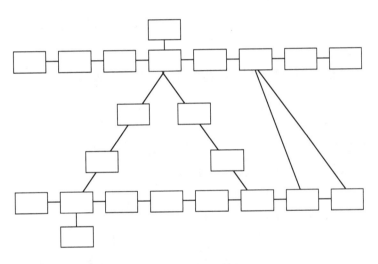

Figure 20-4. Mixed-stack organization

Neither approach is inherently better than the other, and sometimes you may want to mix the two approaches, using separate stacks with stacks that have cards of two or more backgrounds. How will you make these decisions? There are no hard-and-fast rules, but here are some principles you can use in deciding on the best approach for your stack:

1. A single stack with multiple backgrounds increases retrieval speed, usually reduces scripting, and makes copying and downloading your product easier than when multiple stacks are used.

2. Multiple stacks make the best sense when data can be subdivided and some or all users might not want or need to access certain parts of the data.

3. Another place multiple stacks make good sense is where the user may wish to look at two or more cards at the same time. In HyperCard 2.0, the user can open multiple stacks at one time, but each stack can display only one card at a time. Therefore, a multiple-stack design makes the best sense when the user wants to compare, contrast, or view more than one card of information at a time.

4. The minimum overhead for a stack is about 8K of disk space, so using multiple stacks can become costly in terms of disk storage.

5. The standard HyperCard **find** command will not work across stack boundaries, so if this is the primary or sole means for your user to navigate through your application, a single stack is dictated. The same is true of the **print** command. (You could, of course, write a handler to extend HyperCard's **find** or **print** command to cross stack boundaries.)

▶ Consistency in Layout and Design

You should strive for consistency in your stack designs so that users are comfortable with how your stacks work and can focus on their content and substance rather than their form. Consider this consistency issue in relation to background layouts, navigation techniques, restoring the system to its original state, and the user interface.

▶ Background layouts

Basic stack design begins with the background. Most stacks have only one background, though easy but clever approaches can make them appear to have more than a single background.

An easy mistake to make in designing stacks, particularly when you first begin to explore the power of HyperCard, is to over-design the backgrounds. If you have too many varieties of backgrounds or backgrounds that are simply too intricately designed and cluttered, you will confuse the user. When you analyze the data that the stack will present, you can generally find ways of dividing the information conceptually into a small number of subclasses. Use backgrounding or separate stacks for those divisions and leave the rest of the stack as a unified, consistent-looking whole.

▶ Navigation techniques

As users navigate through the stack, they should be comfortable with each card as new information of the same kind is presented. The only time the stack or card design should cause the user to stop simply flowing along with the presentation of information is when the nature of the information changes. For example, when you move from the annual calendar to the weekly calendar to the daily appointment list or notes, the background could change. The user needs to be aware that the rules may have changed; navigation is different now and the information is different as well. On the other hand, if you have different backgrounds for June's calendar and December's, you ought to have a very good reason for that and the reason ought to be one your user can understand.

▶ Leaving things as they were

Another aspect of consistency has to do with a fundamental principle of HyperTalk design: Leave things as they were. If the Message box was visible when the user started using your stack, make sure it's still there when the user quits your stack. If the user's access level was set to authoring (that is, 4) before the user opened your stack, be sure to return it to that level at the end of your stack.

Beginning with Version 2.0, it is particularly important that you not leave the menubar in a strange or unanticipated state when the user leaves your stack. Be sure to "clean up after yourself" with a **reset menu** command that will restore HyperCard's original menus and menu items.

If you do anything to alter the environment during your stack's execution, do yourself and your user a favor. Store the original state of things, and return to that original state as part of an **on closeStack** handler. Be sure to include in this original state the tool that was in use. This will almost always be the browse tool, but be certain that users don't find themselves unable to do something just because you've changed the tool and failed to return it to its original state.

▶ Usage management

During usage of your stack, be sure that things the user notices and uses are consistent from card to card and background to background. This usually requires moving handlers higher up the hierarchy than might at first seem necessary.

For example, if a field on a card is always the one users want to enter information into first, make sure the insertion point always appears in that field when users change cards or add a card. This usually means that the handler that puts the insertion point in the right place belongs at the background or stack level and not at the card level where it could be inadvertently modified during development or later maintenance and where it must be repeated on each card. With the object-like nature of HyperTalk, later modifications are much easier if you keep these handlers high enough in the hierarchy rather than distributing them throughout the cards.

▶ A tip: protect the form

It is important that you design your stack so that the casual browser cannot inadvertently change something that makes the stack work consistently and predictably. Lock elements of the design that you don't want users to modify. If there will be an occasional need for users to modify the design, give them the means — probably with a password check — to do so.

You can lock text fields, cards, or backgrounds using the appropriate "Info..." option from the Objects menu. Stack protection was discussed in Chapter 9.

▶ User-Oriented Button Design

Virtually all of the user's interaction with your stack — at least in terms of directing its activities and processing — comes through pressing buttons on cards and backgrounds. It is therefore important that the design and use of buttons be well thought-out as part of your script design. Consider the issues of consistent use of standard HyperCard buttons, feedback when the user pushes a button, and standard implementation of familiar Macintosh button types in carrying out dialogs with the user and in employing custom menus.

▶ Using HyperCard buttons consistently

The HyperCard buttons that most stacks include are

- arrow buttons (forward, backward, beginning of stack, end of stack, and return to where the user came from last)
- the Home button

Many other buttons are arguably HyperCard "standard" buttons, but they are used far less frequently than these.

Good stack design dictates that you use arrow buttons as users expect in each stack. An arrow pointing to the right ought to result in users feeling that they have turned a page or moved one step farther into the stack (see Chapter 13 for a discussion of accompanying visual effects). Similarly, a left arrow should move users toward the top of the stack and give the impression of flipping the pages of the book back toward the front cover.

This is not to say that you can't be creative with button design for navigation. But if you decide to do so, be sure that your creative choices are intuitive to the user and that you don't use a standard button in a way that is nonintuitive.

The Home button is not furnished in all stacks but probably ought to be. Users can always get to the Home stack with a Command-H key sequence, but why not make life easier and more HyperCard-like for them? And don't have a house icon on the stack mean anything other than "go to the Home stack." We've seen one stack that uses the Home button to take you back to the beginning of the stack. That approach is bad HyperCard design.

▶ Feedback to the user

All buttons that are not transparent — and some that are — should probably highlight when the user presses them. Unfortunately, HyperTalk is designed in such a way that automatic highlighting is turned off for buttons, so you almost always have to turn it on.

In addition to highlighting buttons when they are pressed, consider whether a sound effect accompanying a button's push might have value. The user of your stack feels more comfortable when, having pushed a button, something happens fairly soon. This is especially important in view of HyperCard's very deliberate (and good) design decision to have most actions require only a single click when most users are accustomed to double-clicking. If the user doesn't get some feedback on a single click, you may find your stacks not working properly because the user continues to click and ends up activating something accidentally by pushing a button on the next card.

▶ Consistency with the Mac interface

Anyone who uses a Macintosh for any length of time becomes closely acquainted with check boxes and radio buttons. It is therefore important that your stack's use of these buttons is consistent with the "normal" Macintosh approach users expect.

Don't use radio buttons or check boxes for navigation or to pass commands. These buttons are primarily useful for setting up parameters and properties. The difference between the two types is that only one radio button in a collection of such buttons can be selected, or "on," at one time, but in any group of check boxes, as many as the user wants can be checked at the same time. If you have a situation where you want to use a button to turn a condition on or off, use a check box rather than a single radio button. Radio buttons are not correctly used alone.

Another aspect of consistency with the Macintosh interface involves the use of Cancel in **ask** commands and in other places where the user is providing some information to your script. This is particularly important in HyperCard since the program automatically saves changes while it runs. The user needs a way to say, "I didn't mean that!"

▶ Communicating with the user

It is generally not a good idea to use the Message box to communicate information to the user. Too often the information you want to convey is overtyped the instant the user presses a key. At the very least, it is impossible to prevent the user from typing information into the Message box, so it is bound to happen at inopportune times.

Use **ask** and **answer** dialogs (see Chapter 11) to get information from the user when you really need it. On the whole, however, interrupt the user to obtain information only when there is no smooth way to let the user supply data without interruption. Also, don't let yourself be carried away with overly long messages in these dialog boxes. Beginning with HyperCard Version 2.0, you can use quite long strings with these interface elements, and the dialog box will resize to accommodate the string. But a long string takes the user a long time to read, and slows down interaction with your stack. Ultimately, the user may even decide it's more efficient to accomplish a task without the computer if you make these interruptions too long.

If you run across a place in your design where you wish you could use a Macintosh dialog box, don't just wish — do it. You can create virtually the same effect as a standard dialog box with creative card design. This is one of the most underutilized aspects of HyperCard stack design.

▶ Care in use of customized menus

Beginning with Version 2.0, HyperCard permits you to completely customize the menubar (see Chapter 12). This has resulted in a tendency among some stack builders to replace the standard HyperCard menubar with a custom menubar so that a user's choices are limited in that stack. This is, generally speaking, a bad idea. At a minimum, you should keep some basic principles in mind when you decide to customize any part of the menubar.

First, it is generally considered bad form (and a violation of Apple's *Human Interface Guidelines*) to remove the File or Edit menu from the menubar. You can do these things in HyperCard 2.0, but resist the temptation.

Second, you should avoid conflicts with the names or Command-key equivalents of HyperCard's standard menubar unless you have a very good reason to deliberately override the normal, expected menu behavior. Users become accustomed to the fact that Command-3 takes them to the next card, for example, and if you create a menu item that beeps 3 times when the user presses Command-3, you are going to confuse your users.

Third, you should keep the names of menu items as short as possible while ensuring that they are clear and informative. The longer a menu item's name, the longer it takes the user to read it each time it appears. This slows down your user, who may become aggravated with your design as a result.

Apple's *Human Interface Guidelines* have much more to say on the subject of good menu usage. You should obtain a copy of these guidelines and follow them.

▶ Maintain Display Compatibility

Beginning with Version 2.0, HyperCard lets you create cards that are of arbitrary size. This is a mixed blessing. In earlier versions of the program, stack designers did not need to concern themselves with whether their stacks would operate on all kinds of Macintosh and third-party display screens because all cards were fit to the standard Macintosh nine-inch monochrome display. Now, however, you'll have to take into account the possibility that people with various sizes of displays may well wish to use your stacks.

Unless you are certain that nobody with a standard Macintosh nine-inch screen will ever want to use your stack, you should plan it so that it is usable on that size display. On larger screens, you or the user can make the card window larger and you can even move objects around under script control so that they make better use of the screen real estate. But as a rule, keep your stacks usable on the lowest common denominator screen.

▶ Other Design Considerations

This chapter has scratched the surface of design issues in building HyperCard stacks. We hope it has supplied some insights that may not have occurred to you before.

Keep an eye on other people's stacks. When you find yourself working with a stack intuitively and smoothly, with the substance dominating the form, analyze the reasons for it and then try to emulate some of those design approaches in your own stacks.

▶ Summary

In this chapter, you learned about the basic ideas in HyperCard stack design. You saw that the design of a stack is quite often related to the nature of the data and how it is best organized. You also looked at some of the trade-offs in deciding whether to add backgrounds or stacks when data becomes complex.

You learned how to make your stacks consistent both internally and with the user's expectations. Finally, you learned some principles of good user-oriented button design and how to use dialogs to communicate with the user from your script.

Chapter 21 concludes our study of HyperTalk by discussing how to obtain and use resources such as icons and external routines in your stacks.

21 ▶ Extending HyperTalk with Resources

In this chapter, you will learn

- what resources are and how they figure into HyperCard stacks
- where to find resources
- how to create some kinds of resources yourself, either within Hyper-Card or using other programs
- two techniques for moving resources into your stacks
- how to create palettes in HyperCard 2.0
- the basic concepts involved in creating external commands, functions, and windows
- how to use resources after they are in your stack

▶ Resources and HyperTalk

The idea of a *resource* is central to Macintosh programming. If you were developing applications on the Mac without the benefit of HyperTalk, you'd be spending a good deal of time defining, setting up, and managing resources. As it is, HyperTalk does all the required resource management for you. But adding things like palettes, color pictures, special sound effects, icons, and cursors to your stacks can make your stacks more interesting and effective.

▶ What's a resource?

"Everything is a resource." That statement is only a slight simplification of the crucial role played by resources in Macintosh programming. All icons, cursors, windows, dialog boxes, controls, menus, and other visible elements of a Mac program are or can be resources. In addition, program code itself is a resource.

In some ways, resources resemble HyperCard fields and buttons. They have a type, a name, an ID, and a position relative to their surroundings.

▶ Where are resources stored?

But just saying "everything is a resource" and enumerating things that are resources hardly defines the term in any helpful way. You can think of resources in another way that might help you understand them better. But to understand this discussion, we need a slight diversion into the world of Macintosh files.

Every Macintosh file, without exception, has two *forks:* a data fork and a resource fork (see Figure 21-1). The data fork is managed by the program without any built-in or automatic assistance from Macintosh system software. The resource fork, on the other hand, is managed and accessed by means of the system's Resource Manager, a part of the powerful and extensive User Interface Toolbox that exists primarily in ROM on a Mac.

Information peculiar to the program, managed by application

Menus, window, dialogs, fonts, icons, cursors, sounds, and program code, managed with help of Mac's Resource Manager.

Figure 21-1. Two forks in a Mac file

Quite often, a Macintosh program has an empty data fork. We don't know of any applications that have empty resource forks, though documents often do, particularly if they contain only text.

The nonempty resource fork of any Macintosh file has a structure like that shown in Figure 21-2. Each resource in a fork has two entries: a *resource map* entry that tells the system the type, number, name, and attributes of the resource, along with a pointer to the resource data itself and a *resource data* entry that completely describes the resource. Each type of resource — and there are several dozen identifiable types, some application-defined — has its own resource data format.

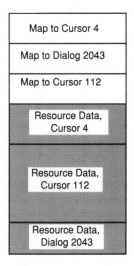

Figure 21-2. Structure of the resource fork

When you add resources to a stack, you are simply bringing in a new resource data entry describing that resource, and the Resource Manager builds an entry in the resource map to access that resource. Then, when you want to use the resource, all you do is tell the Resource Manager, in effect, "Go get me cursor 2983," and it knows where to find it and what to do with it.

▶ The role of resources in HyperCard

When you define a new button and click on the Icon button in the Button Definition dialog, you may notice that the buttons to which HyperCard takes you have numbers associated with them (see Figure 21-3). Each number is a resource identifier. In Figure 21-3, the icon has ID number 7012.

There are a great many kinds of things that you'll find in HyperCard stacks that are resources. Cursors, sound effects, palettes, and external functions, commands, and windows are the most common examples.

You can think of resources in HyperCard as being of two basic kinds. The first could be termed "integrated resources." These are resources that are either included in their entirety in HyperCard (for example, icons, an external command to deal with pictures, or an external command to create and use palettes) or that allow you to create and manipulate resources entirely within HyperCard (for example, the built-in icon editor). The second kind are purely external resources, including XCMDs, XFCNs, and external windows (all discussed later in this chapter), as well as cursors and sound effects. Some resources can fall into either category. For example, although HyperCard comes with both a collection of icons that you can associate with buttons and its own built-in icon editing capability, you can still use icons from external sources and import them into your HyperCard stacks using one of the techniques discussed later in this chapter.

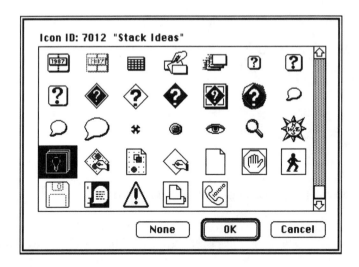

Figure 21-3. An icon has a resource number

▶ Where Do Resources Come From?

Now that you have an idea about what resources are, you might be interested in adding some nifty new resource to the prize-winning stack you're constructing. But where do you find resources? There are at least four sources:

- HyperCard itself includes quite a number of resources.

- Other people's stacks often contain useful resources that you can copy using one of the techniques described later in this chapter. Even non-HyperCard applications have usable resources that you can obtain. (Remember the caveat we mentioned earlier about copyrighted material; some resources are copyrighted.)

- Some special stacks contain only resources that you can use in your stacks. (Again, be sure about ownership before you use these in a commercial product.)

- You can create your own resources using specialized tools, including some that come with or are designed specifically for use with HyperCard.

If you use a stack or another Macintosh application that has an icon or a cursor you particularly admire or find suitable for your stack, and assuming the owner of the resource permits its use, you can use one of the techniques defined in the next section to copy that resource directly into your stack.

▶ Special stacks for resource use

From the early days of HyperCard, many people began to build stacks with the express purpose of offering resources you could use in your own stacks as well as some excellent facilities for moving these resources into your stacks.

There are numerous stacks that are either public domain or shareware products that allow you to experiment with and add such things as animated cursors, sophisticated sound effects, simulated speech, and icons to your HyperCard stacks.

One interesting commercial product is Icon Factory from Hyperpress Publishing (1166 Triton Dr., Suite F, Foster City, CA 94404). Figure 21-4 shows one of the cards from the numerous icon libraries included with this product. More than 2,000 icons come with Icon Factory, most of them usable in your stacks without further permission once you own the program. It also includes capabilities for things like creating and editing icons; however, these functions are somewhat obsolete in HyperCard Version 2.0, which includes built-in facilities for these operations. But the wealth of icons in the libraries gives you a great starting place for customizing your own icons.

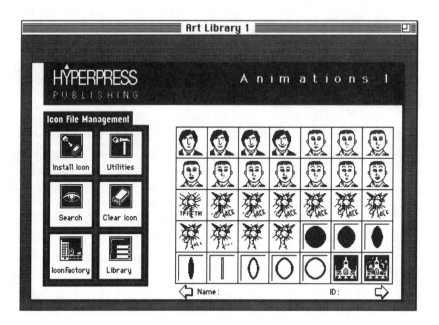

Figure 21-4. Sample card from Icon Factory stack

▶ Creating your own resources

Several commercially available and public domain or shareware programs enable you to create resources. Apple Computer distributes a program called RMaker through the Apple Programmer's and Developer's Association. It is part of the Apple-developed Macintosh Programmer's Workshop (MPW) product line.

With the release of Version 2.0, Apple Computer added the built-in ability to create and edit icons within the HyperCard environment. Since this process involves no HyperTalk programming, a description of how to do this is beyond the scope of this book. But you should know that when you or the user creates a new icon or modifies an existing one and then attaches it to a stack, you can use the techniques described later in this chapter for moving that icon from one stack to another. It is a resource, like all other icons.

Creating sound effects is a little more difficult, as you can imagine, but there are some commercial products to assist you. One of the most versatile and affordable approaches is Farrallon Computing's MacRecorder. This product consists of a sound digitizer with a built-in condenser microphone and a jack for connecting it to external sound sources such as stereos. It comes with two major pieces of software to facilitate both the editing and customizing of recorded sounds and their conversion to appropriate formats for HyperCard use. Many HyperCard designers have adopted MacRecorder as their sound digitizer of choice.

▶ Moving Resources

A number of programs on the market enable you to move resources such as icons, sound effects, and cursors between Macintosh files. The most widely used is probably Apple Computer's own ResEdit (for Resource Editor). Figure 21-5 shows a typical ResEdit screen with an icon selected and ready to be copied to another application. ResEdit can be obtained through your Apple dealer, APDA, or packaged with *ResEdit Complete* by Peter Alley and Carolyn Strange (Addison-Wesley, 1990).

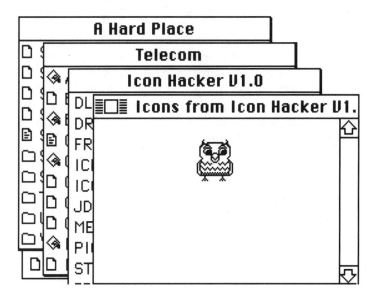

Figure 21-5. Typical ResEdit icon selection session

After you have located the icon or other resource you want to move with ResEdit, simply use the Edit menu commands to Copy it, then open the file in which you want to include it, and Paste it into the right resource type. (This is something of a simplification; you must be concerned about conflicting resource numbers as well, but a complete discussion of the detailed use of ResEdit is not our objective here. If you want to use the program, read the documentation and only work on copies of files that you don't mind damaging if you encounter some difficulty.)

If the resource you want to move is not located in another HyperCard stack, you have to use ResEdit or a program like it. But if you want to shift a resource from one HyperCard stack to another, you may prefer a superb stack called Resource Mover written by Steve Maller. Maller is a well-known Mac guru, author, and trainer who works on the Apple Computer HyperCard team.

Resource Mover is included with HyperCard 2.0 in the Power Tools stack. (Incedentally, this stack contains several extremely useful routines. Exploring it is a good idea.) You are free to use it to copy resources from stack to stack and even from applications into your stack (though you cannot move resources from stacks to applications using this product). But if you wish to distribute Resource Mover with your applications — if, for example, your HyperCard application depends on Resource Mover to allow the user to install certain resources you supply into the user's stacks — then you must make licensing arrangements with Apple Computer.

Figures 21-6 through 21-8 show you how easy it is to use Resource Mover. In Figure 21-6, we have opened Resource Mover and opened a stack called "Addresses" on a disk drive called "OverDrive." (Note the file information under the left-hand scrolling field.) We have also opened another stack called "Dan1" on the same drive, as you can see under the right-hand scrolling field. We have selected an icon called "Small left arrow," which has a resource ID of 20461. Notice, too, that the icon we are copying is displayed just above the "Edit..." button.

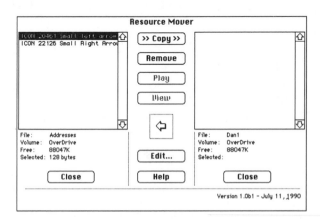

Figure 21-6. Starting the resource copying process in Resource Mover stack

Figure 21-7 shows what the screen looks like after the icon has been copied from its original stack to the destination stack.

If you click on the "Edit..." button in Resource Mover, you'll see a dialog like that shown in Figure 21-8. This dialog lets you either rename or renumber a resource. You may wish to do this to avoid resource ID conflicts (the Mac prohibits you from having two icons of the same resource ID, for example) or to make the name more meaningful in your stack.

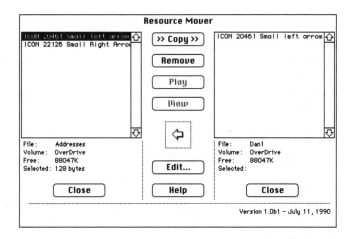

Figure 21-7. Completed resource copying process in Resource Mover stack

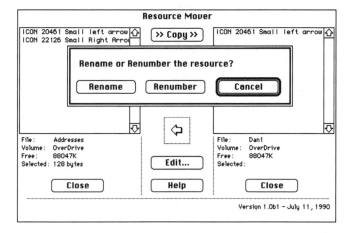

Figure 21-8. Editing a resource's information in Resource Mover stack

Note ▶	You may be tempted to copy these resources into your Home stack where they will always be accessible to all your stacks. That is an acceptable strategy provided you remember that when you sell or copy the stack to someone else, you move the needed resources out of your Home stack and into the new stack. Otherwise, the user will have trouble running your stack.

This discussion of resource movement in HyperCard has not been exhaustive. Additionally, the world of HyperCard programming tools is increasing quite fast, so by the time you read this there may be a dozen slick new ways of moving resources. With the assistance of tools like those discussed here, you can do a lot to make your stacks more effective and efficient without having to do a great deal of heavy-duty Macintosh programming. Consider this a starting point, not the final word.

▶ Creating Palettes in HyperCard

One of the most powerful additions to HyperCard that appeared with Version 2.0 is the ability to create a new type of window, called a "palette," entirely within HyperCard. A palette is a "floating windoid" that remains visible atop any open cards until it is explicitly closed, either by the user (if you provide that capability when you design the palette) or by a script. HyperCard's tear-off menus for tools and patterns are examples of palettes.

HyperCard includes one palette, called "Navigator," with the program as an example of how such palettes work. But it goes beyond that by providing you with a stack containing two external commands that permit you to create and use your own palettes with amazing ease.

▶ The navigation palette

Figure 21-9 shows the Navigation palette provided by HyperCard as it appears in actual use. To make the palette appear, you simply type

```
palette "Navigator"
```

either in a script or in the Message window. The palette then permits users to click on any of its eleven "buttons" to navigate around in the HyperCard environment, exactly as they would from the menu or using Command-key equivalents.

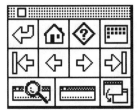

Figure 21-9. The Navigation palette

You can study this palette and how its commands are set up by examining it in the Palette Maker stack, which is discussed in the next section. The Navigation palette appears on the first card in that stack.

▶ Creating palettes

Creating your own palettes using HyperCard's built-in Palette Maker stack is a relatively simple process involving the following steps:

1. Open the Palette Maker stack.
2. Click on the "New Palette" button.
3. Give the new palette a name in the upper-left field on the newly created card.
4. Draw the palette in the workspace provided.
5. Attach buttons to each portion of the palette that is to be treated as if it were a button in the working palette.
6. Program each button with one and only one line of HyperTalk script.
7. Select the appropriate window type for your palette.
8. Click on the "Create Palette" button.
9. Use the "Show Palette...," "Demo this Palette," and "Show Commands..." buttons to confirm that the palette does what you expect.
10. Install the palette in the desired stack(s).

   Most of these steps are self-explanatory, but we'll take a closer look at steps 4–7, as well as 9 and 10.

Drawing the palette

You can draw your palette either using HyperCard's built-in painting tools or by copying and pasting a bitmapped piece of artwork from some other application using the Clipboard or the Scrapbook. Although the Palette

Maker stack provides a specific area for you to draw your palette, it is not mandatory that you do all of your drawing entirely within that area. Any artwork that exists at the card level when you tell this stack to create your palette will be included in the palette.

Figure 21-10 shows what the Palette Maker stack looks like after we've drawn a new palette called "Game Demo" that includes four new controls: one to roll dice, one having to do with money, one dealing with a stack or deck of cards, and one labeled "Quit." All of these objects were drawn in HyperCard using its built-in painting tools.

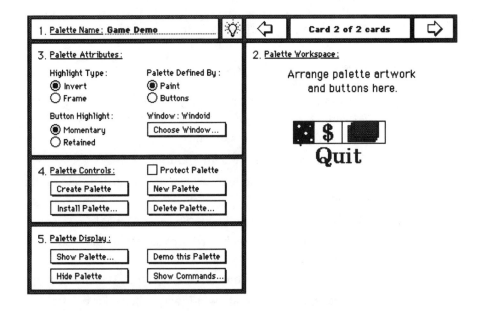

Figure 21-10. Drawing a new palette

Attaching buttons

Once you've drawn the palette as you want it to appear, you create a new button for each portion of the palette that you wish to be active when the user displays the palette and clicks on some part of it. In our sample, we created four new buttons, one to go over each of the areas just described.

You don't have to worry about the style of these buttons, by the way. The Palette Maker will convert them to transparent buttons whose names do not show when it generates the palette for you from your drawing and your buttons. It's probably easier to work with the palette during development if you do define the buttons as transparent without names or highlighting, but it's not essential that you do so.

Programming the buttons

Once you've created the needed buttons, you have to program them so that they'll do what is expected of them when the user clicks on them in a live version of your palette.

Each button can have only one operating line of code to define its behavior. If, for example, you want to carry out a menu action when the user clicks on a button, you can simply code that behavior as the only line in the handler. To program a palette button to delete a card, you could just write the second line of code in this handler, inside the **on mouseUp** and **end mouseUp** lines provided by HyperCard:

```
on mouseUp
   doMenu "Delete Card"
end mouseUp
```

If, on the other hand, you want the button to execute a handler of your own design or to carry out more than one built-in HyperCard action, you should define a handler to execute all of these desired actions, name it, and then give the name of that function or handler as the second line of code in the palette button. For example, if you want to build a function called **rollTheDice** to be carried out when the user clicks on the dice-shaped button in the "Demo Game" palette example, you would program its button as follows:

```
on mouseUp
   rollTheDice
end mouseUp
```

You would then, of course, have to write the **rollTheDice** handler and include it at an appropriate level in your stack. When the user clicks on the button in the palette, HyperCard generates the message called for by the first line of the button's handler and then stops executing.

Selecting a window type

There are two window types available for palettes in HyperCard 2.0. Both are windoids. One includes the title of the palette and the other does not. You can choose which of these you wish to use by clicking on the "Choose Window..." button in the Palette Maker stack. Figure 21-11 shows you what the screen will look like when you click on this button. You can see the two choices of window types. Note that the Palette Maker stack shows you the currently selected window type above the "Choose Window..." button.

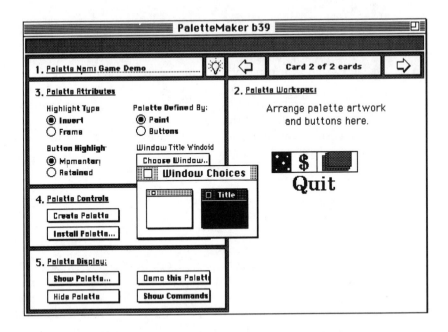

Figure 21-11. Choosing a window type in the Palette Maker stack

Showing and demonstrating the palette

The portion of the Palette Maker stack labeled "5. Palette Display" contains four buttons. The left-most buttons are self-explanatory.

If you click on the "Demo this Palette" button, the palette will appear (if it isn't yet visible) and then HyperCard will simulate the user clicking on each of the buttons in turn so that you can see the appearance of the buttons as they are clicked. No messages are generated, so you need not worry about having the programming completed before using this feature.

The "Show Commands..." button produces a dialog like that shown in Figure 21-12. This dialog simply lists the names of the commands associated with the palette so that you can ensure that you've named them correctly and programmed all the buttons you wish to be active in the palette.

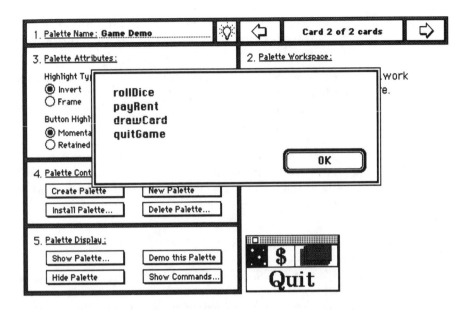

Figure 21-12. The "Show Commands..." dialog in the Palette Maker stack

Installing the palette

As with any other resource, you must install the palette resource where it will be accessible to the stack(s) from which you wish to use it. In the final version of Palette Maker, the "Install Palette..." button will handle the installation process for you. In earlier beta releases of the stack, you must use some other method to copy two resources: the 'PLTE' resource and the 'PICT' resource of the same name.

▶ External Commands, Functions, and Windows

From the beginning, one of the most powerful ideas in HyperCard was the concept of extensibility. Stack builders and others familiar with conventional programming languages like Pascal and C can write routines that extend the capabilities of HyperCard and HyperTalk. There are three categories of external routines:

- external commands (XCMD resources, pronounced "ex-commands"), which are extensions to the HyperTalk programming language that do not return a value when they are carried out

- external functions (XFCN resources, pronounced "ex-functions"), which are other extensions to HyperTalk that do return a value when they are executed

- external windows, which are extensions to XCMDs and XFCNs added beginning with Version 2.0 that allow these externals to create and manage their own windows all but independently of the HyperCard universe

XCMDs and XFCNs can create external windows if they wish or need to do so. But it is equally possible to have external routines that have no custom windows, that is, that operate entirely within the HyperCard environment and use cards as their habitat.

▶ What are externals?

XCMDs and XFCNs are similar to Macintosh programs in that they are written in traditional high-level languages and perform some function. They differ from applications because they have no header bytes. They differ from desk accessories in much the same way, though they more closely resemble desk accessories than they do full-blown Mac programs. (Actually, these external routines can include header bytes as long as the first byte they contain is executable code. The same is true of desk accessories, but in practice this turns out to be a fine point most programmers ignore.)

XCMDs in particular, but also XFCNs, typically rely heavily on HyperCard to furnish a hospitable and manageable environment in which they can reside. Most routines use the user interface built into HyperCard rather than making calls to the Macintosh's ROM Toolbox routines themselves. This means they differ markedly from full-scale applications, which manage the entire user interface. Generally, Mac applications are much larger and more complex than XCMDs and XFCNs.

This is not to say, however, that XCMDs and XFCNs are trivial. On the contrary, we have seen several XCMDs that were more than 1,000 lines long. Such XCMDs can carry out sophisticated processing that is beyond the scope of what HyperCard and HyperTalk were designed to do.

▶ Why design external routines?

HyperCard creates a specialized environment for itself. In doing so, it isolates the programmer from the myriad details contained in more than 900 ROM toolbox calls that facilitate and define the Mac's distinctive user interface. On one hand, this isolation is good; it frees the programmer to concentrate more on solving the problem and less on presenting the solution to the user.

On the other hand, if you need to accomplish something in a script that is outside the range of HyperTalk's built-in commands, you could be quite frustrated were it not for the ability to extend the language through XCMDs and XFCNs.

Specialized math routines, management of color and Color QuickDraw (on the Macintosh II), and the like are all candidates for XCMDs and XFCNs. If you are scripting along and find a need for a command that isn't built into HyperTalk, you might consider tackling the design and construction of an XCMD or XFCN.

▶ The extended external interface of version 2.0

HyperCard Version 2.0 greatly extended and expanded the external interface of HyperCard. Essentially, the new interface allows developers to create virtually full-blown applications that reside in and depend only slightly on the HyperCard environment for their operations.

This extended interface is rich and robust. Its use is well beyond the scope of this discussion. Books will undoubtedly appear that will deal with this new interface in some depth.

▶ Tools for creating externals

In addition to conventional programming languages including both MPW C and Pascal and THINK C and Pascal (the latter from Symantec Corp., 10201 Torre Ave., Cupertino, CA 95014), there are other, less conventional tools for creating external routines in HyperCard. (You should note that while all of these tools work with HyperCard 1.2.5, we do not know the publishers' plans for supporting HyperCard 2.0. Contact the publishers indicated for information.)

The following tools are particularly useful:

- Wild Things (from Language Systems Corp., 441 Carlisle Dr., Herndon, VA 22070), a collection of stacks that includes a number of useful externals, full source code, templates for the construction of externals, and other helpful information

- HyperBASIC (from Teknosys, 3923 Coconut Palm Dr., Suite 111, Tampa, FL 33619, which lets you use the widely popular BASIC programming language to create externals and automatically moves them into your stacks in the most seamless way we've seen

- CompileIt! (from Heizer Software, P.O. Box 232019, Pleasant Hill, CA 94523), which permits you to compile your HyperTalk code into external routines for speed or protection and which also gives you access to virtually the entire Macintosh User Interface Toolbox so that you can create very sophisticated external routines

▶ Using Resources

After a resource has been added to a stack, you can use it like any other resource that was there when you obtained HyperCard or a specific stack. HyperCard cannot tell the difference between "original equipment" and "added accessories" when it comes to resource files.

Thus, if you add a new icon to the repertoire of those available in Hyper-Card, you can use it like any standard icon. For example:

```
set icon of button 4 to "Smiling Face"
```

The same is true of new cursors:

```
set cursor to 603
— Any valid cursor resource number can be used.
```

Sounds are treated the same way as built-in sounds, called into effect with the **play** command

```
play "Applause"
```

and can even use the tempo and note-value arguments that are normally associated with "music." Some startlingly good sound effects are available.

Once a palette has been added to a stack or made accessible to it, you simply use the **palette** external command to cause it to appear and for its scripting to be recognized by the stack.

You can then use **hide** and **show** commands to make the palette visible or invisible, as in the following lines:

```
hide window "Game Demo"
show window "Game Demo"
```

Using the **picture** XCMD and its associated scripting functions to detect and deal with user mouse-clicks within the picture boundaries are discussed in detail in Chapter 13.

▶ Summary

Extending the look, feel, sound, and utility of your stacks with the resources you create or with resources borrowed from others can be fairly easy and quite effective. In this chapter, you learned what resources are, how they are used in HyperCard, and how to move them from other applications and other stacks into your own stacks. You also saw that, from HyperCard's perspective, there is no difference between these added resources and the ones it originally had, so they are used the same way.

We have also examined in some detail how to create and use palettes in HyperCard Version 2.0.

This concludes our discussion of HyperTalk. We trust you have found the experience both enjoyable and rewarding. Happy stacking!

Appendix A
HyperTalk Glossary

This appendix lists all of the commands, functions, operators, key words, and identifiers used in HyperTalk in alphabetical order. The type of word or phrase, its syntax, and notes about its use and effect are also supplied. For page references, see the index.

Note that beginning with Version 2.0, HyperCard permits the creation of custom external windows that may have properties and behavior that are not included in this appendix. These objects may appear to be part of the HyperCard environment, but they are not. Since we cannot anticipate what developers will do with this capability and since each application will be different, we have made no attempt to document these features in this appendix.

Because of its different nature, we have introduced some new uses for italics, brackets, braces, and other special typographic techniques in this appendix. The appendix differs in these respects from the rest of the text in the book.

Italics in this appendix act as cross-references to words and phrases used elsewhere in the appendix. We have italicized only those words that are explained in some depth here and that are particularly relevant to the command or phrase under discussion. Brackets continue to indicate optional material, as in the text. Curly braces, on the other hand, mean that one of the options they contain must be chosen. A bullet symbol (•) follows the names of entries that are new or modified in HyperCard Version 2.0.

Word/Phrase	_Type_	_Syntax_	_Notes_
^	Operator	number ^ number	Returns the first number raised to the power indicated by the second number.
&	Operator	string-value & string-value	Concatenates the two string-values together with no intervening space added. See &&.
&&	Operator	string-value && string-value	Concatenates a space and then the second string-value onto the end of the first string-value. See &.
*	Operator	number * number	Returns the product of the two numbers.
+	Operator	number + number	Returns the sum of the two numbers.
-	Operator	number - number	Returns the difference between the two numbers.
/	Operator	number / number	Returns the first number divided by the second number.
<	Operator	value < value	Compares two values and returns _true_ if the first number is smaller than the second, _false_ if the second number is smaller.
<=, ≤	Operator	value <= value value ≤ value	Compares two values and returns _true_ if the first value is smaller than or equal to the second, _false_ otherwise. The second form of the operator is created with Option-comma.
>	Operator	value > value	Compares two values and returns _true_ if the first is the larger of the two, _false_ if the second is larger.
>=, ≥	Operator	value >= value value ≥ value	Compares the two values and returns _true_ if the first is larger than or equal to the second, _false_ if the second is larger. The second form is created with Option-period.
≠	Operator	value ≠ value	Compares the two values and returns _true_ if they are not equal to one another, _false_ if they are equal. Created with Option-equal sign.
¬	Operator	None	Continuation operator for long script lines. Created with Option-L or Option-Return.

Word/Phrase	_Type_	_Syntax_	_Notes_
abbreviated	Format	abbr[ev[iated]] date	Used with _convert_ to reformat a date field or value. Also used with functions. An abbreviated date formats as Fri, Nov 6, 1987.
abs	Function	the abs of number abs(number)	Returns the absolute value of a number (_i.e._, its value with a positive sign regardless of its original sign).
add	Command	add number to container	Container must have a number in it or an error occurs. Result of addition replaces former value of container.
after	Preposition	None	Used with _put_ to insert material behind (following) current contents of destination container or variable.
all	Adjective	all cards	Used with _show_ and _print_ primarily. Any place a number could be used with _cards, all_ can appear.
and	Operator	expression and expression	Returns _true_ if both expressions are true, _false_ if either is false.
annuity	Function	annuity(rate,periods)	Highly accurate way of calculating the annuity function. Arguments must be numeric. Used to calculate present and future value. See _compound_.
answer	Command	answer "prompt-string" [with option [or option [or option]]]	Displays a dialog with a default OK button if all "with" parameters are omitted. Otherwise, fills the dialog box button row from right to left with parameters. User presses button and result of the button press is stored in _it_. See _ask_.
answer file •	Command	answer file "prompt-string" [of type <string | fileTypeList>]	Brings up a standard file-open dialog (SFGetFile) with the indicated prompt string and showing all files of the type(s) shown in the optional argument, or all files if no _of type_ argument is included. See _ask file_.

Word/Phrase	Type	Syntax	Notes
any	Selector	any chunkExpression	Used in commands to identify, select, or test a random element or chunk.
arrow	Cursor Shape	set cursor to arrow	Changes the cursor to a northwest-pointing arrow. (Note that cursor shape is reset at *idle* time.)
arrowKey	System Message	arrowKey left | right | up | down	A system message sent to a card when the indicated arrow key has been pressed.
ascending	Modifier	see *sort*	Instructs *sort* command to sort its argument in order from lowest to highest, or smallest to largest.
ask •	Command	ask "prompt-string" [with answer] ask password [clear] "prompt-string" [with answer]	Displays a dialog displaying the message in "prompt-string" and allowing user to enter text in response. Places string into *it*. If password form is used, password is encrypted before being returned unless "clear" option is included.
ask file •	Command	ask file "prompt-string" [with <expression>]	Brings up a standard file-save dialog (SFPutFile) with the indicated prompt string and the optional "with" argument as the default file name to use. See *answer file*.
atan	Function	the atan of angle atan(angle)	Returns the arc tangent of the "angle," which must be expressed in radians.
autoHilite	Property	None	Tells whether a button will highlight when pressed or not. Values are *true* and *false*. Read/write.
autoTab	Property	None	Tells how a Return key will be treated when pressed in the last line of a non-scrolling field. True/false. Read/write. Added in Version 1.2.
average	Function	average(number-list)	Returns the average value in the list of numbers supplied as an argument.
back	Identifier	None	Points to card immediately before the current card in the Recent list. Equivalent to *recent card*.

Word/Phrase	Type	Syntax	Notes
background	Object	background bkgnd bg	HyperCard object that contains all objects shared by more than one card, each of which in turn belongs to this background.
barn door	Visual Effect	barn door {open | close}	No default value.
beep	Command	beep [number]	Causes the system to beep number of times. If number omitted, beeps once.
before	Preposition	None	Used with *put* to insert material ahead of current contents of destination container or variable.
bg	Abbreviation	None	Can be used wherever the term "background" would be allowed.
bkgd	Abbreviation	None	Can be used wherever the term "background" would be allowed.
black	Adjective	visual effect to black	Alters the way *visual effects* work. Creates a black screen as an intermediate point for the visual effect before going to the destination card.
blindTyping	Property	None	Global property that indicates whether blind typing is available to the user. Read/write.
bold	Text Style	see *textStyle*	None
bottom	Property	None	Field, button, and window property containing the pixel coordinate of the bottom edge of the object's surrounding rectangle.
bottomRight	Property	bottomRight botRight	Field, button, and window property containing the point coordinates of the lower-right corner of the object's surrounding rectangle.
browse	Tool Name	None	None
brush	Tool Name	brush tool	None
brush	Painting Property	None	Holds a value of 1–32 defining the shape of the brush to be used in paint operations. Read/write.
bucket	Tool Name	None	None

Word/Phrase	Type	Syntax	Notes
busy	Cursor Shape	set cursor to busy	Changes the cursor to a "beach ball" shape which, if used inside a *repeat* loop, will rotate. (Note that cursor shape is reset at *idle* time.)
button	Tool Name Object	button tool btn tool button[s] btn[s]	None
cantAbort •	Property	None	Stack property that determines whether scripts in the stack can be interrupted with the Command-Period key combination. True/false.
cantDelete	Property	None	Stack, card, or background property that determines whether a user can delete the object to which it is related. True/false. Read/write.
cantModify	Property	None	Stack property that determines whether a user can compact, delete, or change the contents of the stack. If the stack is not physically locked, this property is read/write. True/false.
cantPeek •	Property	None	Stack property that determines whether the user can look at the buttons, fields, and scripts of a stack with the Command-Option key combination. True/false.
card	Multiple	card[s] cd[s]	Used in chunk expressions, in *go* commands, with *show*. Also used with *visual effect*, where it is default mode.
center	Text Style	see *textStyle*	None
centered	Painting Property	None	When true, draws shapes from their centers out rather than from their top-left corners. When false, uses standard top-left corner anchor for shape drawing. Read/write.
char	Identifier	char[acter][s]	A character or a group of characters can be selected using one of the chunking techniques. See *word*, *line*, and *item*.

Word/Phrase	_Type_	_Syntax_	_Notes_
chars	Modifier	see _find_	Instructs the _find_ command to search for an exact string regardless of where it appears in a word.
charToNum	Function	the charToNum of character charToNum (character)	Returns the ASCII value of the "character."
checkbox	Button Style	see _style_	None
checkerboard	Visual Effect	None	None
checkMark •	Property	None	Menu item property that determines whether a menu item is displayed with a checkmark. True/false.
choose tool	Command	choose tool-name tool	Selects the named tool exactly as if chosen from the Tools menu. The userLevel must be set to appropriate value to allow access to the named tool.
click	Command	click at point [with keyList]	Simulates the user clicking the mouse at the screen address given in "point." Modifier keys may be added in combination, separated by commas.
clickChunk •	Function	the clickChunk	Returns the chunking expression of the word or phrase where the mouse was clicked.
clickH	Function	the clickH	Returns the address of the horizontal point on the screen where the mouse was most recently clicked. See _clockLoc_ and _clickV_.
clickLine •	Function	the clickLine	Returns the line where the mouse was clicked.
clickLoc	Function	the clickLoc	Returns the address of the point on the screen where the mouse was most recently clicked. Point is in format (h,v).
clickText •	Function	the clickText	Returns the word or phrase where the mouse was clicked. Will return word unless multiple words have a style of "grouped," in which case it returns the entire set of grouped words.

Word/Phrase	_Type_	_Syntax_	_Notes_
clickV	Function	the clickV	Returns the address of the vertical point on the screen where the mouse was most recently clicked. See _clickLoc_ and _clickH_.
close file	Command	close file <_fileName_>	Closes a file previously opened with _open file_.
closeBackground	System Message	None	Sent to card when movement causes the background to change. Can occur on any _go_ command or on a _quit_.
closeCard	System Message	None	Sent to a card when it is closed.
closeField	System Message	None	Sent to a field when the user tabs or clicks out of it and its contents have been changed.
close printing	Command	close printing	Terminates printing and flushes the print buffer to ensure all cards are printed.
closeStack	System Message	None	Sent to a card when the stack is about to be closed by the user opening another stack.
cmdChar •	Property	cmdChar commandChar	Menu item property that defines the Command-key equivalent for the item to which it applies. Requires single-character argument.
commandKey	Function	cmdKey	Returns status of Command key as _up_ or _down_.
commandKeyDown •	System Message	None	Sent to a card when the user types a key with the Command key held down.
compound	Function	compound(rate,periods)	Returns the compound interest factor at "rate" over the number of "periods" indicated. Used in calculating present and future values of annuities. See _annuity_.
condense	Text Style	see _textStyle_	None
contains	Operator	container contains value	Returns _true_ if the text on the left side of the operator is found in the string or container on the right, _false_ if it is not. The _contains_ operator and the _is in_ operator are synonymous except the order of arguments is reversed.

Word/Phrase	Type	Syntax	Notes
controlKey	System Message	controlKey key-number	A system message sent to a card indicating that the Control key has been pressed. Always accompanied by an argument that indicates which key was held down along with the Control key. The argument is the ASCII value of the accompanying key.
convert	Command	convert container to format	Changes format of date/time information in container to format specified: seconds, dateItems, long date, short date, abbrev[iated] date, long time, or short time.
cos	Function	the cos of angle cos(angle)	Returns the cosine of the angle supplied as an argument and expressed in radians.
create menu •	Command	create menu <menuName>	Adds a new menu to the menubar, named the same as the argument, which must be a string or a container or expression that evaluates to a string. See *delete, put,* and *reset menubar.*
create stack •	Command	create stack "<stack name>"	Creates a stack with the indicated name and a blank background. Differs from *doMenu "New Stack..."* in that it does not generate a dialog box for the user to respond to.
cross	Cursor Shape	set cursor to cross	Changes the cursor to a cross-hairs shape. (Note that cursor shape is reset at *idle* time.)
cursor	Property	None	A string or number identifying a cursor resource in the current environment. Write only.
curve	Tool Name	None	None
cut	Visual Effect	None	None
date	Function	the [short	long	abbrev[iated]] date	Returns a string representing the current date in your Macintosh, using one of the formats shown if it is supplied and defaulting to the short format. See *short, long,* and *abbrev[iated].*

Word/Phrase	_Type_	_Syntax_	_Notes_
dateItems	Format	None	Used with _convert_ to cause HyperCard to put a date/time field into a comma-delimited string for extraction and calculation purposes. Returns year, month, day, hour, minute, second, and day of week (Sunday = 1).
dateTime	Sort Type	None	Used with _sort_ to sort stack by treating a chunk expression as a date/time value.
debug checkpoint •	Command	debug checkpoint	Sets a permanent checkpoint for the debugger at this point in the script. Meaningless from the Message box. Debugger will halt execution of the script and stop at the next line to be executed when it encounters this command.
debug hintbits •	Command	debug hintbits	Modifies the behavior of the "Compact Stack" menu option by allowing the designer to examine and change certain characteristics of the compaction algorithm.
debugger •	Property	None	Global property that determines the name of the XCMD containing the debugger to be used. Argument must evaluate to a string. If XCMD not found, HyperTalk loads built-in default debugger.
delete •	Command	delete chunk [of card] delete [<menuItem Identifier> of] <menu Identifier>	Deletes text described by "chunk" expression from current card unless _of card_ parameter is supplied and identifies a different card.
			Second form removes the specified menu or menu item from the menubar. See _create menu, reset menubar_.
deleteBackground	System Message	None	Documented but not functional in any version of HyperCard.
deleteButton	System Message	None	Sent to a button indicating it is about to be deleted.
deleteCard	System Message	None	Sent to a card indicating it is about to be deleted.

Word/Phrase	_Type_	_Syntax_	_Notes_
deleteField	System Message	None	Sent to a field indicating it is about to be deleted.
deleteStack˙	System Message	None	Sent to a card indicating its stack is about to be deleted.
delete menu •	Command	delete menu <_menu name_>	Removes the named menu from the menubar.
descending	Modifier	see _sort_	Instructs _sort_ command to sort its argument in order from highest to lowest, or largest to smallest.
dial	Command	dial number dial number with modem dial number with modem modem-string	Attempts to dial telephone line using built-in speaker tones. If the "modem" argument is omitted, ordinary telephone dialing takes place. With modem command, initialization may be performed with contents of "modem-string."
disable •	Command	disable [<menuItemExpr> of] menu <menuName>	Disables indicated menu or menu item. The menuItemExpr can be the name of the menu item, its position in the menu, or a container or expression evaluating to one of these. The same classes of arguments can apply to the menu. See _enable_.
diskSpace	Function	the diskSpace	Returns the number of bytes left on the currently logged disk drive.
dissolve	Visual Effect	None	None
div	Operator	number div number	Returns truncated quotient of first number divided by second number.
divide	Command	divide container by number	The "container" must have a number in it or an error occurs. Contents of container replaced by quotient.
do	Command	do <expression>	Interprets string, container, or expression as a HyperTalk command and executes it.
doMenu	System Message	None	Sent when the user selects a menu item. Includes one or two parameters. First is menu item name. Second is optional menu name.

Word/Phrase	Type	Syntax	Notes
done	Predefined Value	"done"	The value returned by the *sound* function if no sound is playing.
dontSearch •	Property	None	Background, card, or field property indicating whether text contained in a specific field or in all fields on a particular card or background should be skipped by the *find* command. True/false.
dontWrap •	Property	None	Field property determining whether text in the field should wrap at the right edge of the field or continue in a straight line past the border. True/false.
down	Constant	None	One of the possible values of the mouse button and many keys whose status can be checked with functions. See *up*.
drag	Command	drag from point to point [with keyList]	Simulates dragging with the tool currently in use. Dragging occurs from first point to second. Optional keyList can contain modifier keys, separated by commas. See *choose tool*.
dragSpeed	Property	None	Global numeric property that determines the rate at which dragging will occur, in pixels per second. Read/write. On *idle*, reset to 0.
edit script	Command	edit script of object	Opens script of "object" for editing by user. The userLevel must be set to 5 (scripting) or nothing happens.
editBkgnd	Property	None	Global property that determines whether operations are currently being performed on the background of the current card. Read/write.
eight	Constant	None	Use in place of number 8.
eighth	Selector	eighth chunkExpression	Used in commands to identify, select, or test the eighth element or chunk.
empty	Predefined Value	None	Equals the null string, " ". Used most often with *put* and with conditional tests on variables, containers, and fields.

Word/Phrase	_Type_	_Syntax_	_Notes_
enable •	Command	enable [<menuItemExpr> of] menu <menuName>	Enables indicated menu or menu item. The menuItemExpr can be the name of the menu item, its position in the menu, or a container or expression evaluating to one of these. The same classes of arguments can apply to the menu. See _disable_.
enabled •	Property	None	Menu or menu item property indicating whether the item is enabled or disabled. True/ false.
end	Identifier	end handler-name	Required at the end of all event and function handlers. See _on_, "function."
enterInField •	System Message	enterInField	A system message sent to a field when the user presses the Enter key while the cursor is in the field.
enterKey	System Message	enterKey	A system message sent to a card indicating the Enter key is pressed.
eraser	Tool Name	None	None
exit	Command	exit handler-name	Leaves a handler before the _end_ is reached.
exitField •	System Message	None	Sent to a field when the user leaves the field without having changed its contents. See _closeField_.
exit repeat	Control Structure	exit repeat	Used to exit a repeat loop before the condition that would normally terminate it arises.
exit to HyperCard	Command	exit to HyperCard	Quits all levels of handlers immediately and stops HyperTalk completely.
exp	Function	the exp of number exp(number)	Returns the constant "e" raised to the power represented by number.
exp1	Function	the exp1 of number exp1(number)	Returns the value one less than the _exp_ of the number.
exp2	Function	the exp2 of number exp2(number)	Returns the value of 2 raised to the power specified by the number.

Word/Phrase	_Type_	_Syntax_	_Notes_
export paint •	Command	export paint to file \<fileName\>	Saves the bitmap image of the current card to the file indicated. Only usable when a paint tool has been selected. See _import paint_.
extend	Text Style	see _textStyle_	None
false	Constant	None	One of the two Boolean values returned with true/false tests. See _true_.
fast	Adjective	None	Used with _visual_ to cause the next visual effect to execute quickly.
field	Tool Name Object	field tool fld tool field fld	None
fifth	Selector	fifth chunkExpression	Used in commands to identify, select, or test the fifth element or chunk.
filled	Painting Property	None	When true, any shapes drawn are filled with the currently selected pattern as they are drawn.
find •	Command	find target [in field field-name][of marked cards] find target [of marked cards] find char[acter][s] target [in field field-name] [of marked cards] find word target [in field field-name][of marked cards] find whole target [in field field-name][of marked cards] find string target [in field field-name][of marked cards]	The target is a text string. field-name, if present, must be the name, number, or ID of a field. Without qualifiers, _find_ locates target at the beginning of words. With _chars_, it finds string anywhere in word. With _word_, it finds only whole words that match the target string. With _whole_, it finds only exact matches, including spaces, with word order significant, and requires that the target be found entirely within one field. With _string_ and arguments with spaces, performance improvement is obtained in Version 1.2 and above. Supplying the "of marked cards" option causes the search to be confined to cards previously identified by the _mark_ command.
first	Selector	first chunkExpression	Used in commands to identify, select, or test the first element or chunk.

Word/Phrase	Type	Syntax	Notes
five	Constant	None	Use in place of number 5.
fixedLineHeight •	Property	None	Field property that determines whether the *textHeight* property of a field remains fixed regardless of changes in the *textSize* property of the field. True/false.
formFeed	Constant	None	Can be *put* or concatenated into a string with & to cause the printer to eject a page when it is encountered. See *lineFeed*.
forth	Identifier	None	Points to the next card in the Recent list. If the current card is the last card in the Recent list, returns to Home stack.
foundChunk	Function	the foundChunk	Returns a chunking expression that identifies the location of the last text found with a *find* command (Version 1.2 and later).
foundField	Function	the foundField	Returns the identification of the field in which the last text was found with a *find* command (Version 1.2 and later).
foundLine	Function	the foundLine	Returns the field number and line number on which the last text was found with a *find* command (Version 1.2 and later).
foundText	Function	the foundText	Returns the last text found with a *find* command (Version 1.2 and later).
four	Constant	None	Use in place of number 4.
fourth	Selector	fourth chunkExpression	Used in commands to identify, select, or test the fourth element or chunk.
freeSize	Property	None	Global property indicating how much free space is in the current stack. Read-only.
function	Keyword	function <*function name*>	Key word used to start the definition of a script element that returns a value to the calling function or handler. See *on*.
functionKey	System Message	functionKey number	A system message sent to a card indicating that the function key whose number is indicated has been pressed.

Word/Phrase	Type	Syntax	Notes
get	Command	get source-expression	Puts the value of any literal, constant, function, or container into *it*. See *put*, which is more useful. *get* is not often used and is left over from earlier versions of HyperTalk for compatibility.
global	Command	global name-list	Identifies one or more variables as global in nature, *i.e.*, known and accessible outside the current handler. Command must appear before variable it names is used.
go •	Command	go [to] card-name [without dialog] go [to] stack stack-name [without dialog] [in new window] go [to] card-name of stack-name [without dialog] [in new window] go [to] card-name of background-name [of stack-name] [without dialog] [in new window]	Changes the display to show the designated card in the current or designated stack with the current or designated back ground. If "without dialog" option is specified and destina-tion stack or card cannot be found, HyperCard displays error dialog rather than asking user to find the stack or card. If "in new window" option is specified, stack opens a new window, leaving the current stack open in an inactive window.
gray	Adjective	visual effect to gray (Alternate spelling — grey)	Alters the way *visual effects* work. Creates a gray screen as an intermediate point for the visual effect before going to the destination card.
grid	Painting Property	None	When *true*, constrains some painting operations to a grid with lines at eight-pixel intervals, forcing everything to line up on those grid lines (visible or invisible). Read/write.
group •	Text Style	see *textStyle*	None
hand	Cursor Shape	set cursor to hand	Changes the cursor to a hand (symbol for the *browse* tool). (Note that cursor shape is reset at *idle* time.)

Word/Phrase	_Type_	_Syntax_	_Notes_
hBarLoc •	Property	set the hBarLoc of window	"variable watcher" to <location> Property of the built-in _messageWatcher_ window supplied with HyperCard beginning with Version 2.0. Determines the number of variables that can be seen at one time. See _vBarLoc_.
heapSpace	Function	the heapSpace	Returns the amount of space currently available on the application heap.
height	Property	None	Field, button, and window property containing the height, in pixels, of the object's surrounding rectangle.
help	Command	help	Takes user to HyperCard's built-in Help stack.
help	System Message	None	Sent to a card indicating that Help has been selected from the Go menu.
hide •	Command	hide menuBar hide window hide titlebar hide groups hide object	Removes the designated window or object from view. See _show_. The _window_ may be _tool window_, or _pattern window_ or any valid address for the _Message box_. The "groups" option does not remove the grouped text from view but hides the special underline that identifies grouped text.
hideIdle •	Property	set the hideIdle of window "message watcher" to {true | false}	Property of the built-in _messageWatcher_ supplied with HyperCard beginning with Version 2.0. Determines whether the _idle_ message is monitored during debugging.
hideUnused •	Property	set the hideUnused of window "message watcher" to {true | false}	Property of the built-in _messageWatcher_ supplied wth HyperCard beginning with Version 2.0. Determines whether messages for which no handler is found are monitored during debugging.
hilite	Property	None	Indicates whether a button is highlighted or not. Read/write.

Word/Phrase	Type	Syntax	Notes
home	Identifier	None	Points to first card in Home stack. (There must be a stack called Home for HyperCard to operate.)
iBeam	Cursor Shape	set cursor to iBeam	Changes the cursor to a text-insertion I-beam shape. (Note that cursor shape is reset at *idle* time.)
icon	Property	None	Number of icon resource associated with a button. Read/write.
id	Property	None	Numeric ID of a background, card, field, or button. Read-only.
idle	System Message	None	Sent to a card when no other message is being sent and no other action is taking place. Alternates with *mouseWithin* if the mouse is over a button or a field.
if	Control Structure	if true/false then statement-list [else statement-list end if]	If only one statement in either or both statement-lists, no need for *end if. else* is optional. *then* is required.
import paint •	Command	import paint from file \<fileName\>	Replaces the current card's bitmap with the bitmap stored in the indicated file. File must contain a paint image. Usable only when a paint tool has been selected. See *export paint*.
international	Sort Type	None	Used with *sort* to sort a stack by treating a chunk expression as text but using international sort-sequence standards rather than ASCII. See *text, numeric,* and *dateTime*.
into	Preposition	None	Used with *put* to replace current contents of destination container or variable with value supplied in command.
inverse	Adjective	visual effect to inverse	Alters the way *visual effects* work. Creates a screen that is the inverse of the destination card as an intermediate point for the visual effect before going to the destination card.
iris	Visual Effect	iris {open | close}	No default value.

Word/Phrase	_Type_	_Syntax_	_Notes_
is •	Operator	is {a | an} {number | integer | point | rect | date | logical}	Returns a logical value indicating whether an object is of the selected type.
is in	Operator	text is in container	Returns _true_ if _text_ is found in "container," _false_ if not. The _is in_ operator is synonymous with _contains_ except the order of arguments is reversed.
is not in	Operator	text is not in container	The logical opposite of _is in_. May also use _not (text is in "container")_ to accomplish this goal.
is [not] within	Operator	<point> is within <target> <point> is not within <target>	Returns a logical value indicating whether the point lies within the boundaries of the rectangle.
it	Identifier	None	Default container used by several retrieval and chunking commands. Can also be used explicitly. See _put_ and _get_.
italic	Text Style	see _textStyle_	None
item[s]	Identifier	None	An item is defined as any arbitrary text separated by a comma from other text in a field, line, container, or variable.
keyDown •	System Message	None	Sent to a field when the user presses any alpha or numeric key without holding the Command key at the same time. Also sends a parameter indicating which key was pressed. See _commandKeyDown_.
language	Property	None	Global property containing the language in which activities take place. Must be a language interpreter for the chosen language or an error results. Read/write.
lasso	Tool Name	None	None
last •	Ordinal Selector	last chunkExpression	Used in commands to identify, select, or test the last element or chunk.
left	Property	None	Button, field, or card property containing the pixel location of the left edge of the object's surrounding rectangle.

Word/Phrase	Type	Syntax	Notes
length	Function	the length of text length(text)	Returns the number of characters in the string of *text* supplied as an argument.
line	Tool Name	None	None
line	Identifier	None	A line is a block of text in a field ended with a carriage return.
lineFeed	Constant	None	Can be used with *put* or concatenated with & to cause the printer to skip a line when it is encountered. See *formFeed*.
lineSize	Painting Property	None	Defines thickness in pixels of a line drawn in painting as one of the following values: 1, 2, 3, 4, 6, or 8. Read/write.
ln	Function	the ln of number ln(number)	Returns the natural (base-*e*) logarithm of *number*.
ln1	Function	the ln1 of number ln1(number)	Returns the natural (base-*e*) logarithm of 1 + *number*.
location	Property	[the] loc[ation]	A set of two screen coordinates that define the center of a field or window, or the upper center of a button's outline. Read/write.
lock	Command	lock screen	Equivalent to setting the *lockScreen* property to *true*.
lockMessages	Property	None	Indicates whether *open* and *close* messages will be sent to the card. True/false. Read/write. On *idle*, reset to false.
lockRecent	Property	None	Global property that determines whether the Recent stack, which shows the most recent cards navigated to up to a depth of 42 cards, will be updated or not. True/false. Read/write. On *idle*, resets to *false*.
lockScreen	Property	None	Global property that determines whether the screen will reflect navigation and other on-screen activities that alter the appearance of the screen. True/false. Read/write. On *idle*, resets to *false* with no levels of lock and unlock pending. (See *lock* command.)

Word/Phrase	_Type_	_Syntax_	_Notes_
lockText	Property	None	Field property that determines whether the user can enter information into the field or not. True/false. Read/write.
log2	Function	the log2 of number log2(number)	Returns the base-2 logarithm of the _number_.
long	Format	long {date | time}	Used with _convert_ to reformat a date or time field or value. Also used with functions. Long dates format as Friday, November 6, 1987. Long times format as 9:50:10 PM or 21:50:10.
longWindow Titles •	Property	None	Global property that determines whether the title bars of all windows will show the entire path name or just the name of the stack. True/false.
mark •	Command	mark {<cardIdentifier> | cards where <logical> | all cards | cards by finding <expression>}	Marks cards that match criteria contained in the expression. A logical expression can contain any Boolean logic statement that evaluates to _true_ or _false_. The "by finding" option accepts same syntax and arguments as _find_ command. See _unmark_, _marked_.
markChar •	Property	None	Menu item property that defines the character to be used in check marking a menu item when that item's _checkMark_ property is true. HyperTalk will use only the first character of the string supplied as a value for this property.
marked •	Property	None	Card property identifying whether a card has been identified by execution of a _mark_ command as meeting some criteria. True/false.
max	Function	max(number-list)	Returns the highest value in "number-list," which must be a list of two or more numbers separated by commas.

Word/Phrase	_Type_	_Syntax_	_Notes_
me	Identifier	None	Points to object to which the script is attached. In Version 1.2 and later, is also a container into which information can be placed and which can be used to access the contents of the object when that object is a field.
menuMsg •	Property	menuMsg[s] menuMessage[s]	Menu item property that determines what message HyperCard will send when the menu item is selected. See _create menu, put_.
menus •	Function	the menus	Returns a list of all menus in the current menubar. The word "Apple" is substituted for the Apple logo at the left of the menubar. Inactive menus are included. List is return-delimited.
Message box	Object	[the] message [box | window] [the] msg [box | window]	A window that stays on top of the display at all times.
message Watcher •	Property	None	Global property that determines the name of the XCMD containing the messageWatcher to be used during debugging. Argument must evaluate to a string. If XCMD not found, HyperTalk loads built-in default messageWatcher. See _variableWatcher_.
middle	Selector	mid[dle] chunkExpression	Used in commands to identify, select, or test center or middle element or chunk. Always rounds up if chunkExpression has even number of elements.
min	Function	min(number-list)	Returns the smallest value in "number-list," which must be a list of two or more numbers separated by commas.

Word/Phrase	_Type_	_Syntax_	_Notes_
mod	Operator	number mod number	Returns only the decimal remainder of the division of the first number by the second.
mouse	Function	the mouse	Returns current status of the mouse button as *up* or *down*. See *mouseUp* and *mouseDown*.
mouseClick	Function	the mouseClick	Returns *true* if the mouse button has been clicked since this handler began executing, *false* otherwise.
mouseDown	System Message	None	Sent to an object indicating mouse button is down and located within its boundaries.
mouseEnter	System Message	None	Sent to a button or field when the mouse enters its boundaries. See *mouseLeave*.
mouseH	Function	the mouseH	Returns current location of the mouse pointer in pixels from the left side of the card window. See *mouseV* and *mouseLoc*.
mouseLeave	System Message	None	Sent to a button or field indicating the mouse has left its boundaries. See *mouseEnter*.
mouseLoc	Function	the mouseLoc	Returns the horizontal and vertical coordinates of the point in the card window where the mouse is currently located. The horizontal position is given first in a two-number list, separated by commas. See *mouseH* and *mouseV*.
mouseStillDown	System Message	None	Sent to an object indicating that the mouse button has remained down and within its boundaries since the last time it was checked.
mouseUp	System Message	None	Sent to an object indicating that the mouse button has been released within its boundaries after having been pressed there. See *mouseDown*.
mouseV	Function	the mouseV	Returns the current location of the mouse pointer in pixels from the top of the card window. See *mouseH* and *mouseLoc*.

Word/Phrase	_Type_	_Syntax_	_Notes_
mouseWithin	System Message	None	Sent to a button or field indicating that the mouse pointer has moved within its boundaries.
moveWindow•	System Message	None	Sent to card window when the user or a script changes the card window's *location* on the screen.
multiple	Painting Property	None	When *true*, creates multiple images of a shape as the cursor is dragged after selecting a shape tool. Read/write.
multiply	Command	multiply container by number	The container must hold a number or an error results. Product of multiplication replaces contents of container.
multiSpace	Painting Property	None	Determines the number of pixels (1-9) between multiple images drawn when *multiple* is *true*. Read/write.
name •	Property	None	String identifying a menu, menu item, stack, background, card, field, or button by the name assigned by the developer or the user or the default value if none is assigned. Read/write.
newBackground	System Message	None	Sent to a card indicating that a new background is about to be created.
newButton	System Message	None	Sent to a button as soon as it has been created. To be of practical use, must be in a script at card level or higher.
newCard	System Message	None	Sent to a card as soon as it is created. To be of practical value, must be at the background level or higher.
newField	System Message	None	Sent to a field as soon as it is created. To be of practical value, must be at the card level or higher.
newStack	System Message	None	Sent to a card indicating a new stack is being created. To be of practical value, must be at the Home stack level or higher.
next	Identifier	None	Points to next card in current stack.

Word/Phrase	_Type_	_Syntax_	_Notes_
next repeat	Control Structure	next repeat	Used to cause part of a repeat control structure not to execute and the control value to increment if one is in use. See _repeat_.
nine	Constant	None	Use in place of number 9.
ninth	Selector	ninth chunkExpression	Used in commands to identify, select, or test the ninth element or chunk.
none	Cursor Shape	set cursor to none	Hides the cursor by giving it an empty shape. (Note that cursor shape is reset at _idle_ time.)
normal	Modifier	see _find_	Redundant modifier that simply tells the _find_ command to use its usual, unmodified approach to finding information. See _chars, whole, word, string_.
not	Operator	not (true/false)	Returns the opposite of the result of the true/false expression.
number	Property	None	Backgrounds, cards, fields, and buttons have a number associated with them that indicates the layer within which they are found on the card. This property holds this number for each object. Read-only.
number •	Function	[the] number of objects [the] number of cards of background [the] number of chunks in text-source number(objects)	Returns the number of card or background buttons or fields on the current card, the number of backgrounds or cards in the current stack, the number of cards sharing a current or specified background, or the number of marked cards in the current stack. Can also be used to determine the number of menus on the menubar, menu items in a particular menu, or total windows. When dealing with chunks, returns number of characters, words, items, or lines in a string, variable, or container.

Word/Phrase	Type	Syntax	Notes
numberFormat	Property	None	Global property that uses zeros, decimal points, and pound signs to format numbers for output in the stack. Read/write. On *idle*, resets to "0.######".
numeric	Sort Type	None	Used with *sort* to sort a stack by treating a chunk expression as a numeric value. See *text*, *international*, and *dateTime*.
numToChar	Function	the numToChar of number numToChar(number)	Returns character whose ASCII equivalent is *number*. You can only use one argument even with the second form.
offset	Function	offset(text,string-source)	Returns the number of characters from the beginning of "string-source" at which *text* begins. If *text* is not present in "string-source," function returns 0.
on	Identifier	on handler-name parameter-list statement list end handler-name	See *end*, "function."
one	Constant	None	Use in place of number 1.
open application	Command	open application "*<application name>*"	Opens the named application. The application name may include path information if needed.
open file	Command	open file file-name	Opens any ASCII file called "file-name," which can be a string or a container storing a string. See *read from file* and *write to file*.
open printing	Command	open printing [with dialog] print card-name close printing	Initiates a print job, prints cards that appear in *print* statements before the *close printing* statement. Optionally opens print dialog for user's input.
open report printing •	Command	open report printing [with {template <template name> | dialog}]	Initiates printing of a report using the identified template or allowing user to choose template from dialog. If parameter is omitted, last template used with stack is selected. Printing does not actually get carried out until *close printing* command is encountered.

Word/Phrase	_Type_	_Syntax_	_Notes_
openBackground	System Message	None	Sent to a card when it is opened and its background is different from that of the immediately previously shown card. See _closeBackground_.
openCard	System Message	None	Sent to a card when it is opened by going to it.
openField	System Message	None	Sent to an unlocked field when it has been clicked in or tabbed into.
openStack	System Message	None	Sent to a card when its stack is opened. To be of practical value, usually placed at the stack level or higher.
optionKey	Function	the optionKey	Returns status of Option key as _up_ or _down_.
or	Operator	expression or expression	Returns _true_ if either expression is true, _false_ only if both are false.
outline	Text Style	see _textStyle_	None
oval	Tool Name	None	None
param	Function	the param of number param(number)	Returns the parameter in the _number_ position of the parameter string passed to the currently executing handler. The message name is numbered 0.
paramCount	Function	the paramCount	Returns the number of parameters passed to the currently executing handler.
params	Function	the params	Returns the entire parameter list, including the name, of the message passed to the currently executing handler.
pass	Command	pass handler-name	Sends the handler-name message or command to the next level up the hierarchy.
pattern	Painting Property	None	Sets the current number to a value from 1-40 corresponding to the palette patterns. Read/write.
pattern window	Identifier	None	Used to _get_ and _set_ properties of the pattern window used during graphics operations.
pencil	Tool Name	None	None

Word/Phrase	_Type_	_Syntax_	_Notes_
pi	Constant	None	Value of pi = 3.14159265358 979323846
picture	Identifier	pict[ure]	One of HyperCard's object types. Can be a _background_ picture or a _card_ picture.
plain	Text Style	see _textStyle_	None
plain	Visual Effect	None	None
play	Command	play "sound name" [tempo]["note-list"] play stop	Uses voice identified in sound name to play sounds through the Macintosh built-in speaker or external speaker port. Any sound resource can be used as the sound name. Sound plays until done unless _play stop_ is encountered and stops the music immediately. If note-list is empty, middle C is played. See _sound_ function.
plus	Cursor Shape	set cursor to plus	Changes the cursor to a thick plus shape. (Note that cursor shape is reset at _idle_ time.)
polygon	Tool Name	poly[gon] tool	See _regular polygon_.
polySides	Painting Property	None	Determines how many sides the regular polygon tool will draw. Must be between 3 and 50. Read/write.
pop	Command	pop card [{into | before | after} destination]	Retrieves a card previously _push_ed. If a destination is furnished, card's contents are placed there; otherwise a _go_ to the _pop_ped card is implied. See _push_.
powerKeys	Property	None	Global property that determines whether a user with painting-level or higher access can use one-key power keys during paint operations. True/false. Read/write.
previous	Identifier	prev[ious]	Points to previous card in current stack.
print	Command	print <expression>	Prints the contents of a container or field or a HyperTalk expression.

Word/Phrase	Type	Syntax	Notes
print card •	Command	print card [from \<point> to \<point>] print {number | marked | all} [from \<point> to \<point>] print card-name [from \<point> to \<point>]	Part of *open printing* construct. Orders HyperCard to print the cards current card, some number of cards in the stack, all cards in the stack, all marked cards in the stack, or a specific card whose name or number or ID is supplied. If "from" option is supplied, a bitmap of the rectangular portion of the card(s) defined by the two points will be printed See *open printing, close printing*.
print document	Command	print document with \<application>	Prints the named document using the indicated application, ctly as if ordered from the Finder.
printMargins •	Property	None	Global property used by *print* command and as default during report printing that defines margins on printout. Argument is four numbers, separated by commas, containing, in order, the left, top, right, and bottom margins in pixels. Default is 0,0,0,0. See *reset printing*.
printTextAlign •	Property	None	Global property used by *print* command and as default during report printing that defines alignment of text on printout. Argument is one of left, center, or right. See *reset printing*.
printTextFont •	Property	None	Global property used by *print* command and as default during report printing that defines font to be used on printout. Argument is a string containing the name of an available font. See *reset printing*.
printTextHeight •	Property	None	Global property used by *print* command and as default during report printing that defines line height to be used on printout. Argument is numeric and defines line height in pixels. See *reset printing*.

Word/Phrase	Type	Syntax	Notes
printTextSize •	Property	None	Global property used by *print* command and as default during report printing that defines size of type to be used on printout. Argument is numeric. See *reset printing*.
push card	Command	push card	Saves current card's ID information in memory for later retrieval with *pop card*.
put •	Command	put [expression] [{into	before	after} destination] put "expression" {into	before	after} <menuItem Identifier> of <menu Identifier> [with {menuMsg	menuMsgs	menuMessage	menuMessages <message Identifier>]	With only an "expression," replaces contents of Message box with "expression" value. With "destination," places *expression* contents in place of, preceding, or following contents of "destination." If "expression" contains an arithmetic expression, it is evaluated first.
		put "expression" into menu <menu Identifier>	Second form of command adds a new menu item to an existing menu, optionally identifying the message that should be sent when the user chooses that menu item or a *doMenu* command invokes that menu item. Third form of command replaces all of a menu's menu items with the expression.
quit	System Message	None	Sent to a card when Quit HyperCard is selected from the File menu. To be of practical value, must be at the Home stack level.
quote	Constant	None	Used primarily in concatenation with & and && to place a quotation mark in a string.
radioButton	Button Style	see *style*	None
random	Function	the random of number random(number)	Returns a random integer value between 1 and *number*.
read from file	Command	read from file file-name {until character	for number}	Reads from a text-only ASCII file previously opened with *open*, placing results into *it*. Reading continues until a specified character is reached or until a specific number of characters have been read, depending on form used.

Word/Phrase	_Type_	_Syntax_	_Notes_
recent card	Identifier	recent card	Points to the card immediately before the current card in the Recent list. Identical to *back*.
rectangle	Tool Name	rect[angle] tool	None
rectangle	Property	rect[angle]	Holds the upper-left and lower-right corner coordinates for a field, button, card, or window (built-in or card) as four digits separated by commas.
regular polygon	Tool Name	reg[ular] poly[gon] tool	See *polygon*.
repeat	Control Structure	repeat [for] [number] [times] repeat with variable = start to end repeat with variable = start downTo end repeat while true/false repeat until true/false	Used alone, means "repeat forever." Minimum form is repeat number. See "end repeat," *exit repeat*, and *next repeat* for ways of ending control structure looping.
reportTemplates •	Function	the reportTemplates	Returns a return-delimited list of all report templates associated with the current stack. See *open report printing*.
reset menubar •	Command	reset menubar	Returns menubar settings to their default HyperCard settings, removing any custom menus installed by scripts and resetting the operation of all standard menu items to their default behaviors.
reset paint	Command	reset paint	Returns painting parameters to their original default conditions.
reset printing •	Command	reset printing	Returns printing parameters to their original default conditions, with *printTextFont* to Geneva, *printTextStyle* to plain, *printTextSize* to 10, *printTextAlign* to left, *printTextHeight* to 13, and *printMargins* to 0,0,0,0.
result	Function	the result	Returns a string explaining any error caused by the previous command. If no error occurred, the value of *the result* is *empty*.

Word/Phrase	_Type_	_Syntax_	_Notes_
resume	System Message	None	Sent to a card to indicate that HyperCard has resumed operations after being _suspend_ed.
resumeStack •	System Message	None	Sent to a stack to indicate that the user has chosen its open window and made it the currently active stack. See _suspendStack_.
return	Command	return result	Used in function handlers (see _function_) to identify the value to be sent to the calling handler routine.
return	Constant	None	Used primarily in concatenation with & and && to place a carriage return in a string.
returnInField	System Message	returnInField	A system message sent to a field whenever the user presses the Return key with the pointer positioned in that field. (Version 1.2 and later.)
returnKey	System Message	returnKey	A system message sent to a card indicating that the Return key has been pressed.
right	Property	None	Button, field, or card property containing the pixel location of the right edge of the object's surrounding rectangle.
round	Function	the round of number round(number)	Returns _number_ rounded to the nearest integer.
round rectangle	Tool Name	round rect[angle] tool	None
roundRect	Button Style	see _style_	None
screenRect	Function	the screenRect	Returns four integers separated by commas indicating the top left and bottom right corners of the display. (Version 1.2 and later.)
script	Property	None	Enables the retrieval and modification of the script of any object: stack, background, card, field, or button. Read/write, but must use a container for modification.

Word/Phrase	Type	Syntax	Notes
scriptEditor •	Property	None	Global property that determines the name of the XCMD containing the script editor to be used. Argument must evaluate to a string. If XCMD not found, HyperTalk loads built-in default script editor.
scriptTextFont •	Property	None	Global property that determines the font to be used in displaying the text of scripts in the script-editing window. Argument must evaluate to an available font name.
scriptTextSize •	Property	None	Global property that determines the size of type to be used in displaying the text of scripts in the script-editing window. Argument must be numeric.
scriptTextStyle •	Property	None	Global property that determines the style(s) of text to be used in displaying the text of scripts in the script-editing window. Argument must be a comma-delimited list of style types. See *textStyle* for options (except "group" is not permitted here).
scriptWindowRects	Property	None	Global property that holds the location of script-editing windows. The built-in HyperCard script editor uses this global to position windows to avoid two script-editing windows occupying the same screen positions if possible.
scroll	Visual Effect	scroll {left | right | up | down]	No default value.
scroll	Property	None	Field property that determines the number of pixels of text that have scrolled above the top of the field's visible area. Read/write.

Word/Phrase	Type	Syntax	Notes
scroll •	Property	None	Card-window property that determines the number of pixels vertically and horizontally that the card's image is scrolled within the card window. When card and card window are same size, value is 0,0.
scrolling	Field Style	see *style*	None
second	Selector	second chunkExpression	Used in commands to identify, select, or test the second element or chunk.
seconds	Format	sec[ond][s]	Used with *convert* command to cause HyperCard to change a date/time field to total number of elapsed seconds since 12:00:00 a.m. on January 1, 1904. Used for calculations.
seconds	Function	the sec[ond][s]	Returns an integer containing the number of seconds between the Macintosh start date of midnight, January 1, 1904, and the date currently set in your system.
select	Tool Name	None	None
select	Command	select object select [before | after] location of field select [before | after] text of field	First form selects the appropriate tool (field or button) and then the designated object. Second form uses location as a chunking expression to position the cursor in a field, selecting the text designated by position if *before* and *after* are omitted, or inserting a blinking cursor *before* or *after* the chunking expression. Third form selects all text in a field or positions the cursor at the beginning (*before*) or end (*after*) of the field.
selectedChunk	Function	the selectedChunk	Returns a chunking expression that identifies the location of the currently selected text, if any. Returns *empty* if no text is selected (Version 1.2 and later).
selectedField	Function	the selectedField	Returns the identifier of the field in which the currently selected text is located. Returns *empty* if no text is selected (Version 1.2 and later).

Word/Phrase	_Type_	_Syntax_	_Notes_
selectedLine	Function	the selectedLine	Returns the line and field numbers of the currently selected text, if any. Returns _empty_ if no text is selected (Version 1.2 and later).
selectedLoc •	Function	the selectedLoc	Returns the lower-left point of the text selection in a field if there is one. Result is empty if there is no selection.
selectedText	Function	the selectedText	Returns the currently selected text, if any. Returns _empty_ if no text is selected (Version 1.2 and later).
selection	Container	None	Contains the text currently highlighted (selected) on the card.
send	Command	send message-name [parameters] to object	Directs a message-name at a particular object in the hierarchy, overriding normal passage of control. Message-name must be one word with no spaces. It must not end with a special character.
set	Command	set property of object to value	Alters condition of "property" associated with "object" so that it equals _value_. If no change is needed, none is made.
seven	Constant	None	Use in place of number 7.
seventh	Selector	seventh chunkExpression	Used in commands to identify, select, or test the seventh element or chunk.
shadow	Text Style	see _textStyle_	None
shadow	Button Style Field Style	see _style_	None
sharedHilite •	Property	None	Background button property that determines whether the state of the button (see _hilite_) is saved for each card on which the button appears. True/false.
sharedText •	Property	None	Background field property that determines whether the text entered into this field will appear on all cards or whether contents will be card-specific. (Attempt to set or get property for card field is ignored.) True/false.

Word/Phrase	Type	Syntax	Notes
shiftKey	Function	the shiftKey	Returns status of Shift key as *up* or *down*.
short	Format	short {time | date}	Used with *convert* to reformat a date or time field or value. Also used with functions. Short dates format as mm/dd/yy. Short times format as 9:50 PM or 21:50.
show •	Command	show menuBar show window [at point] show object [at point] show titlebar show groups show card window [at point] show {number | marked | all} cards	Displays a specified object or window at an optionally specified location on the screen. Displays a specified number of cards or all cards in the current stack. If "card window" is shown, point is in global coordinates, with upper-left corner of screen 0,0 and "point" giving offset of upper-left corner of card. The "groups" option produces a special underline that identifies grouped text.
showLines	Property	None	Field property that determines whether the lines within a field will be visible or invisible. Has no effect on a scrolling field. True/false. Read/write.
showName	Property	None	Button property that determines whether the button's name will be shown as part of the button display. True/false. Read/write.
showPict	Property	None	Card or background property that determines whether the corresponding *picture* is visible or invisible. True/false. Read/write.
shrink •	Visual effect	shrink to {top | center | bottom}	None
sin	Function	the sin of angle sin(angle)	Returns the trigonometric sine of the "angle," which must be expressed in radians.
six	Constant	None	Use in place of number 6.
sixth	Selector	sixth chunkExpression	Used in commands to identify, select, or test the sixth element or chunk.

Word/Phrase	Type	Syntax	Notes
size	Property	None	Property holding the size of the stack in kilobytes. Read-only.
sizeWindow	System Message	None	Sent to a card window when it is resized by the user or from a script.
slowly	Adverb	slow[ly]	Used with *visual* to cause the next visual effect to execute slowly.
sort •	Command	sort [[marked | all] cards of [this]] [stack | background] [ascending | descending] [sortType] by sortValue sort {lines | items} of \<container> [ascending | descending] [sortType]	First form sorts all or marked cards in a stack or belonging to a particular background. Assumes ascending order. "sortType" may be *text*, *numeric*, *international*, or *dateTime*, and if omitted, defaults to *text*. The "sortValue" can be any field identifier or chunk expression or a source of such an identifier or expression. It can also be the name of a user-defined function that produces a sorting algorithm. Second form sorts the lines or items in a container.
sound	Function	the sound	Returns the name of the currently playing sound or *done* if none is playing.
space	Constant	None	Used primarily in concatenation with & and && to place a blank space in a string.
spray	Tool Name	spray [can] tool	None
sqrt	Function	the sqrt of number sqrt(number)	Returns the square root of *number*.
stacks •	Function	the stacks	Returns a return-delimited list of the stacks that are presently open.
stacksInUse •	Property	None	Returns a list of all stacks in the current inheritance path as a return-delimited list. Read-only. See *start using* and *stop using*.
stackSpace	Function	the stackSpace	Returns the amount of memory currently available in your system's stack.

Word/Phrase	_Type_	_Syntax_	_Notes_
start using •	Command	start using <stack identifier>	Adds the named stack to the message-passing hierarchy. See _stop using_ and _stacksInUse_.
stop using •	Command	stop using <stack identifier>	Removes the named stack from the message-passing hierarchy.
startUp	System Message	None	Sent to the first card shown when HyperCard is started. Normally, this is the top card in the stack called Home, but it will be passed if no handler for it is present in this card.
stretch •	Visual Effect	stretch from {top | center | bottom}	None
string	Identifier	find "string"	Used only with the _find_ command to gain a performance improvement when searching for combinations of characters including spaces.
style	Property	None	For buttons, determines whether button is transparent, opaque, rectangle, shadow, or scrolling. For fields, determines whether field is opaque, rectangle, round rect, check box, radio button, or scrolling. Read/write.
subtract	Command	subtract number from container	The "container" must hold a number or an error condition results. The result of the subtraction replaces the contents of "container."
suspend	System Message	None	Sent to a card when Hyper Card is about to be suspended by operation of the _open_ command that launches another application.
suspended	Property	None	Global property indicating whether HyperCard is presently suspended.
suspendStack •	System Message	None	Sent to a stack when the user chooses a stack in another window, or opens a stack in a new window without closing the current stack, causing this stack to become inactive. See _resumeStack_.
tab	Constant	None	Used primarily in concatenation with & and && to place a tab in a string.

Word/Phrase	Type	Syntax	Notes
tabKey	System Message	None	A system message sent to a card indicating the Tab key has been pressed.
tan	Function	the tan of angle tan(angle)	Returns the trigonometric tangent of the "angle," which must be expressed in radians.
target	Function	[the] target	Returns a string identifying the original recipient of the current message. In the case of card, background, field, or button, returns a string like "card field id 2578" but may also return "this stack." If message has been passed up hierarchy, use this function to identify the original recipient. The use of *the* is required in versions earlier than 1.2. After Version 1.2, *target* accesses the contents of *the target*, which continues to refer to the object itself and not its contents.
ten	Constant	None	Use in place of number 10.
tenth	Selector	tenth chunkExpression	Used in commands to identify, select, or test the tenth element or chunk.
text	Sort Type	None	Default type of *sort*. Sorts stack by ASCII sort sequence. See *numeric*, *international*, and *dateTime*.
text	Tool Name	text tool	None
textAlign	Property	textAlign [of object]	Sets alignment of text in an object to left, right, or center. If no object is specified, it is a painting property. Read/write.
textArrows	Property	None	Global property implemented in Version 1.1 that determines if arrow keys will be used as cursor-moving keys in text-editing mode or only for navigational purposes. True/false. Read/write.
textFont	Property	textFont [of object]	Sets the font to the resource font name to be used. If no object is specified, this is a painting property. Read/write.

Word/Phrase	Type	Syntax	Notes
textHeight	Property	textHeight [of object]	Determines the line height (leading) between baselines of text. If no object is supplied, this is a painting property. Read/write.
textSize	Property	textSize [of object]	Determines the font size of text. With no object specified, this is a painting property. Read/write.
textStyle	Property	textStyle [of object]	Sets the style of text in a button's name, a field, or a menu or menu item to any combination of bold, italic, underline, outline, shadow, condense, extend, or plain. If the object is omitted, this is a painting property. If the object is a field, text may also be assigned the style value of grouped. Read/write.
the	Keyword	None	See text discussion of when *the* is required, when it is optional, and when it is incorrect.
then	Control Structure	None — part of structure	See *if*.
there is •	Operator	there is {a | an} {<object identifier>}	Returns true or false value identifying whether a particular window, menu, menu item, file, card, background, button, field, or stack exists.
third	Selector	third chunkExpression	Used in commands to identify, select, or test the third element or chunk.
this	Identifier	None	Points to current card.
three	Constant	None	Use in place of number 3.
ticks	Function	the tick[s]	Returns number of ticks (1 tick = 1/60 second) since the Macintosh was turned on or re-booted.
time	Function	the [short | long] time	Returns the current time as a text string. See *short* and *long* for those formats.
titlebar •	Object	None	The portion of a card window that contains the name of the stack. May be the object of a *hide* or *show* command.
to	Preposition	Various usages	None

Word/Phrase	_Type_	_Syntax_	_Notes_
tool	Function	the tool	Returns the name of the currently selected tool. See _choose tool_.
tool window	Operator	None	Used to _get_ and _set_ properties of the Tool Window used during graphics operations.
top	Property	None	Button, field, or window property containing the pixel location of the top edge of the object's surrounding rectangle.
topLeft	Property	None	Button, field, or window property containing the point at which the upper-left corner of the object's surrounding rectangle is located.
traceDelay •	Property	None	Global property that determines the time (in ticks) between execution of HyperTalk statements when tracing is in effect during debugging.
transparent	Field Style Button Style	see _style_	None
true	Constant	None	One of the two Boolean values returned with true/false tests. See _false_.
trunc	Function	the trunc of number trunc(number)	Returns integer portion of _number_ without rounding. See _round_.
two	Constant	None	Use in place of number 2.
type	Command	type text [with key-list]	Simulates character-by-character typing of _text_ as if from the keyboard, using one or more optional modifier keys in a comma-separated list.
underline	Text Style	see _style_	None
unlock	Command	unlock screen [with [visual effect] _visual effect_]	Unlocks the screen after a _lock screen_ or _set lockScreen to true_ command has been issued. Alternatively, may include a _visual effect_ to be displayed as the screen is unlocked. In latter case, the key words _visual effect_ are optional.

Word/Phrase	_Type_	_Syntax_	_Notes_
unmark •	Command	unmark {<cardIdentifier> | cards where <logical> | all cards | cards by finding <expression>}	Unmarks previously marked cards that match criteria contained in the expression. A logical expression can contain any Boolean logic statement that evaluates to _true_ or _false_. The "by finding" option accepts same syntax and arguments as the _find_ command. See _mark, marked_.
up	Constant	None	One of the possible values of the mouse button and many keys whose status can be checked with functions. See _down_.
userLevel	Property	None	Global property containing a number between 1 and 5 and determining the user's level of access to HyperCard. Read/write.
userModify	Property	None	Global property that can be set to _true_ to allow the user to make temporary changes to a locked stack. Changes made by the user will not be retained. Ignored in an unlocked stack. Reset to _false_ when user leaves a stack. True/false. Read/write.
value	Function	the value of string value(string)	Evaluates _string_ as a numerical expression and returns the result.
variable Watcher •	Property	None	Global property that deter mines the name of the XCMD containing the variableWatcher to be used during debugging. Argument must evaluate to a string. If XCMD not found, HyperTalk loads built-in default variableWatcher. See _message Watcher, variable Watcher, message Watching_.
vBarLoc •	Property	set the vBarLoc of window "variable watcher" to <location>	Property of the built-in _variableWatcher_ supplied with HyperCard beginning with Version 2.0. Determines the width of the window and contributes to how much detail can be seen in the window. See _hBarLoc_.

Word/Phrase	Type	Syntax	Notes
venetian blinds	Visual Effect	None	None
version	Property	the version [of this stack] the long version	Global property containing the version of HyperCard currently in use or, when applied to a stack, the version used to create that stack. With *long* modifier, returns a list of five numbers reflecting the version(s) used to create and modify the current stack.
very fast	Adverb	None	Used with *visual* to cause the next visual effect to execute more quickly than when the adjective *fast* is used. Difference probably only noticeable on a Macintosh II.
very slowly	Adverb	very slow[ly]	Used with *visual* to cause the next visual effect to execute more slowly than when *slowly* is used.
visible	Property	None	Determines whether a field, button, or window is visible or invisible to the user. Read/write.
visual	Command	visual [effect] effect-name [speed] [to image]	Defines visual effect to take place on next card switch. The "effect-name" must be a valid effect. The *speed* parameter can be *very slow[ly]*, *slow[ly]*, *fast*, or *very fast*. The *image* parameter can be *white, gray, black, card,* or *inverse*. Effects can be accumulated and stay in effect until replaced in another handler.

Word/Phrase	Type	Syntax	Notes
wait	Command	wait [for] number [seconds] wait until trueFalse wait while trueFalse	Pauses script execution either for a specific amount of time or based on Boolean expression value. If *seconds* is not added, ticks (1 tick = 1/60 second) are assumed. With "until," waits for *trueFalse* to become true; with "while," waits for *trueFalse* to become false.
watch	Cursor Shape	set cursor to watch	Changes the cursor to a watch face. (Note that cursor shape is reset at *idle* time.)
white	Adjective	visual effect to white	Alters the way *visual effects* work. Creates a white screen as an intermediate point for the visual effect before going to the destination card.
whole	Identifier	find whole	Used only with *find* to force HyperCard to locate target string only where it appears exactly as provided in argument, in same word order, in same field.
wideMargins	Property	None	Field property that determines whether text abuts both the left and right margins, or is indented slightly from them. True/false. Read/write.
width	Property	None	Button, field, or window property containing the width, in pixels, of the object's surrounding rectangle.
windows •	Function	the windows	Returns a list of all open windows, in back-to-front order. List includes all built-in palettes, whether open or not. List is return-delimited.
wipe	Visual Effect	wipe {left | right | up | down}	None
word	Identifier	None	A word is defined as any string beginning and ending with a space.
write to file	Command	write text to file file-name	Writes *text* on a previously opened file. See *open file, read from file*, and *close file*.
zero	Constant	None	Use in place of number 0.
zoom	Visual Effect	zoom {open | out | close | in}	No default value.

Afterword by Scott Knaster

Dan Shafer's book reminds me that for someone interested in neat computer products, working at Apple is like hanging around the back room at the world's best toy store, except that you get to open all the boxes. There are so many interesting things going on that it's easy to spend your spare time looking at all the new goodies, hardware and software, that smart folks are creating.

Back in 1986, I had a chance to look at something called WildCard that was cooking at Apple. It was supposed to be pretty intriguing, and Bill Atkinson was working on it. Unfortunately, I never made the time to look at WildCard — I was too busy doing real stuff, things that I got paid for. So I missed an opportunity to see something great in the making.

WildCard got its revenge on me later. In 1987, after WildCard had been renamed HyperCard and was shipped to the world, I had a spare hour and a fresh new copy of HyperCard on my desk, so I plunged right in. It took me about fifteen minutes to decide that it was the neatest piece of software I had ever seen, and I was completely hooked on HyperCard, especially the HyperTalk programming language, which was my favorite part.

After discovering HyperCard, I resolved to find an excuse to spend a lot of time with it. This excuse turned into a book with HyperTalk's creator, Dan Winkler, and I really got to explore this fantastic language. I also got to watch as HyperTalk evolved into Version 2.0, with more power, more speed, more features — you know, all those standard good things. When I started using HyperCard 2.0, I was awed by it all over again.

In addition to being beautiful and wonderful, HyperTalk is seductive. It makes you think that programming is easy and just like writing English. Of course, the truth is that HyperTalk is real programming. It's easier than most other languages, but you can still get caught by old-fashioned programming problems.

That's where this book comes in. Dan Shafer tells you about HyperTalk and shows you how to write scripts (a more civilized kind of programming). He explains the furious world of stacks and their cards, backgrounds, fields, and buttons, where a zillion messages are darting around getting work done, all while presenting the user with flashy and elegant things to look at.

I hope this book will help you become one of the thousands of folks who love to work and play with HyperCard, if you're not one of us already. As for me, HyperCard 2.0 is the repository for my life-long project: a complete guide to 35 years and 300 issues of *Mad* magazine. Now, if I can only find a spare hour to work on it . . .

Scott Knaster
Macintosh Inside Out Series Editor

Index

W

X

Z

Other Books Available in the Macintosh Inside Out series

▶ **Programming with MacApp®**
David A. Wilson, Larry S. Rosenstein, Dan Shafer
Here is the information you need to understand and use the power of MacApp, Apple Computer, Inc.'s official development environment for the Macintosh. The book discusses object-oriented concepts, using MPW with MacApp, the MacApp class library, and creating the Macintosh user interface. All examples are in Apple's Object Pascal language.
576 pages, paperback
$24.95, book alone, order number 09784
$34.95, book/disk, order number 55062

▶ **C++ Programming with MacApp®**
David A. Wilson, Larry S. Rosenstein, Dan Shafer
In this book you will find information on using MacApp with C++, the up-and-coming language for Macintosh development. The book covers object-oriented techniques, MPW, and the MacApp class libraries. All program examples are in C++.
600 pages, paperback
$24.95, book alone, order number 57020
$34.95, book/disk, order number 57021

▶ **Elements of C++ Macintosh® Programming**
Dan Weston
Macintosh programmers will learn just what they need to take the step from C to C++ programming, the future of Macintosh development. The book covers the basics and then teaches how to design practical programs with C++.
464 pages, paperback
$22.95, order number 55025

▶ **Programmer's Guide to MPW®, Volume I**
Exploring the Macintosh® Programmer's Workshop
Mark Andrews
Learn the secrets to unlocking the power of MPW, Apple's official integrated software development system for the Macintosh. The book begins with fundamental skills and concepts and then progresses to more advanced examples culminating in a fully functional application.
608 pages, paperback
$26.95, order number 57011

▶ **ResEdit™ Complete**
Peter Alley and Carolyn Strange
This book/disk package contains the actual ResEdit software along with a complete guide to using it. The book shows you how to customize your desktop and then moves on to cover more advanced topics such as creating standard resources, designing templates, and writing your own resource editor.
560 pages, paperback
$29.95 book/disk, order number 55075

Order Number	Quantity	Price	Total
_____	_____	_____	_____
_____	_____	_____	_____
_____	_____	_____	_____
_____	_____	_____	_____

Name _____

Address _____

_____

City/State/Zip _____

Signature (required) _____

TOTAL ORDER _____

___Visa ___MasterCard ___AmEx

Shipping and state sales tax will be added automatically.

Account # _____ Exp. Date _____

Credit card orders only please.

Offer good in USA only. Prices and availability subject to change without notice.

Addison-Wesley Publishing Company
Order Department
Route 128
Reading, MA 01867
To order by phone, call (800) 477-2226